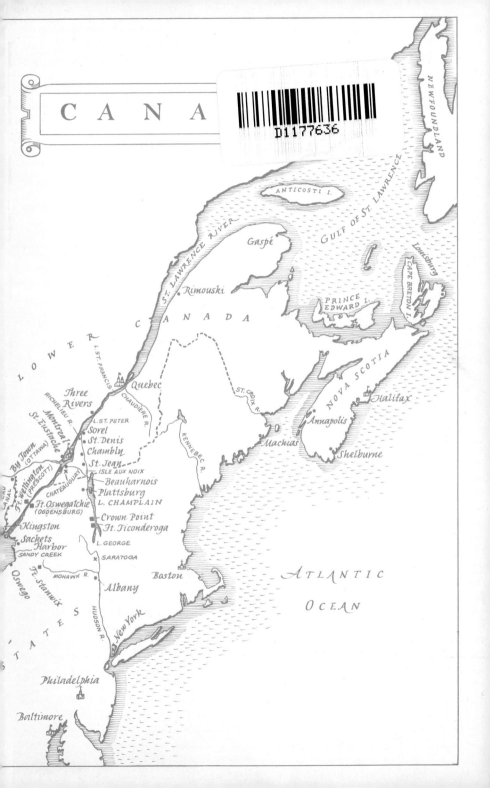

THE PATH OF DESTINY

CANADIAN HISTORY SERIES

Edited by Thomas B. Costain

VOLUME ONE

THE WHITE AND THE GOLD

The French Regime in Canada

THOMAS B. COSTAIN

VOLUME TWO

CENTURY OF CONFLICT

*The Struggle Between the French and British
in Colonial America*

JOSEPH LESTER RUTLETGE

VOLUME THREE

THE PATH OF DESTINY

*Canada From the British Conquest to
Home Rule: 1763-1850*

THE PATH
OF DESTINY

*Canada from the British Conquest
to Home Rule: 1763-1850*

by

THOMAS H. RADDALL

DOUBLEDAY CANADA LIMITED
Toronto
1957

CONTENTS

LIST OF MAPS

CHAPTER I

1763 — 1774

*Governor Carleton — The Quebec Act
— Trouble in America*

AFTER the Treaty of Paris in 1763 a small British garrison sat
in easy occupation of the old French colony along the St.
Lawrence and the Great Lakes. Nobody saw much value in it.
Voltaire had dismissed the lost colony as so many acres of snow and
most people in Europe and America saw it in the same light. During
more than a century of backwoods warfare the French troops and
their savage allies had made Canada a crown of thorns to the American colonists, but now, with the thorns removed, the menace and the
pain were gone and the Americans had another crown to think about.
For ten years after the Treaty of Paris the old French domain lay
quiet and almost forgotten in a new and rising quarrel to the south.
In the next year, 1774, two measures of the British Government gave
it a sudden interest.

On the eve of the American Revolution the region then called
Canada stretched along the St. Lawrence and the Great Lakes and
thrust a deep wedge down into the heart of the continent between
the Mississippi and Ohio rivers. Except for this wedge, clearly
marked by the rivers, the Canadian borders were as vague as the
edges of a cloud, but roughly they included what are now the
provinces of Quebec, Ontario, and Manitoba, the present states of
Wisconsin, Michigan, Illinois, Ohio, and Indiana, and parts of
Pennsylvania and New York.

Originally the French domain had reached all the way down the
Mississippi to the Gulf of Mexico, where the Canadian brothers
Le Moyne founded New Orleans and other settlements between
1698 and 1716. After Canada fell to British arms France wrote off
the southwestern half of her domain ("Louisiana") and handed it
over to Spain; an enormous gift, for in the airy theory of those days
"Louisiana" included all the continent west of the Mississippi. The

rest of French North America was Britain's by conquest, and in
1774 the territories from Gaspé to Manitoba and from the Great
Lakes to Kentucky and Missouri were placed under the command of
Guy Carleton, captain general and Governor of Canada.

Carleton's rule did not extend to Hudson Bay, where the scattered
posts of a British trading company sat in the bleak sub-Arctic air
and looked to England for orders and supplies. Nor did it cover the
old French province of Acadie, which included the present-day
Maritime Provinces of Canada and parts of Gaspé and of Maine. This
region was officially the British province of Nova Scotia, with a
governor of its own at Halifax. Thus the Canada of Carleton's time
had some curious limits and still more curious inclusions in the light
of the present day.

The North American continent was largely an unknown wilderness, to European eyes as remote as the moon, a shaggy green moon
of mountain, forest and prairie, explored in threads by fur traders
and other adventurers, and haunted by ferocious savages. The
English colonies were still confined between the Allegheny mountain
chain and the Atlantic, a ribbon of settlement two thousand miles
long and at most a tenth as wide. The French Canadians clung to the
St. Lawrence Valley, another slender ribbon ending just above
Montreal. Some foot-loose Canadians had wandered along the Great
Lakes and into the prairie country, others had gone down into the
Middle West and settled on the Mississippi near the present city of
St. Louis, and a few Hudson's Bay Company men had penetrated
into the barrens between the prairies and the Arctic Sea.

On the distant south the Spaniards of Mexico had a fringe of
missions and trading posts in what are now Texas, New Mexico, and
California. On the far and chilly northwest the mysterious Russians
had found their way from Asia to Alaska and were trading down that
coast. Between the Spanish and the Russian explorations on the
Pacific shore was a gap and an interesting myth, the rumor of a
waterway reaching far into the land, a sort of St. Lawrence of the
West. This tale had trickled across the continent by way of gossip
from tribe to tribe and on the lips of Canadian travelers like the La
Vérendryes. The famous British-American ranger, Robert Rogers,
had heard it at Mackinac in 1765 and sent an unsuccessful expedition
to find the wonderful stream. He was the first white man to use the
name Oregon for it, and like La Salle and others before him he
dreamed of a northwest passage to the China Sea, a series of streams

and portages through the heart of the land, linking the Great Lakes with the fabulous river of the West.

The typical French Canadian and Anglo-American knew little and cared less about these legends from the hazy distance to the west. In 1774 the talk in their parishes and on their village greens was all of matters closer to home. Among other things the Quebec Act, like a sudden wind in aspen trees, had set tongues and broadsheets fluttering all the way from Laborador to Florida.

The Act in its origin was made with good intentions, but like so many intentions of that kind it paved a path to heat and pain. Hence it was praised and damned from the moment it appeared. The good intentions had begun soon after the conquest of Canada, when Wolfe's brigadier, Murray, became the first British Governor at Quebec. James Murray was a Scot with a warm heart and a hot head. A wit said of him that he had every soldierly virtue except prudence, a point that Murray had proved in the bloody snows of Ste. Foy. He admired his old foes and had nothing but contempt for his Anglo-American camp followers — "the Licentious Fanaticks trading here" — who had come up from Albany and elsewhere to profit by the conquest.

Most of the "Fanaticks" had gone to Montreal, where they could seize the rich St. Lawrence fur trade. They had come to stay and they proposed to rule the country. The last bayonet had hardly been sheathed when they began to demand government by an assembly drawn from His Majesty's loyal subjects, meaning themselves alone, with all their greed, their Protestant bigotry, and their contempt for the conquered French. Among themselves they could muster at most five hundred men, yet they proposed to dominate ninety thousand Canadians. To do this they required the active support of the British garrison.

The garrison had other views. The British officers and men found the Canadians law-abiding and hospitable. In the pleasant years of peace many of them had married Canadian women and spoke French as their second tongue. In any case Murray and his soldiers had much more in common with the Canadian *seigneurs* and militiamen who had fought in some fashion for their country, than with the English-speaking, English-shouting claque from Albany who had not shown their noses past Ticonderoga until the last shot was fired.

Unfortunately for the ardent Murray, the "Fanaticks" had powerful mercantile voices in New York and London. In vain he defended his view of the Canadians, "a Race who, could they be indulged with a few privileges which the Laws of England deny to Roman Catholicks at home, would soon get the better of every National Antipathy to their Conquerors and become the most faithful and useful set of Men in this American Empire." At last he was recalled and Guy Carleton took his place; but before Carleton had been in the governor's seat very long he came to share Murray's views, although he chose to express them more discreetly. In the year 1770 he went on leave to England, where he could talk directly to the men concerned with Canada's future.

Carleton's leave of absence extended to four years, a momentous interlude for him and for the empire. During that time the middle-aged soldier met and married a slip of the English aristocracy, a girl (oddly enough) educated in the French court at Versailles. In somewhat the same spirit Great Britain decided to woo and wed the new province of Canada. In Britain's case the wedding licence was an Act of Parliament, and in framing it the British Government had the advice of Murray and Carleton, of Canadians like the *seigneur* Chartier de Lotbinière, and of the British legal officials at Quebec.

Through the influence of these men the Act killed officially a fatuous idea, born in the first flush of conquest, that the Canadians could be drawn away from their language and religion and transformed into English-speaking Protestants. Taking a more realistic view, the Act confirmed to the Canadians the free use of their tongue, their customs, their devotion to the Roman Catholic Church. It granted them most of the old French civil laws, including the seigneurial tenure of land. It ensured the right of their clergy to collect tithes. It offered the people an oath of allegiance that contained no insulting religious clause.

The matter of an elected assembly was by-passed like a porcupine met in the Canadian woods, and for much the same reasons. It prickled all over and was especially dangerous in the tail — the tail of English-speaking malcontents in Montreal and Quebec. Other than priests and *seigneurs* very few of the Canadians could read or write; they had no knowledge of democracy or the principles on which it worked; they were used to rule by a king's deputy and his little court at Quebec, and so long as that rule was light they wanted nothing else. As for the notion of an assembly drawn entirely from the English-American group, that was preposterous in a country where the French were thirty to their one. Hence the Quebec Act provided rule by a governor and council to be appointed by the British Crown.

All of this was a matter of plain justice to the Canadians and a sensible effort to make the weight of the British imperial hand as light as possible. The Act then went further. There were other people to be considered in the old French-Canadian empire; the original owners, the Indians. Most of them lived in the great pocket below the Great Lakes, a group of proud tribes, not yet stupefied by the white man's rum nor enfeebled by his diseases. The British had cause to respect their strength and their resentment against white encroachments on their hunting grounds. These were the people stirred to war in 1763 by the eloquence of Pontiac, that remarkable Indian seer, with bloody results to the American frontier folk and to the redcoats in the outposts. Now again the frontiersmen were pushing forward with their queer following of rum traders, thieves, fanatical preachers, speculators, absconding debtors and other outcasts from the American towns; and British soldiers in America foresaw another uprising of the tribes unless something drastic was done to prevent it.

In the very year of the Quebec Act a party of white scamps in the Ohio country shot down the Shawnee chiefs Bald Eagle and Silver Heels like a brace of partridges and brought on a dangerous quarrel. The Indians swarmed to fight. The British governor of Virginia, Lord Dunmore, had to send a strong force of militia to put them down, and his two thousand sharpshooting Virginians put them down bloodily. One of the Shawnee warriors killed in this affair left two small sons to be brought up with a hatred of the "Long Knives," the Americans. In a long time ahead the British and the Long Knives came to know them well. They were the Prophet and his brother Tecumseh.

Of such was the problem in the Middle West; and to the British Government in London and their military advisers in America there was plainly one solution. The tribes must be secured in the possession of their lands, and the obvious way to do it was to resume the old French authority in those parts and place them under the British governor at Quebec. The Indians could then look for justice and support from Canada, as they had in the past, and the restive American frontiersmen must halt their advances at the line of the Ohio River.

In the slow and cumbersome way of British imperial machinery
in the eighteenth century, these important decisions dragged at their
conclusion for more than a decade after the peace with France and
the war with Pontiac. Then, suddenly, they came to a point. The
reason was a new and ominous condition in America that in itself
had nothing to do with Canadians or Indians.

The political views of the American colonists had been changing
swiftly since the end of the French wars. Always independent of
mind as individuals, Americans had begun to see their country as a
chain of semi-independent provinces or states with conflicting local
interests but one common bugbear — taxation of any sort and
especially taxation from abroad. The London view was the old
Roman one that colonies must render unto Caesar whatever Caesar
had spent in their defense.

This seemed plausible to the British taxpayer, groaning under the
debt of the Seven Years' War. What he and his government failed
to see or would not see was that British manufactured goods and
shipping services enjoyed a monopoly of the American trade, by
imperial law as well as colonial custom; and (despite the notorious
American habit of smuggling) the colonies were paying an enormous
tax every year in the form of profit to the merchants and shipowners
of Britain. The colonists were well aware of it. They also were
becoming aware of their own strength.

The fourteen colonies from Georgia to Nova Scotia had a combined population of about three millions, and with immigration and
a prodigious birth rate the figure was rising fast. This created an
American problem. The shelf between the sea and the Allegheny
mountain chain was too narrow for an active people of that size,
and the Americans were eager to burst across the mountains and
spread into the West. Their frontiersmen already had crossed the
barrier, and wherever they went their women were eager to follow.

The Canadians, in contrast, were content to find room for their
own swelling population close to the St. Lawrence. The restless
few, the *coureurs de bois*, wandering off into the continent, had
to satisfy themselves with Indian women, leaving a half-breed race
(métis) scattered all through the West. The Canadians had a deep
distrust and fear of *les bastonnais* (the Bostonians), their common
name for all the American colonists to the south of them. It was a
feeling bred in all the wars since the time of Frontenac. When the

final invasion came in 1759 they were relieved to find that their
conquerors were British regulars not *les bastonnais;* and since the
conquest, a brief experience of British rule under Murray and Carleton had given them a trust in British justice to protect their dearest
interests.

On the other hand the three million Americans saw nothing to
fear on the continent now that the French King's armies were gone
forever. They knew they could thrash the Indians any time they
chose and they were itching to do it. As for British rule, the American experience was a long one under governors and councils, sometimes good, usually mediocre, often bad, and nearly all operating
in an aura of polite jobbery and snobbery that excited the colonists'
contempt. Moreover the Americans had nothing of the patient
feudal outlook of the *habitants* of Canada. They sprang from an
impatient and determined folk, English, Scotch-Irish, German,
Dutch, and Huguenot, who had crossed the sea to get away from the
religious and political restraints of the old world, and they bristled
at any restraint here in the new.

The causes of the American Revolution were many and complex,
but in their final essence they came to a single fact. The English-
speaking colonies had grown up. Like any strong young man of
twenty-one they felt their future in their own hands and they would
have no more of father's interference. The presence of so many
Loyalists ("Tories") among them — perhaps one million of the
three — made no essential difference. Most of the American Tories
shrank from the radical Whig ideas not so much because they loved
rule by a king and parliament across the sea as because they feared
mob rule at home.

By one of the odd turns of human fate this crisis in British
imperial history came at a time when the Americans had in their
midst men of bold political genius like Benjamin Franklin, John
Adams and Thomas Jefferson; gifted agitators like Samuel Adams,
Patrick Henry and Thomas Paine; and first-rate soldiers or potential
soldiers like George Washington, Benedict Arnold and Daniel
Morgan; while Britain had a dunderhead King, a reckless Cabinet,
and with few exceptions the most incompetent military staff that
ever disgraced British arms.

In America the gifted agitators had been busy ever since France
withdrew from the North American scene. The Stamp Act sent
them into full cry, and they achieved their first result in 1770 when

a mob of toughs provoked a British guard into firing upon them in a Boston square. After that the Revolution came on apace, with the ministers in Britain doing their part by passing one after another the famous "Coercive Acts," the "Intolerable Acts" that set the American woods afire. The hottest torch was the Quebec Act, which in its origin, as we have seen, was an act of simple justice to the Canadians and Indians. As an act of justice it had been long delayed; but in the excitement of 1774 the British ministers suddenly found a most important virtue in it and jammed the Act through Parliament.

The newly seen virtue of the Quebec Act was fantastic. By a stroke of pen it would restore the old menace on the north and west which had kept the American colonists in check for half a century. The ministers assumed with a quite false optimism that the *habitants* of Canada would be ready to fight, if necessary, to support the British Crown which had granted them this boon; and that merely placing the fierce tribes of the Middle West under the old auspices of the Château St. Louis would hold quiet forever the turbulent American frontiersmen, the best fighting men in the colonies.

Thus the Quebec Act lost its original innocence and became a challenge to rebellion, and in America the gifted agitators fell upon it with fury and with glee. All the old passions of the French and Indian wars were dragged out of their dusty cupboards and rubbed hot. The fundamental justice and common sense of "No Taxation without Representation" received some strange embroideries. King George (that stubborn Protestant) was pictured as a plotter hand in hand with the Pope on one side and a naked savage on the other. Religious liberty for French Canadians became political tyranny to Americans. Property rights for Indians beyond the Ohio became a theft of American birthrights everywhere.

In all this hubbub some Americans kept their heads. Franklin, Washington and others knew that Canada should be wooed, not insulted, if the North American colonies were to speak as a whole against interference from abroad. But there were other Americans who believed that the time had come to toss into the ocean not merely British tea but British rule, and that Canada must be drawn into the act, if necessary by force.

Thus on the rock at Quebec another realist found himself in a strangely fitting pair of shoes, the shoes of Montcalm, who had died in them.

CHAPTER 2

1774

Canada on the eve of the American Revolution

WHEN Guy Carleton returned to his post in Canada with his new wife and his wide new responsibilities under the Quebec Act he was fifty and Lady Maria was barely twenty. He was an Ulsterman, the son of a poor country gentleman in County Tyrone, and he had spent most of his life in the British Army. She was a petite blond daughter of the blue-blooded Howards, a precocious girl well taught in the arts and graces of French court society and untainted by its habits.

People in England told a story of Carleton's marriage with a plot as witty as any play in London at the time. Act One; the stalwart middle-aged soldier, the "grave Carleton" of Wolfe's letters, coming home on leave from Canada and calling on his old friend Howard, Earl of Effingham. Carleton finding Effingham's two lively daughters grown up and beautiful. Carleton falling in love at first sight of the older daughter, Lady Anne, who is (alas) in love with Carleton's nephew. Carleton telling his modest tales of service in the wars abroad, a red-coated Othello bearing the scars of wounds received in France, in Cuba, and in that wild adventure with Wolfe on the Plains of Abraham. The two young girls listening; Lady Anne with half her mind (for her best thoughts are on the nephew), and Lady Maria with all of hers, Desdemona-like, loving Carleton for the dangers he has borne and because he is not merely brave but wise and kind.

Act Two; Carleton (grave Carleton) drawing Lady Anne aside and making a formal proposal of marriage. Lady Anne in tears. Lady Anne bursting out of the room and into the presence of Lady Maria and a talkative Miss Seymour. Lady Anne exclaiming that she's just been obliged to refuse the best man on earth, meaning Guy Carleton of course, the second-best man. Lady Maria, eighteen, all golden curls and bright blue eyes, retorting scornfully, "The more

fool you! I wish he'd given me the chance!" Curtain and an interlude. Months passing. Noises off, including some chatter of Miss
Seymour to the rejected Othello.

And then Act Three. Carleton calling once again on the Howards
of Effingham. Carleton proposing again, this time to young Lady
Maria. Maria accepting him promptly and with ecstasy. Wedding
bells, and the happy pair moving off to Canada. And as a final note
of tender comedy, Lady Anne marrying the young man of her
choice, a soldier like his uncle, and Nephew getting an appointment
to serve on the staff of the captain general and governor of Canada.
As Macaulay said of another matter, so much is history stranger than
fiction, and so true is it that nature has caprices which art dare not
imitate.

Portraits of Guy Carleton show a man with a certain resemblance
to George Washington. There is the same calm unsmiling mouth, the
bald sloping brow, the sagacious nose, the set mouth, the steady
gaze, the grizzled side locks brushed forward over the ears. And their
inner qualities were much the same; the common sense, the ability to
regard a wide scene and pick out the vital points, the patience with
fools and knaves relieved by a burst of hot impatience now and then,
the courage in adversity, the sober caution in strategy, the outward
stiffness, the humanity under the crust.

Common sense was such a rare quality in British soldiers and
governors of the time that it shines in Carleton even now. So it
shone at the beginning and at the end of the American Revolution.
Manifest Destiny is an American phrase, but it applies to Canada as
much as the United States. Borne out by history the manifest
destiny of the continent north of the Rio Grande was that it
should be ruled by two nations, not one, just as Canada itself was to
be ruled by two and not one predominant race. Guy Carleton
secured the destiny of Canada in 1775, when he defended it successfully against absorption from the south. He confirmed that destiny
at New York in '83 when he sent the displaced persons of the
Revolution, the swarm of American Loyalists, to root themselves
firmly on the north.

These developments were hidden in '74 but there were omens.
One was a letter to Carleton from Thomas Gage, the British
Governor of Massachusetts, who was deep in trouble there. He had
the job of enforcing another of the "Intolerable Acts," an Act
closing the port of Boston as a belated punishment for the famous

tea party; and his cry was for more troops. Already he had stripped
Nova Scotia of its garrison to overawe the Bostonians, and those
tumultuous Yankees had shown no awe whatever. Indeed they
seemed ready to show fight. There was a sound of fife and drum, of
marching and drilling, in every village of New England.

The letter asked for Carleton's best troops, the 10th and 52nd
regiments. Gage added casually, "I am to ask your opinion whether
a body of Canadians and Indians might be collected and confided in
for the service of this country should matters come to extremities."
A delicate matter, this. In the meantime Carleton sent off the re-
quested troops at once, an example rarely followed by British
generals in the war that was to come. The transfer left him, for the
whole defense of Canada, two weak battalions of redcoats, the 26th
Regiment scattered in posts along the St. Lawrence and up the
Richelieu, and the 7th Fusiliers in Quebec citadel.

In his early days as governor, and as a matter of soldierly routine,
he had sketched the state of Canadian defense. The fortifications
were chiefly "the flimsy wall round Montreal" and the ramparts of
Quebec, damaged by Wolfe's shot in '59, and since by years of
frost and thaw. His regular garrison was small, but he had placed a
hopeful reliance on the Canadians themselves. They could, he believed, "send into the field about eighteen thousand men well able
to carry arms; of which number above one half have already served
with as much valour, with more zeal, and more military knowledge
for America than the regular troops of France that were joined with
them."

This kind of wishful thinking persisted in British minds, as Gage's
letter showed. A little research into Canadian history would have
shown how false it was. The experience of Montcalm was plain
enough. Most of the Canadians were of quiet peasant stock, Norman,
Breton, Biscayan, with a leaven of French gentry and of soldiers
discharged after regular service in the colony. They had among
them a portion of bold adventurers, the kind who explored the
West to the Rockies, the Midwest to the Gulf of Mexico, and in
time of war made forays against the American frontier. These men,
tough and fearless, the leatherstockings of Canada, had struck an
impression on Anglo-American minds out of all proportion to their
numbers.

The rest of the Canadians, the majority, clung to their small farms
by the St. Lawrence, peaceful, happy-go-lucky, content with a rude

subsistence and no more, suspicious of all foreigners, devout in their religion while grudging the parish tithes, obedient to the *seigneurs* while resenting their authority. They had the peasant's dislike of the *corvée*, which forced them to work on the roads without pay, and of war, for the militia system of the French regime had demanded the armed service of all able-bodied males from boys of sixteen to gray heads of sixty. These two things had put in their hearts a deep hatred of conscription in any form that holds to the present day.

As a result Montcalm had found his Canadian militia uncertain in the field, depending on the class from which they were drawn. There was a revealing incident during Montcalm's attack on the British fort at Oswego in the old war. His regulars had pressed forward regardless of the British fire. His militia chose to stay at a safe distance, whooping and sniping like Indians from the shelter of the trees, and rushing in at the surrender to claim the victory and the loot. The French regulars were contemptuous, and to the end of the war they had a gibing name for the Canadian militia, *chouayens*, possibly a twist of *chouan*, a Breton word for the owl, the bird that hoots and swoops by night but is timid in the day, or a French attempt at the savage name which the English pronounced Oswego. (Quaintly enough, the word *chouayen* survived on the lips of the French Canadians themselves; it was much used in the rebellion of 1837-38 and it continues to mean skulkers, the men who hang back from a fray until the issue is past doubt.)

This contempt was part of the usual attitude of regular troops toward raw militia anywhere; the British redcoats had much the same opinion of Americans; but it had a point in Canadian as well as American history. If Montcalm had found too many *chouayens* among the Canadian militia in the supreme struggle against the English, what could Guy Carleton expect when the war was not for France but for one *anglais* faction against another — King George against *les bastonnais?* True, the Canadians had been given remarkable concessions under the Quebec Act, to which the Americans were so violently opposed. But the *habitant* asked, "What's in it for me?" and he could not see much.

His faith and language were his own in any case; no Act framed in London could give him back what he had never lost. On the other hand he grumbled at paying tithes, which the Act upheld; and he resented the power and privileges of the great landowners, which the Act upheld also. The cold truth was that the Quebec Act, with all its good intentions, had gained for the British the ardent support of the clergy and *seigneurs*, but no one else. The *habitant* remained unmoved.

There remained the class of adventurers; the forest rangers, the hardy fishermen and sailors of the coast, the sprinkling of bold and restless young fellows to be found in any staid farming community. These *canadiens* were first-class fighting men. But for whom would they fight in the event of "extremities"? The stolid British with their penny-pinching London government? Or the Americans, who could offer better pay and more adventure and another kind of freedom altogether?

One thing was certain. Even if the Canadians rallied *en masse* against a serious attack by the Americans, Carleton could only hope to hold the strip along the St. Lawrence. The huge expanse of the Canadian empire beyond, which looked so fine on the maps in London, was like an inflated bladder suspended over the Long Knives. One prick would leave nothing but the neck. In all the space beyond Montreal there was no settled white population except a few hundred Canadians at Detroit and perhaps a thousand others far down the great pocket on the left bank of the Mississippi. Many of these had Indian wives. All lived a semi savage existence, hunting and fishing, raising small crops, carousing on the traders' bad brandy or on wine made from wild grapes, knowing little and caring nothing of affairs so far away as Quebec or Philadelphia or New Orleans. The so-called "forts" in the pocket were stockaded trading posts in which the distant British authority was represented by an easygoing Creole agent or the factor of a fur merchant in Montreal.

As for the Indians, they were a shabby puzzle. By this time most of the tribes between the St. Lawrence and the American settlements had lost their old fighting power, debauched by white contact and chopped small in past wars. The best of them, the Iroquois group, were divided in their sympathies. Only the Mohawks in upper New York, under the direct sway of the Johnson family, could be counted upon to fight for the British King, and these were so reduced by disease and war that they could raise no more than one hundred fighting men.

The tribes of the West, those fierce proud creatures, still nursed the spite of Pontiac's war, in which the redcoats and the Long Knives had combined to put them down. The pocket between the Ohio and the Mississippi was shaped somewhat like a hornet's nest and it had the same meaning for British and Americans alike. Whoever stirred it up might well be stung himself.

Indeed in this whole matter of employing Indians in the approaching civil war in America there were wise men on both sides hoping to keep the savages quiet, just as there were others striving even now to enlist them in one cause or the other. Britons and Americans afterward engaged in a pot-and-kettle business of accusing each other on this point. The fact was that both parties bribed and used Indians from the start. The main difference was in the savage mind. The Indians had much more resentment against the Long Knives, who took their lands, than against the stolid redcoats, whose only desire was to draw their pay and drink their grog and get back to England as soon as their time of service passed. For that reason many more Indians took King George's gifts and fought in the Great White Father's cause; but the stain was on both flags throughout the war, and the victims suffered one as much as another.

All this was merely a foreboding in 1774. The immediate and obvious facts about his situation were quite enough to occupy Carleton's mind. In the little viceregal court that pirouetted about the Château St. Louis things looked deceptively well. His known sympathy for the Canadians, his part in framing the Quebec Act, his charming little wife with her fluent Parisian French, all gave Carleton the friendship of the *seigneurs* and of the Catholic hierarchy. Outside this circle (although he was still writing hopefully to London about battalions of Canadians) he could count on nothing but the bayonets of his redcoats.

Meanwhile the first Congress of the American colonies was wending its way to Penn's city of brotherly love. Invitations had been sent to Canada and Nova Scotia so that the Congress might be truly continental, but the North was silent and no delegates appeared. The Americans who went to Philadelphia knew they were risking their properties and perhaps their lives. Some were timid, some doubtful; the majority had the courage of their convictions, but they also had the inconsistency that goes with desperation.

On October 21, 1774, the Congress passed "An Address to the People of Great Britain" full of harsh words about the Quebec Act ("that worst of laws") which supported in America a religion that had spread "impiety, bigotry, persecution, murder and rebellion throughout every part of the world."

Four days later the same men passed "An Address to the Inhabitants of the Province of Quebec," in which nothing was said of
impiety or murder but a good deal about liberty and brotherhood.
"Seize the opportunity presented to you by Providence itself," this
document urged. "You are a small people compared to those who
with open arms invite you into fellowship. A moment's reflection
should convince you which will be the most for your interest and
happiness, to have all the rest of North America your unalterable
friends or your inveterate enemies. The injuries of Boston have
roused and associated every colony from Nova Scotia to Georgia.
Your province is the only link that is wanting to complete the bright
strong chain of union. Nature has joined your country to theirs. Do
you join your political interests."

This official invitation, with its hint that Nova Scotia already was
linked in the chain of union — Nova Scotia, whose territories then
ran from Gaspé to the sea and commanded the St. Lawrence mouth
— was followed up zealously by the American traders in Montreal.
Other American agents soon were busy in the countryside, passing
broadsides in French, even pinning copies to the church doors. The
habitant could rarely read, but there were Canadians ready to inter-
pret for him, for even among the *seigneurs* there were certain ones
nursing old grudges against the British.

This paper snowstorm blew into Canada by the old invasion route
from the American colonies, the long slit in the shaggy frontier hills
where Lake Champlain and the Richelieu River led the way to
Montreal. Therefore the region about Montreal was most exposed
to it, while Quebec, far down the St. Lawrence, was most aloof. This
had an effect on Canadian attitudes later on when American armies
followed up their notices.

The Champlain pass, the Canadian Khyber, was wide open. True,
the old French forts built to guard it were still there, Crown Point
on the western shore of Lake Champlain and Ticonderoga near its
foot, each with a bristle of cannon that had been silent fifteen years.
But the only soldiers there were a few British caretakers, thirty or so
at Ticonderoga and a baker's dozen at Crown Point, all bored with
solitude, suspecting nothing. Before their idle gaze the long lake
flashed like a silver tadpole in the ditch through the rugged hills,
with a wriggle of tail toward the Hudson Válley and its mouth
toward Montreal.

CHAPTER 3

1775

*Ethan Allen in the Champlain pass — Benedict Arnold
plans a dash on Quebec*

A S SOON as the New England snow was off the ground in
April '75 General Gage's "extremities" came upon him with a
bang, the fusillade at Lexington. The Revolution was off to
a first-class start, with the redcoats performing their drill-book
evolutions on the muddy New England roads and the rustic minutemen discovering that anyone who knew the value of a stump or a
stone wall could regard the fight for freedom as a glorified turkey
shoot.

As the months passed each side learned something from the other.
Sharp experience taught the British to raise light troops, especially
among the American Loyalists, who knew the country and could
move and fight and kill in cover. The Congress found that important
battles often must be fought in the open and eventually raised the
steady Continental Line, uniformed in blue and buff, which could
march, wheel, deploy, and charge with the bayonet in the best
manner of the drill books.

In the spring of '75 the struggle was just beginning and neither side
was in a mood to learn. In June the battle of Bunker Hill assured the
British that discipline would beat the rabble, no matter the cost, while
the Americans remained convinced about the turkey shoot. So far the
war had no pattern at all. But between the skirmish at Lexington and
the bloody clash at Boston there was an odd little comedy in the
backwoods toward Canada, and from it came a bold pattern for the
next three years.

The news of Lexington had passed quickly into the hills of Vermont, at that time a no man's land claimed by the colonies of New
Hampshire and New York and occupied by a tough-minded frontier

folk who took a few laws from the Old Testament and obeyed no others. Chief of these people at the moment was a tall wild man named Ethan Allen, the leader of a band of leatherstockings whom he called his Green Mountain Boys, all expert with the musket and the long frontier knife.

Allen and his boys had noted the small number and the stupor of the British guards at Ticonderoga and Crown Point, and on learning the news from Lexington they decided to take action. A camp election made colonels of Allen and his shadow Seth Warner, and soon afterward two hundred and thirty of the boys moved with their silent step from the misty mountain woods to the east shore of Lake Champlain. There they met another colonel, this one from Connecticut by way of Boston. He was Benedict Arnold, a man of parts.

Of the three colonels Arnold was far the ablest soldier, although none had much experience of war. Colonel Allen, in Tyler's words, was "a blustering frontier hero, an ableminded ignoramus of rough and ready humor, of boundless self-confidence, and of a shrewdness in thought and action equal to any emergency." These qualities made him hostile not only to King George but to the New Yorkers, to the Massachusetts Committee of Safety and anyone else who did not see things in a pure Green Mountain light. Colonel Warner's light also was pure green. Colonel Arnold was the many-colored man, the quick darting chameleon of the Revolutionary War, its brightest genius and eventually its blackest traitor. For instinctive military skill and energy Arnold stands out among the ruck of commanders, British and American, to this day.

When the Revolution opened Arnold was thirty-four, captain of the local militia company, and at the news from Lexington he mustered his men and marched to Cambridge. There he found an American army composed or rather discomposed of small groups like his own, with others coming in every day. The officers were elected by their own men, who proposed to run a war on the principles of a town meeting. The battle of Bunker Hill was as yet unfought. The American army camped and squabbled outside Boston while, inside, Thomas Gage built up his forces. The Americans were short of many things besides discipline and leadership, but what Arnold quickly noted was the shortage of artillery. His businesslike mind went to the depots on Lake Champlain. He put the matter before the local board of strategy, the Massachusetts Committee of Safety, and the delighted committee made him a colonel and sent him off to raise four hundred men in the mountains for the job. This was on April 29, just ten days after Lexington.

Arnold took horse for Vermont. There he met Allen and Warner and their boys, an "army" in their own right, not to be impressed by a paper colonel from some obscure committee in Cambridge. When Arnold offered to take command they said "No." When he insisted they offered to put him under arrest. It was Arnold's first encounter with lesser men who refused to see his worth in the national cause, and it was to be repeated as time went on; but in these early stages of the war he was able to keep his temper and to offer his services in any capacity so long as the job was done. He was a handy man at organizing anything, especially transportation, and so Allen put him in charge of the boats on Lake Champlain.

Allen's scouts, posing as simple forest wanderers, had gone over the lake to Ticonderoga and sauntered about the fort, chatting amiably with the little garrison. The bored men in the red coats had just passed a winter in these northern solitudes and they were glad to see anyone from outside. They even believed a backwoods tramp, one Phelps, who said he was looking for a barber, although he seemed more interested in their musket rack and the condition of the gate. Everything about Ticonderoga was known to Ethan Allen, while very little was known to Guy Carleton, absorbed in his worries at Quebec. Carleton had done the best he could with what he had, spreading his redcoats like a too-thin smear of cherry jam over the enormous slice of his responsibilities; and now that the country was emerging from another winter he could only hope that each lone post was alert.

On Lake Champlain the posts were not. The captain and thirty men in charge of two hundred cannon at Ticonderoga suspected nothing in the countryside. Thirteen soldiers in charge of a hundred and thirteen cannon at Crown Point were just as innocent. So were the ten men in charge of the fort and the armed sloop at St. Jean, where the Richelieu flowed out of the big lake toward Montreal. Artillery enough for a powerful army lay in these last-war posts along the water pass to Canada, with no guard but a handful of dreamers, and watched now by a picked force of catfooted mountaineers very much awake. The outcome was simple and, over the distance of time since, a hilarious farce. The shabby pink mice, still blinking after the winter's hibernation, were swallowed by the Green Mountain cat in three easy gulps.

Arnold brought the boats to Allen's rendezvous on the ninth of May, and that night they crossed the lake to Ticonderoga. The fort was dark and silent as they approached. The British sentry was awake, but the night's mist had dampened the powder in his musket pan and when he pulled the trigger nothing happened. He was knocked down in a moment, and the rest of the garrison were taken in their beds. Allen himself, knowing every inch of the fort, went to the captain's quarters, rattled the door with a gun butt, and called on the sleepy man within to surrender "In the name of the great Jehovah and the Continental Congress!" (At least that was what Allen always said afterwards.) At all events the British captain had no choice but to pull a dressing gown over his nightshirt and surrender. Colonel Warner had the same success in his pounce on Crown Point.

Then Colonel Arnold had his turn, passing up the lake to capture ten bewildered redcoats at St. Jean, together with their cannon and the useful sloop. In the whole operation from one end of the lake to the other, a distance of one hundred and twenty-five miles, hardly a shot was fired. The vital pass and its forts and stores were all in American hands by a stroke of magic. The very ease of its capture suggested that Canada itself might be taken in the same way. Allen boasted that he could seize Montreal with his Green Mountain Boys alone. Arnold knew better. Montreal, even with its "flimsy wall," was better garrisoned than the posts on Lake Champlain. The alarm had now gone down the Richelieu, Carleton's troops were mustering, and already a loyal and energetic French Canadian, De Belestre, had gathered a company of militia and was on the march from Montreal to St. Jean. Still, Carleton's forces were known to be small. If he marched them to Lake Champlain he must risk the lower St. Lawrence and Quebec. On that fact Arnold based another plan.

George Washington had heard the news of Bunker Hill as he rode from Philadelphia to take command of the American Army, and now that single-minded man found himself with a rabble of sixteen thousand militia outside the town of Boston. Inside were ten thousand British troops, well armed and disciplined, and a quartet of generals, Gage, Howe, Clinton and Burgoyne, each with a different theory of the way to win the war. And there, wrapped up in one package, with most of the principal characters, was the story of British defeat in the next six years.

The costly and empty success at Bunker Hill had discredited Gage, and his successor Howe had no intention of risking a Bunker Hill himself. Privately he deplored the quarrel in America, and quite publicly he and his mistress, Mrs. Loring, were enjoying the hospitality of the Boston Loyalists. The rebels outside had no cannon. If he could not break out, they could not break in, and he was content with that. The summer went by very pleasantly. The cool Virginian in the rebel headquarters at Cambridge was satisfied to see it go. The Ticonderoga cannon could not be moved to the siege of Boston until winter hardened the backwoods roads. Meanwhile he trained and disciplined his rustic troops.

And now came Arnold with his scheme for Canada, and the Virginian lent an ear. The classic pattern for the invasion of Canada had been set by geography and the experience of all the colonial wars against the French. It was as formal as a game of chess, with many petty moves but only two decisive ones, by sea to Quebec and overland by the Champlain pass to Montreal. Properly timed, with the proper force at each end, these twin moves won the game, as Wolfe and Amherst had proved.

But the Americans had no fleet and the British held the sea. Britain could ship troops and stores into Canada by way of Quebec and the great river, while every American soldier and every scrap of his supplies must travel the long country route to Lake Champlain. If Canada was to be taken, something had to be done about Quebec, and without ships. Arnold had the answer.

In these days of sail and wooden hulls the sea approach to Quebec was valid only five months in the year, beginning with the breakup of the winter ice and ending with the first autumn gales; for shipmasters feared the difficult navigation of the gulf and river after mid-September, and every year on the tail of the hurricane season came the frosts, which closed river and gulf until the following April or May.

It was now the beginning of September and Arnold proposed to take two thousand men through an almost unknown wilderness, traveling up the Kennebec River to its source, over the height of land to the source of the Chaudière, and down that ramping river to its meeting with the St. Lawrence just above Quebec. He would arrive there in October, when Quebec could look for no help by sea for the next six months. By that time other American forces, already assembled by Philip Schuyler at Albany, would have moved against Montreal through the Champlain gap. With any luck Arnold would burst out of the wilderness to find Quebec stripped of troops for the defense of Montreal and he could take the place in a leap. If Quebec proved strong, then Montreal must be weak. In that case Schuyler could destroy the small British force on the upper river and move down to join Arnold, bringing with him a siege battery from that great store on Lake Champlain. Either way Quebec was doomed before the winter's end.

On a much larger scale the proposed raid on Quebec was just the kind of gamble that had paid off so handsomely at Ticonderoga and Crown Point, and if anyone could win it Arnold was the man. So Washington approved and Arnold moved. His troops were picked largely from the army outside Boston. The problem of supply up the Kennebec compelled him to cut the proposed force to about eleven hundred men. Most of them were New Englanders, a mixture of fishermen, woodsmen and townsmen; but a company of Virginian riflemen under an able frontiersman, Daniel Morgan, led the march. Arnold started from Cambridge on September 13, an unlucky day.

CHAPTER 4

1775

Arnold's march to Quebec—Montgomery captures Montreal — Carleton's dramatic escape

ARNOLD's dash to Quebec remains a remarkable feat. All he had to guide him was a rough map and the notes of John Montrésor, an adventurous Englishman who, with Indian guides, had crossed that way from Quebec fourteen years before. The distance turned out to be nearly four hundred miles by the winding and turbulent courses of the rivers and the rough march over the height of land. (The names of the rivers alone were significant; Kennebec means "the rattlesnake" and Chaudière "the boiler.") The streams were swollen under the autumn rains and already snow was blowing in the hills. The supplies for eleven hundred men had to be moved in boats, against the current, up the whole length of the Kennebec. On its lower reaches the men could travel in the boats sometimes for miles, but above they had to drag their craft by track ropes, scrambling along the thickly wooded banks. Montrésor's map was vague between the rivers, and after a month of hard travel the army was lost for days in a maze of dismal ponds and muskegs at the head of the Chaudière. They were drenched with rains and chilled with snows. The supplies ran out, and at the height of land they had to abandon most of their boats.

At the end of October a starving mob straggled out of the forest upon the Canadian settlements along the Chaudière. Desertion, sickness, and death on the march had reduced their force by half and the survivors needed food and rest before they could go on. Fortunately for them the *habitant* farmers had in their cellars a winter's provisions, and Arnold had managed to drag a chest of hard cash through the wilderness. The attitude of the Chaudière people was typical of the *habitants* throughout Quebec province during the American occupation. Some hastened off to warn the British at

Quebec. Others as readily went back and forth as spies and couriers in American pay. The majority shrugged and sold their provisions for the best possible price.

The American view of them appears in the diary of one of Arnold's soldiers;

"The French Inhabitants Carried all our Provision and Baggage and were very kind and hospitable to us. All camped in the French houses and bought Bread Milk Eggs Potatoes Rum Brandy Sugar Turkeys Fowls etc. Their Fences are made of Ceader Stakes Drove Down into the Ground about 2 inches from each other. All their Farming Tools and household furniture is very Poor. They draw their Oxen by the horns. Their Houses and Barns are Chiefly Thatched and very Poor. They Lodge Chiefly on Straw Beds which are raised on Bedsteads about 2 feet high. Their Windows are Chiefly Paper but Some Glass. A Good Chunked Breed of horses. Small Cattle. Poor Hogs. Very Good Fowls of all sorts. No Chairs to Set on. All Set on blocks & Stools etc. It is to be observed that the French in these Back settlements are very Stupid, not one to 400 that could read one word, but were very Precise in Saying their Prayers Counting their Beads and Crossing themselves."

At St. Georges de Beauce (called St. Egan or Sartigan by the Americans) Arnold harangued a gathering of savages, closing with, "Now if the Indians, our brethren, will join us, we will be very much obliged to them, and will give them one Portuguese [a gold coin worth about $8.80] per month, two dollars bounty, and find them their provisions, and they liberty to choose their own officers." On these promises fifty warriors joined the Americans and went with them down the Chaudière.

On November 8, marching through the light snow of early winter in their broken shoes, Arnold's men arrived at Point Lévis and gazed across the broad St. Lawrence to the spires and citadel of Quebec. They were late and their force was down to 650 men, of whom a hundred were still unfit to fight, but on the whole the American strategy was working well.

The column from upper New York, moving into Canada through the Champlain pass, had drawn Carleton away from Quebec with most of his troops. His deputy at Quebec, Captain Hector Cramahé, had managed to snatch away all the boats from the Lévis side of the river before the Americans got there; but Arnold's Indians had brought their canoes, and other canoes and boats had been picked

up along the Chaudière. According to Arnold's plan, all that remained was to repeat Wolfe's tactics exactly and the prize was won.

On the night of November 13, two months after leaving Cambridge on that other ill-omened day, Arnold crossed over the great
stream and led five hundred men up the Heights of Abraham. The
famous path was still there, slippery but unguarded, and in the
morning the little army of Americans marched boldly across the old
battlefield, formed up just out of gunshot from the ramparts, and
gave three lusty cheers. It was an invitation to the garrison to rush
out, as the French had rushed out in '59, to be destroyed by one or
two sharp volleys on the plain.

But Captain Cramahé knew the lesson of '59. The walls of Quebec
were not to be tumbled by a noise, like those of Jericho, nor by the
mere apparition of an army on the plain. Obviously the men who
had come so far through a wilderness had brought nothing but the
muskets in their hands. The nearest American supply of artillery was
on Lake Champlain; hence everything now depended on the fight
for Montreal, 150 miles upriver. Cramahé manned the ramparts and
sat tight awaiting news from Carleton, and Arnold had to content
his restless energy in cutting off the town from its country supplies
and finding quarters for his men among the farms.

Some ardent souls in the American force were for storming
Quebec at once, but Arnold's spies in the town had sent bad news.
Cramahé's soldiers had been joined at the last moment by several
companies of the newly raised Royal Highland Emigrant Regiment
under a fighting veteran, Colonel Allan Maclean, moving swiftly
down the river from Sorel; and from the other direction a company
of recruits for Maclean had arrived by sea from Newfoundland just
before winter closed the gulf. Also Cramahé had levied within the
town a battalion of French-Canadian militia and another of British
Canadians. In all, said the spies, he had more than fifteen hundred
men under arms. They added however that six hundred of these, the
French-Canadian conscripts, would join the Americans at the first
chance. In this the spies were indulging an amiable fancy; but the rest
of their information was correct and it spoiled any hope of taking
Quebec in the easy manner of Ticonderoga. So Arnold sat tight
also, awaiting the news from Montreal. It was on the way.

The New York troops mustered by Schuyler had marched for
Lake Champlain as early as July, with an order from Congress to
"take possession of St. Johns, Montreal and any other parts of the

country . . . if General Schuyler finds it practicable and that it will not be disagreeable to the Canadians." An order as ambiguous as it was ambitious, for when it was issued Schuyler had only a few hundred men and not even Guy Carleton knew if the Canadians would agree with an American army on their soil.

On the march to Ticonderoga, however, the New Yorkers were joined by a thousand Connecticut Yankees under blustering old General Wooster and by a company of Green Mountain Boys under Ethan Allen and Seth Warner. These made up a considerable force and at once there was a squabble over the command. While this was going on a third general, Richard Montgomery, with a commission from the Congress, arrived on the scene. He was only thirty-eight, a former British officer who had married into the Livingston family, powerful in Whig circles in the Hudson Valley.

Philip Schuyler grew sick of the quarreling and gave up the command, returning to his home in Albany. Wooster, a brave old tosspot, at last agreed to serve under Montgomery, which was just as well for the cause. The expedition needed a leader of skill and sobriety, for in view of Arnold's scheme the original plan was enlarged. The force at Lake Champlain was to seize Montreal and then join hands with Arnold.

On the farther side of the hills and forests Guy Carleton was not idle. The comedy on Lake Champlain in May had been sad stuff to him. With the vital pass in American hands his Canadian empire was open to a quick stab at the throat. The British commander at Montreal, Colonel Templer, had sent nearly all of his small force up the Richelieu to restore the post at St. Jean; and as soon as Carleton learned of Montgomery's march he hurried to support Templer with most of the redcoats from Quebec.

The captain general had written to London for reinforcements, but the return passage in the teeth of the westerly winds at this time of year was a matter of months, and it was plain that he could expect no help from Britain until spring. Therefore he called on his next and last resource, the Canadians themselves.

Most of the *seigneurs* came forward readily enough, and some (but only some) of the adventurous class. The *habitants* as a whole remained stolidly on their farms. It was not their quarrel, they observed. The flutter of pamphlets and the open sedition of American merchants and others in Montreal had reached every parish. Everyone knew that *les bastonnais* had beaten King George's soldiers in open fight at Lexington and Bunker hill, and that in the hours of a night or two they had taken Ticonderoga and Crown Point, those famous strongholds of the old war. They had deposed British governors all the way from New England to Florida. A formidable people. And what was King George doing about all this? He could not even get his Englishmen to cross the sea and fight for him! He was begging the Queen of Russia for troops, he was begging the German princes. Soon, if *les bastonnais* did not get here first, Canada would be swarming with armed barbarians in foreign uniforms. In that case surely the sooner *les bastonnais* arrived the better!

There was more than a grain of truth in this propaganda, including the British bid for Russian troops (which the haughty Catherine refused) and for German troops, which their own greedy princelings were now selling at so much per head for the British service in America. And how was the simple *habitant* to compare the virtues of the Americans as an army of occupation? His priests and *seigneurs* told him that *les bastonnais* hated his language and his religion, but of course the priests and *seigneurs* had their bread buttered on the British side. What to do? Wait and see.

So, while the *habitant* waited and watched, a column of dour redcoats and a few loyal Canadian *capotes* moved out of Sorel and Montreal toward the frontier. From the opposite direction Montgomery's fifteen hundred homespun jackets and hunting shirts were moving up Lake Champlain. The clash came at the village of St. Jean.

St. Jean was at the end of navigation down the Richelieu from Lake Champlain, just as Chambly was at the end of navigation upstream from the St. Lawrence. Between these places the Richelieu tumbled down sixteen miles of impassable rapids. Of the two, Chambly was the more important because its stone fort-barrack covered the lower reach of the Richelieu and the cross-country road to Montreal, a short day's march away. It was garrisoned by eighty redcoats under Major Stopford. Above the rapids at St. Jean stood a weaker fort but a much larger garrison, for this was the place where the invaders must leave their boats and fight. Hence Major Charles Preston was posted there with six hundred men, most of them regulars with a platoon of Scotch Loyalists and ninety Canadian militia under De Belestre.

Montgomery's troops scrambled out of their boats beyond gunshot of St. Jean and quickly surrounded the fort. Preston was invited to surrender. He refused. What was more he held on stoutly

through the months of September and October. The wild man Ethan
Allen soon tired of stuff like this. He was not used to garrisons alert
and shooting and he still thought that he and a band of mountain
boys, with some assistance from inside, could take Montreal in a
jump. He dived into the woods past Chambly, popped up at Laprairie on the St. Lawrence, and began to enlarge his force among
the more credulous *habitants* on a promise of thirty pennies a day
and all the loot they could carry away from the Tory shops of
Montreal.

For their part the rebel group inside Montreal had been active
many months. Their leaders were the American merchant Thomas
Walker; John Brown, an agent for the Boston Committee of Correspondence; and a French Canadian, the radical Valentin Jautard.
Together they had enlisted a following among the French as well
as the English-speaking citizens.

So far the plans of the *congressistes* in and outside Montreal had
gone extremely well. James Livingston, an American merchant of
Chambly, had raised a battalion of Canadians and joined Montgomery. Moses Hazen, another American merchant on the Richelieu,
was raising a Canadian battalion of his own. In Montreal itself there
were others preparing to play Trojan horse when the invading
army appeared on the farther bank.

In the meantime Montgomery, like the well-trained soldier he was,
concerned himself with cutting off St. Jean and Chambly from
Sorel, the British base at the mouth of the Richelieu. He could not
march for Montreal with seven hundred British troops on his line of
communication with Lake Champlain. Instead it was Ethan Allen,
with his strangely mixed following of mountain boys and armed
habitants, who appeared before Montreal and sent word across the
river to the committee. From that point things went astray. Thomas
Walker and his wife did most of the talking for the rebel group in
Montreal, but John Brown was the appointed leader for action, and
John Brown's body had no desire to molder in the grave. He saw
through Allen's bravado at once. As a result the Montreal *congressistes* failed to appear in arms. What did appear was a mixed
column of British soldiers, loyal Canadians, and refugee backwoodsmen from the Mohawk Valley in New York State, about three hundred in all, under the command of Major Carden, one of Wolfe's
veterans.

These came up with Allen's force at Long Point, and after a smart fight (in which Carden was killed) the rebel *habitants* fled into the woods and Jehovah's witness and his eighty mountain boys surrendered. Carleton shipped his remarkable prisoner off to England, where he spent the next two or three years in the confinement of Pendennis Castle, Cornwall, a sad change from the green hills of Vermont.

This skirmish had some far-reaching results. Joseph Brant, the young Mohawk chief, returning from a visit to the Indians of Lake Ontario, had stopped for a talk with the British officers in Montreal; and he was there when the whole town saw a band of the dreaded American leatherstockings trailing off as prisoners. The British officers now invited Brant to visit England and see for himself the power and grandeur of the Great White Father; and Joseph went, in one of the last ships out of Quebec.

That winter Brant was the handsome brown lion of the London drawing rooms. James Boswell was one of his friends. Romney painted his portrait. He was laden with gifts, including a silver-hilted dagger, a brace of double-barreled pistols, and an astonishing musket that could fire fifteen shots from a single loading. When Brant returned to the Mohawks in the spring of '76 he was convinced of the British wealth and power, and if there had been any doubts in his mind about his own course in the war, those doubts were gone.

Meanwhile, as Allen and Brant went off to England (Allen in handcuffs and Brant the captain's honored guest), the American cause in Canada took a sharp turn toward success. On October 18 a small company of Americans and Canadian *congressistes*, by-passing the stubborn Preston at St. Jean, appeared before the post at Chambly trundling two light field guns. The guns could do little more than knock chips off the stone walls of the barrack, but the weak-kneed Stopford surrendered at the end of thirty-six hours. He was well supplied with food and ammunition, which the Americans needed very much and were thankful to get, and his abject surrender exposed Sorel and Montreal and left the gallant Preston in a hopeless position up the river at St. Jean.

At Montreal Carleton had been mustering a force for Preston's relief. He had only two hundred regulars, but the local *seigneurs* by a combination of eloquence and threat had managed to scrape up twelve hundred *habitant* militia. This seemed a sufficient force, but as of old the militia had a high proportion of *chouayens*. There was much grumbling because the *seigneurs* had dragged them away from their fall plowing. There was a suspicion among them that certain *seigneurs* were secretly in league with the Americans. It was true in at least one case, that of Saint-Luc de la Corne. (Carleton wondered why so few of the Indians in the Catholic missions across the river had answered his call to arms. Saint-Luc had persuaded them to ignore it.)

Some of the Canadian militia were ardent enough, like Simon Sanguinet of Montreal, who wanted to cross the river and attack the American army at once. Most of them were cold. Exaggerated tales of the size of the American army were drifting down the Richelieu. The militia deserted by scores each night. The small band of Indians crept away. When Carleton sent a patrol to test the river crossing they were driven back by sharp American musketry from the other bank.

Under the gray rainy skies his "army" melted away. On November 3, after a stoic defense at long odds and on thin supplies, Preston surrendered at St. Jean. The attempt to hold the Canadian tip of the Champlain pass had cost half the regular garrison of Canada, and already the Americans were in Sorel and had sent a force cross the St. Lawrence at Berthier.

Carleton could do nothing now for Montreal; he could only try to save Quebec. He was still unaware of Arnold's daring march. He was not even sure how far Montgomery's forces had progressed on the St. Lawrence below him. On November 11 he bade farewell to the band of Loyalists in Montreal, loaded his stores and ammunition on a few sloops at the waterfront, and marched the remnant of his regulars aboard, 130 officers and men. On the following day, catching a momentary wind, he began to run the gauntlet down the river.

On November 13, the very day that Arnold crossed the river to Wolfe's Cove, the eight or nine thousand inhabitants of Montreal watched a long column of American muskets winding through the streets to the Place d'Armes. It was a motley march, for among the homespun jackets and the fringed hunting shirts were many Americans wearing in triumph the red coats taken from the prisoners at St. Jean. The *congressistes* of Montreal were jubilant.

General Montgomery proclaimed that his forces had come to give liberty and security to the province of Quebec. The *congressistes*, speaking through Valentin Jautard, replied with fervency that "our hearts have always desired union ... and receive the troops of union as our own men." Montgomery, an Ulsterman and a veteran of

Wolfe's army like Carleton himself, observed privately that "the Canadians will be our friends as long as we are able to maintain our ground."

The Church, personified by M. Montgolfier, vicar-general of Montreal, remained vigorously hostile to the Americans and especially to the local *congressistes* with their Voltairian spokesman Jautard. Most of the inhabitants, as Arnold had found along the Chaudière, were indifferent. So long as the farmer could take his pigs to the best cash market, it mattered nothing whether *les anglais* talked through their noses or their teeth.

The Americans and their *congressiste* allies down the river at Sorel were soon informed of Carleton's run for Quebec. The St. Lawrence at that point, where it entered Lake St. Peter, was choked by a cluster of islands, and the passages between them were easily commanded by cannon. It was a perfect trap, for the Americans had found the necessary cannon in the abandoned British camp at Sorel. All they required was a few days' time to raft and drag them into place, and time they got by favor of the weather — for even the weather was against the British now.

Carleton's sloops, held up by head winds soon after leaving Montreal, came down to the islands at last, to find the batteries placed. Both banks of the river were swarming with Yankee riflemen and with eager *congressistes*, among them John Brown of Montreal. These beat off an attempt of the British to land on the north shore and make their escape through the woods. The soldiers and crews of the sloops had no choice but an ultimate surrender, for the trap was closing behind them as well as in front. Yet there was still a chance that a few men might slip through, and Carleton took it.

One of the sloop captains, Bouchette, better known on the river as the Wild Pigeon, offered to take Carleton past the islands in an open boat by night. His chosen crew for the adventure were all Canadians, and Carleton dressed as one of them in blanket coat and sash, *bonnet rouge* and moccasins. In the chill November dark the boat crept into the passage between Ile St. Ignace and Ile du Pas. At the place of greatest danger the Pigeon ordered his men to cease rowing and paddle with their hands. So, almost under the American gun muzzles, the captain general and governor of Canada slipped through Montgomery's grasp.

In the morning the boat came to Three rivers, where by the erratic fortune of war the British ship *Fell* lay ready to drop down the river.

There was danger below, where Arnold's troops waited outside Quebec, but the *Fell* went through and on November 19 Carleton stepped ashore in the lower town. On the same day, far up the river, the crews of the sloops and the British soldiers dumped their gunpowder into the river and surrendered. From that moment, in all the great map empire of the governor's command, the British flag flew over the citadel of Quebec and nowhere else except Niagara, Detroit and a few other small posts cut off in the heart of the continent.

CHAPTER 5

1775

The attack on Quebec — Montgomery's death
— The capture of Daniel Morgan

IN THE diary of Thomas Ainslie, captain of militia at Quebec, appears this November entry: "On the 19th (a Happy day for Quebec!) to the unspeakable joy of the friends of the Government and to the utter Dismay of the abettors of Sedition and Rebellion, General Carleton arrived in the *Fell*, arm'd ship, accompanied by an armed schooner. We saw our Salvation in his Presence."

The man with the sachem nose and the small tight mouth did not disappoint them, although Cramahé had saved Quebec in the first place by his quick measures for defense and by his firm front in the face of Arnold. Carleton himself wrote generously, "I find everything has been done in my absence for the Defence of this Place [that] the unfortunate Situation of Things would permit; could the people of the Town and seamen be depended upon I should flatter myself we might hold out till navigation opens next spring, at least till a few Troops might come up the River, for I fear the delays commonly attending a large armament; but tho' the weather is far advanced we have so many Enemies within and foolish People, dupes to those Traitors, with the natural fears of Men unused to war; I think our Fate extremely doubtful to say nothing worse."

The populace were certainly divided. Some of the British merchants slipped away with their families to the safety of well-stocked farms on the Island of Orleans. American merchants in the town naturally gave every possible aid to their friends outside. Many of the French-Canadian townsmen believed that the Americans were bound to win the city and hoped that Carleton would surrender quickly to save them the terrors of a siege. Others went further and sought the good graces of the invader by acting as spies within and messengers without. On the other hand there were many *Quebecois* proud of spirit and loyal to Guy Carleton if not entirely to the King across the sea, and there was a considerable group of British merchants, clerks, and officials ready to fight for both.

To muster a full garrison Carleton scraped the Quebec barrel to the bottom — the very ships at the wharves. What he got was an odd collection, but it stood up to the rigors of a winter siege, and when the time for fighting came it fought. All told, the garrison came to 1800 men. Of these only 448 were regulars, including two companies of the 7th Fusiliers, the small battalion of Highland Emigrants under Colonel Maclean, and parties of engineers and artillerymen. Two naval ships, the *Lizard* and *Hunter*, provided 400 seamen and 35 marines. There were 50 merchant seamen, 543 French-Canadian militia under Colonel Noel Voyer, and 330 British-Canadian militia.

On the second day of December, Montgomery took Arnold's men under his own command at Pointe aux Trembles, 20 miles above Quebec. Their united forces were perhaps 2000, including Canadian *congressistes*, whose numbers varied but were certainly 400. Disease and the harsh cold of the northern winter were at work on the Americans and as the weeks went on the sick list grew. Arnold's troops, weeded out and hardened by their desperate march, were by far the best in Montgomery's army. They had arrived at Quebec ragged and almost barefoot, and although they had covered their feet with the raw hides of Canadian cattle slaughtered for their mess pots, they were still poorly clad. Montgomery was able to supply them with captured British jackets like those worn by many of his own men, and over these in bad weather most of the American soldiers wore typical *habitant* blanket cloaks, bought or stolen in the countryside.

Thus when the invaders drew up to the fortress the troops on both sides looked quaintly alike; the British regulars on the ramparts in red jackets, and the Quebec militia in green or the common gray homespun of the country; the Americans on the plain in captured scarlet, in homespun, in green hunting shirts; and on both sides the useful *capotes*. These similarities made it hard to distinguish one from the other even in close encounter, and for their own benefit the Americans stuck sprigs of hemlock in their hats whenever they skirmished up to the walls.

The rocky height of Quebec rose three hundred feet sheer above the St. Lawrence and sloped to about one hundred feet above the valley of the little river St. Charles, which flowed into the St. Lawrence on the seaward side of the town. The citadel stood on the crest with the upper town close behind it, and at their feet lay the lower town by the water. Outside the defenses on the St. Charles side was the straggling suburb of St. Roch. The ramparts ran about a thousand yards across the high neck of the cape. Inside them, even after the flight of the timid, Carleton had to feed and warm five thousand people, of whom more than three thousand were non-combatants.

Outside the walls, the Americans occupied St. Roch and extended their siege lines across the plains of Abraham at a quarter-mile distance from the ramparts, mounting their siege guns chiefly on a wooded spur beside the road to Sillery. Their troops, billeted on the *habitant* farmers, amused themselves in looting the country homes of well-to-do Loyalists in Quebec. At first they were able to pay for supplies in cash, but when their cash ran out they had only the celebrated Continental paper dollars which (in the pungent phrase of the time) were not worth a Continental damn. The *habitants* had suffered from paper currency in the days of the old French regime; at one remote time, well remembered, their ancestors had even been forced to accept "money" printed on playing cards, which in the upshot had more to do with knaves than kings. As the American occupation went on, with its hungry demands and paper pay, the *habitant* came to take a dubious and then a sour view of his liberators.

Montgomery's artillery, shipped down from Montreal before ice closed the river, was unable to breach the hard-frozen walls of the fortress. For their part, the British gunners on the ramparts could only search for American batteries hidden in trees or masked by slabs of ice and snow, with occasional pot shots at buildings known to be used by the enemy or at parties moving in the open. It was a slow game at long bowls played in the bitter air of a Canadian winter, and with time on his side Carleton was content to play it.

The American troops quartered about the countryside and carousing in the drinking dens of St. Roch began to suffer from smallpox, a disease more or less endemic in those days in all the seaports of the continent. The crammed confinement of winter quarters and a complete lack of sanitary discipline changed a scattered infection to a scourge. With dismay Montgomery saw his effective strength shrinking as the December days went by. And now the short enlistment period, that bane of American military operations, began to suck away the ardor of the troops, even of Arnold's tough men. Many of them reckoned their time of service finished at the year's end.

The pillaged wine, the rude fare of the farms, the occasional embraces of a fuddled hag in St. Roch were all very well; but they were bored with their long vigil on the bleak plateau, in the sharp cold that came on the northwest wind from Hudson Bay, and with the alien feeling they all had in a country where not even the dogs understood a word they spoke. Even officers talked openly of packing off for home as soon as the new year came.

This growing *malaise* in his troops, even worse than the smallpox, drove Montgomery toward a rash decision as Christmas approached. In a few more days the American army would melt away as Carleton's had melted at Montreal. Their cannon balls could not damage the frozen ramparts and the mortar shells they tossed like explosive footballs into the town could only hurt a few inhabitants in the streets. Carleton seemed well supplied with food and ammunition, for he had treated every demand for surrender with contempt.

Montgomery could not afford to hesitate now, although as a soldier familiar with the town he must have known the madness of the plan. It was to occupy Quebec by night, stealing past the citadel on both sides and dashing into the lower streets. According to his chief advisers, a pair of Montreal *congressistes* named Antell and Price, the seizure of the lower town would scare the Quebec militia out of their wits; the merchants among them would be fearful for their shops and warehouses, the rank and file for their homes; and under their pleas or actual desertion Carleton must give up, for his regulars and sailors were too few to man the ramparts and the upper town as well.

With the plan chosen, Montgomery and Arnold soon worked out the details. Livingston, the American merchant from Chambly, was to lead four hundred Canadian *congressistes* in a demonstration against the citadel from the Plains of Abraham, where the British would expect attack. A battery of mortars in St. Roch would lob bombshells into the upper town. At the Palace Gate on that side, Jerry Duggan, a former barber, would make another demonstration with a party of *congressistes* and Arnold's Indians.

With Carleton's attention thus diverted, Arnold and six hundred men, including Morgan's sharpshooters, would slip from St. Roch into the dark streets of the lower town and press on to the docks. From the other side Montgomery and five hundred men would make their way along the base of Cape Diamond and link with Arnold's force at the foot of Mountain Street. The combined troops would then scramble into the upper town, where all would be confusion and dismay, and Carleton would be caught in front and rear, the final application of those pincers which had started from Boston and Albany.

For success the attempt required a night of wind and snow to blind the British sentinels and hush the attackers' footsteps. Such a night came on December 30, a neat coincidence, one day before so many of the American enlistments expired and the night before hogmanay, when presumably Carleton's Highlanders would have begun drinking to the folk at home with any substitute for whiskey they could find.

At two o'clock on the morning of December 31, in the wild gusts of the snowstorm, the Americans and their *congressiste* and Indian allies moved to the assault. Hemlock twigs were useless in the dark. For mutual recognition many of the Americans pinned to their hats a slip of white paper on which as an extra flourish they had written *Liberty or Death*. Montgomery's column went down to the river by way of the famous path at Wolfe's Cove and crept along to the foot of Cape Diamond with the storm in their teeth. This took much time, and it was five o'clock in the morning when they shot into the air the green rockets which were the signal for the general assault.

On the plateau Livingston's battalion of Canadians immediately opened fire against the ramparts, at the same time whooping and cheering as if the whole American Army were afoot across the plain. The battery in St. Roch began to fling bombs into the upper town, with Jerry Duggan's party yelling and firing muskets at the Palace Gate.

Arnold slipped forward along the street that wound around the St. Charles shore of the town. Montgomery's men followed the narrow beach under Cape Diamond itself.

Unluckily for Montgomery the British sentries were alert. If the Highlanders had found any whiskey for a premature toast to hogmanay, it had merely sharpened their wits for war. And unluckily some too eager American symphathizers in the lower town had begun to show lanterns below the citadel for Montgomery's guidance in the storm; these were glowing an hour before Montgomery sent up his rockets. When the Highland sentries on Cape Diamond reported the strange lights to Captain Malcolm Fraser, that alert officer turned out his guard and passed the word to head-quarters. By the time Montgomery gave his signal the church bells of Quebec were already clanging the alarm and Carleton was mustering his reserve troops in the Place d'Armes. The uproar of Livingston's and Duggan's men was impressive for a few minutes, but when they continued their random shooting from the cover of the dark it was obviously a feint.

The chance of American raids into the lower town had been fore-seen and the shore approaches on both sides were barred. The ap-proach from the foot of Cape Diamond had a timber barricade and blockhouse at Près-de-Ville, with four small cannon to sweep the path along the beach. On the St. Charles side the road from St. Roch followed a narrow shelf under the cliff called Sault au Matelot (Sailor's Leap); and here were two barricades, one just before the Leap and the second and larger one around the corner. The larger barricade stretched a hundred yards between the river and the foot of the cliff, with loopholes for musketry and raised platforms for cannon. All these defenses of the lower town were manned by small groups of sailors and militia, some of whom were seminary students.

Montgomery's column, winding between the St. Lawrence and a sheer rock face, hacked their way through a fence of wooden stakes and there halted sharply at the sight of the Près-de-Ville barrier on the other side. The silence of the blockhouse and barricade was ominous. The American advance guard hesitated. To start them forward Montgomery whipped out his sword and led the way shout-ing, "Come on, brave boys! Quebec is ours!"

Behind the Près-de-Ville barricade stood thirty Canadian and eight British militiamen in charge of Quebec volunteer officers Captain Chabot and Lieutenant Picard. With them were nine seamen and a sergeant of Royal Artillery manning the four cannon. They had seen the head of the American column through the swirl of snow, but they held their fire until Montgomery's shout. The passage between river and cliff was only fifty feet wide, and Montgomery's men were treading on each other's heels along the winding length of it when the barrier cannon blazed and the night's storm became a blast of grapeshot.

The advance party, including Montgomery, went down in a bloody heap. At a second blast the rest of the column turned about and vanished into the storm the way they had come, dragging their wounded with them, and that ended their part in the night's affairs. After daylight a garrison patrol found a hand showing through the drifted snow and uncovered Montgomery's body. He had been killed instantly by bullets through his head and thighs and lay on his back two paces from the water's edge. Nearby were the bodies of two of his staff officers and ten American soldiers.

On the other side of the town the resolute Arnold was having his own difficulties. The route from St. Roch forced his men to pass close below the Grand Battery, whose walls were lined with British sailors shooting at the dim forms flitting between the houses in the street beneath. The Americans pressed on dragging a cannon on a sled and came to the first barricade at the Sailor's Leap, which was defended by sixty Quebec militia with two cannon.

Arnold's cannon stuck in the deepening snow, and for an hour the Canadians at the barricade beat off all attacks. The Americans suffered severely. Among others, Arnold himself went down with a bullet in his leg and was carried away from the fight. The tall roaring figure of Daniel Morgan now took charge. With a well-timed rush in the snowy dark at a moment when the barrier cannon were being reloaded he and his riflemen overran the post at last.

Moving on swiftly, they surprised and captured a reserve company of amateur soldiers, all Quebec merchants, posted in a building beyond the barrier. The Americans' musket pans were wet with snow, and their leading troops took the dry weapons of the merchants for an attack on the second barricade. This was the more formidable of the two, running across two streets between cliff and river, with its cannon on high platforms and with a hundred muskets flashing from the loopholes and from the upper windows of the houses.

Again Morgan led the assault. His Virginian marksmen shot the gunners off the platforms, but the defenders under Captain Dumas held on stubbornly at the loopholes. The wooden pickets of this barricade were twelve feet high, and the ladders dragged forward by the Americans were thrown down or in some cases actually seized and pulled inside by a giant Canadian named Charland.

In the east a gray light began to gleam through the still-driving snow. The night had gone, and soon the garrison could shoot with better skill, not only from the barricade but from the Grand Battery where the American support line was exposed. Some of Morgan's men tried to steal around the end of the barricade on the ice floes at the water side, but in the snowy morning dusk they blundered among the mooring ropes of ships tied to posts and shanties and were discovered.

Carleton, matching reports from the whole noisy perimeter, now knew the situation. Already part of his reserve had gone down to support the little group at Près-de-Ville in case Montgomery's troops attacked again, and a reinforcement of Fusiliers and Highlanders had reached the gallant Dumas at the foot of the Sault au Matelot.

The rest were few but they were enough. Captain McDougall of the Highlanders and Captain Lawes of the Royal Engineers sallied out of the Palace Gate with 120 men to take Morgan in the rear. Jerry Duggan's *congressistes* and Indians were placed to hold that point, but they fled over the ice floes in the mouth of the St. Charles, two desperate miles, and scattered into the country on the other side. Lawes and McDougall were able to capture half of Morgan's column with ease. As one American rifleman put it, they "most fairly and handsomely cooped us up."

Morgan himself, with the fighting front of the column, had taken to the houses before the Sault au Matelot post, shooting from the windows and hoping still that Montgomery's men were in the lower town and moving up to take the barricade in the rear. They were soon disillusioned. Parties of Highlanders appeared and began to storm their way from house to house, clearing the rooms with the bayonet. The Americans fought back fiercely. When Lieutenant Anderson of the Royal Navy with a party of seamen tried to force his way along the open street Morgan shot him dead and led a counterattack that drove the sailors back to the barricade.

But now the British sortie under Lawes and McDougall came up at Morgan's back. The big Virginian and his men held on in the houses until ten o'clock in the bleak winter morning and then surrendered. It had been a bold try and a stubborn one. Had Montgomery's men at Près-de-Ville possessed half the spirit of their own commander, the Americans must have taken the lower town. In that event, however, they would have lost their whole army instead of Arnold's half. The Quebec militia, fighting in their own streets, had shown a spirit beyond all expectations; combined with Carleton's soldiers and sailors they made a stout garrison, and any American attempt to storm the steep street leading to the upper town would have perished. The precarious paths along the shore by St. Roch and below Cape Diamond were easily cut off once the Americans were inside, and Livingston's *congressistes* on the Plains of Abraham were too few to extract them.

So ended Canada's year 1775, with its governor and garrison confined like their own prisoners within the ramparts of Quebec, with the Americans still in control of the St. Lawrence from Wolfe's Cove to the rapids above Montreal, and winter ruling all. In the vast Canadian landscape these struggles of men at St. Jean, at Chambly, at Montreal, and at Quebec had been no more than the pricking of a few fireflies in the immensity of a summer night.

Indeed the sublime comedy of the American Revolution, as of the Seven Years' War before it, was that armies seldom larger than a few hundred men, never more than a few thousand, moving like thin files of hostile ants in the fields and woods of the Atlantic strip, claimed to be battling for a continent whose extent they did not know and which in its greater part knew nothing of their existence.

Even among men in touch with British-American politics and war there was complete indifference on the part of those who measured the size of the continent against the ants. One of these, a Spaniard named Heceta, sailing up the Pacific coast from Mexico, had seen this year the mouth of a mighty river which might be the long-sought "Oregon" at last. Another, the Englishman James Cook, after a three years' voyage in the great South Sea, was in England planning a new expedition. It was sponsored by the British Government but it had nothing to do with the rebellious colonists across the Atlantic. Cook was to search the vague west coast of North America and to solve from that side, once and for all, the puzzle of two centuries, the existence of a northwest passage.

CHAPTER 6

1776

Benjamin Franklin's mission to Montreal — Carleton breaks the siege of Quebec — The Affair at The Cedars

ON THE second day of the new year Arnold wrote to the senior American officer Wooster at Montreal, giving the detail of his disaster, and adding, "Our force at this time does not exceed eight hundred men, including Colonel Livingston's regiment of two hundred Canadians, and some scattered Canadian forces amounting to two hundred more. Many of the troops are dejected and anxious to get home, and some have actually set off . . . For God's sake order as many men down as you can possibly spare consistent with the safety of Montreal, and all the mortars, howitzers and shells that you can possibly bring. I hope you will stop every rascal who has deserted from us and bring him back again . . . I think it will be highly necessary, with the reinforcement which I make no doubt Congress will send, that they should order all the large mortars and howitzers at Crown Point, Ticonderoga and Fort George on to this place. Monsieur Pelissier, who has a furnace at Three Rivers, assures me that he can cast any size and number of shells between this and the beginning of April. I hope the honourable Continental Congress will not think of sending less than eight or ten thousand men to secure and form a lasting connection with this country."

Arnold was still determined to take Quebec and seal the conquest of Canada, wounded though he was and shattered as his forces were. In a long view his assurance was justified. The St. Lawrence would be choked with ice for another four months, during which the winter road by horse and sled from the American colonies to Montreal was at its smooth-gliding best and the ice of lake and river could support the movement of heavy cannon. He had all the resources of the colonies to draw upon, for the only other British army in America was shut up in Boston, just as Carleton's garrison was shut up in Quebec; and Arnold could scrape the resources of Canada as well. He could even add, in a note to the Congress, "The forts at Niagara and Detroit are an object which I make no doubt the honourable Congress have in view. Mr. Antill, now on his way down, can inform you in regard to their strength, stores, etc."

Carleton made no move to break the siege. Apart from military considerations Carleton had a personal quirk shared by Howe at Boston. He still regarded the American Revolution as a dangerous riot, nothing more, to be resisted firmly but with the least possible bloodshed and hard feeling. He clapped some of his American prisoners into chains when they formed a plot to break out, but even then he persisted in treating them all like boys caught breaking windows, unruly but good lads at heart, who would remember his kindness when he let them go home in the spring. And when British troops came overseas to him in the spring he would shepherd Arnold's remaining Americans and misguided *congressistes* back toward their homes in much the same spirit. Meanwhile the rigors of winter in their exposed lines would chasten them properly.

So the winter and the siege dragged on. Carleton's only sign of distress was a want of fuel, which drove his working parties under cover of night to tear down some of the battered houses in St. Roch. Arnold took the first chance to set the suburb afire, and the whole of St. Roch burned to a black shell. As the weeks passed, the snow deepened until it covered the *habitant* fences in the fields, and the continual winds whirled it about the ramparts and the siege lines and made drifts in places twelve feet high.

By the end of February Arnold was able to hobble about his room. A few hundred reinforcements, partly American, partly Canadian, had reached him from Montreal, where the *congressistes* were still actively recruiting among the population. General Wooster had given them a good talking point this month when he commanded free elections in the Canadian parishes, cutting away the last traditional authority of the *seigneurs* and of the governor. The *congressiste* merchants of Montreal were busy supplying Arnold's army from their own stocks and with provisions gathered in the countryside. At Three Rivers the ironworks of Christophe Pélissier were casting mortars and bombshells and making various military tools for Arnold's use. These forges, employing four hundred to eight hundred Canadians, remained an arsenal for the Americans during the whole period of the occupation.

Not all the Canadians were so complaisant. Many, given leadership, were ready to fight the invaders even now, when outside the lone dot of Quebec almost the whole country was in American hands. This feeling was especially noticeable in the region of Quebec itself. Late in March 1776 the *seigneur* of Crane Island, forty miles below Quebec, marched with 350 *habitants* and supplies for Carleton. They were betrayed however, and a prompt movement of Arnold's troops crushed them. In early April a parish priest, Father Bailly, led fifty *habitants* against the American outposts. These too were trapped and overwhelmed.

The spring sun was now warm on the snow, which melted fast in the fields. The bibulous Wooster, after a snug winter in Montreal, came down to take personal command of the siege forces and Arnold limped away to Montreal in some disgust. His fierce will had kept the siege going in spite of difficulties, and by this time, in addition to the guns on the Plains of Abraham, he had mounted batteries at Lévis and at the mouth of the St. Charles. He had even prepared a stock of scaling ladders for another assault, for he imagined thousands of fresh American troops coming north for the final blow.

When Wooster arrived at Quebec the margin of time was getting slim and there was remarkable news from Boston. American troops under John Thomas had seized Dorchester Heights, which commanded that town; and the guns of Ticonderoga, dragged by sled over the winter roads and mounted on the heights, had forced the British to withdraw. General Howe with his whole army and an unhappy throng of Boston Loyalists had sailed late in March for Nova Scotia. On the face of this British retreat Washington was now free to send the reinforcements for which Arnold had been begging. But it also meant that a strong British army, complete with transports, was now at Halifax, Wolfe's old sea base — and soon the ice would be drifting out of the Gulf of St. Lawrence.

On this news the Continental Congress aroused themselves to the situation on the north. Their title remained false until Canada and the seaboard colony of Nova Scotia had been secured to the American cause. Nova Scotia would have to wait because Howe's army and fleet were there, but Canada lay almost entirely in American hands and there was still a month's time to make the capture whole.

The Congress set troops afoot for Montreal, including several regiments of the newly trained Continental Line. And at this late moment, after all Arnold's urgent letters and the personal pleas of ardent Canadian *congressistes* like Antell, Walker, James Price, and Saint-Luc de la Corne, who had traveled all the way to Philadelphia to set forth their views, the Congress awoke to the political siege of Canada as well.

The seed of revolt had found a rather cold soil in the St. Lawrence Valley, although there were promising sprouts about Montreal. Several hundred Canadians had joined the American army, and Arnold talked hopefully of two more Canadian regiments. Some civilians like Pélissier and Jautard were firm in the American cause which offered them so much profit or local power. Most of the *habitants* were willing to do business with the American army for cash. But the Roman Catholic Church in Canada was still opposed to the invaders; the *seigneurs*, although stripped of their nominal power, still held influence with their tenants; and now with the melting of snow and ice the people were turning a curious attention to the sea gate of the St. Lawrence, where in a few more weeks British ships were sure to appear.

In April, therefore, Congress hurried off a commission of three men, the best it could select, to win over the Canadians who really mattered. The chairman was none other than Benjamin Franklin, the shrewdest apostle of democracy; the others were Samuel Chase, the eminent Maryland jurist, and the wealthy landholder Charles Carroll, also of Maryland, the English colony in which the Roman Catholic Church had its oldest and strongest influence. With them went Carroll's brother John, educated like himself in French Jesuit colleges and now a priest, one day to become the first American bishop of his Church; and Fleury Mesplet, a migrant French printer, who was to spread the gospel of revolution from a press in Montreal.

Franklin himself had long been interested in the vast country to the north. He was busy in land speculation in Nova Scotia as far back as the 1760s, when he and his Philadelphia associates sent Anthony Wayne (the gallant "Mad Anthony" of later days) to that province as their agent; and now with his international outlook, and with the forthcoming Declaration of Independence in his mind if not in Thomas Jefferson's words he could see the present issue better than any other American of his time.

But April 1776 was much too late. The time for winning friends in Canada had gone with the last days of '75. If the spectacle of their British governor cooped up in Quebec was not an edifying one to the Canadians, the magic of American invincibility had been shattered by the volleys at Près-de-Ville and the Sault au Matelot. Moreover in the long months of winter the *habitants* had come to know the harsh facts of life under occupation by undisciplined troops; for the American soldier drank and stole as carelessly as any other, with less fear of punishment, and he had no respect for a religion in which he did not believe or a language he did not understand.

The *congressistes* in the population were no better examples of the American ideal. Most of them were too obviously adventurers on the make. What Franklin wrote of Thomas Walker and his wife could have been said of nearly all; "I think they both have an excellent talent in making themselves enemies, and I believe they will never be long without them." Finally the *habitants* could not help comparing the senior American officer in Canada, David Wooster, who roistered in the lowest pothouses, with the dignity of Carleton, who was so much like the *noblesse* of the old regime.

Thus Franklin and his commission came up against a frigid wall when they entered Canada after their long journey from the South. The Montreal *calèche* drivers refused to take their fare in Continental paper dollars and the populace took the same view of other Continental promises. The Church in Canada was not to be moved by the Church in Baltimore, however fluently its ambassador spoke French. Charles Carroll, himself a *grand seigneur* in Maryland, could hardly expound democratic views to *habitants* filled with notions of freedom in land tenure. And Poor Richard of the *Almanack*, seeing at close range the native caution of the Canadians in continental politics, must have reflected on one of his own proverbs:

> *Vessels large may venture more,*
> *But little boats should keep near shore.*

One week after Franklin's mission arrived in Montreal the defenders of Quebec heard a knocking of signal guns at their long-frozen front door, the river reach below the island of Orleans, and the flowing tide carried among the last broken floes of the winter ice three British warships with clusters of redcoats on their decks. It was the sixth of May. The siege was almost five months old.

The American siege forces had been growing slowly through the spring. Wooster had been displaced and the commander now was General John Thomas, fresh from his success at Boston. The advance party of the British relief force was small, a few companies of the

29th Regiment and of marines from the three ships, but their appearance on the scene was enough. Where some had come, more would
follow. And now the sun itself, which had opened the river to the
British, was melting to mud the long-frozen backwoods roads by
which all American supplies and reinforcements had to come.

Carleton moved to break the siege at last, marching out with every
man who could carry a musket and put one foot before the other.
Five months shut up in the town had left them in poor condition for
marching or fighting in the open. Had Arnold been there it might
have been a different affair, for the American troops were equal in
number and shooting from long-prepared trenches and covered posts.
But the American commander was Thomas, uneasy and lost in this
northern scene, so different from Dorchester Heights; and like his
men he could not put out of mind the nightmare of a great British
army coming up the gulf.

So the long-awaited battle on the plain was no battle at all. A
splutter of muskets and it was all over. Thomas gave the word to
retreat, and in an hour the retreat became a frantic rush for Montreal. The American army abandoned their cannon and stores, their
sick and wounded; and the astonished *habitants* in the small white-
washed farmhouses along the Sillery road beheld their winter guests
streaming past the billets and throwing off their equipment as they
went.

The British warships sailed up the river to harass the retreat, and
had the pursuit been as vigorous by land the whole American army
must have been destroyed. Many of the Quebec garrison were in-
capable of a day's forced march, but a more daring or a more blood-
thirsty British commander would have pressed on with the active
men, knowing by the litter along the road that the Americans could
not make a stand anywhere short of their armed camp at Three
Rivers.

Carleton, the stiff professional soldier, could plan and carry out
a campaign with regular troops and do it reasonably well; but he
could never grasp the qualities or inspire the daring of irregular
troops as men like Arnold could. There lay one of his weaknesses.
The other was his Dutch-uncle view of the invaders, which he
summed up a few months later when he freed his prisoners and sent
them home by land and sea. He accepted without the slightest doubt
their promises not to fight again and addressed them thus:

"My lads, why did you come here to disturb an honest man in his government, that never did you any harm in his life? I never invaded your property nor sent a single soldier to distress you. Come, my boys, you are in a very distressing situation and not able to go home with any comfort; I must provide you with shoes, stockings and good warm waistcoats. I must give you some good victuals to carry you home. Take care, my lads, that you do not come here again, lest I should not treat you so kindly."

So in all ways the invaders of Canada were allowed, indeed encouraged to escape. Unfortunately for them they had another enemy, this one ruthless. The smallpox, which had been among them all winter, seemed to pick up a new virulence in the heat of flight, and it struck them down all the way along the St. Lawrence and later up the Richelieu. One of the victims was General Thomas himself, who died miserably, blind and delirious, in the camp at Sorel.

Carleton followed slowly as far as Three Rivers; and there, having secured the valuable forges, he halted his march. Pélissier had fled like many another of the *congressistes*, a strange little exodus to the English-speaking world on the south. His wife, more adaptable, remained behind as the mistress of his assistant Laterrière, who continued to operate the forges and collect the profits until 1779, when he, Valentin Jautard and Fleury Mesplet were arrested by the British on new charges of treason.

During the winter 1775–76 the small British posts on the Great Lakes had remained quiet, keeping a wary eye toward Montreal. Arnold had asked the Congress to send an expedition to crush them, but nothing had been done beyond The Cedars, the rapids above Montreal, where the American major Butterfield had established himself with 350 men. The supposition was that when Quebec fell the small western posts of the British would simply wither and perish on a severed vine. With the relief of Quebec and the British advance up the St. Lawrence came at last a chance for action, however small, from the west. Captain Forster, the British commander at Fort Oswegatchie (the modern Ogdensburg) had only forty soldiers, but he gathered a hundred Canadian *voyageurs* and two hundred Indians and moved down the river as soon as he got the news.

The appearance of this wild crew coming out of the long-silent wilderness upstream startled Butterfield out of his wits. His force was more than equal to Forster's rabble, and he had a strong stockaded fort and two cannon while Forster had nothing bigger than a musket. Yet in two hours Butterfield surrendered fort, cannon, stores, and men. He made one condition, that the prisoners were to be exchanged for an equal number of British soldiers taken in last year's campaign.

Forster promptly laid an ambush for an American reinforcement marching up from Montreal and captured them also, adding another eighty prisoners to his bag. Hardly a shot had been fired. It was as good a comedy as Ethan Allen's coup on Lake Champlain. Unfortunately there was no humor in the Indians, greedy for spoil and furious at the surrender terms. The sequence was grimly familiar in forest warfare; the robbing of the prisoners, first for small trinkets and then their clothes; and then amid the jostling and the protests a sudden lifting of tomahawks. Many of the Americans were stripped and some killed before the angry Forster could restore order, a bloody stain on his little victory.

Forster's coup had no effect on Montreal. The new troops sent by Congress already were passing through the Champlain gap and down the Richelieu, and in Montreal itself the efforts of Franklin and of Benedict Arnold had put new heart into the fugitive troops from Quebec. General John Sullivan, the able lawyer-soldier from New Hampshire, was now in command of the whole American army in Canada, including four full regiments of the Continental Line smartly uniformed in blue, with coat facings of white and buff and crimson, and equipped with new muskets and bayonets.

These regulars were a strange sight to the Canadians, whose view of American troops had been limited to straggling companies of men in everything from buckskin to captured British coats, and armed with a variety of muskets, rifles, tomahawks, and knives but seldom with the bayonet. The change was an omen of the changing nature of the war. Another omen was just landing at Quebec — regiment after regiment of regulars from Britain, of the hitherto mythical Germans, and the sprightly figure of General John Burgoyne, Carleton's new second-in-command.

CHAPTER 7

1776

The fight at Three Rivers — General John Burgoyne and his army — The naval battle for Lake Champlain

WHEN Carleton halted at Three Rivers he was following his usual prudent course. The town was about halfway between Quebec and Montreal, at the foot of that swollen pool of the St. Lawrence which is called Lake St. Peter. Thirty-five miles away, at the head of the lake and on the other side of the St. Lawrence, were the town of Sorel and the broad mouth of the Richelieu, the final outlet of the Champlain pass. He could not march on Montreal with his flank exposed to fresh American forces coming through the pass; therefore he threw up defenses and awaited the reinforcements arriving at Quebec.

These began to reach him in the last days of May, and in his methodical way he planned the next move, the capture of Sorel. But while he was waiting and planning the Americans moved first. General John Sullivan was scornful over the wild American flight from Quebec. He was convinced that the unfortunate Thomas had run away from no more than a small detachment of Howe's army at Halifax, and that the tale of a new British army arriving from the other side of the Atlantic was merely a rumor put about by Carleton.

Also he had a letter from Congress dashed off at the news of John Thomas' flight, telling him forcibly; "Should our troops retire before the enemy and entirely evacuate that province, it is not in human wisdom to foretell the consequences. In this case the loss of Canada will not be all — the whole frontiers of the New England and New York governments will be exposed, not only to the ravages of Indians but also the British forces. Congress are determined not to relinquish the expedition or give it up."

With these convictions and his own, and with his disciplined new regiments, Sullivan decided to attack and destroy the British forces

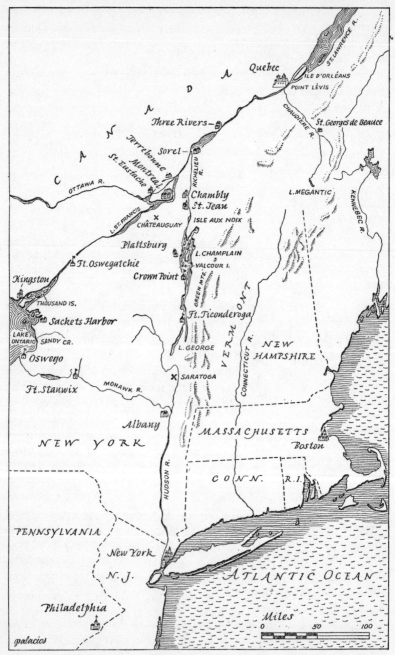

CANADA

Quebec
ILE D'ORLÉANS
POINT LÉVIS

ST. LAWRENCE R.

CHAUDIÈRE R.
St. Georges de Beauce

Three Rivers

Terrebonne
Montreal
St. Eustache
Sorel
RICHELIEU R.

OTTAWA R.

Chambly
St. Jean
L. MEGANTIC
KENNEBEC R.

L. ST. FRANCIS
CHÂTEAUGUAY
ISLE AUX NOIX

Plattsburg
L. CHAMPLAIN
VALCOUR I.

Ft. Oswegatchie
Crown Point
GREEN MTS.

Kingston
THOUSAND IS.

Sackets Harbor
Ft. Ticonderoga

LAKE
ONTARIO
SANDY CR.
L. GEORGE
VERMONT
CONNECTICUT R.
NEW
HAMPSHIRE

Oswego

Ft. Stanwix
MOHAWK R.
SARATOGA

Albany
MASSACHUSETTS

Boston

NEW YORK
HUDSON R.
C O N N.
R. I.

PENNSYLVANIA
New York
N. J.
ATLANTIC OCEAN

Philadelphia

Miles
0   50   100

palacios

The river invasion routes to Lower Canada

where they were. He would then pass on to an undefended Quebec and, as he had promised in a dispatch to George Washington, "Put a new face on our affairs here."

He crossed the lake by night and marched for Three Rivers. But the luck in the dark that came to him later in New Jersey was not with him in Canada, that tomb of military hopes. His guides proved incompetent or false, his new regiments wandered in nine miles of woods and bogs. When they emerged on the road beside the St. Lawrence they came under the fire of British warships at close range, and when at last, fagged by their journey, they attacked the British positions they were stopped hard in front and assaulted from the flank. Like other soldiers when the dice were wrong they found that courage was not enough, and they turned and fled. Carleton was absent in Quebec, but his subordinates Fraser and Nesbit followed his policy exactly. About two hundred prisoners were taken on the spot including General Thompson, Sullivan's second-in-command; but there was no attempt to chase and destroy the shaken American force and the exhausted Continentals got back safely to the camp at Sorel. But there in the infected huts of Thomas' men the smallpox was awaiting them, and it spread like a fire in dry grass. Diseased, short of supplies, with the population about them changing from passive to active hostility as their own distress increased, with the *congressistes* already fleeing the country to avoid the British wrath, with Carleton's forces joined by six thousand British troops under Burgoyne and four thousand Germans under the Baron Riedesel, there was no hope now for the American army in Canada except retreat. Sullivan still favored holding on but Arnold, no coward, wrote him earnestly; "The junction of the Canadas with the colonies is now at an end. Let us quit them and secure our own country before it is too late." These few hasty lines scratched with a soldier's quill were the notice of divorce between Canada and the United States, a forced and uneasy marriage from the first, with no offspring but the adopted children, the handful of *congressistes* who fled and found homes under the American flag, and at the very end the fifty thousand American Loyalists or Tories who transferred their lives and fortunes to the north.

So the retreat from Canada began. Franklin and his fruitless commission quitted Montreal in May, taking with them the fugitive (and ungrateful) Thomas Walker and his wife with their three wagonloads of household goods. The American troops left Sorel on June 14, Montreal the next day, Chambly two days after that, and St. Jean on the eighteenth. Carleton as usual (and to the great scandal of John Burgoyne) made no effort to catch them on the move. Like Wellington long after him Carleton's forte was the set battle, not pursuit.

Sullivan gave him a last chance; after leaving St. Jean the Americans paused for a time at Ile aux Noix, a swampy island placed like a cork in the Richelieu River neck between St. Jean and Lake Champlain. In gathering up the various American troops in Canada, including the *congressiste* battalions under Livingston and Hazen, Sullivan had with him about eight thousand men. Of these two thousand were sick and many dying of the smallpox, and all were starving. Although he had carried away or destroyed every sloop, boat, and canoe at St. Jean, the British had only to march a few miles along the banks of the river to trap him on Ile aux Noix, or force him to make off down the lake and leave his sick behind. But Carleton halted at St. Jean and again Sullivan escaped.

Despite all this Carleton was not the fool he seemed to the impatient Burgoyne, nor the coward he seemed to arrogant Lord George Germain, the Secretary of State for the Colonies. Canada had been saved by a hair in the winter past and Carleton did not propose to lose it by a scalp in the present summer. He was now nearly 200 miles by river and portage from his sea base at Quebec. The lake before him was 125 miles long, and Ticonderoga near its south end was the focal point of American forces moving inland from New England and up the Hudson River from New York.

The importance of the Champlain pass was as clear to the Congress as it was to the captain-general of Canada; the Americans were bound to put up an all-out fight for it when the moment came, and in their preparations they had the resources of a large population and a country so far unhurt by the war, while Carleton had behind him a small and none too co-operative people and a countryside ravaged by the past campaign. His ultimate supply base was in England, an ocean away, and from Quebec every ounce of salt beef and biscuit, of powder and ball, had to be boated and carried and constantly traced by vigilant quartermasters all the way to his troops in the frontier woods.

There were no roads then along the shores of Lake Champlain. An army moving up or down the pass needed water transport and

armed ships to cover it if the movement was to be secure. Montgomery's troops had moved up the lake with ease in '75 because the
only British warship on it, the *Royal Savage* of twelve guns, had
fallen into American hands. This ship and the two other sailing
vessels on the lake were still in American hands, and the amphibious
Arnold was in charge of them now and with his usual energy
preparing to build and arm more. Therefore the next British move
had to be a naval one.

It was a tantalizing problem for the man on the spot. At Sorel
lay all the shipping he needed, including naval craft; but no ships,
however small, could get up the Richelieu past Chambly, where the
river boiled down the rocky staircase from St. Jean. British naval
parties tried to haul some small vessels over the portage on skids,
and failed. There was a choice of two things; to take ships apart
plank by plank, drag the materials in wagons up the portage and put
them together again at St. Jean; or to gather carpenters at St. Jean,
cut timber and build new ships on the spot.

Carleton used both means. It was not easy either way. The Americans had burned the St. Jean docks and barracks and workshops
when they left. To hurry the naval work and to maintain supply to
his army, Carleton used the old *corvée* law and conscripted twelve
hundred Richelieu laborers, carpenters, loggers, wagoners and blacksmiths. At the south tip of the lake the Americans were busy also.
Hundreds of axmen labored in the woods. Scores of ship carpenters
drawn from their seacoast hammered away at sloops, galleys and
gunboats, guarded by the fort at Crown Point and by the troops
concentrating at Ticonderoga. Sullivan was gone, and a bluff gray-
haired man with a slight stoop and an English accent now commanded the American army on the lake. He was Horatio Gates, a
former British officer who had served as aide to Edward Cornwallis
at the founding of Halifax in Nova Scotia in 1749. He had come a
long and strange way since, in allegiance and in rank.

All through the summer days a dogged building race went on.
Spies were busy at both ends of the lake, and each end strove to
outdo the other in the number, size and armament of its ships. The
original plans of both British and Americans expanded as the campaign season shrank week by week. Meanwhile there was important
news from the Atlantic coast. General Howe had left Halifax in
June and, with an army swelled by troops from England and
Germany, turned up outside New York harbor. Washington had

guessed this move long before and his army had marched down from Boston in the spring. So there they were, the old opponents, with another city to fight for. Howe landed on Staten Island on July 2. Two days later Congress retorted with the Declaration of Independence. From that moment every American had to make up his mind and take his Whig or Tory stand.

The sounds of carpentry at Lake Champlain went on, and wagon trains groaned up the backwoods roads with cannon, stores, anchors, sails, and cordage for the ships. And still the only news of battle came from the coast, where toward the end of August Howe won a victory on Long Island. By mid-September Washington was forced out of New York. One heavy British foot was planted now at the Hudson mouth, while the other shuffled among the chips and shavings at the northern end of Lake Champlain.

There was still no grand purpose in the British movements. Carleton had been given an army to drive the Americans out of Canada and seize the Champlain pass to make sure that they stayed out. Howe had taken the other British Army to New York because it offered a base where Loyalists were more numerous than rebels, because his presence at New York would be a threat to the Congress just across the New Jersey neck in Philadelphia, and because he still hoped with a show of force to induce them to make peace.

October came. The hardwood leaves made daubs of bright paint on the lake slopes, and snow gleamed on the Adirondack and Green Mountain peaks. It was now or never. On October 5 Arnold sailed with his fleet, a strange mixture of schooners, lateen-rigged galleys, and gondolas — "gundelows" in the spelling of the time — manned partly by seamen from the coast and partly by American soldiers. He came about halfway up the lake and then swung in to the western side, anchoring his ships in a careful array behind the concealing hump of Valcour Island.

Carleton sailed down the lake with his own odd mixture, the full-rigged sloop of war *Inflexible*, the armed schooners *Lady Maria* and *Carleton*, a large gondola of six guns and a great fleet of whaleboats and gunboats, each with a single cannon mounted in the bow. These were manned in part by naval and merchant seamen and partly by soldiers, including some German artillerymen. The man o' war and the two schooners had been taken to pieces below Chambly, carted up to St. Jean, and there put together again. The smaller craft were built at St. Jean. The *Inflexible* was Carleton's ace of trumps in the game that had taken so long to prepare. She carried thirty cannon and bowled along under a spread of square sails on three tall masts, a tremendous sight on Lake Champlain.

Lurking behind Valcour Island, Arnold let the ponderous *Inflexible* go by on a stiff north wind before revealing his own leading ship to the British squadron. The big square-rigger had to beat back slowly before she could get into action, and Carleton decided to play his game without the ace.

Arnold fought with courage, but he could not match Carleton's guns and gunners, even with *Inflexible* out of range. His own best ship, *Royal Savage*, taken from the British in the spring, was run aground and captured. The rest of his ships and their crews were badly torn when the early autumn dark shut down and the firing ceased. The British ships anchored in line across the main channel between Valcour Island and the western shore and waited for morning to finish off the day's work. Their officers and men were much too confident. While they rested, the wily Arnold was awake and determined to escape. Quietly slipping his anchors, moving his battered craft close inshore with greased and padded sweeps (long oars, each plied by two men), he crept past the British fleet in a dank night mist. When the mist cleared in the morning the British made sail angrily toward Crown Point. They deserved no success after the night's stupidity, but Arnold's luck was out. The wind and the chosen course of the British headed him off from Crown Point. The lake was narrow. The American ships were overtaken and this time Carleton had his *Inflexible*. At the end, beaching his damaged craft, Arnold set the hulks afire and with the survivors of his crews trudged through the woods to safety. Only the galley *Trumbull* and four smaller craft managed to escape destruction. The British were supreme on the lake. It was the thirteenth of October, another of Arnold's unlucky days, and one of Carleton's best.

The British fleet and army now moved to attack Crown Point. And now Carleton met a foe very like himself, the canny Gates with his British birth and army training, his American experience, and his preference for a battle based on mathematical certainties. When Gates gave up Crown Point without a fight and drew his forces back to the more powerful Fort Ticonderoga (for there were cannon in those embrasures again), Carleton must have worn a frosty smile. It was just what he would have done himself.

The irony went further. It was Quebec all over again, with everything reversed and all the numbers magnified; the Americans sitting tight in a fortified camp, the British in hostile country hundreds of miles from their base, with winter creeping down from the white tops of the hills. And the scene had the same importance, for Ticonderoga on its point commanded not only the lean tail of Lake Champlain but the portage to Lake George and the Hudson Valley. There was one great difference. Carleton at Quebec had been nipped between the besiegers and the gulf ice, which shut off all supply and reinforcement. General Gates at Ticonderoga had behind him the open road to Albany and the whole resources of the colonies.

To defend this strong position Gates had nine thousand troops, with more on the way. A chained boom, watched by cannon, closed the narrow end of the lake to Carleton's ships and boats. In numbers the opposing forces were about equal, but Carleton's German regiments had a large proportion of beggars, criminals, and casual wanderers snatched up by their princes (known in Germany and among their troops as the *menschen-verkäufer*, the man-sellers) and sent across the sea. The German officers were brave enough, but they were out of their element in these strange lakes and forests, and with the riffraff in the rank even they doubted the fighting value of their troops. Burgoyne was to discover this later on. *Chouayen* means the same thing in all languages, and no doubt the Germans had a word for it.

To Carleton's regular mind Ticonderoga required a formal siege, with trenches and saps to be dug and cannon to be dragged up the forest slopes and placed in well-constructed batteries. At this late season it meant winter operations for which his troops had neither the clothing nor the supplies. His second-in-command was eager for an immediate assault. John Burgoyne's early military experience was that of a light dragoon dashing about the open valleys of Portugal, and he could never quite get down from his horse, even in the rough woods and bogs of America.

Carleton, always the plodding infantryman or the careful quarter-master, counting the paces and the odds, the biscuits and the cart-ridges, encamped his army at Crown Point and looked the whole thing over. Every scout's report showed the American strength. A careful scratching in the fallen leaves before the defenses would have shown something else, the skulls and bones of Abercrombie's men, slain in just such an attempt against Montcalm in '58. (Abercrombie lost in a single day 1944 killed, wounded and missing, and his army of 15,000 had failed to crack Ticonderoga).

Weighing all the chances, Carleton made up his mind on November 2. He struck his tents, embarked the troops, and floated back to winter quarters at Ile aux Noix and Montreal. Burgoyne was scornful. Throbbing with indignation and with wonderful ideas, he took ship for England to express them. Carleton returned to his little court at Quebec and the arms of young Lady Maria. In the tents and huts of Ile aux Noix and in billets in Montreal the army grumbled over a campaign with no victory. The citizens grumbled at soldiers who stole their washing and seduced their servant girls. Along the Richelieu the *habitants* grumbled over a whole crop season wasted in army labor without a penny of pay, not even a scrap of paper. Even *les bastonnais* had been willing to pay in paper.

There was no grumbling at Quebec, however. The Roman Catholic Bishop held a service of thanksgiving. The captain-general gave a public feast and a dinner and ball to mark New Year's Eve, the first anniversary of the victory over Arnold and Montgomery. The Church, the *seigneurs*, and Carleton himself had much to be thankful for. Canada had been cleared of invaders. The great river had been reopened to the valuable trading posts of the West. A strong army stood guard at Montreal and in the Champlain gap, with a ready-made fleet to command Lake Champlain as soon as the ice went out of it. And the very presence of the army, spending its pay and buying supplies in sound British coin, gave the country's business a circulation of cash that it had not seen since the peace of '63.

Elsewhere, as in Canada, '76 had been a year of strange developments. In England, Arthur Lee, the agent of Massachusetts in London (where in the curious manner of the times he had been allowed to remain and work), had opened talks with France on behalf of the rebellious colonists; and in December a French agent, Archard de Bonvouloir, an appropriate name, had appeared before Congress, assured them of his country's sympathy, and hinted at French supplies.

In the spring of '76 the white patron of the Mohawks in upper New York State, Sir John Johnson, had been warned of rebel troops on their way to seize him and his Scotch and English retainers; and he had fled with them to Canada, along with the Mohawks, a tough and angry company.

In '76 Tom Paine had published in Philadelphia his pamphlet *Common Sense*, henceforth the new testament of the Revolution. Congress had issued the Declaration of Independence just as the British general Howe encamped at Staten Island with his army and his odd commission to seek peace. Toward the end of the year the Congress had retired from Philadelphia to the safer distance of Baltimore; and Washington had crossed the Delaware.

Far away in the blue waters of the Indian Ocean, after rounding the Cape of Good Hope, James Cook was on his way to the Pacific coast of North America.

CHAPTER 8

1777

*Burgoyne plans a new campaign — Barry St. Leger — The
capture of Ticonderoga — Burgoyne's disaster at Saratoga
— France prepares to join the war — Carleton resigns*

WHEN Handsome Jack Burgoyne reached England after his
rough winter passage of the North Atlantic he spent two
months amid the gaieties and the hot medicinal waters of
Bath, which he found, he said, "requisite to my health and spirits."

His health and spirits seemed to thrive in hot water, for soon he
was seen riding with King George in Hyde Park, and not long
afterward he presented his famous *Thoughts for Conducting the
War from the Side of Canada.* It was a pleasant pastime for him, for
George III, and for Lord Germain, running light fingers over a map
of North America and discussing a grand strategy for ending the
struggle across the sea. Burgoyne, fresh from the scene, could claim
local knowledge and experience; and Guy Carleton was too far to
be consulted and in any case too cautious to be believed in the light
of Burgoyne's brilliant arguments.

Burgoyne proposed a two-fisted attack from Canada into the
upper Hudson Valley, to be timed with Howe's fist punching up the
Hudson from New York. Any American forces between them would
be crushed, the rebellious colonies would be split in half, and after
that the end was sure. It was all quite simple on the map, and
Burgoyne was a good spokesman with tongue or pen, for he was
as handsome as his nickname, with a cultivated mind and a great
facility for dashing off plays and verses, as well as a snowstorm of
letters. On the military side he had his dashing record in Portugal
and his experiences in Boston and in Canada. On the personal side
he was notoriously a reckless and unsuccessful player at the gaming
tables, but in the British Army that was not a drawback.

So the plan was approved. On May 6, 1777, Burgoyne arrived

back in Canada with a new commission as general officer commanding the expedition. Carleton thus was deposed and confined to his duties as captain-general and governor of Canada only. These, he discovered, involved raising a force of Canadians and Indians for Burgoyne's support, and arranging the whole matter of Burgoyne's supplies.

In the alternate rain and sun-heat of the early Canadian summer the *habitants* along the Richelieu watched a long south-moving procession of British infantry, of German infantry and cavalry, batteries of artillery, ammunition wagons, supply wagons, sutlers' wagons, Lady Henrietta Acland following her gallant husband to war in "a two-wheel tumbril which had been constructed by the artificers of the artillery", the Baroness Riedesel and her children in a *calèche;* General Burgoyne's mistress (the wife of a commissary) riding in one of his carriages along with his wines and his several chests of uniforms; and three hundred other wives and *vivandières* in every sort of conveyance known to the Canadian woods.

The troops marched and later sailed down the lake to the music of their bands. Those who had wintered in Montreal and marched by way of Chambly must have been glad to see the boats at St. Jean, for black flies hung like smoke about the columns in the wooded stretches of the road, and every infantryman sweated in a long-tailed coat of blue or scarlet, a waistcoat, tight breeches and high-buttoned gaiters, with a stock knotted tight about his throat, and burdened with musket, bayonet, and canteen, with five dozen rounds of ball cartridge, with a haversack at his side and a knapsack and folded blanket on his back, the whole load weighing a good sixty pounds. The Brunswick Dragoons were short of horses and many of them had to march in their enormous cocked hats, thick coats, leather breeches, and jack boots rising to bucket tops above their knees.

In addition to the dogs that followed every regiment, the Germans during their idle months in Canada had caught and tamed a number of raccoons and bear cubs, and such other odd pets as an eagle with clipped wings; and all these went along. What with the troops in their bright uniforms and pipe-clayed belts and shoulder slings, the gold lace and silver gorgets of the officers, the polished brass of the field cannon, the ladies, the horses and dogs and other pets, the regimental flags, the trumpets, the fifes and drums, the Canadian *coureurs de bois* in buckskins and colored sashes, and a greasy swarm of Indians with war paint daubed over the grime of a winter's fires, Burgoyne's command was like nothing so much as a traveling circus. All of this was wafted down Lake Champlain in Carleton's well-organized ships and "gundelows," whaleboats and canoes.

Apart from its cumbrous accessories, the army consisted of 4000 British soldiers, 3000 Germans, 150 Canadians and 500 Indians. This was the main fist of Burgoyne's thrust into the Hudson Valley. The second was a miniature almost as picturesque. For the right hook Colonel Barry St. Leger had 200 British redcoats, 300 Würtembergers in blue, a company of Sir John Johnson's Loyalist rangers in green and buckskin, a group of Canadian boatmen and axmen, and a flock of savages, mostly Missisaugas from Canada and Senecas picked up along the way, stripped and painted for war, with dyed turkey feathers in their topknots and varying in number from 400 to 700 as the march progressed.

St. Leger's route from Montreal went by way of Lake Ontario and the abandoned fort at Oswego, thence up the Oswego River to Oneida Lake in the backwoods of the New York colony. The road from there to the Mohawk Valley was guarded by an American outpost at Fort Stanwix. According to Burgoyne's plan St. Leger would take Fort Stanwix easily with the aid of his two light field guns, sweep down the Mohawk Valley enlisting a host of armed Loyalist farmers as he went, and join the main British Army exactly where the Mohawk River flowed into the Hudson, a few miles above Albany.

Campaigns planned with a light finger on a map seldom work out on the ground, especially when there is an active enemy on the ground. In the first stage of his gamble Burgoyne had a gambler's first run of luck. Washington was too concerned with Howe's movements about New York to spare many troops for the Champlain pass, and the American garrison at Ticonderoga had been scraped down to about two thousand men under an indifferent general named St. Clair. Both Washington and the Congress had an impression at this time that the British, having made Canada secure, would do the logical thing and send most of their northern army by sea to join Howe at New York. But the British seldom did the logical thing in this war.

Burgoyne's luck was still with him when his glittering show floated on to Ticonderoga. Within cannon range of the fort rose a steep isolated crag called at various times Rattlesnake Hill, Sugarloaf

Hill, and Mount Defiance. It was said to be accessible only to a goat, but Burgoyne's artillery officer, Phillips, took a careful look at it and observed, "Where a goat can go a man can go; and where a man can go he can haul up a gun." By the sweat of hundreds of men, hoisting the ponderous weight by ropes and blocks fastened to trees on the face of the crag, Phillips got a battery of heavy guns up there, and when the guns opened fire on Ticonderoga with ball and shell it was like tossing pennies into a hat.

St. Clair had no choice but to get out, and he fell back toward the Hudson, fighting off the British pursuit. This easy capture of the famous fort with all its cannon (Montcalm's "Carillon") tolled a passing chime for Carleton's military reputation in the War Office and rang a triumphant peal for Burgoyne's. American geography was vague in England, and Ticonderoga with its rolling syllables had been a magic word ever since the old French wars. There was rejoicing and pot tossing in every London tavern; and in the palace itself George III ran into his Queen's apartment crying, "I have beat them! Beat all the Americans!" — forgetting that an American prisoner lately at Pendennis had once taken that magic name with no more than a few poked rifles and a yell.

And now Burgoyne, sure of his destiny, dived into the swampy wilderness south of Lake Champlain instead of taking the easy roundabout route by Lake George. Meanwhile many leagues through the forest to the southwest Barry St. Leger with his wild following had come upon something unexpected. Fort Stanwix proved to be a large structure of heavy squared logs banked with sods and defended by 750 American muskets and 14 cannon. St. Leger's two field guns were useless against it. The Indians amused themselves in burning the buildings outside, which merely gave the defenders a clear field for shooting.

St. Leger's scouts, moving past into the Mohawk Valley, now discovered something else. Burgoyne's fanciful host of Loyalist farmers did not exist. The ardent "Tories" had been jailed or driven off to Canada in the past two years. The rest of the Mohawk farmers, aroused by the appearance of Indians, were actually marching to attack them. St. Leger's rangers and Indians managed to drive back these militia at Oriskany Creek, but the butcher's bill was heavy on both sides, and from that moment the Indians lost heart. Less than three weeks later, at a mere rumor that General Arnold was marching up from Albany with five thousand men, the gaudy-feathered savages flew away through the woods like a flock of startled parakeets.

St. Leger might have risked a hand-to-hand assault on Fort Stanwix with his small force of whites. Instead he sensibly fell back to Lake Ontario. He was censured for this afterward, but the fault lay in Burgoyne's fatuous ideas. The American army poised at Albany could always strike hard up the Mohawk Valley and still have their troops within recall for the vital battle on the Hudson.

St. Leger's failure was the first breakdown in Burgoyne's wonderful scheme. The other was fatal. Lord George Germain, intent upon a country holiday away from London, had neglected to send Howe any word about the proposed move up the Hudson. Left to his own devices in New York, Howe had chosen the opposite direction and marched gaily off to Philadelphia with his bundle on his shoulder like the Irishman in the song, the bundle in his case including a charming baggage, not his wife, known to the British soldiers as the Sultana.

His subordinate in New York, Sir Henry Clinton, received at last a message of distress from Burgoyne, carried at great risk through the American lines. Clinton did what he could up the Hudson, but it was a feeble effort much too late. When Burgoyne's ponderous cavalcade stumbled out of the bogs and black creeks south of Lake Champlain (his pioneers had been obliged to build forty bridges, one of which was two miles long) the circus found a most unwelcome audience gathered on the Hudson slopes. Gates was there with an army in strong positions chosen by the Polish military engineer, Kosciusko. Arnold was back from his successful bluff against St. Leger. Daniel Morgan was there like a ghost from the Sault au Matelot with a bigger and better corps of his deadly riflemen; and Stark and Warner were on the way. In fact the backwoods roads from every part of New England were alive with American muskets hustling to the scene like mosquitoes to warm flesh. Altogether Gates mustered fourteen thousand men.

Now the gambler's luck was out, and alas the springs of Saratoga were not the soothing ones of Bath. In the fighting pinch his Germans failed him utterly, his Indians deserted (he had actually trusted Saint-Luc de la Corne to lead them) and with his cumbersome tail of artillery, baggage wagons, and camp followers there was no hope of retreat. Burgoyne was brave and gay and his soldiers loved him, but they would have been better off if he had stuck to writing plays. Outnumbered, outfought and out of fortune, the gambler threw down his dice at last on October 17, 1777 — a cast of unlucky sevens. The remnant of his army, 5700 men, were to be shipped home according to the surrender terms, but Congress welshed on the terms and Burgoyne's soldiers pined in prison camps for years. Cannily, the Congress offered to let the captured Canadians go home, at the same time offering them good pay and prospects in Moses Hazen's battalion of exiled *congressistes*. Many of them chose to join Hazen and what was now obviously the winning side.

Burgoyne had left a rear guard in Ticonderoga, the one wise decision of his whole campaign (although he complained that Carleton should have sent a garrison from Canada), and these troops, about nine hundred men, retired up Lake Champlain to Ile aux Noix and St. Jean, where they could cover the Canadian end of the pass. The autumn leaves now were on the ground, and winter shut down. Once more Carleton was left to consider the defense of his Canadian empire with a force entirely too small — and with a new unrest in the population.

His new troubles sprang from the fiasco at Saratoga. To supply Burgoyne on his march, Carleton again had been obliged to conscript hundreds of Canadian laborers, wagoners and boatmen, and this unpaid *corvée* added to that of '76 enraged the *habitants*.

The forced and unpaid labor, the pilfering and other misdeeds of the British and German soldiery during the past winter's idleness in Canada, the news of St. Leger's flight and Burgoyne's surrender, and the prospect of a new American march to the St. Lawrence, all aroused in the *habitant* mind a hostility to Carleton's government where before there had been nothing but indifference.

The news of Saratoga had buzzed a whole winter in the capitals of Europe, especially in Paris. In March 1778 France announced a treaty of friendship and commerce with the United States of America. It was in fact a secret military alliance. The first hint of the alliance was an order to detain all British ships in French ports. The first clear proof came in April, when a vigilant British frigate challenged a ship under French colors slipping along the Nova Scotia coast. The Frenchman's answer was unsatisfactory and a running fight began at once. At last in desperation the French ship ran into the harbor mouth of Liverpool, Nova Scotia, where she struck a reef and surrendered. She proved to be the transport *Duc de Choiseul* of the French Navy, crammed with cannon, muskets, ammunition, and other army stores, with a curiously large list of officers, with the new American colors in her flag locker, and a letter from Silas Deane, the busy American agent in Paris, addressed to Gouverneur Morris of the Continental Congress.

With this discovery the Franco-American cat was out of the bag, all claws and teeth. A few weeks later British and French fleets battled openly at the mouth of the English Channel.

We must now consider a well-born young French officer, Lafayette, a captain of dragoons. When the United States issued their Declaration of Independence in '76 Silas Deane presented him with a commission as major general in the American Army and Lafayette hastened overseas. George Washington hardly knew what to do with a major general of nineteen who spoke little English and did not know a square inch of the country in which he proposed to make war. Lafayette solved his embarrassment by serving as a volunteer officer in the American line, and in September '77 he was wounded at the battle of Brandywine when Howe was on the march to Philadelphia.

Thus the boy learned quickly, and in the early frosty months of '78 he was given command of the American forces at Albany and told (by Gates, who was now president of the Board of War) that he would lead an expedition into Canada at once. This sounded magnificent; but Lafayette found at Albany no more than twelve hundred troops, poorly clad and supplied, and without sleds for transport through the frozen Champlain pass. Possibly the whole thing was a plan to discredit him. The intrigues of Gates and the Irish adventurer Conway against Washington still smelled in the American air, and Lafayette's devotion to Washington was well known. Also well known was the basic situation in the colonies, now recognized by both sides. The Americans had burned their fingers along the St. Lawrence banks and the British had burned theirs at the south end of the Champlain pass. Plainly the war was not to be won in the direction of Canada.

There was another aspect. The Americans were ready to welcome French troops and ships, but it was no part of their plans that France should regain her old dominion and put the North American calendar back to 1758. For that reason when French forces did arrive they were employed a long and discreet distance from the Canadian borders and facing the other way. Lafayette's presence at Albany, the recognized base for operations against Canada, was a matter of suspicion to every American over the age of thirty; and when, wisely, he gave up that dubious post, there must have been a general sigh of relief.

In Canada, however, the effect of his close presence was remarkable. The bush telegraph between the Hudson and the St. Lawrence, sped by *congressiste* couriers and financed by secret agents of France, filled the Canadian towns and villages with golden rumors of a French march from the south. Added to their present disgust with British rule, this propaganda worked strongly upon the Canadians, high and low. The position of the unhappy governor became more and more uncomfortable as the spring of '78 wore on. He tried to soothe the *habitants* by paying them for the *corvées* of '76 and '77. He tried to stimulate their loyalty by offering pensions to volunteers for military service. But he could not wipe away the mirage of the old regime with its French and Catholic appeal. Many of the clergy and the *seigneurs* turned away from him now. The older loyalty was rising like a ghost from the grave of '63, as if the Americans and their continental ambitions did not exist any more, as if the blundering British with their precious Quebec Act, which had cost their American cause so much, were the only enemy in sight.

Guy Carleton had been at sharp pen points with Lord George Germain ever since the retreat from Ticonderoga in the autumn of '76. He was at hot odds face to face with Livius, the New Hampshire Tory who had fled to Canada and received, by Germain's favor, the important office of chief justice. And now he saw the Canadians, for whom he had worked and fought so long, turning their backs on him and all he represented.

With all his virtues, Carleton was too stiff a man for a situation of this kind. He could sense the just thing, the generous thing, and follow it with all his powers of heart and mind; but he did not know how to flatter or persuade. And so he resigned. He had to wait until June '78 for his successor to arrive, and then he boarded a ship for England. When Canada saw him again the world had changed.

CHAPTER 9

1778

*Canada loses the "Illinois Country" — The Loyalist rangers
at Niagara — The propaganda of Lafayette
and Admiral d'Estaing*

THE new captain-general and governor was Frederick Haldimand, one of the able Swiss soldiers of fortune who entered
the British service during the old French war. He had served
five years in Canada after the conquest and then transferred to
imperial service elsewhere. He was now a bachelor of sixty, a solid
gray man with a stake in the country, for during his previous stay
he had bought a seigneury in Gaspé and lands at Shepody in Nova
Scotia. He spoke French as his native tongue, which went a long
way in Canada, even for a Protestant in a red coat; and his past
experience here, at Boston and New York, and as governor of
Florida, had given him a broad knowledge of American affairs.

The inflated Canadian domain set up by the Quebec Act was now
in its last days. The undefended posts in the huge wedge between the
Ohio and Mississippi rivers had survived the war so far because they
had not been attacked; but as Haldimand walked into the Château
St. Louis a band of Kentucky riflemen were on their way down the
Ohio, led by George Rogers Clark. They had no trouble in winning
over the happy-go-lucky French and *métis* settlers, and in six weeks
every post between the rivers was in American hands. Colonel
Henry Hamilton, commanding the British fort at Detroit, led a
party of soldiers and Indians deep into the country and recaptured
Vincennes in December; but two months later the Indians deserted
and betrayed him there and he was captured.

Thus the great midwestern belly of the Canadian empire vanished
from the British maps, never to return. Mackinac, Detroit, Niagara,
and other fortified posts along the Great Lakes remained in British
hands throughout the war; but all of them were on the wrong side

of the water when the peace commissioners drew the boundary through the lakes, and eventually they, too, passed into the possession of the United States.

While the war lasted, however, Haldimand nourished the Great Lakes posts with care, and built a new one (Fort Haldimand) with a barrack and dockyard on Carleton Island near the outlet of Lake Ontario, to guard their water line with Montreal. With this line secure the Canadian trade with the West was made safe also, and by way of Mackinac and Lake Michigan the Montreal merchants continued to tap the flat reaches of "the Illinois Country" for years.

Niagara now had another part to play. Since 1775, groups of Loyalist refugees had been trickling into Canada. After '77 the trickle became a stream. Burgoyne's surrender in the Hudson Valley and Howe's retreat from Philadelphia had left the Loyalists of those parts in a frightful position. They had declared themselves openly at the approach of the British troops, only to find themselves at the mercy of their Whig neighbors when the redcoats vanished. A savage Tory hunt was in full cry all through New York, New Jersey, and Pennsylvania. The refugees from the coastal area could make their way to the British lines about New York City, but those in the back country had to flee through the woods to Canada.

They came over the old Mohawk trail, they came up the valleys of the Susquehanna and Chemung, heading for Lake Ontario by way of the Finger Lakes. This was the country of the Iroquois confederacy, all friendly except the Oneidas. The well-built villages of the Senecas, Cayugas, and Onondagas especially, with their pleasant orchards, their carefully tended patches of corn, squash, beans, tobacco and sunflowers, were hospitable staging camps for the fugitives on the trails to Canada. On reaching Lake Ontario, some of the Loyalists made for Carleton Island and Montreal. Others chose the fertile region where the Niagara River boiled into Lake Ontario.

Governor Haldimand, with a slim garrison to guard a long frontier, could make no large attack to assist the British army at New York; but he could harass the American back country, especially the valleys of Pennsylvania and northern New York which supplied so much foodstuff to Washington's army. To do this, Haldimand chose the old Canadian mode of warfare, tried and proven under the French regime, when hard-hitting parties of rangers and Indians kept the American back settlements in an uproar and pinned down hostile forces out of all proportion to their own.

There were Canadian *coureurs de bois* ready to raid the American hinterland by way of the Champlain pass, but they were few. Haldimand now discovered a keener weapon at his right hand. The Loyalist refugees at Niagara were familiar with the country, hardened by their experiences, and eager to avenge them.

Here was one of history's most caustic examples of the evil in civil war. These people were mostly Americans by birth, representing all classes, the rich, the middle class and the poor, and they came from the town, the farm, and the frontier. Right or wrong, they had opposed the Revolution. Few of them loved King George, an almost mythical personage three thousand miles or more away. Most of them were democrats by instinct and habit. Their objection to the Revolution was a matter of politics, local and American. They believed that whatever the injustice of taxation from abroad, there was greater danger in any disturbance that threatened law and order at home. In an eighteenth-century way they were little different from the equally sincere twentieth-century American who sniffed communism under every liberal bed. Among them were officials with London appointments or merchants with government perquisites too valuable to be lost without a fight, or merely people of British birth and strong old-country loyalties. But these were a minority. In the main the Loyalist was a born American of strong opinions, little wealth, a suspicion of local demagogues, a conservative instinct for law and order, and a hatred of being (in the modern phrase) "pushed around."

A man like this, who has been beaten for his political opinions; who has been tarred and feathered, pilloried, or dangled for hours from a gallows with a rope under his armpits (some Loyalists were actually hanged by the neck until dead); who has been ridden out of his own village on a sharp wooden rail to the tune of fife and drum and amid the jeers of his personal enemies; whose property has been confiscated and sold for a song to some political informer or mob leader; who has been forced at last to flee with his family through a harsh wilderness to safety — such a man is bound to seek revenge and show no mercy when the chance comes. Most of the Loyalists who gathered about the British posts on Lake Ontario during the war were of this kind.

Clad in uniform green jackets and buckskin breeches, furnished with weapons from the British army depot in Montreal, trained in companies and battalions under Sir John Johnson, Major John Ross,

Colonel John Butler, his handsome son Walter Butler, and other officers most of whom were American refugees like themselves, these resolute and bitter men carried war into the valleys of New York and Pennsylvania from 1778 until the peace was signed.

Niagara was their base. Their outposts lay among the friendly Indians about the Finger Lakes in New York State, and with the aid of Joseph Brant they enlisted parties of the Iroquois to join their raids. Often the exploits of the Loyalist rangers and their Indian companions were heroic in the classic sense of the word. As often they were marred by savage cruelty. Always they were carried out over great distances of lonely forest trails, in all weathers, often the man-killing weather of the northern winter, and in spite of the dangers of interception by the watchful American militia in the country they attacked.

Their military value was clear. For example, in the year 1780 Sir John Johnson's rangers and Indians destroyed eighty thousand bushels of grain in the Schoharie Valley alone, and this loss, Washington himself confessed to the Congress, "threatened alarming consequences."

Contemporary American writers and historians condemned the backwoods campaign as a deliberate policy of murder and rapine instigated from London and directed from Quebec, and in their efforts to keep American opinion inflamed they did not hesitate to accept any wild story from the frontier or twist the truth to fit the charge.

The truth was that the Loyalist rangers worked under a hard discipline of their own; without it they could not have carried out their long and dangerous journeys; and usually they had with them picked squads of British regular officers and men from the forest-wise garrisons along the Great Lakes. Nevertheless there were men among them who in the flurry of an attack, especially at night, were able to indulge an instinct for slaughter without regard to their orders. Such crimes were censured by Haldimand in severe terms and he did not hesitate to call Butler and other Loyalist officers to account for them.

Nothing excused the use of Indians by the British or for that matter by the Americans. Most of the savages had old grudges to pay off against the "Long Knives" or the English or each other, and in this recrudescence of the old-time frontier warfare they took the opportunity. This was true also of various white outcasts like

Simon Girty in Kentucky, who joined the western savages in their old vendetta against the Long Knives. The turmoil of the time gave room to all sorts of private quarrels which had nothing to do with the Congress or the King. One thing is notable. The Loyalist rangers operating from Canada, and certain groups in the Carolinas, were the only American frontiersmen fighting on the British side. All the rest, with the same frontier mixture of heroes and ruffians, fought for the United States.

In the autumn of '78 Governor Haldimand had another matter to think about. If Washington and the Congress took a cold view of French ambitions for the recovery of Canada they did nothing to prevent French agents using the powerful names of Lafayette and Admiral d'Estaing (who commanded the French fleet in America) in letters and pamphlets addressed to the Canadians, calling up glamorous memories of the old regime. Lafayette was declared to be leading a combined sea-and-land expedition to recover the lost province. This declaration was followed by broadsheets headed *Declaration addressée Au Nom du Roi à tous les anciens François de l'Amerique Septentrionale*, and signed with simple importance *Estaing*.

These were circulated widely in the Canadian towns and parishes. "You are French," the admiral declared. "You cannot cease to be so." He went on to say, "As a nobleman of France I need not say to those among you born to the same rank [this was of course aimed at the *seigneurs*, whether they had noble origin or not] that there is but one august house under which a Frenchman can be happy and serve with pleasure. Could the Canadians who saw the brave Marquis [Montcalm] fall in their defence be the enemies of his nephews, fight against their old leaders and arm themselves against their relations? At their very name the weapons would fall from their hands!"

All of this had an emotional appeal to the Canadians, *habitant* and *seigneur* alike. The war was no longer a noisy squabble amongst *les sacrés anglais* but a cry from Mother France to her children long lost in the Canadian snows. It was also a cry to the Church. Haldimand wrote to London, "However sensible I am of the good conduct of the clergy in general during the invasion of the Province of the year 1775, I am well aware that since France was known to take part in the contest, and since the address of the Count d'Estaing and a letter of M. de La Fayette to the Canadians and Indians have been circulated in the Province, many of the Priests have changed their opinions, and in the case of another Invasion would, I am afraid, adopt another system of conduct."

He feared another American invasion to take advantage of this sentiment, and asked London to send him an army of eight thousand men. A hopeless request, this. London had sent one army to Canada, only to see it swallowed up, and was not likely to send another. The vital field of war was about New York and in the new hopeful British venture to Georgia and Carolina, where their troops could march free of ice and snow and winter gear. Fortunately for the little garrison of Canada this was also the view of the Americans, who were satisfied to post a force at Albany to watch the Champlain pass and the Mohawk Valley. So Haldimand went on breathing uneasily in his own camp at Sorel, guarding St. Jean, posting a few troops on the upper Chaudière in case the New Englanders made another wild dash that way, striving to keep alive the string of posts along the Great Lakes, and (this became his greatest burden) feeding and housing the growing host of Loyalist refugees.

All this time the traders about Hudson Bay and the Great Lakes went on with their business, war or no war. In 1778 the fur trader Peter Pond reached the Athabaska. On the Pacific side James Cook with his ships *Resolution* and *Discovery* coasted as far as Bering Strait without finding the fabulous passage to the American east coast. He had missed the mouth of the Columbia River, on which the tales were based, but he charted much of the coast of what is now British Columbia and visited the Russians in their Alaskan posts. Long ago Cook had sailed with the fleet that carried Wolfe, and he had spent the better part of two years charting the mouth of the St. Lawrence and the adjacent shores of Nova Scotia and Newfoundland. It would have been a satisfying personal triumph to find the mythical *other end* of that great waterway.

CHAPTER 10

1775

Nova Scotia, the fourteenth American colony

I T IS time now to look at Nova Scotia, the fourteenth and last American colony in the long chain extending up the coast from Florida. "It was formed," said Edmund Burke in a famous speech, "by overflowings from the exuberant population of New England." Which in general was true.

At the beginning of the Revolution, Nova Scotia included (with the peninsula and the island of Cape Breton to which it is now confined) the whole of New Brunswick, much of the Gaspé Peninsula, and part of the state of Maine. It was, in fact, the old French province of Acadie under another name, and from Halifax a British governor and his council ruled the old Acadian domain in its entirety.

Acadie under the French regime, with a mainland rubbing hard against the outer settlements of the New Englanders and a peninsula aimed like a cannon at their Boston heart, had been a menace to generations of spirited Yankees, and for generations they strove to abolish it. In 1710 they captured the ancient Acadian capital (Port Royal, which they renamed Annapolis), only to see the French retire to Cape Breton and build a bigger and more dangerous sea fortress at Louisburg.

In 1746 the New Englanders went on to capture Louisburg, a feat that astonished Europe, the first hint of the new power rising in America. An absurd government in London traded it back to France for concessions elsewhere, a bit of empire shuffling that enraged the American colonists, so that Parliament felt obliged to set up a military and naval base on the Nova Scotia peninsula as an offset to Louisburg. The chosen site was a magnificent wooded fiord known to the Indians as Chebucto, and there in 1749 a strong expedition of British settlers and troops created the town of Halifax, the new capital of the province.

Thus in its first aspect Nova Scotia was the northeastern bastion of New England, an outer warden against attacks by sea from France or Canada. But soon the British and their American colonists saw the real significance of their prize. It was the key to Canada, for it commanded the Gulf of St. Lawrence. Their next step was to clear the flank in Acadie by seizing Fort Beauséjour at the isthmus and expelling thousands of the dour French settlers from the Bay of Fundy. This was in 1755. A third step came in 1758 when Wolfe and Amherst, moving from Halifax, assailed and destroyed the Louisburg sea fortress guarding the approach to the St. Lawrence. The final step came in 1759 when Wolfe's army, again operating from Halifax, sailed up the St. Lawrence and took Quebec.

Nova Scotia's peculiar value was now proven. In any strategy for the defense or conquest of British North America it had the sinister importance of a two-edged dagger, for its ports and hinterland commanded not only the throat of Canada but the main sea approach to New England. For that reason, lest the French plan a reconquest, the British maintained after 1763 their garrison and naval base at Halifax, the only establishment of its kind in North America.

As the years went by, with the British flag snapping in every breeze from Hudson Bay to Florida, the lesson of history faded into a peaceful feeling of assurance. When the American Revolution sent a violent ripple along the colonial chain the significance of the fourteenth and last link was so far forgotten that the British shipped their Nova Scotia garrison to Boston, while for their part the Americans devoted themselves to a wild-goose chase to the St. Lawrence.

In the whole story of the Revolution this is perhaps the most ironical chapter. It has been estimated that five thousand American soldiers perished (mostly of hardship and disease) in the futile adventures along the St. Lawrence in 1775–76. A force of that size could have seized and held Nova Scotia, aided by a population two thirds of whom spoke their own tongue with the familiar nasal accent and regarded New England as their home. With Nova Scotia fixed in American hands the British fleet would have lost its last winter mooring post on the continent north of New York, thus changing the whole face of the war and of the subsequent peace; for the British peace commissioners were in no mood to haggle over an established fourteenth star in the American flag.

All of this belongs to the realm of what-might-have-been; but a history that includes "the war of lost opportunities" must consider the first and perhaps the greatest opportunity of them all. The future of Canada hung upon what happened in Nova Scotia between 1775 and 1783.

In 1775 Nova Scotia was peopled by fifteen to twenty thousand whites and about three thousand Indians. Two of every three whites were Yankee settlers who had moved there from the New England colonies, some as early as 1713, most of them since 1758. Some had planted themselves on the old Acadian farm lands about the Bay of Fundy and up the St. John River. More had chosen the stony harbors on the Atlantic face of the peninsula, where they could fish the great cod banks. Halifax, settled originally by Englishmen in 1749, now had an active majority of citizens who styled themselves Americans in every census; and in town and country the Yankee settlers with their native drive and shrewdness had gathered into their hands the greater part of the arable land, of the fishery, and of the lumber and shipbuilding trades.

In the other third of the population the largest groups were the much-abused Acadians (survivors of the great expulsion and their children) and the Huguenots and Germans of Lunenburg County. These people clung to their native tongues and customs and looked upon British rule very much as they regarded the English tongue, an awkward necessity of which the least smattering was enough. About the shores of Minas Basin were some settlements of Ulstermen, most of whom had come to Nova Scotia after a stay in New Hampshire; and all of these were alive with the truculent spirit of independence which marked the Scotch Irish everywhere in America.

The Indians hovered in ragged groups about the coastal settlements or camped in their separate clans, Micmac and Malecite, on the Miramichi, the St. John, and other rivers of the mainland. They had fought devotedly for the French in the old wars and their chiefs had made a formal peace at Halifax after the collapse of the French regime. They had no allegiance now to anyone, and in the sudden quarrel between what they called the *Aglaseayoo* (English) and the *Bostoonkawaach* (Americans) they saw a chance of profit, playing one side against the other, for they were greedy for gifts.

Thus the only people in Nova Scotia in 1775 with a fixed loyalty to the King were some newly arrived Yorkshire settlers at the isthmus, some Scots at Pictou and in Cape Breton, a scatter of British army and navy veterans discharged in the country after the last war, and the small circle of Halifax officials and merchants whose fortunes were bound up in British Government salaries and perquisites.

The predominant Yankee population of the province lived chiefly on the western shores of the peninsula, where they traded freely with Newfoundland, Labrador, and the West Indies, and with their friends and relatives in New England, visiting back and forth across the mouth of Fundy and smuggling their rum, tea, and other luxuries in the accepted American fashion. They governed their settlements in the New England way, by town meetings at which any man could have his say, and by elected committees whose word was law.

There were few roads in the country. Nearly all traffic was by sea; and because manufactured goods and foodstuffs other than fish were cheaper in New England than in Halifax, most of their supplies were fetched by sea from the older colonies which the Nova Scotians still considered home. In a careless and spasmodic way they sent representatives to the provincial assembly at Halifax, but they knew the assembly for the futile thing it was. The province was ruled by a governor and council appointed from London; and it was financed from London, partly by direct subsidy and partly by the sums spent every year on the Halifax garrison and fleet. Most of this money eventually found its way into the pockets of the officials and their merchant friends.

This little coterie, firmly established since the foundation of Halifax, did themselves well on His Majesty's bounty. In the shabby wooden town on the slope of Citadel Hill their houses alone were luxurious; their carriages in summer and their fur-piled sleighs in winter flashed and jingled in the narrow streets, and at their frequent balls and dinners they entertained lavishly the officers of His Majesty's Army and Navy. In the frugal setting of the fourteenth colony they stood forth like a little bit of fashionable London transported across the sea. Almost to a man and woman their sole dream was to make a fortune and sail away to a well-nourished retirement in England.

In the favored group however there was one man notable for his difference. Michael Francklin had come to Halifax as a young Englishman with a few pounds in his pocket, determined to make a fortune. In his business and political dealings he was as greedy as any other in the manner of the time; but he had something the others lacked, a genuine interest in the country. He traveled the province widely in a time when it was dangerous to do so; indeed in his early experience he had been captured by Indians and held a prisoner in peril of his life for months; and it was typical of him that he spent his captivity in learning the Indians' language and customs thoroughly, and that he parted with them on terms of friendship. This friendship he maintained throughout his life.

Unlike most of the others, too, he had married a Yankee wife, a granddaughter of Boston's famous Peter Faneuil. He had a country mansion at Windsor and maintained a horse-breeding farm in the meadows of Minudie beside the Bay of Fundy. These interests outside the capital and his frequent travels gave him the friendship of the American settlers in the province, something withheld from others of the Halifax oligarchy. When the impending revolution began to throw its shadow across the mouth of Fundy he was the one man in the province who could claim trust from both Crown and people.

In the year 1773, however, a new actor stepped upon the Nova Scotian scene, a British army officer whose kinsman, the Earl of Dartmouth, had secured him the post of governor. Francis Legge assumed the office at a time when the British Government was at last disturbed about the greedy coterie at Halifax which had cost and was still costing the British taxpayer such enormous sums. Before embarking, he had been charged to clean up the whole mess of provincial administration and finance. Legge was an honest but stupid man, ugly and obese, more used to scaring soldiers of the line than dealing with smooth knaves of the Halifax sort or with colonial settlers who disliked the Halifax knaves as much as he did, but who also despised him for a bully and a fool. His investigations proved the ruling group in Halifax to be a gang of pompous thieves; but the thieves were very loud in their loyalty to King George at a time when His Majesty's government had begun to feel a sudden need for friends in America, and London hesitated.

Legge and the Nova Scotians, especially those natural democrats the Yankee settlers, were natural allies in the struggle against the clique at Halifax. But in '75 the news of Lexington and Bunker Hill turned Legge's suspicions to the whole province. The garrison had gone to Boston, leaving him little more than a corporal's guard, and amid so many people whose sympathies obviously lay with the New England rebels he felt himself naked. When he tried to raise a regiment in the province his recruiting officers met with utter failure, and in the Nova Scotians' reluctance to take up arms against their Yankee brethren he saw a deep conspiracy against His Majesty's rule.

He did not cease his vendetta against the parasites of Halifax, but now he extended it to the people of the province, butting fiercely in all directions like the honest but bewildered goat he was. The settlers were harried with demands for an oath of allegiance, abnegation and supremacy, the oath including a vow to fight His Majesty's enemies with no limitations; the familiar and necessary traffic with New England was hobbled by a rigid system of passes, inward and outward, and all public meetings, including town meetings, were forbidden.

The shrewd rogues of Halifax were quick to see their opportunity. In January 1776 a delegation went to London to press for Legge's recall, pointing out that his policy was driving the Nova Scotians toward revolt, which was the truth; and London, suddenly alarmed, gave in. Legge was recalled. He left amid the abuse and curses of a Halifax mob while the oligarchs laughed in their drawing rooms and countinghouses. Michael Francklin, the lieutenant governor, was the obvious man to take his place. But London had determined to make a clean sweep. Francklin was deposed also, and his post went to a naval officer, Arbuthnot, who knew nothing of Nova Scotia or its people, whose view indeed seldom went beyond the Halifax dock-yard gate.

All these matters left the Nova Scotians in a cynical and watchful mood. They had shared the general American unrest over the Stamp Act in '65. At Halifax the semi-official *Gazette* had declared the indignation of the town and province at this attempt at taxation from abroad. When it persisted in this strain the printer was deprived of his contract and replaced by another direct from England, on whose loyalty the government could rely. Henry the printer had only given utterance to the sentiment of many Haligonians at this time; and they went on to expressions of their own, burning an effigy of the local stamp master on the slope of Citadel Hill, and dangling an old boot from a gallows in derision of Lord Bute, the unpopular favorite of King George. Indeed opinion in Halifax was so strong that the authorities had to put a military guard over the stamp master's house. When the Stamp Act was repealed the Nova Scotians rejoiced as much as their brethren in the other colonies. The Boston Tea Party had its echoes in Nova Scotia also. These and other signs of Nova Scotian accord with the other colonies were all noted by the government long before the Revolution.

Soon after the outbreak at Lexington the busy Committees of Correspondence in Massachusetts got in touch with the Nova Scotians, urging open revolt. Later on, with the sanction of George Washington, the Congress sent agents to sound out the feelings of the Nova Scotians and to examine the state of the garrison. These went no farther than Machias, a hotbed of revolt on the vague borderland between Nova Scotia and what is now the state of Maine; but there they found people in close contact with the Nova Scotians, all urging that the province was ripe for rebellion.

In reality the Nova Scotians were in the painful dilemma that had ruined the Acadians before them, caught as they were between two powerful and opposed national interests; and they well remembered what had happened to the Acadians. Of all the continental colonies theirs was the nearest to England and so the most exposed to the British fleet and to troops coming in by sea. Their population was small and scattered about the coast, with no settled interior on which they could subsist in arms, as could the other American colonists.

There were hotheads among them, like Jonathan Eddy of Cumberland and Parson Seccombe of Chester, ardently preaching rebellion; but more typical were Malachi Salter, the Yankee merchant of Halifax, and Simeon Perkins, the Yankee merchant of Liverpool, whose voluminous diary still tells the story of his time. These were cautious, measuring their American sympathies against the British strength by sea, and hoping that somehow the Nova Scotians could stay neutral in what seemed to them a ruinous brawl.

CHAPTER II

1775 — 1781

*Rebellion in Nova Scotia — Attack on Fort Cumberland
— American privateers — The turn of the tide*

IN THE late summer of 1775 George Washington at his Cambridge headquarters outside Boston had two proposals before him. One was Benedict Arnold's scheme for an overland blow at Quebec. The other, known as Colonel Thompson's plan, was for the seizure of Nova Scotia. The Thompson plan required one thousand troops, four armed ships, and eight transports, moving from an advanced base already established in Maine by the ardent revolutionists of Machias. The American troops would proceed up the Bay of Fundy and into Minas Basin. There they would seize the port of Windsor (where they could rouse and arm the American settlers of the Annapolis Valley and Cumberland, and the Ulstermen of Truro and Cobequid) and thence march on Halifax.

The Thompson plan was much more sound than Arnold's in spite of Washington's caution about any scheme that depended on movement by sea. The British fleet at that time was too busy convoying supplies to the besieged army in Boston to give much attention elsewhere, and in any case the British naval commanders had a healthy aversion to the upper parts of the Bay of Fundy on account of its dangerous fogs and tides. In Nova Scotia the Americans would find themselves among a friendly people who spoke their own tongue and had small respect for His Majesty's government. Most important, there were no British troops left in the province except the guard at Halifax, and as late as November 4, 1775, the garrison of Halifax consisted of 390 men, of whom only 126 were fit for duty.

The voice of the dashing Arnold prevailed however, and Washington rejected the easy prize of Nova Scotia. Thus one opportunity passed, and when the British army withdrew from Boston to Halifax in the spring of '76 the would-be rebels among the Nova Scotians had to lie low. Another opportunity came that summer, when Howe went off with all his forces to New York.

This time, other than 300 British soldiers in Halifax, there was a single company of the Royal Highland Emigrants posted at Windsor and a weak battalion of the Royal Fencible American Regiment guarding the isthmus at Fort Cumberland. The Highlanders, newly recruited in Nova Scotia and Prince Edward Island, were poorly armed and without uniforms. The Royal Fencible Americans, commanded by Colonel Joseph Gorham, had been recruited in the streets of Boston before Howe's withdrawal, a mixed lot of Loyalists, vagabonds and foreigners, about 250 in all. A single regiment of well-armed rebels with a battery of field guns could have overrun them all.

Again Washington was urged to send such a force to bring the fourteenth colony into the continental fold. Nova Scotian emissaries Jonathan Eddy, John Allan, and their Acadian colleague Isaiah Boudreau, visited Boston and pointed out the ease with which it might be done, pledging the support of hundreds of Nova Scotians who only awaited arms and ammunition. But Washington was now concerned with New York, and the costly failure of the St. Lawrence venture was fresh in his mind. He referred the Nova Scotia matter to Congress. Congress shuffled it off to the legislature of Massachusetts. A Massachusetts committee in turn were glib with promises of troops, arms, and supplies to the Nova Scotian representatives. In the actual rebellion none appeared.

All that appeared in the autumn of 1776 was a small band of reckless frontiersmen from Machias, guided by Jonathan Eddy. They visited the settlers on the St. John River enroute, and turned up in Cumberland in the last days of October, announcing themselves as the advance party of a strong American army. The intention of this army, they declared, was to liberate Nova Scotia, and they called on all "Friends of America" to rise and take up arms in their support.

Fort Cumberland with its guns and bastions, its earthern ramparts built in the favorite star shape of French engineers in the old regime (it was the famous Fort Beauséjour of former times), guarded the Nova Scotia isthmus on a ridge in the Fundy marshes. It was held by Colonel Gorham, an indifferent soldier, with his shabby battalion of Bostonian refugees.

About the edge of the marshes and along the ridge lived a farming people of various origins, of whom some Yorkshiremen, newly settled in the country, remained aloof. The other settlers mustered an earnest but poorly armed force for the siege of Fort Cumberland. Indictments for treason afterward drawn up for the Halifax courts described them as, "... a great number of traitors and rebels against our Sovereign Lord the King ... to the number of three hundred persons ... being armed in a warlike and hostile manner with drums beating and with guns, swords, pistols, pikes, clubs and other weapons."

The guns were mostly fowling pieces, the swords and pistols relics of the old French war. They had no cannon at all. Nevertheless they captured fifty of Gorham's men, seized a ship laden with his winter food supplies, besieged him and his garrison for three weeks, and in the dark of one November night made a wild and badly managed attempt to storm the fort.

There was great alarm among the Loyalists at Halifax. Michael Francklin hastened to raise the militia of the Annapolis Valley and Minas Basin for Gorham's relief; but even his influence could not move them. To a man the settlers refused to muster. Indeed some of the Ulstermen of Minas Basin were marching to join the Cumberland rebels. For a time it seemed that Eddy's bold enterprise would take Fort Cumberland and roll on to Halifax like a snowball in March, gathering volume as it went, despite the nonappearance of the American army.

General Massey at Halifax took a chance. His garrison there was small and worthless and the town itself buzzing with American sympathizers. The only reliable troops on hand were two companies of Royal Marines, landed from warships in the harbor. These he sent hotfoot through the woods to Windsor, where they joined the little company of Highland Emigrants for a voyage up Fundy Bay to Cumberland. The Highlanders' ship went astray in bad weather, but the marines reached Cumberland at night and landed secretly on the marshes below the fort.

The Cumberland rebels kept a careless watch in the winter weather. Gorham had shown no desire to sally forth and attack their crude siege lines, and after the failure of their own attempt to rush the fort they were content to wait for Gorham's food and fuel to run out. The marines and the pick of Gorham's men, led by Major Batt, stole along the edge of the marshes before dawn, passed the flank of the poorly manned rebel line, and at daylight fell on the camp where most of them were asleep. In an hour the Cumberland "Army of Liberty" was flying through the woods, and the vengeful redcoats were burning farm after farm along the ridge.

Gorham, himself a Nova Scotian of Yankee origin, was more merciful, offering amnesty to all the local rebels hiding in the woods and marshes if they surrendered with their weapons in four days. Most of them did. The chief leaders of the revolt, Eddy and Allan, had escaped to the St. John. The British soldiers gathered up some lesser culprits and sent them to Halifax for trial, but there again a wise clemency prevailed. In various ways the trials were abandoned and the prisoners allowed to escape. One of them, young Richard John Uniacke, eventually became attorney general of Nova Scotia, a Tory of Tories and a power in the land.

Jonathan Eddy did not stop his flight until he reached Machias. Allan, a man of better fiber, halted on the St. John River with some other refugees from Cumberland and began to recruit another force among the settlers at the river mouth and in the villages upstream. He also sought aid from the Malecite Indians of the St. John and the Micmacs of Miramichi. These activities went on undisturbed through the winter and spring of 1777.

There was still no sign of the promised American troops, but Massachusetts was alive to the importance of keeping at least some of the Nova Scotians in revolt and of winning the Indians, who were masters of the forest between the Bay of Fundy and the St. Lawrence. Hence Allan received some arms and ammunition for his followers, and belts of wampum, blankets, and other gifts for the savages.

If Massachusetts and the Congress remained blind to their opportunity in Nova Scotia, the British authorities at Halifax had their eyes wide open after the Cumberland affair. During the winter and spring General Massey recruited vigorously among the Scotch settlers of Nova Scotia and Newfoundland and called ashore the marines of every warship that came into Halifax. By the early summer of '77 he had six hundred marines and four hundred Royal Highland Emigrants, besides Gorham's garrison at Fort Cumberland.

A large part of these troops had to be kept at Halifax, where, in addition to the naval base, Massey now had to guard several hundred American prisoners taken at sea and in Howe's operations at New York. However he detached a force of marines and Highlanders, ordered Gorham to send a picked company of his Fencibles, and in

June embarked them all for the St. John in the warships *Vulture*, *Mermaid*, and *Hope*.

The blow fell suddenly. Allan's little "Army of Liberty" made a brief stand at the mouth of the St. John and then fled up the river. British troops under the Loyalist Major Studholme followed swiftly in boats and canoes. Here and there a party of the rebels halted on the bank of the broad stream. All were attacked and overrun, and again the soldiers burned every farm that sheltered them.

Allen had sent a last desperate appeal to Boston but it was hopeless. A gaudy pageant had begun to move down Lake Champlain and the forces of New England were scrambling inland to meet it. If Massachusetts had ever intended sending troops to Nova Scotia, the intention blew away on the brassy wind of Burgoyne's trumpeters.

Allen's last hope was the tribe of Malecites, whose town of Aukpaque, the largest in the country, lay far upstream. But the Malecite chiefs Ambroise and Pierre Tommo had witnessed the siege of Fort Cumberland, and those canny warriors had come away with mixed impressions. Also Michael Francklin, working from Halifax, had sent gifts from the Great White Father to match those of the *Bostoonkawaach*. Thus when Allan and his harried band arrived at Aukpaque, a few miles above the present city of Fredericton, he found the Indians divided in their councils. About half the tribe, led by the chief Ambroise, joined Allan and retreated with him up the river. The rest, under Pierre Tommo, joined the advancing British troops.

Allan made his last stand at the site of an old French settlement afterward known to the Loyalists as King's Clear. His Indians deserted him and the British troops, guided by Pierre Tommo, fell on the remnant of Nova Scotia's "Army of Liberty" and destroyed it. Allan and a few others managed to escape to Machias, where they arrived in mid-August. Even there they had no rest or safety. Machias had been the base from which the Nova Scotia rebellion was plotted and sprung, and the British command at Halifax was well aware of it. Over the seaward horizon came Sir John Collier with a squadron led by his big flagship *Rainbow*, and when his ships departed Machias was a smoking ruin.

Thus perished the lone armed rebellion of the Nova Scotians.

Like many another battle of the Revolution, in which small bodies of armed men gambled in a wilderness for tremendous stakes, the rising in Nova Scotia had a deep significance. Had the Cumberland affair succeeded (as it nearly did) and had there been any substance in the promised support from New England, the American flag must have been planted firmly at Halifax, and the flag itself would have borne a fourteenth star for Nova Scotia.

As it was, the failure of the rebellion and the emptiness of all the promises from the other colonies caused the Nova Scotians to reflect somberly on their position. The old ties of blood and trade with New England were strong. With few exceptions village after village still refused to take the oath of allegiance, which demanded among other things that the Nova Scotians take up arms against the King's enemies whenever called upon. In every coastal settlement the illicit trade with New England continued, and on these voyages scores of American prisoners escaping from the hulks at Halifax were smuggled home.

But a new factor had entered the Nova Scotian problem and it came from the other side. The successful rebels of New England, now that the tide of war had rolled away to New York, were sending armed ships to prey on British sea-borne trade. Some of these privateers had the written sanction of the Congress or their own states. Some had the doubtful authority of a scrawl from a local Committee of Safety or some other self-appointed body in their own town or village. Most had no authority at all and were in fact pirates flying the Congress colors instead of the Jolly Roger.

These began to harry the Nova Scotia coast. The pretext was that their Bluenose cousins had not sent a representative to the Congress and therefore must be enemies of the United States. It was an excuse of thieves. As far back as August 11, 1775, George Washington himself had declared, "That province has not acceded, it is true, to the measures of Congress, but it has not commenced hostilities against them nor are any to be apprehended. To attack it therefore is a measure of conquest rather than defence."

The sea marauders from New England found a handy source of plunder across the broad mouth of Fundy Bay. They began by seizing Nova Scotia trading vessels bound to or from the West Indies. From this they went to harrying the inshore trade, lurking in uninhabited harbors or islands on the long coast line. The British fleet, busy convoying storeships to New York or carrying troops in Howe's amphibious operations far to the south, could spare few ships for the Halifax station, and these were too clumsy to deal with the nimble Yankee privateers. Made bold by their immunity and by the easy profits, the raiders turned their attention to the shore itself, robbing the defenseless towns and settlements. The chief outports, Charlottetown, Lunenburg, Liverpool, Yarmouth, Annapolis, all were attacked at various times and most of them pillaged, together with many small hamlets of the fishermen. In the autumn of 1776, at the very time when the Nova Scotia rebels were besieging Fort Cumberland and watching in vain for armed help from New England, the celebrated John Paul Jones was seizing unarmed vessels along the east coast of Nova Scotia and burning the small sloops, sheds, and cod-oil barrels of the poor fishermen of Canso. Charlotte-town suffered as early as 1775, when American raiders kidnaped some of the leading inhabitants along with the plunder. The affair came to the notice of Washington in his camp at Cambridge, however, and that sage man denounced the raid and sent the prisoners home.

But as the war went on a swarm of freebooters descended upon the fourteenth colony. Vainly the Nova Scotians wrote misspelled but earnest protests to the state legislatures and to various Commit-tees of Safety and other local bodies in New England. Vainly they traveled in person to plead before those bodies. All was useless. The state legislatures were helpless to control their privateers, and in most cases the local Committeemen were themselves actively sharing in the loot.

In self-defense the Nova Scotians had to muster their militia to fight off the raids. The next step was obvious. A fleet of Nova Sco-tian privateers, armed from the naval stores at Halifax and furnished with "letters of marque and reprisal" by the governor, began to prey upon the coast of New England. By the war's end the Nova Scotian Yankees were embittered and veteran enemies of the United States, a fact that saddened men like Perkins. The separation of their colony from the American group to which they belonged by all the ties of blood and geography was nothing less than a tragedy to the older men, and its future offered no light.

Had the Americans played their cards with more insight, there is little doubt that Nova Scotia would have become part of the United States. In Britain itself long before the war's end there were powerful voices urging the abandonment of the province. The cost of holding that strategic bulb of rock and forest which commanded the Gulf of St. Lawrence had run to an appalling sum by 1780, when Edmund Burke arose in the Commons and cried, "Good God! What sum the nursing of that ill-thriven, hard-visaged and ill-favored brat has cost this wittol nation! Sir, this colony has stood us in the sum of not less than seven hundred thousand pounds. To this day it has made no repayment. It does not even support those offices of expense which are miscalled its government; the whole of that job still lies upon the patient callous shoulders of the people of England!"

Fortunately for the future Canadian nation, England forbore to write off the ill-thriven brat and New England chose to drive it off. The turn of events (and the influx of exiled Loyalists from the older colonies) made Nova Scotia more fiercely British than the British themselves.

Thus instead of a fourteenth American state commanding the Gulf of St. Lawrence, which would have doomed Canada in 1812 if not in 1783, there remained a solid British bastion on the Atlantic coast of North America.

The Loyalist flight to Nova Scotia had begun with Howe's retreat from Boston, but the real hegira came when the news of Yorktown reached the refugees crowded inside the British lines at New York. By the winter of 1783 not less than thirty-five thousand American men, women and children had moved to the lone province on the seaboard still flying the British flag. Of these about ten thousand founded the city of Shelburne, on the south shore of the peninsula. Another fourteen thousand settled on the St. John River and in various other places on the north shore of the Bay of Fundy from St. Stephen to Cumberland. Cape Breton received about three thousand. The rest went to Halifax and other parts of the peninsula, and to Prince Edward Island.

For a generation their life was hard. Too often the chosen place for settlement had a stony soil or an exposed harbor, and there was much drifting to find a better site. Shelburne's population dwindled to a few hundred within ten years; thousands who spent the first winter at Halifax scattered later into the countryside or removed to Upper Canada. The weaker spirits crept back to the United States as soon as the wartime rancor faded. Most of the Loyalists stayed in the keen air of the North.

The access of population from the older colonies made the Halifax government unwieldy, and in 1784 all of Nova Scotia lying north of the Bay of Fundy was set off as a separate province under the name of New Brunswick. In the same year Cape Breton also became a separate province, although it rejoined Nova Scotia later on. Prince Edward Island had received its own government in 1769.

CHAPTER 12

1778 — 1781

*The cold war against Canada — Creation of the Provincial
Marine — Horatio Nelson — The war ends*

THE tramp of armies and the sounds of battle were dim to the
southward after 1778, but Canada remained the target of a
cold war waged by both partners in the Franco-American
alliance. It was a cross fire of threat and intrigue aimed at the French
Canadians and Indians. Haldimand's troops watched the Champlain
pass and the upper reach of the Chaudière, but his enemies made
much use of a secret route through the high forest between the
headwaters of the Connecticut River and those of the St. Francis,
which flowed into the St. Lawrence a little below Sorel.

Guy Carleton had found the Indians of Canada shifty at best, and
some openly hostile when the test came in '75. The St. Francis tribe
throughout the war acted as messengers and guides for French and
American agents passing through their country. The traffic was so
easy that on one occasion a mixed party of Canadians and Indians
made a conducted tour through the United States to view the
French fleet and army on the Chesapeake, returning with powerful
impressions of the Franco-American alliance.

The effect of all this was plain in Canada. As Haldimand wrote to
London, "It is with much concern I acquaint Your Lordship that I
have myself perceived Secret Pleasure from the hope Strongly
marked in the countenances of many who make their Bows to me."
He increased his frontier watch. Parties of troops with British and
canadien rangers sought out the secret routes, and until the war's end
there was an armed game of hide-and-seek in the frontier hills with
false trails blazed in the woods to mislead one side or the other,
with messages concealed in hollow trees, in walking canes, even
written in milk between the lines of a French song.

Carleton's easy policy after the American retreat in '76 had left many *congressistes* free to carry on quiet propaganda against the British regime. Fleury Mesplet, brought into Canada by Benjamin Franklin expressly for that purpose, was able to remain and in 1778 to begin publication of the Montreal *Gazette*, an apparently innocent sheet; and on the other hand, with the aid of Jautard, to issue such things as the pamphlet entitled *Tant pis Tant mieux*, which defamed British officials from the governor down. Thus, too, Laterrière was allowed to stay in charge of the St. Maurice forges near Three Rivers; Dr. Pillon of Montreal kept up his correspondence with Washington and Lafayette; Francis Cazeau remained a spy for the Americans; so did the Scotsman Charles Hays at Quebec and the clever and plausible Pierre du Calvet, who supplied the American troops in Montreal in '75 and afterward boasted that he was the only Canadian creditor ever paid by the Congress.

Haldimand imprisoned some of these in '79 and others later when Benedict Arnold, having changed his coat, gave the British a list of his secret allies in Canada in '75 and '76. The arrests were a sensible precaution although they came late in the war, and naturally the guilty ones and their friends raised a great outcry at Haldimand's "tyranny."

The frontier watch became more difficult than ever in the latter part of the war, due to the curious position of Vermont. Ethan Allen had bobbed up there after his release from prison in England, and in 1780 he and his brother Ira opened a flirtation with Governor Haldimand. The Vermonters had always resented the claims of New York upon their territory, and from the beginning of the Revolution they demanded recognition as a separate state. In this they were opposed by New York and other strong voices in Congress, and in March 1781 Allen issued his famous threat. "I am as resolutely determined to defend the independence of Vermont as Congress that of the United States, and rather than fail will retire with the hardy Green Mountain Boys into the desolate caverns of the mountains and wage war with human nature at large."

Allen played his double game with gusto; now offering to join the British with four thousand armed men on their recognition of Vermont as a separate Canadian province, now avowing his devout loyalty to the Congress. Haldimand himself had a sour view of the Mountain Boys — "a profligate banditti" — and he posted Colonel Barry St. Leger at Crown Point with a thousand troops lest they try a second seizure of the Champlain pass under this mask of friendship.

Allen had no intention of turning British. His forces actually were weak and he feared a British move to occupy Vermont as a flank defense of the pass. The result of his artful *contredanse* was that Haldimand, on instructions from London, was obliged to treat Vermont as neutral ground on which not a single soldier from Canada could set foot; and French and American agents passed through Allen's country without hindrance until the war's end.

Amid all these distractions Haldimand went on doggedly trying to secure the defenses of Canada, not only along the St. Lawrence watershed but on the Great Lakes. Lake Ontario was the vital area, with its key forts at Carleton Island and Niagara, and at these places he built ships to command the water and to move his soldiers and supplies back and forth.

These ships were manned by the Provincial Marine, a creation of Carleton's under British naval officers. Navigation of the inland seas with their sudden gales and quickly rising waves was a problem always difficult and often dangerous (the *Ontario*, of twenty-two guns, was lost in Lake Ontario with all on board in 1780), but there were other difficulties in the passage of troops and stores to the West. The turbulent rapids between Montreal and Lake Ontario remained an expensive obstacle, for here every ounce of stores had to be dragged upstream in *bateaux*, and carried past the worst places on the backs of men. Hundreds of Canadian *voyageurs* were so employed. The great St. Lawrence Waterway, which was to come true in the twentieth century, was in Haldimand's day a wish, not a hope; but he gave it a start by blowing out rocks and digging small boat canals across the more dangerous points between Montreal and Lake St. Francis.

Thus, not for the first or last time in history, the demands of war created something to serve the longer use of peace. The busy traders of Montreal were quick to take advantage of the improvements on the river, and although they had to pay a toll of 25 shillings per boat they sent on the average 260 laden *bateaux* each season through Haldimand's crude little canals. Until the Revolution the Montreal merchants had worked in frantic rivalry for the profits of the West. In 1779 some of them began to co-operate loosely, and after the peace of 1783 they tightened their organization as the North West Company, a powerful name on the Great Lakes and far beyond in the years ahead.

The "Nor'westers" sought a direct route through the Great Lakes, avoiding the long loop by way of Niagara (with its falls) and the Detroit River. The old Indian route by way of the Ottawa River and Lake Nipissing was used more and more and they explored another route by the old Toronto portage of the savages, crossing the Ontario peninsula by way of Lake Simcoe to Lake Huron. They also built ships for the navigation of Lakes Huron and Superior. Already their eyes were on the woods and plains of Manitoba. So far the Hudson's Bay Company had drawn most of the trade in that wild region to its own posts on the bay. With their improved passages to the head of Lake Superior the Nor'westers now had an inside track, and they made the most of it. The unwritten motto of the fur traders was Business As Usual, even in the midst of a war that threatened not only their communications but their richest trading grounds. Other frontiersmen were more concerned with the hostile power to the south. The raids of Loyalist rangers from Niagara (and their Indian allies from the Iroquois country) had proved so galling by 1779 that the Americans made a sharp thrust toward Lake Ontario. An army of five thousand veteran soldiers under General Sullivan marched to the Finger Lakes that summer. Colonel John Butler and Brant with a small force of rangers and Indians tried to halt them at the site of Elmira, New York, but they were driven back. Sullivan went on through the villages of the Senecas and Cayugas, burning their houses, hacking down their orchards, and destroying their crops all the way to the Genesee River, which flows into Lake Ontario. Had he pushed on with his full force he could have taken Fort Niagara, the seat of the raids; but in mid-September he turned back, and Haldimand breathed again.

The desolation of the Indian villages did not stop the raids. The Senecas and Cayugas were furious and more determined than ever. But indirectly Sullivan's campaign threw a heavy burden on Haldimand's commissariat at a point where the problem of supply was most expensive. The Indians of the ravaged tribes, men, women and children, flocked to Niagara in the bitter winter of 1779–80. This Indian migration, and the continued arrival of Loyalist families in flight from New York and Pennsylvania, made Niagara almost as much a headache to Haldimand as it was to Washington.

However Sullivan's march was the war's last threat against the long Canadian line. From that time until the peace Haldimand's outposts heard many rumors of attack, but none appeared. The Americans and their French allies were too deeply occupied toward the south.

The sea war against Canada and Nova Scotia crackled briskly to the end. Chiefly it was waged by the swarm of American privateers, but French warships also prowled about the coasts, and British warships prowled in search of them. An account of these activities would fill a volume, but their chief effect was upon the Nova Scotians and it has been noticed in chapters 10 and 11. Two incidents were noteworthy for the chief actors, minor characters in this war but famous afterward. One was the French sailor La Pérouse, who in the summer of 1782 threaded his perilous way through the ice of Hudson Strait and destroyed York Factory and Fort Prince of Wales, the chief posts of the Hudson's Bay Company. The other was Horatio Nelson, then a young frigate captain, who convoyed some merchantships to Quebec when La Pérouse was on his way to Hudson Bay.

From Quebec Nelson sailed on a long cruise against American privateers off the coast of Nova Scotia and Cape Cod. The crew of his *Albemarle* at last began to suffer scurvy, and Nelson returned to Quebec in September '82. He stayed a month of the delightful Canadian autumn, fell in love with the country ("fair Canada") and with a fair Canadian, sixteen-year-old Mary, daughter of "Sandy" Simpson, provost marshal of the Quebec garrison. Nelson in his impetuous way decided to marry the girl then and there. His friends, notably Alexander Davidson, a prosperous merchant of Quebec, strove to talk him out of it. Marriage — marriage at all in this early stage of his career and especially marriage for love with the penniless daughter of the Quebec provost — seemed likely to blight the future of a young captain who even then impressed everyone he met as a man of destiny. According to legend the persuasion was not without dust and heat, nor influence from high quarters. It has even been suggested that Nelson's friends, naval and civil, bundled him off to sea with more than the mere force of words. Whatever the persuasion, Nelson sailed away in the chilly air of mid-October and never saw fair Mary or fair Canada again.

For the American war was over now. On April 12, 1782, peace talks had begun informally in Paris between Richard Oswald for Britain and Benjamin Franklin for the United States. Across the sea Sir Henry Clinton, who had so badly bungled the British campaigns in the crisis of the war, was relieved of his command; and Sir Guy Carleton, recalled from retirement in England, arrived in New York on May 9 to wind up the whole sorry affair. The job before him was the evacuation of the British troops and disposal of the huge throng of Loyalists gathered at New York. The troops were no problem, a matter of transports and discharge certificates. The Loyalists were another matter. There was no hope or even safety for them in the thirteen colonies. Where could they go? Some of the southern Loyalists had made their way to the West Indies, where the climate was congenial. Most of the wealthier class had removed to Britain, where in London they formed a colony of American exiles in the empire's heart. The refugees within the British lines at New York wished to stay in America under the British flag. For these the only hope lay to the north, in Nova Scotia and Canada, where some thousands already had gone. But would the British flag fly there? At the peace table in Paris Benjamin Franklin insisted that Canada must be ceded to the United States. Manifest Destiny as a phrase belong to a later time, but as a theory it was in the front of Franklin's mind. The French had gone. The British must go. The Spaniards could be dealt with at some later time. The United States must rule the continent.

On their part the British Government were in a mood for peace with the Americans at almost any price. For years now, while burdened with an expensive and disastrous war in America, Britain had been fighting France, Spain, and Holland. The British were still fighting them, and the homeland was separated from hostile armies only by the narrow width of the Channel.

CHAPTER 13

1783

The strange Peace of Paris — The Loyalists

THE story behind the peace of 1783, which had such vital consequences for the United States and for Canada, is a curious tale.

In giving up her American empire twenty years before, France had reserved the right to fish in the Gulf of St. Lawrence and on part of the coast of Newfoundland, and she had retained two islands (St. Pierre and Miquelon) off Newfoundland from which to exploit those rights. In an age when the Canadian codfish was a staple of food and a source of wealth to many people on both sides of the Atlantic this was a rich concession, and France held it watchfully.

New England, the source of the American Revolution, with a block of powerful voices in the Congress, also held the codfish sacred. Therefore the Americans at the peace conference in Paris determined to secure their right of fishery in the Gulf of St. Lawrence and on the coasts of Newfoundland and Nova Scotia — precisely the grounds of the French claims, not to mention the rights of the British fishermen living in those parts. Thus one of the chief bones of contention between Britain, France, and the United States at the peace table was, of all things, a fishbone; and it stuck in the French throat. The Revolution had revealed the unsuspected power of the Americans. France had begun to suspect their ambitions.

For quite different reasons so had Spain, with her holdings in Florida and her claim to the lands west of the Mississippi. If in defeat the British withdrew from the whole continent, as France had done in '63, the Spanish empire must face alone the inevitable expansion of the United States in the time to come. Apart from this bogey, Spain had something painful and immediate to consider. Like France, she had lost heavily in the war from which their American allies had gained so much; and she had nothing to show for it, not even Gibraltar, where the long fruitless siege went on all through the summer of 1782.

With these reflections France and Spain found themselves in an odd position as the war in America dragged to a close. They wanted British defeat in America — but not too much defeat. They wanted British defeat in Europe and on the seas — and they could not get enough. The danger now was that Britain might yield everything across the Atlantic, call home her fleet and armies, and face her European enemies with all her strength.

In Britain the state of affairs and the affairs of state were just as divided and as strange. The ministry of Lord North, which had undertaken the war in America with such recklessness and mismanaged it with such stubbornness, had fallen at last. Rockingham was in power with a ministry determined to end the war. Charles Fox, who had opposed the American war from the start, was made Secretary for Foreign Affairs. By an awkward division of authority Fox could deal direct only with France, Spain, and Holland in the matter of peace. Lord Shelburne, as Colonial Secretary, was the man to deal with the Americans.

For Britain it was important that these two should work in harmony, but they did not. Fox believed with passion that as a gesture of good faith Britain should recognize at once, before any formal peace conference, the independence of the United States. Shelburne, seeing the whole thing as a game of cards, held that such a gesture would throw away a valuable trump which might be decisive at the peace table. He opened the game by sending Richard Oswald as his private agent to interview Benjamin Franklin in Paris.

His choice was poor. Oswald was no match for Franklin. The Englishman knew little of North American geography and less of the human issues at stake there. In his innocence he accepted a paper in which Franklin laid down the surrender of Canada as a prime basis of the peace. He took this back to London and passed it to Lord Shelburne. Shelburne probably showed it to King George, but he concealed it like a guilty secret from his fellow members in the Cabinet, including Fox. In his view Canada, and the case of the homeless Loyalists, were matters that could be sacrificed if necessary to the interests of the empire at large. The whole British trade with Canada at this time was less than that with the single island of Jamaica in the West Indies.

On May 8, 1782, Fox's own private agent Thomas Grenville arrived in Paris to join the talk. What he heard was surprising. He found Oswald admitting naïvely to the shrewd Franklin that Britain was sick of fighting one nation in America and three in Europe, and that she must have peace; and he was appalled when Oswald casually revealed to him the existence of the Canada paper. He informed Charles Fox at once, and that fat, intelligent, but hotheaded man flew into a rage. Shelburne had refused, on a cardsharper's grounds, the immediate recognition of American independence; yet his blundering agent had revealed the British war-weariness and accepted tacitly the cession of Canada — all before any formal peace conference began.

Fox vented his rage in the Cabinet, once more demanding recognition of American independence but nothing else before the formal peace commissions met in Paris. But if the Cabinet were shocked at Shelburne's duplicity they were not willing to repudiate anything he had done. Fox in his disgust wished to resign, and he refrained only for the sake of Rockingham, who was gravely ill. When Rockingham died in July, Shelburne succeeded him as Prime Minister, and Fox was out.

Meanwhile Benjamin Franklin was wrestling with his own embarrassments in Paris. He loved France and everything French. The treaty of 1778 between France and the United States had stipulated that neither party should make a separate peace with Britain. Yet he could not fail to notice the jealous French interests in America, especially in the direction of Canada, nor to foresee the clash of American interests there. To strengthen his advice he called in John Jay from Holland, and Henry Laurens from home. These formed the American peace commission.

Lord Shelburne, with full power in his own hands at last, now recalled Fox's agent and sent Alleyne Fitzherbert to Paris in his place. The game was getting brisk. Some fortunate news from the West Indies gave the British a good card at the table. Admiral Rodney had thrashed the French fleet under De Grasse, the very man who had bottled up Cornwallis at Yorktown, that place of disaster, less than a year before; and Rodney, writing home, had pointed out significantly, "In two little years I have taken two Spanish, one French and one Dutch admiral." In truth the European allies of the United States were in sorry case for bargaining. They had every reason to hang back now, to let the war drag on in the hope of better fortune for themselves, just as the Americans had every reason to end it while the British were in a mood to give up all they asked.

The Congress made no bones about it. Franklin was told that the time for peace was now. His fellow commissioners, fresh from Spain and Holland and sniffing the political air of France, were aware of the reasons behind the Europeans' reluctance to make peace now. At this point Mr. Fitzherbert played another surprising card. It was a letter captured by a British cruiser in the Atlantic, written by M. de Marbois, secretary of the French legation at Philadelphia, and clearly part of a correspondence between the French ambassador and Vergennes, the French Foreign Minister. It had to do with that most touchy of Franco-American subjects, the fishery in Canadian waters, and it spoke of American claims to that fishery with the utmost contempt.

Whatever Franklin thought of this, John Adams (the future second President of the United States) was a New Englander not only by birth but in every fiber of his being, hotly conscious of the ancient enmity between the Yankees and the French and very much alive to the Yankee stake in the fishery. To him the letter was a personal slap in the face. To the others it was a slap in the American face. Laurens was still on the sea.

The French army under Rochambeau had wintered in Virginia after the final victory of Yorktown. It was still on American soil in the spring of 1782 when Franklin, Jay, and Adams began to see the wide angle between the peace aims of the United States and those of France and Spain. Aside from their touchy interest in the Canadian fishery the French were contending for certain ancient rights they had given the Indians between the Alleghenies and the Mississippi, and for the broad rights of Spain at the mouth of the Mississippi and beyond. To Jay and Adams this was a scheme to set up the old barriers which had kept the American colonists from marching west.

In their anger they determined to make a separate peace with Britain, even at the cost of some concessions. Franklin was loath to abandon France, and he still felt that a stubborn face at the peace table would give the Americans all they wanted, including Canada.

But here the history of the past five years came into play. Another kind of destiny had been at work when the Nova Scotians changed their original sentiments and set their faces against the United States, for without their corridor to the sea Canada was isolated by winter itself for six months in the year, and open to a throttling American attack at any time.

As it was, the Nova Scotian domain from Cape Sable to Gaspé gave the British a firm land hold between the St. Lawrence and the open Atlantic, and with that in their hands there was the chance of salvaging Canada and some part of the West from the general wreck of their American empire. On this point they now held firm. On the others they gave way so completely that Vergennes, learning the terms, exclaimed, "The English do not make peace — they buy it!"

The chief items of the treaty were these: (1) Britain would recognize the independence of the United States. (2) The boundaries were to be as follows: the St. Croix River dividing Massachusetts from Nova Scotia; the height of land between the St. Lawrence River and the Atlantic watershed; the 45th parallel of latitude; a line drawn through Lakes Ontario, Erie, Huron, Superior and the waterways connecting them; a line from Lake Superior to the headwaters of the Mississippi; a line down the middle of the Mississippi to the 31st parallel, to be the boundary with Spanish Louisiana; and the 31st parallel and the St. Mary and Apalachicola rivers to be the boundary with Spanish Florida. (3) United States fishermen were to have the right to fish on the banks off Newfoundland and Nova Scotia and liberty to dry their catch on any unsettled shore in Labrador, the Magdalen Islands, and Nova Scotia. (4) All debts between private citizens in the United States and those in British territory were to be valid, one with the other. (5) Congress would "earnestly recommend" to the various state legislatures a complete restoration or compensation for property and other rights taken from Loyalists who had not borne arms against the United States. (6) Hostilities were to end, and the British land and sea forces were to be evacuated from United States territory "with all convenient speed."

The preliminary articles of peace were signed by Oswald and Strachey for Britain, and by Franklin, Jay, Adams, and Laurens for the United States, in November 1782; and the terms remained unchanged when the general peace treaty was signed in September 1783.

Time proved the document a faulty one in many ways. The boundary definitions left gaps for argument running far into the future — argument always pursued with uncompromising vigor by American representatives and usually accepted by men appointed from Britain, whose interest was in the empire at large and not in the coldest and apparently the most barren part of it. With an exception here and there, the border disputes were decided always to the advantage of the United States at the cost of Canadian territory and without reference to Canadian interests.

The loose definition of American fishing rights remained a source of unending quarrel with the fishermen of Newfoundland, Nova Scotia, and the Gulf of St. Lawrence, for the seafaring New Englanders were ever ready to poach in the shadow of the treaty wherever the fishing was good or the shore offered an advantage, a habit that continued far into the twentieth century.

The Loyalists' rights in the United States were never considered. The treaty's promised "recommendation" was purely cynical, for Franklin and his fellow commissioners knew that none of the states would restore a pennyworth of the confiscated "Tory" property, whatever the treaty said. Over the distance of time one can almost see the British shrugs of Oswald and Strachey as they signed away the Loyalist claims in that empty clause.

In the back districts of the colonies south of the Potomac a stream of dispossessed "Tories" poured through the mountain gaps into Kentucky and other parts of the West, where their political taint could be lost in the anonymity of the frontier. From the country north of that river some thousands already had made a perilous way to Canada. The refugees from the coastal regions had collected at New York, where more than thirty thousand remained to be evacuated with the British troops. Nearly all of these sailed to Nova Scotia and New Brunswick, and from there a large number shifted later up the St. Lawrence to Ontario. Including the considerable groups who, after much hesitation in the States or wandering abroad, finally came to Canada in the five years after the peace, about fifty thousand displaced persons left the United States to make a new life under the British flag in the North.

They brought with them a mixture of frontier skills and urban culture that the raw Canadian provinces needed and could use. They carried with them also a blind hatred of the United States that persisted for generations and led some into a blind worship of

British rule, however good or bad that distant rule might be, which Canada could have done without. In its final result the migration of the Loyalists was to create a new nation in North America, where before there had been only a glum province of conquered French on the St. Lawrence and another of insular Yankees and "Dutch" on the Nova Scotia coast.

CHAPTER 14

1781 — 1791

*Settling the Loyalist exiles — The Canada Act — Canada
divided into two provinces*

NOT since the flight of the Huguenots had the Western world
seen such a large and unhappy migration as that which came
to Canada during and for some years after the American
Revolution. With the flock of civilian refugees came soldiers of the
Loyalist regiments, veterans of eight hard years of civil war, with
their wives and families. Along with these came the families of men
of the Royal Navy and of various British and German regiments
who had chosen to take their discharge on the west side of the
Atlantic.

Fortunately for all of them, the close of the war had left the
British commissary with a large stock of salt provisions, hardtack
biscuit, blankets, tents, clothing, weapons and tools. These were
removed to Canada and distributed to the refugees. The food supplies (described by one disgruntled Loyalist as "His Majesty's rotten
pork and weevily biscuit") were carefully rationed and lasted almost
three years.

Each family received an ax, hammer, saw, hoe, and spade, a
quantity of nails and a pair of door hinges. Each group of five
families got a whipsaw for making plank and a gun for hunting.
Eventually there was a gun for every family. Without a supply of
wild game to eke out the pork and biscuit ration, none of them
could have survived the first hard years before the newly cleared
soil could yield a winter's food.

A fair distribution of these rations and materials was difficult over
the long distances between the seaports and the new settlements, and
it was hampered by the delays and quibblings of red-tape-bound
officials on the route. Again and again Haldimand and the other

governors had to tear the tape aside merely to keep the people alive, risking censure from loftier authorities across the sea.

For the benefit of settlers along the shores of the upper St. Lawrence and Lake Ontario the government built gristmills at Cataraqui (Kingston) and elsewhere within boat reach of the farms, and the pioneers in more remote districts were able to get hand mills for grinding their own small crops of grain. Cattle were few and almost impossible to obtain. Even the seed for wheat had to be sought in (of all places) the Mohawk Valley, where only a short time ago the Loyalist rangers and Indians had waged their destructive campaigns.

For years it was a hand-to-mouth existence, and 1788, when all the crops failed, was long known as the Hungry Year. Financially one hope was held out to them. After the "rebels" failed to recognize the Loyalist claims, the British Government (which had signed those claims away) decided in a twinge of conscience to compensate them. A commission was appointed to travel about the country inquiring and weighing the Loyalist losses. Some were huge, for not a few of the Loyalists had risked large fortunes and lost all; but most of the claims were modest, and in the final payment even these were whittled down. The inquiry dragged on through the hard Canadian seasons year after year, and if hope deferred maketh the heart sick then indeed the Loyalists' hearts were sick. No doubt the British Government clung to a dream that the victorious States eventually would do something about the property rights of these former citizens. The inquiry begun in 1783 did not finish its leisurely course until the year 1790. The payments came slowly after that.

When the war ended, the largest groups of American exiles were at Sorel, Machiche, and St. Jean in the province of Quebec, and in the St. John Valley of New Brunswick. Governor Haldimand, fearing friction with their late foes, refused to let any of the refugees settle in the so-called Eastern Townships, along the newly drawn frontier between Quebec and the United States. Instead he offered them lands on the bank of the St. Lawrence above Montreal and along the north shore of Lake Ontario; or if they preferred the older and more settled parts of the country they could have lands about Sorel and in Gaspé, where Haldimand himself had a seigneury.

A number of Loyalist frontiersmen and their families had settled at Niagara, and a few had gone on to Detroit. These people had found the richest soil and the finest climate in the country, for the lower parts of the Ontario peninsula were in a latitude far south of

Quebec and Fredericton, with summer heat and winter cold tempered by the massive waters of the Great Lakes. Trees and shrubs and plants typical of the American Midwest flourished there and nowhere else in Canada.

But to most of the refugees, accustomed to life in the Atlantic colonies, the sea had a nostalgic importance and they did not want to get too far away from it. The stretch of inland water between Montreal and Kingston, or the broad reaches of the St. John River, were far enough into the wilderness. There they chose their grants, settling group by group and regiment by regiment as if in peace they must cling together as they had in war.

Haldimand's chief surveyor, Major Samuel Holland, and a small staff laid out a string of townships above Montreal during the winter of 1783 and the spring of '84. As in Nova Scotia and New Brunswick, these surveys were made in a hurry; there was no time for careful measurement or compass adjustment; and the errors of this haste were a sore trouble to future generations. Each township was divided into lots of two hundred acres, with the townsite set apart and itself split into building lots. When the refugees arrived the men drew their lots simply by picking paper tickets out of a hat; and these tickets had to be kept as evidence of title, for the Crown Land offices did not provide individual deeds for years. (In the case of Tarleton's Legion, settled in Nova Scotia, the tickets were scrawled bits of paper torn from old commissary forms, and some of these were still preserved by their descendants in 1956.)

The most wretched of the Loyalists were people of comfortable means reduced almost to beggary, amateur officers accustomed to command and to steady pay during the long war, and other misfits who could not or would not adapt themselves to a frontier life. Many of these drifted back to the United States or across the sea to Britain. Others hung about the Canadian towns and villages living any way they could and filling the air with their complaints. From such as these came a nickname for the old fourteenth colony — "Nova Scarcity."

In the year 1786 Haldimand gave up his post to Guy Carleton, who returned to Canada with a new title in the British peerage as Lord Dorchester and with a wide new authority as governor general. Henceforth the Canadian provinces from the Atlantic to Lake Ontario were to be ruled by lieutenant governors under his supreme command. It was the first blind step toward a political union of what remained of British North America. Dorchester's absence had made the French-Canadian heart grow fonder. They had disliked Haldimand. Dorchester was even more welcome to the Loyalists; the man who had saved a future home for them by his defense of Canada in '75, who had got them out of New York in '83, whose favor at the British court might get them, even now, full payment of their losses in the war.

But if all was smooth on the surface of Canadian affairs at Dorchester's return, there were deep stirrings that soon boiled up to disturb it. Until 1783 the population was overwhelmingly French and Catholic, dreaming of the old regime, hoping vaguely for its return, but in the meantime satisfied with the easy British rule set forth in the Quebec Act. With their solid mass and their busy cradles there was no cause to doubt that, if not a colony under the French King, at least a French-Canadian race would spread and fill the whole region of the St. Lawrence and the Great Lakes and probably the West.

Now there was violent change. An inpour of people most of whom were neither French nor Catholic had filled up Nova Scotia and New Brunswick and was spreading rapidly west of Montreal. To priest, *seigneur,* and *habitant* alike, there appeared almost by magic a human wall of foreigners between them and the sea, and another on the west toward the lakes. On the south stood *les bastonnais,* bitter haters of all things French and Catholic. On the fourth side lay the frosty barrens of the North. Their last link with Catholic France was broken by the French Revolution in 1789. From that time the *Quebecois* saw themselves as a race alone, closed off in a hostile continent. This claustrophobia was to affect all their thinking far on into the twentieth century.

The settlers of Ontario disliked a status which made them part of the province of Quebec and subject to French-Canadian laws and customs. Although they were not solidly English-speaking or Protestant (there were large German groups among them, and many of the Highlanders were Catholic and spoke Gaelic), their views and attitudes were those of the American states from which most of them had come. The seigneurial tenure of land in Quebec was to them a feudal monstrosity. The French measure of land was the *arpent* and the French laid off their farms in narrow ribbons running back from a river or a road. The Loyalists measured by the acre and laid out their farms rectangular or square. On the spiritual side there was a profound difference in their attitudes toward Caesar and God. To the French their Church was the supreme authority on earth, which did not leave them much room for obeisance to a king, especially a British king. To the devout upper-class Loyalists the King and God were a kind of Anglican partnership. To the common run of Loyalists, struggling for life among the stumps in the wilderness, the first consideration was mankind itself at war with the elements, with respectful service to God and King George after that; and they could nod understandingly at the rugged old Catholic Highlander who avowed three leaders in his world, "The Chisholm, the King, and the Pope — in that order."

None of this made for co-operation between the old inhabitants and the new. The Upper Canadians demanded a separate province and a local assembly to rule it. The *Quebecois* were indifferent. They had not asked *les anglais* to come and live among them. And what good was an assembly? They had never had such a thing and they had got along very well without it. The English-speaking minorities in Montreal, Sorel, and Quebec on the other hand were loud for an assembly to be chosen entirely among themselves; failing that, they opposed a separate province on the upper river, fearing that they would be swamped by the French majority where they were. The wrangling went on until 1791, when the gods spoke from Olympus with the voice of Britain's Parliament, setting off Upper Canada as a separate province under the Canada Act, and leaving Quebec with its basic laws and customs — and with a new assembly of its own — as the province of Lower Canada.

The Canada Act, or Constitutional Act as it is usually known, was a poor makeshift in the long view of things to come. What should have been done, the bold and wise thing, was a federation of all the British North American colonies (including Newfoundland) each with its own assembly and lieutenant governor, and the whole to be ruled by a federal assembly under a governor general. Actually this had been proposed by Canada's new chief justice, William Smith, a Loyalist from New York. But it was not to come for many years. Meanwhile the provinces were to blunder along in their separate ways, at odds with each other and at the same time trying to present a good face to the world, especially to the watchful republic on the south.

None of the provincial assemblies had real power, because they had no real purse to control. The British Government paid and for decades continued to pay all the defense bills and most of the civil bills. The provinces themselves did not raise much more than a fifth of the annual expenses. With that condition it was obvious that the British Government would insist on appointing its own councils over the heads of the assemblies and arming them with the power of veto over any assembly bill. So democratic government was a long way off. However the assemblies made good speaking trumpets for the voice of the people; and the people soon began to speak, in English and in French.

CHAPTER 15

1783 — 1794

*The Indians — Joseph Brant — The slaughter at Fallen
Timbers — Jay's Treaty*

THE Treaty of Paris in 1783 had made no mention of the
Indians. For the Indians that was ominous. The tribes in the
old Canadian tract between the Ohio and the Mississippi still
trusted in the guarantee of their lands given by British proclamation
in 1763. To these people, fierce and proud, the British cession of their
country to the Americans, the Long Knives, was a betrayal; and if
another war prophet like Pontiac arose their wrath would be shared
by all the tribes about the lakes. To the thin line of new British
settlements creeping along the shores of Lake Ontario and the
Niagara River, that could be highly dangerous. For the Canadian
trade with the West it would be fatal.

Until now the water route by the St. Lawrence and the lakes had
given the Canadians a trade monopoly in the West. The American
colonists had no such entry. At the end of the Revolution they were
still confined to the Hudson watershed; they had not been able to
establish themselves beyond Fort Stanwix at the head of the Mohawk
Valley. Yet a few men sitting over a table in Paris had conveyed to
the United States an immense region below the lakes, long traveled
by Canadian priests and traders, but in most of which no American
— not even the riflemen of George Rogers Clark — had ever set
foot.

From the Canadian point of view, to yield up tamely to American
garrisons the whole string of ancient army posts from Oswegatchie
(Ogdensburg, New York) to Mackinac in the purse neck of Lake
Michigan was to admit two evils; first, that the British had suffered
a defeat at the hands of the Long Knives humiliating beyond anything imagined in the savage lodges of the West; and second, that in
a panic for peace the British had broken all their Indian promises.

Haldimand and after him Dorchester shrank from these dangerous admissions. They had in their ears the constant warning of the Montreal traders that the posts must be held or all Canadian interests in the West must perish. All this was made clear to the government in London.

As it happened, the Long Knives themselves provided an excuse for British retention of the forts. The Americans had broken the Treaty of Paris, in British eyes at least, by their failure to pay for the confiscated Loyalist properties and their refusal to recognize a huge sum in pre-war debts owed (chiefly by the southern states) to British merchants. On the strength of this the British kept their soldiers in the lake posts.

A quibble is never good business. It was only a matter of time, and not very much time, before the Indians discovered that the British guarantee of 1763 had no more meaning. The American frontiersmen were on the move toward the West. Sooner or later the tribes would have to fight them or abandon their rights in the rich Ohio plains. Undoubtedly they would fight, and when they did they would expect support from their British friends. If the British refused, they would be damned in the eyes of every tribe about the lakes. If they gave the Indians so much as a gunflint or an ounce of powder they would be damned in the eyes of the Americans.

Thus, especially after 1790, the British governors of Canada were in an evil position that steadily became worse. The American settlers, moving eagerly into the Midwest and swelling in numbers with every passing summer, had a growing voice in the ear of Congress. Eventually the voice was to have a name, the War Hawk party; and already it insisted that American progress in the West could never be safe while the British remained in contact with the western tribes. In that, like the leading edge of a cloud shadow running over the land, was the shape of war to come, the War of 1812.

The American frontier march toward the Great Lakes had long been barred by the league of the Iroquois. That had been swept aside by the Revolution. The two most numerous tribes, the Senecas and Cayugas, had been broken and their country ravaged by American troops. The Mohawks and other remnants had fled to Canada with Joseph Brant. Of all the Iroquois who fought against the Americans, only the Senecas remained as a whole tribe in American territory, and they had drawn back to the upper Genesee Valley, wounded and astonished, watching an endless migration of Long Knives taking up their old lands along the south side of Lake Ontario and moving on toward Erie.

Governor Haldimand did his best for the Iroquois refugees in Canada, especially Brant, whose name as a warrior was respected by all the Indians in the country of the Great Lakes. Haldimand first gave Brant and his people a choice tract of land on the north shore of Lake Ontario, and furnished them with food, clothing, blankets, and weapons. Later on (1785) they were given lands and a church near Lake Erie, for they were Christians of the Anglican faith and in their retreat to Canada they had been careful to bring the great Bible and the communion silver given them long ago by Queen Anne. (Thus the first Protestant church in Ontario was provided for the redskinned Loyalists, not the whites.)

When the Senecas learned of Brant's decision to settle his exiles on the north side of Lake Ontario they were alarmed. At a Niagara conference they made an outcry, reproaching their Iroquois brothers for leaving them alone and friendless in the path of the Long Knives. Brant heard them gravely and offered a shrewd compromise. He would arrange with the British to resettle most of his people on the Grand River, which flows through the pleasant Ontario countryside to Lake Erie at a point about thirty miles from the head of the Niagara River. There they would be no more than an easy day's paddle and another day's march from the fringe of Seneca villages in American territory. And this he did, getting a grant of land six miles wide on each side of the Grand River from source to mouth, where he could keep in contact, not only with the Senecas, but with the large and still undefeated tribes to the West who shared the Senecas' suspicion of the Americans.

This arrangement did not escape the notice of the Americans, who saw it as part of a diabolical British plot. The truth was that Brant knew the full extent of the British defeat in the Revolution, and he realized that the only hope for the western tribes was a firm defensive league on the lines of the old Iroquois confederacy.

In 1785–86 he made another trip to England, where again he was lionized, but where he saw, too (especially under the guidance of the profligate Prince of Wales), the corrupt side of Britons in high places. In his splendid dress, half Indian, half European, and with his fighting reputation, the English lords and ladies patronized him as a handsome savage with an interesting civilized veneer. Few saw him as the shrewd and farseeing backwoods statesman that he really was, politely regarding British interests, gravely considering the opposed American interests, and keeping close at heart the interests of his own people. In that respect Brant was the first of a long line of Canadian diplomats who, one after another, inherited exactly the same position.

He was ambitious. The example of Pontiac as the trusted prophet and leader of all the tribes between the Ottawa River and the mouth of the Mississippi had occurred in his own time. As a child he must have heard the half-legendary tales of Hiawatha, who lived three centuries before him, the founder of the Iroquois league and in Indian eyes the symbol of all human progress in the face of evil. With some such figure of himself in mind, he began to knit together the Indians on both sides of the artificial and unnatural boundary drawn in Paris, so that they could treat with the whites, especially the powerful and exuberant Americans, as a single race too strong to attack and therefore well able to assert its claim to human justice.

In November 1786, soon after he returned from England, Brant attended a council of the western tribes at Huron Village on the Detroit River and he was probably the author of their written declaration of independence addressed to the Congress of the United States. In it the Indians avowed themselves a united people and declared that the Americans must treat with them as a whole. They expressed a wish for peace but not at the cost of their birthright in the land of Ohio.

These were brave words and for a time the Americans were impressed. But the Indians were not a single people. Intertribal feuds and jealousies rooted deep in the past were still alive and not even Brant's eloquence could stifle them. Within three years of this bold declaration an American frontier officer, General St. Clair, was able to inform Congress that he had made separate deals with two of the Ohio tribes. He added, "I am persuaded their general confederacy is entirely broken. Indeed it would not be very difficult, if circumstances required it, to set them at deadly variance."

It was the old game of divide and rule. But as the impatient frontiersmen began to press boldly into Ohio, three strong tribes (the Shawnees, Potawatomis, and Miamis) arose together and thrashed the white invaders. This was disconcerting. In view of his own statements St. Clair felt bound to move and in 1791 he marched to the Wabash River, southwest of Lake Erie. There he met in battle the Shawnees and Miamis, who killed or wounded eight hundred of his troops and drove the survivors in flight back to Fort Jefferson.

The slaughter on the Wabash convinced Congress that Brant had brought about a union of the western tribes too powerful to be taken lightly. Several of the western chiefs were invited to Philadelphia for peace talks. The American Secretary of State wrote particularly to Brant; "I can assure you that the President of the United States will be highly gratified by receiving and conversing with a chief of such eminence as you are, on a subject so interesting and important to the human race."

Brant went, making the long journey mostly on horseback by way of his old home in the Mohawk Valley. He arrived in Philadelphia in June 1792, an almost fabulous figure of the bloody story of the Revolution, moving with dignity in the midst of his old foes.

The United States Government, following the example of the British in London, made every effort to please and flatter the great war chief and to outbid the British for his services. According to Brant himself, "I was offered a thousand guineas down, and to have the half-pay and pension I receive from Great Britain doubled, merely on condition that I would use my endeavours to bring about a peace. But this I rejected." The Americans then offered a large grant of land in addition to the cash. Brant knew that a switch to American pay, however peaceful the motive, would ruin his standing with his own people in the West as well as the British in London. In the end he accepted nothing, but he promised to counsel the Ohio tribes to make peace.

This pledge he carried out in the summer of 1793, when he urged a great powwow of the Miamis and their allies for their own sake to put down the hatchet and treat with an American commission waiting in the offing. The tribesmen were hot with their wrongs and with a false sense of their own power after the victory over St. Clair. They would not permit the American commissioners to approach their camp. Even Brant was suspect among them after his visit to the grand council of the Long Knives. (The Indians interpreted the stars in the American flag as the council fires of so many white tribes.) And suspicion of Brant was not confined to the Indians. Contrary to American belief, which always saw the British hand in hand with the savages, Lieutenant Governor Simcoe of Upper

Canada took a hostile view of Brant's visit to Philadelphia and his effort to unite the tribes. He never trusted the Mohawk chief afterward and sought every means to curb his influence.

Thus Brant's long views and hopes were doomed. So were the Ohio tribes. In 1794 the Americans marched against them with crushing force, including a large body of Kentucky sharpshooters mounted on horses and moving swiftly through the parklike woods of the plains. The leader this time was no St. Clair, but the able and resolute Anthony Wayne of the Revolutionary War. The Indians, a mixture of tribes, Miamis, Delawares, Shawnees, Potawatomis, Chippewas, Ottawas, and Senecas (and with them a few Canadian adventurers), chose to stand on the bank of the Maumee River, not far from the site of the present city of Toledo. At this point a recent tornado had blown down a wild tangle of forest in which the Indians hoped to hold off the American horsemen, and the place was called Fallen Timbers. These hopes, all their hopes, were groundless. Outnumbered more than three to one, they were beaten in battle and slaughtered in flight, and Wayne went on to destroy their villages and their winter stores of corn. In the following year, after a forlorn and hungry winter, several of the chiefs submitted to Wayne in the famous Treaty of Greenville, whose terms included the surrender of enormous tracts of land.

From his retreat in Canada, Brant could only watch the ruin of his dream. But there was another dreamer now. Among the Indians who survived the fight at Fallen Timbers was the Shawnee warrior Tecumseh, whose father had been slain by the Long Knives on the Ohio long ago. He was twenty-six, half the age of Brant, with all of Brant's lost fire and ambition. Unlike the Mohawk chief, settled and prosperous on the British bounty in Canada, Tecumseh and his brother the Prophet wandered poor and foot-loose in the midwestern wilderness with nowhere and yet everywhere to lay their heads. Of such stuff were the Hiawathas and Pontiacs of Indian story. In time Tecumseh was to take his place in that story, and in the histories of Canada and the United States.

For Canada the disturbing feature of these affairs was not only the clash of Indians and Americans along the hitherto untroubled shore of the Great Lakes but the lonely and conspicuous presence of British soldiers in the old forts there. History gives no valid evidence that the British garrisons helped the Indians in the battle for their lands, but their sympathy was open enough; the Canadian traders about their posts were ready enough to sell knives, hatchets, guns, powder, and shot, all staples of the fur trade; and certainly some white and half-breed adventurers were fighting with the tribes. For their part the Americans always believed that Canada's governor supplied the Indians with British army weapons and stores and even permitted soldiers, disguised as Indians, to take part in the fighting.

American suspicion was sharpened by the presence of a new British army post on the Maumee River a few miles from Fallen Timbers, where the Indians had chosen to make their stand. After the battle a party of American horsemen dashed up to the post, and Major Campbell's little company of redcoats cocked their muskets and poised a linstock over their cannon, expecting an attack. It was a delicate moment. Wayne had Washington's orders to avoid any clash with the British posts along the lakes; but the British were not supposed to be on the Maumee, the American troops were fierce and eager, and they had force enough to smash Campbell's group and their weak stockade in a few minutes. One shot could have shattered the peace of North America, for at that moment Lieutenant Governor Simcoe, having misinterpreted a dispatch from Lord Dorchester, was hastily mustering troops, artillery, and boats in the full belief that war had begun and that Wayne intended to seize not merely the Maumee outpost but Detroit itself.

As it happened Wayne drew back in accordance with his orders, and when the hotheaded Simcoe arrived on the Maumee scene the incident had passed. Simcoe had been full of brave and foolish plans for his little army, although later on he admitted, "I think no force in this country could resist Wayne's direct attack."

It was the truth. With the defeat of the Indian confederacy and the presence of a strong and well-equipped American army at the base of the Michigan peninsula, the whole situation was changed. The British footing on the southern side of the lakes, untenable in law after 1783, was now untenable in fact.

A solution was on the way. In the summer of 1794, at the very time when Wayne was preparing his powerful stroke, a special American envoy, selected by Washington himself, was on the far side of the ocean urging the British Government to give up the embarrassing forts. He was John Jay, an old hand at dealing with the British and now chief justice of the United States. The time was well chosen. Britain was again at war with France, this time with the rampaging citizen armies and warships of the Republic, a new and explosive force among the ancient states of Europe; and the British had no energies to spare for a fight or even a show of force in the heart of North America. There were various matters to argue, but the chief results of Jay's negotiation were that the United States Government agreed to smooth the way for payment of the pre-Revolutionary debts of the southern states (an old sore with the British) and Britain agreed to evacuate the Great Lakes forts by 1796. Thus Jay's Treaty saved for a time the peace of Canada and the United States.

But only for a time. During the next eighteen years the Canadians watched uneasily an American multitude hustling into the Middle West, cutting wagon roads, clearing the forest, dotting the old Indian lands below the lakes with prosperous towns and villages, and in the process closing up to the weak spots in any defense of Upper Canada, the narrow waters of the Detroit and the Niagara rivers.

CHAPTER 16

1786 — 1794

Lord Dorchester returns — Prince Edward and his mistress

WHEN Lord Dorchester came back to rule what was left of British North America in 1786 he was sixty-two, an age when old wounds and a life's campaigns have their inevitable effect. With a brief interlude of service at New York he had spent the past eight years quietly on his estates in the mild English climate, and now that he had to face again the rigors of Canada he was content to face them from the comfort of the Château at Quebec, surrounded by his court and traveling as little as possible. He made a dutiful round of his domain, visiting the raw settlements toward Lake Ontario in one season and the Maritime Provinces in another, but that was all.

His former impression of an immutable French-speaking and Catholic Canada under the British flag had been changed by the Loyalist migration, but he found the new creation in the North a kind of Frankenstein monster and it puzzled him. If not a born aristocrat he was one by instinct and now by formal patent of the King, and he leaned toward what he called "the gentlemen." There were gentlemen among the French Canadians and among the Loyalists, but the masses left him cold. He despised men of business (especially Montreal business) and he saw in the common run of Loyalist settlers a democratic turn of thought that disturbed him.

The new Canada was a curious sum and he could not add it up. In a country that should have been a field for French and English gentlemen-adventurers, a sort of bilingual Hudson's Bay Company equipped with clean shirts and a polite turn of speech, it was disappointing to discover that the gentlemen were not adventurers and the adventurers were not gentlemen. He recoiled from the sweating hard-grubbery of the majority of his subjects and from the amazing quarrels that arose among them.

The Upper Canadians shouted down the river for a separate province and an assembly of their own. The merchants of Montreal objected violently to separation, declaring in the same breath that if there was to be a province of Upper Canada, then Montreal must be a part of it. The French Canadians of Montreal, who were the majority, blew down their noses at the very thought. In the sprawling Quebec countryside the *habitants* merely shrugged. They no longer listened respectfully to their *seigneurs* — "the gentlemen" — but lent a willing ear to a rising caste of village notaries and small-town lawyers; and the lawyers, seeing the approach of an elected assembly, began to see also the approaching power in their hands, the chance to confound the English with their own machine, the vote.

The Catholic Church in Canada, watching anxiously the swarm of Protestants on one hand and the frightful heresies of the French Revolution on the other, was drawing in upon itself, stiffening its attitude and its hold as a Canadian Church that had nothing to do with France or England, that had no outside tie except the supreme one with His Holiness in Rome. The Anglican Church in Quebec, to be personified soon by a bishop with a tremendous name, Jacob Jehosaphat Mountain, was insisting on all sorts of privilege in defiance of French-Catholic feelings and despite the fact that the Anglicans of Quebec, including the garrison and His Majesty's governor general, were pitifully few.

To further complicate religious matters, there was the problem of the valuable Jesuit Estates, which had been left in a sort of suspension between earth and heaven when Pope Clement XIV suppressed the order in 1773, ten years after the British authorities put a cold finger on the Jesuit activities in Canada. The *canadiens* insisted that these properties be used for the support of education in their province, where not one man in five could read or even write his name. Jeffrey Amherst had claimed the Jesuit Estates long ago as a reward for his services in the conquest of Canada; and in 1787 that aged warrior renewed the claim, pushing it with the power and prestige of his post as commander in chief of all the British Army.

In Upper Canada the people were largely Protestant but of the dissenting faith, not that of which His Majesty was the sworn defender. Their tendency was Methodist, and the preachers now arriving among them were not the safely English and soundly Wesleyan kind but something distinctly American and therefore republican, the horseback prophets common to the American frontier, roaming the backwoods trails, holding forth in wayside shacks and at fantastic camp meetings where people prayed and sang and groaned in the light of fires and torches.

Down on the Atlantic coast the Nova Scotians, still mostly Yankee in origin and rugged democrats by instinct, looked askance at the Loyalists who had come among them, especially the refugees who had lost fat jobs and perquisites in the old colonies and were busy pulling transatlantic strings to get the same things here. The New Brunswickers were mostly Loyalist with an older fringe of French; but even there the men seemed to have brought the dangerous seed of democracy northward in their knapsacks. Had not Benedict Arnold settled among them still wearing his rank of brigadier general in the British Army, and had not they called him Traitor in the streets and ostracized him and finally caused him to sell up and go to England? Shadows — shadows everywhere, even in the little garden of the gulf, Prince Edward Island, where the settlers were in a fury against the great absentee landlords, British and Loyalist, who by favor of His Majesty owned all the better soil.

In the other direction, in the Far West, there were the fur traders, mostly Scots, living like rough backwoods kings, knowing no law but their own, with their sporrans open to any sort of profit and closed to any sort of tax. And the Indians, those brown creatures of the forest on both sides of the lakes, what could a British gentleman make of them? There had been promises (and a gentleman lived up to promises), so he had done his best to honor old pledges to these crapulous and unclean creatures upon whose whim the western trade depended.

But how far could one trust them — even Brant, who was a gentleman? There was a strong suspicion that Brant would stop at nothing in his dream of uniting the tribes, even at the cost of starting another war between the British and the Americans, playing the white men at their own game of divide-and-rule.

With all these squabbles and suspicions darkening the Canadian sky, Lord Dorchester no doubt was glad of an excuse to take another long leave in England. The excuse came in the summer of 1791 in the tall and handsome person of Edward, one of His Majesty's headstrong sons, who had been transferred from Gibraltar to command the Canadian garrison at His Majesty's own request. The move relieved Dorchester of his military duties, though not of his over-all responsibilities. It was pleasant now to think of a long leave on his English estates. The lieutenant governors could deal with the petty civil worries of the provinces and the long delays of the Atlantic mail would stave off the major ones for a whole year at a time. The Dorchesters packed up and sailed away, not to return until the autumn of 1793, when a new French war demanded the presence of the governor general at his Canadian post.

When he came to Canada Prince Edward was twenty-four, and he had been trained in the harsh German military system from the age of seventeen. Unlike most of his brothers he had no weakness for drink or prostitutes, but like them he had quarreled with his father; hence, as a soldier, it had been convenient to send him on service abroad, first to the rock of Gibraltar and then to the rock of Quebec. In his public relations he was amiable, if pompous. He was always heavily in debt, for he had not the faintest idea of the value of money, and he was always obsessed with his own importance. His worst fault was his Hanoverian notion of discipline. He had swallowed a ramrod in his teens and by twenty-four the iron had passed into his soul. As a result wherever he went in the world he left a trail of debts and a rumble of mutinous troops.

To the British army officer at this time Canada — cold Canada with its dreary distances and savage forests — was the last post on earth, with scope for neither comfort nor ambition. For a prince of the royal house however there was something else. Edward was surprised and pleased to find in Quebec a polished society and a vice-regal court which under the influence of Lady Maria Dorchester had become a charming miniature of the courts of London and Versailles — especially of Versailles.

He took to this society, English and French, like the proverbial duck to water. Before long he dived deeply in love with a vivacious and cultured *canadienne*, and because as a king's son he was not permitted to marry a commoner, the lady agreed to be his mistress. This was in the tradition of the old regime and, far from disapproving, the *canadiens* took it as a compliment. The lady (who called herself Alphonsine Thérèse Bernadine Julie de Montgenet de St. Laurent, Baronne de Fortisson) was Julie to her lover and Madame St. Laurent to everybody else. Her exact origin has always been something of a mystery because it was carefully obliterated by her own family and by the British royal house. Certainly she was one of the old seigneurial class, and through her Edward made lasting and affectionate friendships with the De Salaberry and other families of the Canadian *élite*. And their own liaison was no mere affair. Edward and Julie remained faithful companions until he was past middle age, when, like his portly graying brothers, he was ordered to put his mistress aside, marry an authentic princess, and produce if possible an heir to the British throne. This, the only important act of his life, produced, of all people, Queen Victoria.

With Edward and Julie installed in a romantic country house overlooking the beautiful falls of Montmorency, the society of Quebec was able to bask in the magic aura of royalty, something never conferred upon it by the old regime. There was a round of dinners, dances, musical *soirées*, shooting parties, sleeping parties, and other activities to pass the brief summers and the long months of cold. Edward did not confine himself to the *élite* but mingled with the people, English and French. He was not above passing buckets at a fire, or mounting a chair in the street to quell an election riot with his booming voice — "Let me hear no more of these odious distinctions of French and English. You are all His Britannic Majesty's beloved Canadian subjects" — which was true, if somewhat obvious. And if his friendship with His Majesty's *canadiens* was also obvious, it did not prevent him from practicing freemasonry in their midst or attending with punctilio the services of Bishop Mountain or establishing Sunday free schools, none of which could be regarded with enthusiasm by the Catholic hierarchy.

His chief activity however was with his military toys. Like a child with a box of bright red wooden soldiers, he never tired of arranging and drilling and marching and countermarching them from morn to night. The mere sight of troops on parade always sent him slightly mad. His eyes would sparkle at a perfection of stiff drill movements. He would fly into a rage at the sight of a missing gaiter button or an improperly combed and powdered pigtail, and his punishments kept the cat-o'-nine-tails slashing at naked backs in every barrack yard. At Quebec as at Gibraltar, the incessant drill and the brutal punishments dismayed the more humane officers and finally drove the rank and file to mutiny. A group of soldiers plotted to seize and kill him. They were betrayed and punished with savage floggings; and their leader, a private named Draper, was made the victim of a macabre ceremony which must have astonished the *Quebecois* as it angered the troops.

With the tall prince on his charger at their head, the whole garrison marched to a spot two miles outside Quebec, where a gallows had been erected and fitted with a hang rope. At the tail of the troops trudged the miserable Draper in a white burial sheet, with his coffin on a wagon before him and a regimental band behind playing the doleful music sacred to military funerals. In the shadow of the gallows the prince addressed the wretched man thus; "Draper, you have now reached the awful moment when a few moments would carry you into the presence of the Supreme Being. As the son of your Sovereign whose greatest prerogative is the dispensation of mercy, I feel myself fortunately able to do that which, as your colonel, the indispensable laws of military discipline rendered it impossible for me even to think." With this ponderous mouthful the man who had suffered a thousand deaths on the long slow march from the citadel received the prince's pardon. The whole sadistic performance was typical of Edward's worst side (he arranged a similar show on a larger scale at Halifax some years later), and its effect upon the troops was surely not what he planned.

Indeed the chief effect of Prince Edward's command in Canada was to make the smallest army post in the woods a miniature German barrack square. The peculiar problems of Canadian defense were lost to sight in the rigid formula of a European grand review. And this at a time when the constant danger was a war with the active and uninhibited Americans, a war that would be fought, if fought at all, in the Canadian frontier woods and farms.

Prince Edward could not see an American war. He could hardly see Canada. His back was always toward the continent and his mind's gaze across the sea. Despite his quarrel with his father he had a devout faith in the divine rights of royalty, and as the sprig of a royal house himself he was furious when the French beheaded their King and Queen. He thirsted for action against them and he wrote to England demanding a chance. Unfortunately for himself the War Office had no great opinion of him as a soldier, and King George, who had not forgotten his son's impertinence, insisted that Edward must be kept in service far from England.

In these circumstances the best the impatient young warrior could get was a posting to join a small British expedition against the French West Indies. It was in the winter of 1793 and the St. Lawrence was frozen. There was no time to be lost. Edward gathered an elaborate equipment of hats and boots and uniforms, of bed and table linen, of silverware and chinaware, of books on military tactics, of maps and geographies, of saddles, swords, pistols, wines, and cordials; and with all this piled on three large sleds, and himself leading the procession in a spanking cariole, he set off overland for Boston by way of the Champlain pass. It was Burgoyne's old route and an evil fate seemed to hang over it for the next dashing British officer to come that way. A midwinter thaw had weakened the ice on Lake Champlain, which let the cariole glide past but broke under the weight of the three overburdened sleds. The whole magnificent equipment vanished, and the prince arrived in Boston with little more than the clothes he wore.

However, still determined, he took ship for Guadeloupe. For the next two or three months he served with Sir Charles Grey's expedition, a futile business of small skirmishes among the hot islands where there was far more danger from mosquitoes than the bullets of the French. He sailed north in the summer of 1794, but not to Quebec. He had secured a new appointment to command the troops in Nova Scotia. Another bee was buzzing in his stiff cocked hat. He was convinced now that the red republicans of France were about to send a fleet and army across the sea for the reconquest of Canada, and he foresaw that they must seize Nova Scotia first, as the British had done. It was a glorious dream. He saw himself at Halifax like another Heathfield at Gibraltar, sustaining a long and famous siege, hurling off attack after attack, and winning an imperishable name for himself in a lonely outpost of the empire. At Halifax he built another lovenest for Julie, and for the next six years he remained there, harrying his troops and engineers, throwing up all kinds of expensive forts, batteries, barracks, depots, and stables, and hacking an avenue through the forest for a chain of visual-signal stations reaching from Halifax to Fort Anne, and around the Bay of Fundy and up the St. John Valley toward Quebec. If the French had come he would have put up a magnificent battle, signaling a blow-by-blow description through the woods. But they never did.

CHAPTER 17

1793 — 1796

*The intrigue of Citizen Genêt — Vermont plans a war on
Canada — The comedy of the Olive Branch*

PRINCE EDWARD'S obsession became an expensive joke with
the rapid growth of the British fleet and the rising star of
Nelson, but at first it had some grounds. The explosive energies
of the French Revolution reached far and wide, and the western
side of the Atlantic was not immune. In the autumn of '92 the
National Convention of the French Republic declared their intention of war to the death against all kings and kingdoms, and they
began by putting their own King through the busy guillotine in
January 1793. Ten days later they opened war on Britain. At the
same time they sent off a minister with credentials to the United
States. He was Edmond Charles Genêt, a man with the red fire
of revolution in his belly and some very hot plans in his head. In
the interests of *Le Peuple Français debout contre les Tyrans* he
would bring about, by every possible means, a war between the
United States and Britain. This meant, of course, chiefly a war
against Canada. And he could promise a French fleet.

In the United States the memory of their own revolution was
still fresh and hot. The southern states, especially Virginia, then the
most populous state in the union, owed large debts which their
stubborn British creditors were still trying to collect and which
another war would bury for good. In the West the American
frontiersmen were embroiled with the Indians and inflamed at the
sight of British redcoats still holding the Great Lakes posts. Even
in the cooler northern states there were many people who saw
in the French revolution a true reflection of their own. Was not
their own prophet of rebellion, Tom Paine, now carrying the torch
of liberty in France, indeed sitting in the convention as a deputy
from Calais? Was not stout old Rochambeau in arms again, this

time commanding a French republican army, and was not Lafayette commanding another?

At this time the American people had begun to divide politically into two parties. Hamilton and others called themselves Federalists and supported Washington's administration. Their appeal was to businessmen, manufacturers, shipowners, and in general the urban population whose interest was in trade abroad and a strong central government at home. Their opponents, led by Jefferson, called themselves Republicans although they were, oddly enough, the progenitors of the modern Democratic party. They stood for the agricultural interests, the plantation owners of the South, the small farmers of the North, the land-hungry backwoodsmen of the frontier. Their policy was Jefferson's own; isolation from Europe, ruthless expansion in North America.

The author of the Declaration of Independence was to many Americans the very incarnation of their own Revolution; and as the unrelenting enemy of kings and kingdoms, especially the British kingdom, Jefferson was naturally an ardent admirer of the French Revolution. The Terror with all its bloodshed failed to shake his admiration. It was not until Napoleon seized power and became an open and unblushing dictator that Jefferson cooled. Even then he could not lose and he never lost his anti-British bias. This was partly, perhaps chiefly, fed by the British presence in Canada and their influence with the Indians of the West. Tall, lean, brilliant, many-sided, thoroughly dedicated to the theory of Manifest Destiny although not the author of the phrase,[1] Jefferson in 1793 was set on one immediate thing—to seize the Indian lands in the old Canadian tract between the Ohio and Mississippi. If that meant war with the British in Canada, so much the worse for the Indians and them.

Into this useful situation sailed Citizen Genêt. He landed in

---

[1] At the time of the Louisiana Purchase (1803) Jefferson wrote to his envoy James Monroe, "The future destinies of our country hang on the event of this negotiation." But the first use of the actual words "Manifest Destiny" came nearly twenty years after Jefferson's death. They were part of an editorial in the *United States Magazine and Democratic Review*, July–August 1845, in which the writer declared that "foreign governments" were anxious to check "the fulfillment of our manifest destiny to overspread the continent." The phrase became popular in the United States during the Texas and Oregon disputes. Its first utterance in Congress was in 1846, when Massachusetts representative Robert C. Winthrop, in a debate on American versus British claims in Oregon, referred to "the right of our manifest destiny to spread over this whole continent."

Carolina in April and traveled through the South to Philadelphia, getting enthusiastic ovations all the way. Even before presenting his credentials to George Washington, he was busy whittling at American neutrality. There were French merchant ships in various American ports and their crews were eager to earn prize money. It was easy to purchase American guns and stores, to fill out the crew lists with American adventurers, to commission the ships as privateers of the French Directory flying the French republican flag, and to send them forth against British shipping from the security of American ports.

At Philadelphia Genêt demanded boldly that the Americans repay in kind the fighting help they had got from France in 1778–83. President Washington received this with a formal politeness in which there was a certain chill. The France represented by Citizen Genêt was hardly the France of 1778. Already the news beating slowly across the Atlantic told of very strange developments. The French Revolution had begun to devour its own children. Washington's old friends Rochambeau and Lafayette had both resigned their commands and were in danger of their heads, indeed Lafayette had felt obliged to flee the country. This was not the spirit of '78. The full story of the Terror had yet to unfold, but Washington scented mischief in the person and actions of Citizen Genêt. He refused the French minister's demand, and for emphasis proclaimed the neutrality of the United States in the present war.

Genêt then worked along the devious but more practical lines which had offered him a pattern from the first. In spite of a warning from the United States Government (conveyed by Jefferson himself, significantly enough), Genêt went on with commissions to privateers operating out of American ports. These ports included Boston, and very soon the merchant skippers of Nova Scotia and New Brunswick were under surprise attack not only on their long passages to and from the West Indies but on their own coast. Here was the very seed of a British-American war. With privateers flaunting the *tricolore* under the nose of the Halifax admiral and slipping back to Boston with their prizes, the presence of British warships off Cape Cod was bound to follow.

With this seed well planted, Genêt turned to another promising field, the land of the French Canadians. The French Revolution had aroused a keen interest in Lower Canada and the interest was followed by a good deal of sympathy when France declared war on

Britain in the early part of 1793. Was not the French Republic fighting for survival in the face of its enemies, especially the ancient British enemy—just as the *canadiens* themselves were struggling for survival under British rule?

Citizen Genêt left them no doubt about it. With the aid and ideas of a republican sympathizer in Montreal the busy French agent addressed them thus, in a pamphlet entitled, *The Free French to their Brothers of Canada.*

"Follow the example of the peoples of America and of France. Break with a government that grows worse from day to day and has become the most cruel enemy of the liberty of peoples . . . It is time to upset the throne on which hypocrisy and imposture have sat too long. Do not fear George the Third or his soldiers, who are too few to check your courage . . . rebellion is your most sacred duty. Remember that as French-born people you will always be suspected and persecuted by the kings of England . . . Canadians, to arms! Call the Indians to your help. You can count on the help of your neighbors and of the people of France."

Survival, that pet word of nationalistic *canadien* orators, writers, and demagogues in after years, never made much sense in the light of fact, especially the fact of 1774, when the Quebec Act sealed the rights of the French Canadians in their religion, language, laws, and customs. True, a clique of the British governor's favorites secured all the fat jobs and contracts for themselves; but that was true in the other provinces which were neither French nor Catholic; and graft and favoritism were not unknown in Quebec long after French-Canadian democracy was firmly in the saddle.

When the first Quebec Parliament met in 1792 one half of the upper House and two thirds of the lower were French Canadians, and their first debate decided that the speaker of the assembly was to be a French Canadian and that the French language must be recognized equally with English in all their proceedings. With that condition henceforth the word *survival* was absurd. The proper word was *revival,* for after the mental depression of the conquest, the French Canadian was able to refresh his spirit in the very halls of Parliament set up for him by the conqueror.

Thus when Citizen Genêt and his *agents provocateurs* began their propaganda in 1793 they were thumping a scarecrow stuffed with their own straw. Nevertheless the magic word *français* as opposed to *anglais* had its appeal, especially to those who saw the French

Revolution as a breaking of mankind's chains. After 1794, when the horrid facts of the Revolution drifted across the sea, the Republic of France became anathema in Quebec. Indeed the worst effect of Genêt's seditious effort was upon the minds of the English, not the French. Beginning with Lord Dorchester a long succession of British officials in Canada during the wars of the French Revolution saw a red republican under every Canadian's *bonnet rouge*.

The suspicion reached its height in the person of Sir James Craig, the bull-minded governor who tramped ponderously into the Quebec china shop in 1807. This man, more than any other, aroused in the French Canadians a hatred instead of a mere dislike of British rule, a fanatic belief in the word *survival*, and a sullen spirit of non-co-operation with the English-speaking Canadians that was to survive for generations.

As in the American Revolution, the work of French agents plotting trouble in Canada was made easy by the position of Vermont. Ethan Allen, that wild man of the mountains, had died in 1789. Two years later Vermont was admitted a state in the American union, thus receiving the fourteenth star that might have been Nova Scotia's in '76. Ethan Allen's brother Ira was very much alive, the new leader in the Green Mountain state, and busier than ever with the old intrigues.

The boundary set by the Treaty of Paris in 1783 had placed Lake Champlain in American territory, so that the famous pass to Canada was not only in American hands but controlled by the Vermonters. The long wedge shape of Vermont forced their trade to move in opposite directions, the southern traffic going to Boston or down the Hudson, the rest reaching the sea through Canada by way of the Richelieu River and the St. Lawrence. Ira Allen and his Green Mountain Boys lived in the upper part of the state, with covetous eyes on the Richelieu Valley and Montreal.

Nowadays, comparing the proportions of Vermont and Canada, the notion of war between them seems ridiculous. In 1793 it was a serious matter, and so weak was the British position in Canada that the odds were on Vermont. The population of Lower Canada at this time was about 160,000, of whom only 10,000 were of British origin. Upper Canada had only 10,000 people, largely of British origin, but including a considerable French-Canadian group at Detroit. The attitude of the French Canadians was doubtful. Ira Allen and the French secret service were sure that the Canadians of French origin were ready to revolt as soon as weapons were put in their hands. The British governor could count on nothing more than a scatter of English-speaking militia.

As for the people of the United States, officially neutral in the war between Britain and France, sentimentally they were on the side of France—and the southern and western Americans were in favor of war with the British. If the Vermonters succeeded in their private invasion of Canada, even for a few weeks, they were sure of strong support from the Jeffersonian party throughout the other states. Moreover the population of Vermont itself was now formidable. From about 7000 in 1771 it had swollen to more than 85,000 in 1791, and already its land-hungry frontiersmen were spilling quietly over the unmarked border into the St. Lawrence plain.

Thus for the British Canadians there was every cause for alarm. Dorchester could not forget that Ethan Allen's absurdly easy seizure of the Champlain pass in 1775 had led to a general American invasion. There seemed no reason to doubt that Ira Allen's ambition to seize the Richelieu would set another afoot in '93. Governor Haldimand's policy, which forbade any Loyalist settlement close to the border, had left a vacuum in the so-called Eastern Townships; and for years now, with the aid of greedy land speculators in Montreal and Quebec, the Vermonters had been moving in to fill it. Ethan Allen's old ambition to seize Montreal as a natural outlet for Vermont trade was very much alive in brother Ira, and (as if its chanted "*Ah! ça ira, ça ira, ça ira!*" were something personal) the French Revolution seemed to him an opportunity. So the situation grew into a plan real in intent and frightening in its implications. It was for a large armed invasion from Vermont to be timed with a general uprising of French Canadians and Indians along the lines of Genêt's proclamation.

Rumor of Ira Allen's intentions began to reach Quebec soon after Lord Dorchester resumed his Canadian post in '93, and it was followed by rumor of a powerful French fleet and army coming across the sea—the very tale that had so impressed Prince Edward among the mosquitoes of Guadeloupe. By the spring of 1794 Dorchester was so alarmed that he called out two thousand provincial militia to guard the border. What followed was revealing.

As in '75 some *canadiens* turned up promptly to defend their country. The majority refused. At Charlesbourg near Quebec three hundred men armed themselves, not to defend the country but to resist any attempt to make them obey the militia law; and their phrase, *In the name of the people, which is above the law,* sounded suspiciously like Citizen Genêt. In the region about Montreal, horsemen galloped through the parishes like so many *canadien* Paul Reveres, calling on the countryfolk to rise against the British governor who ordered them to war.

The *habitant* disliked the English-speaking people across the border as much as those at home, and he remembered sourly the American invasion of '75, but he hated conscription. The fact that under American rule he would have to muster in state regiments in time of war did not occur to him at all. (Later generations of French Canadians settled in New England found this out, submitted without question, and made very good American soldiers.) Dorchester wisely did not enforce the militia muster and the agitation simmered down.

The Vermonters were not ready to march. They needed a stock of weapons for themselves and for the host of French Canadians who were to join them in sweeping the British out of Canada. The problem was to get the arms. Washington was watching Vermont almost as uneasily as Dorchester himself and any attempt to get a large supply of arms in the United States was sure to meet his frown.

It was not until 1796 that Allen and the French secret service hit on a solution. The French Directory would supply the arms at a French port and Allen would get them across the sea and into the proper hands. Ira promptly set off for France. In December he sailed from a Channel port in a ship named *Olive Branch* with twenty thousand muskets and a supply of ammunition under the hatches. The name of this explosive package was droll enough. What followed was the kind of historical farce and twist of plot that fiction dare not imitate.

The French Directory had many irons in its bright red fire. One was a sponsored rebellion in Ireland and the British Navy was watching Irish waters with care. As the *Olive Branch* drew toward the toe of Ireland on her westward passage she was stopped and searched by a British warship; and there below the hatches were just what the British were looking for. Ira found himself charged with smuggling arms to Ireland, a charge that properly belonged to a gentleman named Wolfe Tone. He could not explain his real purpose without letting the Canadian cat out of the bag and exposing himself to the same charge in a court at Quebec, where the punishment would be death. (One of Genêt's dupes, David McLane, was tried and hanged at Quebec for treason in July 1797.)

Ira Allen took the British sentence, jail for five years, and when he returned to Vermont in 1801 he came like a Yankee Rip van Winkle to find that the times had changed, that he was half forgotten and his influence gone. Strange things had happened in his absence. In 1798 the United States Government had passed a Sedition Act with stiff penalties for anyone, citizen or alien, who attempted or aided "any insurrection, riot, unlawful assembly or combination." Apart from that the lawless behavior of French privateers in the Atlantic had created an unofficial but hot little sea war between France and the United States that lasted from 1798 to 1800. The songs and dances of the French Republic were no longer popular in American drawing rooms. In Vermont the old invasion scheme was dead. To avoid being jailed for debt Ira had to flee to Philadelphia; and there he died in 1814, amid the thunders of a war that he had tried to provoke before its time.

What might have happened if Allen had got his muskets safely into the hands of the Green Mountain Boys and their prospective Canadian allies is an interesting speculation. Dorchester had few troops to stop them and the fiasco of the militia muster seemed to show how little support he could expect from the Canadian people. The margin between farce and bloody drama can be very narrow, as history has often shown. As it was, these alarms and excursions between 1793 and 1796, the Vermont affair, the French privateers out of American ports, the tramp of American troops toward Detroit, the hot scurry of Simcoe, and finally the flutter of the Stars and Stripes over every key fort on the Great Lakes, all made a nightmare preview of 1812.

Meanwhile there was a breathing space. In 1796 Lord Dorchester left Canada forever, taking with him that peculiar blend of soldierly and diplomatic qualities—and luck—which somehow had carried the country through one crisis after another. He was followed by a succession of governors who lacked his balance; soldiers with no diplomacy, diplomats who were bad soldiers. None of them had his luck.

CHAPTER 18

1791 — 1792

Upper Canada at the time of the Canada Act
— Governor Simcoe

WHEN the country west of the Ottawa River became the province of Upper Canada most of its ten thousand people had settled since 1783 along what they called the Front, meaning the river front from Montreal to Kingston. In the eight years of their occupation they had cleared a narrow belt of farm land by the water, where they could boat their grain to the grist-mills and receive trade goods from Montreal.

Passengers and merchandise from Montreal still traveled by *bateaux*, passing the roughest rapids by portage paths and Haldi-mand's little canals, and threading their way through the Thousand Islands to Kingston, a trip that took twelve days. At Kingston they transferred to schooners of the Provincial Marine for the passage up Lake Ontario. The unit of freight measurement was the barrel of rum, the most popular commodity on the frontier, which cost three dollars to move from Montreal to Kingston.

The only towns beyond Montreal were Kingston and Niagara, each with less than four hundred people. Both derived their importance from the military posts and the small dockyards of the Provincial Marine at each end of Lake Ontario. As a defense measure dating from the American Revolution, the only sailing vessels permitted on the lake were ships of the Marine, which thus had a monopoly of the bulk carrying trade. Indeed this was now their chief activity. The naval efficiency of the service had vanished since the American war. With few exceptions the officers were no navigators in the naval sense, the ships were badly designed, worse kept, and manned by crews of backwoods misfits who preferred a small wage and all the rum they could steal to the rigors of farming in the bush.

The ease of lake transport compared with the rough forest trails kept almost the entire white population close to the waterside. The interior remained a hunting ground for Indians. From Kingston around the shore to Niagara there was little or no settlement; the forest came down to the bank untouched except for the clearings of a few outcasts and wanderers and the charred knots that marked the old French trading post (Fort Rouille) on Toronto Bay.

At Niagara the settlement was chiefly about the fort, on the "American" side of the river. On the Canadian side opposite Fort Niagara was the little village of Newark (now Niagara-on-the-Lake), which contained the rude wooden barracks put up by Butler's Rangers during the late war, and the dock, store sheds, and barracks ("Navy Hall") of the Provincial Marine.

The people here were Loyalists from the Mohawk Valley and other parts of New York State, with some descendants of the original French inhabitants and a curious rag, tag and bobtail of Indians, portage men, and Negro slaves carried off with other loot to Canada in the raids of the American war. Farms stretched along both sides of the river below the falls and there were orchards of apple, peach, and cherry trees.

A small post called Fort Erie stood at the head of the Niagara River on the Canadian side. Transportation on Lake Erie was entirely by boat or canoe and there was no settlement between Fort Erie and Detroit. At Detroit, chiefly below the fort on the American side of the river, lived two thousand people, the largest settlement in Upper Canada, of ancient origin and composed of French Canadians, *métis*, and a few families of Loyalists. Here again were farms and orchards on both sides of the river, with some substantial houses. The home of Colonel Francis Baby, built on the Canadian side in 1790, was the first brick house in the western district of Ontario.

Beyond Detroit a wilderness of lake and forest stretched away into the blue. A lone British army post sat on the limestone cliffs of Mackinac Island near the entrance to Lake Michigan. Between Lakes Huron and Superior there was a portage road and a fur post at the Sault Ste. Marie rapids, both on the American side of that river. From the head of Lake Superior a chain of North West Company trading posts extended over the Grand Portage and through the forests and lakes toward the mysterious regions of the plains. Even here the British hold was precarious, for the boundary line so blindly accepted by the British in Paris was found (after

1796) to place the Pigeon River end of the Grand Portage in American territory also.

The chief route of the traders from Montreal to the Far West ran up the Ottawa River, thence by a series of portages and streams through Lake Nipissing to Lake Huron, and so on to the head of Lake Superior. The Nor'westers had explored a tentative short cut, the old Indian route from Toronto Bay overland to Lake Huron. Various other canoe routes threaded the forest between the Ottawa and the lakes, used mostly by wandering Indians. The portage paths and hunting trails of the savages, and the crude wagon tracks linking one farm with another in the settlements, were the only means of land travel. There was not a real road in the country.

The political separation of Upper from Lower Canada came at a time when the four million people of the United States had burst the Allegheny barrier and were spilling into the Middle West. Nearly half of them lived north of the Potomac and their geographical thrust was toward the Great Lakes. To these people, especially the million New Englanders and New Yorkers, the peninsula of Ontario jutting across their westward path like a down-turned thumb was an interesting prospect for three reasons. It had good water connections with the sea; it had a much better soil and climate than their accustomed part of the country; and it had no desperate Indian problem like the lands beyond the Ohio.

The country was British, but the settler's only concern was land, and one of the charms of western land was that no government, whether in Philadelphia or London or Quebec, had much authority. A man could hack out a clearing, build a shanty, raise a crop among the stumps, catch some fur in the winters to trade in the springs, and live from one year's end to another without seeing a politician or a tax gatherer. Hence at the very birth of Upper Canada there was a large potential immigration crowding about the east end of Lake Ontario and along its southern side.

Such was the situation when John Graves Simcoe came to take up his new post as lieutenant governor of Upper Canada. Here was a remarkable personage, a thickset ruddy Englishman with the blunt features of John Bull himself, and with the mind of a minor Caesar. He had physical and moral courage. His mind in some ways was as broad as Lake Ontario, in others as narrow as his own sword edge. He could be generous, he could be blindly stubborn, he could be calm and sensible in debate and again intolerant and bombastic in every word he said and wrote. As an administrator he combined flashes of geographical insight worthy of a Nor'wester with the parochial views of an English country squire.

Simcoe had served with distinction as commander of the Queen's Rangers, a Loyalist corps in the American Revolution, and he was only twenty-nine when the rangers became prisoners in the surrender at Yorktown. This affair left a permanent mark on Simcoe's life. Cornwallis had tried to protect the Loyalists in his army by stipulating in the surrender terms that they were not to be punished for their service in the royal cause. Washington had replied stiffly in refusal, declaring it a matter "altogether of civil resort"; and the Loyalists were treated as civilians taken in arms. Simcoe as a British regular officer was permitted to go on special duty to New York. His men were jailed like common criminals and several were hanged. He never forgot it and never relaxed his hatred of republicans in general and George Washington in particular.

His animosities were not confined to the American camp. Another thing he never forgot or forgave was some slight, real or fancied, from Sir Guy Carleton toward certain officers of the Queen's Rangers with regard to rank and pay. His appointment to Upper Canada had a single drawback—that it placed him once more under Carleton's command. However Carleton, now Lord Dorchester, was enjoying his long leave in England. Two years were to elapse before he and Simcoe crossed pens and wills in Canada.

Simcoe had been M.P. for St. Maws, Cornwall, during the whole debate in Parliament over the Canada Act in the spring of 1791. He had applied for the lieutenant governor's post and his appointment followed soon after the passing of the Act. He spent that summer drawing up his plans and needs and discussing his ideas with officials of the Colonial Office. His information about his new field was patchy and it was reflected in his written notions, "worth the attention of the new settlers in Upper Canada." He had sound ideas about developing the salt springs known to exist, and seeking for iron deposits and building forges, and encouraging the settlers to grow flax and hemp for British naval use; but his notion of supplying the Indian trade with rum made from parsnips was hardly a thing to impress the settlers, least of all the rude Nor'westers.

Simcoe left for Canada with his wife and two children in September 1791. His equipment included what he called his "canvas house," a large marquee that had been used in the Pacific by the famous Captain Cook, purchased at a sale of Cook's effects in London. He arrived at Quebec on November 11. He could not take office until his executive council had assembled to administer the oath, and while four of these had been appointed in England, only one had yet crossed the sea. Still in England also was the regiment being raised for his service. He was obliged to spend the winter as an appanage to Prince Edward's staff at Quebec, a bad experience, for Simcoe was impressed with Edward's Hanoverian discipline and polish.

In the time to come Simcoe obliged his troops in the forest to keep the Edwardian level of smartness. He kept the cat-o'-nine-tails swinging in his barrack yards. His deserters were hunted down by Indians like runaway dogs, and after court-martial some were shot like dogs, even though it was a time of peace. One received a quite Edwardian execution. A private who deserted his sentry duty over some boats at Fort Erie was taken down the river to Fort Niagara and shot kneeling on his own coffin.

All of this was in store when Simcoe's new regiment arrived at Quebec in the early summer of 1792. He gave them the title of his old Loyalist corps, the Queen's Rangers, and gave commissions to several of his former officers. At about the same time a quorum of the new executive council arrived, and with these and his staff and family Simcoe set off for Upper Canada. On July 26 he reached Niagara, the temporary military and civil headquarters of his new domain. The permanent capital was still a question. Dorchester had suggested Kingston. To Simcoe that was impossible, first because Dorchester favored it, and second because in the event of war with the United States an American force could cross over to Kingston on the winter ice.

Niagara was a beautiful spot and life was pleasant there, but the old fort must be surrendered sooner or later in accordance with the Treaty of Paris and then the village of Newark and Navy Hall would be at the mercy of American guns across the river. Clearly the capital of Upper Canada must be safe from a quick American attack and a site must be chosen somewhere in the interior. In the meantime Niagara must suffice. Simcoe set his army carpenters to work repairing and changing Navy Hall for use as a temporary Government House, and while the work was in progress he and his family camped in Cook's old marquee on a bluff overlooking the Niagara River. Elizabeth Simcoe was a lively and intelligent woman, and her journal and sketches give some interesting pictures of the life and scene.

Among his foibles Simcoe had a starched conviction of the evils of democracy and the virtues of the English class system. In Upper Canada he decided to establish, while the country was young, an aristocracy of squires and supersquires with hereditary titles and privileges, all under the benign but authoritative shadow of an established Church of England. From these (and with a careful admixture of gentlemen direct from England) would come the executive council, like a backwoods House of Lords, to watch over the measures of an elected assembly. He talked of this a good deal, seeing in the course of a few generations another England in the heart of the American land mass, strong enough to resist the republic on the south and to offset on the east what he called "the miserable feudal system of old Canada . . . too firmly established by a sacred capitulation to be openly got rid of." Here was a source of trouble to come. What Simcoe planted in Ontario was an English feudal mentality as objectionable as the French one in Quebec. A future generation of Upper Canadians called it a "Family Compact" and got rid of it.

CHAPTER 19

1793 — 1796

Simcoe explores the wilderness — Choosing the site
of Toronto — Simcoe's wild plans for war — A new inpour
of American settlers

FOR several months Simcoe was busy at Niagara with the first session of his miniature legislature and a mass of new matters ranging all the way from courts of justice to an annual agricultural fair. In February 1793 he was free to make a frontier inspection. At this season, when swamps were frozen and the snow leveled the rough face of the country, it was possible to travel by horse and sleigh over the backwoods trails. With half a dozen of his staff and a retinue of servants Simcoe reached the Mohawk village on Grand River in three days. Here Brant greeted them, and together they attended divine service in the Mohawk mission church.

A sudden thaw made further sleigh travel impossible and after three days the party set off around Lake Erie on foot, with Brant and some of his Mohawks. Simcoe reveled in the life on the winter trail, making careful note of such things as a salt spring and a place where petroleum seeped to the surface. They traveled hard, sending Indian messengers ahead, and on February 18 they were met by a train of horses and sleighs which took them the rest of the way to Detroit. Like the post at Niagara the fort at Detroit was on the wrong side of the river, and in American hands it would cover an easy approach to Upper Canada. The Ohio tribes were still confident after their victory over St. Clair, but General Wayne was known to be mustering an American army in the West, and the chief villages of the Indians were on the Maumee River not fifty miles from Detroit. If Wayne was victorious, many of the Indians would flee to safety in British territory. Where would Wayne halt his pursuit? This was the question in every British officer's mind on the frontier in 1793, and Wayne's approach in '94 made it hot and pertinent.

On the way back to Niagara, traveling some distance inland from Lake Erie, Simcoe's party came to the Thames River and halted for a day at a spot that he "judged to be a situation eminently calculated for the metropolis of all Canada." It was the site of the present city of London, Ontario; but Simcoe's dream, in which he persisted for years, was never to be realized.

The journey had taught Simcoe a good deal about the frontier country and the handicaps of its defense, and he saw at once the need of roads for moving troops toward Detroit from Lake Ontario. He set his Queen's Rangers to work cutting the first road in the summer of 1793. It ran from Burlington Bay to the Mohawk village on Grand River. His idea was ambitious—to link Burlington with Detroit by way of the proposed "metropolis" on the Thames, and in the other direction with Kingston along the shore of Lake Ontario —and he called this narrow slash in the forest "Dundas Street" in honor of Britain's Secretary of State for War.

Had Simcoe commanded people and material enough during his five years in Upper Canada, he might have wrought the same kind of miracle that Anthony Wayne performed in Ohio, creating a rich and populous state in the heart of the lake country. As it was he could only make the most of his small means and show the way to those who followed him. The threat of another war with the Americans hung over the new province almost from the start, and while building a civil framework in the wilds Simcoe had to see all things with a soldier's eye.

He foresaw that the seat of government should be well removed from the frontier and placed so that troops could move quickly to the Niagara and Detroit danger points, hence "Dundas Street" and the dream site on the Thames. He foresaw that the defense must be amphibious, with warships on Erie and Huron as well as Lake Ontario, hence his chosen sites for naval bases at Long Point, Penetanguishene, and Toronto Bay. In choosing the latter, he sailed up the lake shore from Niagara in May 1793. The bay was sheltered by a long marshy point, the home of huge flocks of wild fowl in the summer season. Except the small clearing about the vanished French trading post the forest came down to the lake bank, and an Indian path led off through the trees toward Lake Huron.

Simcoe chose a townsite in a grove of oaks at the waterside

and hurried back to Niagara, where a commission of American officials had arrived to treat for peace with the Lake Erie tribes. Simcoe gave them a polite hospitality and arranged meetings with Brant and other chiefs, but he was suspicious. A dispatch from Quebec had warned him of the new war with France, he knew that the Americans were mustering an army in the West, and he suspected a connection between the two. The American commission went up Lake Erie and returned in mid-July admitting that their journey had been fruitless. Obviously now the United States would resort to force, and again the question arose: if they defeated the Ohio tribes would they stop short of Fort Detroit, which by treaty belonged to them? And what about Fort Niagara? Simcoe suspected his guests of spying. With Britain again at war with France, the shadow of the old Franco-American alliance loomed like a ghost from the field of Yorktown, that scene of his indignant memories.

It was important now to get a safer base established in case of war. He kept his rangers busy clearing the Toronto site and on July 30 he removed his wife and family there while he superintended the work. Like all his ideas, the plan for the new town was ambitious. He laid out a site on a scale undreamed west of Montreal and drew up strict building regulations. As for a name, Toronto would never do. On August 26, 1793, he proclaimed it York—"in compliment of the Duke of York's victories in Flanders."

The settlers at the other end of Lake Ontario were not impressed. The Kingston merchant Richard Cartwright wrote to Montreal describing the visionary man "at present at Toronto, where he has laid out a town plot which he has called York, and where I am told he intends to pass the winter in his canvas house, for there is yet no other built, nor preparations for any; his regiment also is to hut themselves there. You will smile perhaps when I tell you that . . . a town lot is to be granted only on condition that you shall build a house of not less than forty-seven feet front, two stories high, and after a certain order of architecture . . . it is only in the back streets and alleys that the tinkers and tailors will be allowed to consult their tastes and circumstances."

Of the proposed "metropolis" in the wilds of the Thames River he was even more scornful—"a piece of political quixotism, a scheme perfectly Utopian, unless Montgolfier's ingenious invention could be adopted to practical purposes and air balloons converted into vehicles of commerce."

In the conservative air of Quebec, where progress had been a leisurely affair through almost two centuries, Lord Dorchester, too, had a skeptical view of his flea-hopping subordinate in the West, and tried in his cold formal letters to pin him to earth. Simcoe was oblivious. The air of Upper Canada had a dynamic quality, especially west of Kingston.

With the rangers' log huts rising at York, with his marquee pitched in a scene never contemplated by Captain Cook (and sheathed with boards against the coming cold), Simcoe was off again, this time to explore the Indian route to Lake Huron. He traveled thirty miles afoot and the rest by canoe through Lac aux Claies (which he renamed Lake Simcoe) and down the Severn River. He found a good site for a Lake Huron naval base at Penetanguishene. It would need a road from York and so another military "street" was born, this one named in honor of another British cabinet minister, Sir George Yonge.

All his plans, in which the ax was so much more important than the musket, went to the winds in the spring of 1794. After spending a hard winter at York with his family and the rangers, Simcoe received an alarmed dispatch from Lord Dorchester. The Vermont invasion scare was at its height and so was the unrest among the French Canadians. Dorchester at the age of seventy was not the graven image of 1775. He was badly rattled. He now had word of a definite American march toward Detroit as well as Ira Allen's preparations in Vermont, and he assumed that Canada was about to be invaded east and west. To safeguard the approach to Detroit and make a link with the friendly tribes in Ohio, he ordered Simcoe to establish an outpost on the Maumee River.

To the brisk and peppery Simcoe these instructions could only mean that war with the United States was definite and he assumed the shooting would start when General Wayne's army came upon the new British outpost in Ohio. He set off for Lake Erie and in three weeks he was watching Major Campbell and a small company of redcoats setting up their lone cannon behind a stockade on the Maumee. There was no sign of Wayne's army. He hurried back to Niagara, checked defense matters there, and went on to York. There was still no word of actual war when the small legislature of Upper Canada met at Niagara in June. Simcoe spent the summer by the river almost sniffing the wind for the first whiff of gunpowder and making fantastic plans. It seemed to him that the only hope was a bold offensive as soon as the fighting began. When the news of Wayne's march reached him late in August he packed off his wife and children to Quebec for safety, hurried troops and field guns up to Fort Erie, and embarked with them in boats toward the farther end of Lake Erie and the Maumee River.

Fortunately for everyone, Washington's strict orders and Anthony Wayne's common sense had saved a clash with Campbell's redcoats at the Maumee stockade, and when the fire-breathing Simcoe came on the scene there were no American troops in sight. How far things might have gone Simcoe revealed later in a private dispatch over Dorchester's head to the Duke of Portland, an amazing mixture of petulance, bombast, and rash military speculation. He had prepared to launch raids by parties of rangers and Indians from Niagara, striking deep into the states of New York and Pennsylvania. With these distractions for the Americans in the East, he would have attacked Wayne's four or five thousand troops in Ohio with his own small force of regulars and militia and the Maumee Indians (whom in fact Wayne had already destroyed). He had no doubt that he could destroy Wayne's army or at least put it out of action. He would then have marched on to Pittsburg to join the backwoodsmen of Pennsylvania, who were in revolt (the so-called Whiskey Insurrection) against their own government.

"Supported as these people could easily be by Upper Canada and the Indians, they would present a most systematic and formidable opposition to the United States. I have no doubt that the president, Mr. Washington, in person must have marched to crush it. The first object of my heart would certainly be . . . to meet this gentleman face to face."

It was a plan and a letter worthy of Johnnie Burgoyne; and as it happened Simcoe (if he had got so far) would have met at Pittsburg not "Mr. Washington" but Burgoyne's old nemesis Daniel Morgan, sent there to put down the Whiskey Insurrection. Obviously this fantasy sprang from Simcoe's rankling memories of Yorktown, from an utter miscalculation of Wayne's strength and the Indians' weakness, and from yarns with Butler's old rangers at Niagara.

The London authorities, dealing peacefully with John Jay and preparing to sign a treaty which would give up the western forts and remove all cause for trouble there, were astounded when news of Dorchester's rattled moves and Simcoe's wild assumptions came across the sea. Their censure was severe, and when it came to them the two soldiers blamed each other.

Jay's treaty had settled matters in the West. Nothing appeared to settle Ira Allen and the Vermonters, and Dorchester now drew down to Montreal nearly the whole garrison of Upper Canada. Probably he was glad of an excuse to take these dangerous weapons out of Simcoe's hands, but with them he removed Simcoe's chief means of making roads and opening the Ontario countryside for settlement. Canada had no crowding population, no swarm of eager frontiersmen. Simcoe kept his few rangers hard at work, but their axes could not even scratch the wilderness.

He had lost none of his creative dreams in the wild excitement of '94 and when it was past he turned his mind to other ways and means. With Wayne's victory over the Indians, a mass of American pioneer folk began to roll across Ohio. To get there the New Englanders and New Yorkers had to pass by Lake Ontario, and some of them, seeing more convenient land in the empty woods of Upper Canada, had made their way to the Canadian shore. With a little encouragement others would follow.

Simcoe issued a general invitation. Whatever his prejudice against Americans, he knew that these people made the best possible settlers, bringing with them their own tools, household goods, and cattle. They were in no way different from the Americans who had come to Upper Canada after 1783, and he was ready to believe that these, like the others, were on the move because they disliked life in the republic.

And Americans came in thousands, and they continued to come and to send for friends and relatives long after Simcoe left Canada. The people of the old Loyalist migration viewed all this with some distaste. In 1799 Richard Cartwright noted dourly, "That part of the province which extends from the Bay of Kenty [Quinte, near Kingston] upwards is composed of persons who have evidently no claim to the appellation of Loyalists." By 1812 a large majority of the people in the Ontario peninsula were Americans or the sons and daughters of American parents who had settled there in the past twenty years. With the difference of a flag flying over the modest parliament buildings at York, the upper province had become to all outward appearance a typical part of the American Midwest.

In the summer of 1796 the old lake forts were turned over to soldiers of the United States, and for the first time the Stars and Stripes fluttered in the lake winds all the way from Oswego to Mackinac. At Niagara most of the population moved over to the Canadian side. At Detroit there was a similar movement; of 2200 people only 500 remained on American soil. It was the end of an epoch and apparently Dorchester and Simcoe saw it in that light. They themselves were already part of the past. They had never been able to get along with each other. Simcoe resented Dorchester's authority, Dorchester found Simcoe insubordinate. In 1796, in separate ships, they quitted Canada forever, leaving their separate marks upon it.

Dorchester's influence had obtained much longer, but it was exerted in the somewhat static air of Lower Canada and he could never quite see past Montreal. In his time he had saved the St. Lawrence Valley out of the British-American wreck and that was to be his monument. Simcoe, in only five years, had shaped the future province of Ontario for good and ill and marked out the military paths by which the second northward march of the Americans was to be halted in 1812. That was monument enough for any man. He in turn had never been able to see past Detroit.

Yet the great flank march of the Canadians and Americans across the continent was already in progress, with the Canadians far ahead of their neighbors. In the autumn of 1794 Simcoe had received a passing call from a young Nor'wester named Alexander Mackenzie, who told him quietly that he and his party of Canadians had been across the Rocky Mountains and had stood beside the Pacific. Years were to pass before any American stood west of the Great Lakes.

CHAPTER 20

1785 — 1789

The Nor'westers — Alexander Mackenzie
— "Mackenzie's River"

EVER since the conquest the British governors had been absorbed in local problems. When they looked far, it was
nostalgic gaze toward England or an apprehensive glance
toward the south. The Canadians themselves, largely French, saw
nothing but their small farms along the St. Lawrence or their few
patches on the Great Lakes—except for a single class. The fur
traders looked deep into the West and they saw the country whole.
The spirit of a vast Canada of the future gleamed in these bold
and hardy men. Their vision could leap a thousand or two thousand
miles across the land, and they had the will and the endurance
to get there in spite of every obstacle. Moreover they combined
in their ranks in cheerful comradeship the two races, British and
French. Together they discovered the great Canadian land and
they stamped the Canadian character with their own simple faith
in the country and their ability to do things and do them quietly.

Even in the fur trade however there was a shortsightedness
in the old established Hudson's Bay Company, whose posts were
dotted like nails around the vast horseshoe of the bay itself, com-
municating with Britain by sea in the brief summers. The northern
limit of the Canadian forest avoided their domain, running its irregular fringe below the barren shelf of the bay and slanting across the
great land mass toward the mouth of the Mackenzie River. They
lived and traded on the edge of a dreary maze of lakes, rivers,
muskegs, and tundra barrens in which all human life depended on
the migrant herds of caribou.

To reach the more habitable Canadian world required a long and
difficult journey up one of the rivers that fell into the bay. The
"factors" of the company found it easier to sit in the rude comfort

of their posts beside tidewater and let the Indians and Eskimos come to them. A few of them had the urge to explore. As early as 1691 Henry Kelsey had paddled and scrambled over the rugged face of what geologists call the Canadian Shield (from its shape) and had seen the rich plains of the Saskatchewan. Samuel Hearne, moving from his base at York Factory between 1769 and 1771, had explored the desolate barrens toward the Northwest, had seen Great Slave Lake (which he mistakenly called "Athapuskow") and followed the Coppermine River to the Arctic Sea. But in general the "Bay men" stayed close to the bay.

The fur traders of Montreal had a different outlook although, like the Bay Company, they recruited their agents largely among the hardy fishermen and crofters of Highland Scotland. They had taken over the old French fur trade at the conquest, working mainly about the Great Lakes with a focus at Detroit. Their business was interrupted by the American invasion of 1775-76, but this temporary embarrassment proved a good thing in the end, for they were able to see the folly of their individual rivalries and the advantage of working together. They began to co-operate in 1779. In 1785 they founded in Montreal the famous Beaver Club, and with it the informal but highly efficient association known as the North West Company or simply the Nor'westers.

By 1790 the Nor'westers were firmly in charge of the fur trade about the Great Lakes and deep in the "Illinois country," and from the head of Lake Superior they were pushing into the true northwestern reaches of the continent. The Hudson's Bay men despised what they called the "pedlars" and "packmen" from Montreal, but as time passed they began to realize that the packmen made up in energy what they lacked in easy touch with the sea. The Nor'westers with their canoe crews of tough and cheerful *voyageurs*, willing to paddle all day and half the night, able to carry packs weighing two hundred pounds over the portages, and satisfied along the way with a chunk of salt meat and a few dried peas or a handful of flour, could cover amazing distances in a short time. For these men fifty miles was only a fair day's travel. On good water their express canoes could travel a hundred.

The old Bay practice of waiting for the savages to come down the rivers had lost its complacent ease and profit by 1785. The Nor'westers were taking their goods to the Indian and getting his best furs on the spot, and they were moving freely into the western sources of the Hudson Bay fur supply and diverting more and more of the pelts to Montreal. After 1796, when the Americans took over the Great Lakes forts and began to interfere with the Canadian trade in the "Illinois country," the effort of the Nor'-westers was forced toward the Manitoba plains and they put their main strength and skill in that direction. They had their difficulties. Toward the close of the eighteenth century the Americans dis-covered that the Grand Portage, a pack trail running fourteen miles up the Pigeon River from Lake Superior, lay partly in their territory. By the year 1800 Nor'west fur brigades coming down the portage found a United States customs post at the Pigeon mouth, charging a stiff tariff on all goods passing over it.

The Nor'westers were obliged to move up the Lake Superior shore to the mouth of the Kaministikwia River, which offered a con-siderably longer and more difficult route toward Lake of the Woods and the Far West. Here in 1803 they built a base for their far western operations, calling it Fort William in honor of William McGillivray, one of their partners. From this time Fort William played the same role in the Nor'westers' trade that York Factory played for the Bay men. *Bateaux* coming up the Great Lakes un-loaded here the trade goods from Montreal and carried back the fur bales gathered in the interior. From Fort William westward everything traveled by canoe and portage, a job for the younger and tougher men. In this way the *bourgeois* (partners) divided themselves into two groups; the veterans who made their head-quarters at Montreal and directed North West Company affairs, and the "wintering partners" who traveled through the Northwest as long as the rivers were open and spent the frozen months in rude feast and wassail at Fort William.

In the farthest outposts the wild landscape and the electric air were developing a new kind of man, the young Nor'wester of some education and plenty of daring and energy, faithful to the gods of Beaver Hall but always itching to travel farther and see more. For a time a sort of beaver compass drew these men toward the North, because it was an axiom in the trade that cold country yielded the best fur. As early as 1775 Alexander Henry had re-turned to Montreal with his tale of discovery on the Athabaska River, where the Indians had described another great stream (the Peace) that flowed out of huge mountains in the West. In 1778 Peter Pond reached Lake Athabaska, and by 1786 Cuthbert Grant had been to Great Slave Lake. Meanwhile the greatest explorer of them all had arrived upon the Canadian scene.

Alexander Mackenzie was typical of many young Scotsmen now in the Nor'west service. At fifteen he had sailed to Canada, an emigrant from the stormy Hebrides, and arrived in Montreal in 1779 when the war of the American Revolution was still thundering away. The Nor'westers gave him a clerk's post in one of their warehouses, where he worked hard, saved his wages, and stored his mind with details of the business. At twenty-one he was able to buy a minor partnership and to become a *bourgeois* in charge of the trading post at Detroit; but he was not there long. A young man with brains on an athlete's frame belonged in the front line. The Nor'westers sought such men and pushed them into far responsibilities. In 1785 they sent Mackenzie to build a post called Fort Chipewyan at Lake Athabaska, where their strategic minds had seen a master key to the North.

From Lake Athabaska, like the tentacles of an octopus, a complex of waterways reached in all directions. The Athabaska stream itself came nearly eight hundred miles through the prairie country on the southwest. The Peace flowed a thousand miles out of the west and joined the Athabaska waters just above the lake. The Fond du Lac River and its various portages connected with the Churchill, which flowed a thousand miles east to Hudson Bay. Northward Lake Athabaska emptied into the larger basin of Great Slave, a lake far bigger than Erie or Ontario; and from Great Slave in turn there was a tremendous outpour, the sum of all these tributary waters, gathered in one huge river whose end nobody knew.

The Athabaska had been partly explored. The Peace had not. But it was the giant river flowing out of Great Slave Lake that teased young Mackenzie's mind. Where did it go? To the Arctic Sea? If so, it was too big to be the Coppermine described by Hearne. Or did it turn westward somewhere in its course and pour that vast drainage into the Pacific?

By the summer of 1789, with his fur trade well organized about Fort Chipewyan, Mackenzie was ready to find out. With a German and four French-Canadian *voyageurs*, two of these accompanied by their women (whose native skills were indispensable on a long journey into the North), he set out by canoe from the Nor'west post. It was June 3 and the sub-Arctic summer had barely begun, although the days were long. There was jagged ice along the river-banks, and when they had paddled 230 miles north to Great Slave Lake they found it still covered with the winter sheet except in a narrow belt about the shores. Here they spent two weeks exploring and waiting for the ice to break up.

Toward the end of June they found the lake's outlet and on July 1 they launched down the stream. For a space it flowed west as if it aimed for the Pacific, then it swung more toward the north. Day after day it carried them into the unknown, in rain, in snow, in bitter night frosts, and again in the broad light of the far northern summer where the sun was in the sky twenty hours a day.

There were places where the stream flowed six miles wide. The average width was a mile. Five hundred miles beyond Great Slave Lake they met strange Indians who warned them to go no further, that the river passed through a land without fuel or game, that there were frightful rapids and falls, that evil spirits haunted the passage. The sea was so far away that these Indians had heard of it only in fable, and said that if the voyagers ever got there they would be old men. Mackenzie's companions took a sorry view of all this, but he refused to turn back.

The massive river poured on toward the northwest as if sucked by some powerful Arctic vacuum and their own paddle strokes increased the pace, so that the landscape rolled away behind them swiftly. On July 12 they came to the river's end and a dull anticlimax it was. Instead of belching its farfetched waters into the ocean in one great rush, the stream spread and divided, wandering in shallow channels among flat marshy islands where the rise and fall of a salt tide alone marked the edge of the Arctic Sea. Mackenzie spent three days in this huge and dreary delta under the midnight sun and then turned back. The voyagers reached Fort Chipewyan again on September 12, 1789, and Mackenzie could contemplate his achievement.

He had traced to its mouth one of the greatest rivers in the world. Including the Peace tributary, it flowed 2500 miles, draining part of the Rockies and a large expanse of the Canadian barrens and prairies. Contrary to the warnings of the savages, it was easily navigable for most of its length; the banks were shaggy with forest most of the way (there were trees one hundred feet tall well beyond the Arctic Circle), and more than all this Mackenzie had gone to the northern sea and back again in a single summer and at the ripe old age of twenty-five.

It was not the long-rumored waterway to the Pacific in which so many men still believed. The Nor'west directors considered it worthless, a splendid road to nowhere. It had some curious features and that was all. In one place the voyagers had seen a form of petroleum dripping down the rock like soiled wax. At another a seam of coal burned mysteriously and stank the air—undoubtedly the "evil spirits" of the savages. It did not occur to the Nor'westers that this chilly barren stretching along the Canadian North had under its crust a treasury worth more than all the beaver ever caught.

Meanwhile back at Fort Chipewyan there was another shining query, the water of the Peace. It flowed from the west, from the region of the great mountains. Did it flow through a pass in those mountains? The prairie Indians spoke of the Rockies with a kind of horror as a barrier never meant for man to pass, the wall at the end of the world, with its peaks frozen in a perpetual winter.

And yet that way lay the Pacific.

CHAPTER 21

1579 — 1794

*The Pacific Coast — Sir Francis Drake — The Inquisitive
Russians — Captain Cook — An American finds the "Great
River of the West" — The quest of George Vancouver*

IT IS strange to reflect that nearly thirty years before Samuel
Champlain founded the town and colony of Quebec (and forty-
one years before the Pilgrim Fathers crossed the Atlantic to
Massachusetts) an English adventurer in the Pacific Ocean had seen
and claimed for his Queen the coasts of what are now California,
Oregon, Washington, and British Columbia. He was Francis Drake
in his famous *Golden Hind*, and the year was 1579. With the magnificent impudence of the Elizabethans he had made a foray around
Cape Horn against the Spaniards of Peru and Panama, and now he
was seeking a way home by the rumored northern passage to the
Atlantic. How far north he went is still obscure, but his own words
dismissing the passage as a myth reveal a knowledge of the coast as
far as Alaska that could not have been mere guess.

He turned south again, anchored in what is still called Drake's
Bay near San Francisco, and went through the pleasant ceremony
of claiming for Queen Elizabeth the whole coast north of the
Spanish settlements. He called the country New Albion and sailed
away across the Pacific for home. Nearly two centuries were
to pass before another Englishman came that way, searched New
Albion more carefully, and came to the same conclusion about the
northern passage. He was James Cook in 1778. But after Drake's
visit the Spaniards had been questing up from Mexico and one of
their hired pilots, a Greek they called Juan de Fuca, had reported
somewhere to the northward a great arm of the sea thrusting into
the land. This was thought to be the mouth of the Great River
of the West—the "Oregon" of the Indian tales.

Juan de Fuca's voyage was made about the time (1588) when Spain's naval strength was shattered on the coasts of Britain, and the Spanish empire in Mexico did little in the way of North Pacific exploration for a long time afterward. The Russian empire was much more active in the early part of the eighteenth century, when Peter the Great sent Vitus Bering to explore the Pacific coast of Siberia. The job took Bering many years and Peter died in the meantime; but then the Russians had a new curiosity. What lay beyond Siberia? In 1741 Bering sailed from a port in Kamchatka with two ships, *St. Peter* and *St. Paul,* and with a number of scientists and naturalists for passengers.

The time was propitious. The British were hotly at war with France and Spain (the so-called War of Jenkins' Ear). It was a chance to extend Russian interests to North America while the three nations most interested in that continent were mauling each other in the Atlantic.

Bering's ships reached and explored part of the Alaskan coast in the summer of 1741. On their way back they were lost in the storms and fogs of the Aleutian Islands, and the *St. Peter* was wrecked and Bering perished on the island that still bears his name. The *St. Paul* returned to Siberia with wonderful tales of the American world and with a few pelts of the sea otter, whose fur was coveted by every China merchant. On the Siberian side of the North Pacific the sea otter was comparatively scarce. On the Alaskan side it was to be found in thousands.

Just as the beaver had drawn men deep into North America from the Atlantic side, so now the sea otter was to draw them across the Pacific; but there was a difference. The otter was a beast of the northern coast and islands only, and in any case a mass of prodigious mountains came down to that edge of the Pacific and discouraged anyone from venturing far inland. The Russians, after their secretive habit, kept all this to themselves. For more than a generation their discoveries and their trading activities along what are now the coasts of Alaska and British Columbia were hung about with a mystery as thick as the Aleutian mists.

The man who pierced this curtain finally was James Cook. For years his voyages had ranged about the South Pacific. In the spring of 1776 his sponsors, the British Admiralty, sent him out again, this time to seek the fabulous Northwest Passage from the Pacific side, probing the west coast of America from Drake's "New Albion" to

Latitude 65° North — in other words from California to Bering Strait.

Cook reached the coast of Oregon on March 7, 1778, with the ships *Resolution* and *Discovery*. His crews included a harsh but excellent navigating officer named Bligh (afterward to make famous a ship called *Bounty*), a studious young midshipman named George Vancouver, and a corporal of marines named John Ledyard, a Connecticut Yankee who had run away from college to enlist in His Majesty's sea service.

The tall rampart of the Coast Ranges loomed above the shore and Cook followed it at a comfortable offing, watching for the great gap reported by the vague Juan de Fuca long before. In this way he missed the mouth of the Columbia River, hidden behind a shoulder of the land. Farther on he sighted Cape Flattery, but at that moment a gale rushed down from the mountains and drove him off to sea, and when he made the land again it was at Nootka Sound on the west coast of Vancouver Island. Thus he missed the Strait of Juan de Fuca also.

The harbor at Nootka was a good one and the time was spring, when the island was at its warm and lovely best. Here the voyagers stayed a month, camping on the shore and refreshing themselves after the long weeks on the sea. The natives were an ingenious people who wore toques of straw and frocks of a stuff woven from bark fiber and animal hair. In cool or wet weather they drew about themselves rich capes of otter and other fur. Their houses were built of hewn plank, with roofs sloping from back to front, and in the roomy interiors the white men saw large idols carved from tree trunks in the shape of birds and animals and men, and painted in bright colors.

Apparently Nootka was the center of a large coastal tribe, for men, women, and children flocked there in carved and painted canoes, eager to see the white strangers. Their native tools were of bone and stone, but some of them had scraps of iron, brass, and copper fastened to handles and used as chisels, clear evidence of European contact. At last Cook sailed on, passing a chain of rugged islands. Bering's old landfall Mount St. Elias with its white cap loomed inland. The islands hid a succession of deep fiords running into the mainland, some of them very long, any one of which might have been the mysterious Northwest Passage, and Cook saved a lot of time by what he missed.

His hopes rose in what he called Prince William Sound, a great inlet farther on, where he found people like the Eskimos of Greenland with swords, beads, and other European articles, which he supposed must have come to them through intertribal trade with the Hudson's Bay Company on the other side of the continent. And Cook Inlet, a huge cleft running two hundred miles into the under jaw of Alaska, seemed at first the very passage he was seeking.

Disappointed, he sailed around the Alaskan Peninsula into Bering Strait, where he named Cape Prince of Wales, the grim point of Alaska which comes nearest (fifty-six miles) to Asia. Turning the great north bend of the coast, he followed it almost to Latitude 71°, but there he was stopped by what appeared to be a solid barrier of ice.

He turned back, visited the Aleutian Islands (where he found Russian traders long established), and then sailed away to the fateful bay in Hawaii where he met his death. His ships returned home by way of the Orient, where the sailors found that their souvenirs of otter fur, even the filthiest cloak cast off by a Nootkan Indian, fetched an astonishing price.

When the ships left England in June 1776 the trouble in America seemed an isolated affair. When young George Vancouver reached home again in 1780 he found his country involved in a life and death struggle with France, Spain and Holland as well. He turned to war service, and he was one of Rodney's men in that West Indian sea victory which gave the British commissioners such a handy trump at the peace table.

Meanwhile the yarns of Cook's seamen caused a wagging of tongues in the seaport taverns and countinghouses of Britain, especially those concerned with the China trade. Furs at Nootka, tea in China — and Canton merchants crazy for the fur. These things made a pretty sum. Nothing could be done about it until the war's end, but then British merchants in the China trade began to measure the width of the Pacific and to send a ship or two in the direction of Cook's discovery.

In that year (1783) John Ledyard published in Connecticut a description of his travels. He gave the only eyewitness account of Cook's death and that alone was worth attention; but foremost in Ledyard's mind was the value of otter fur. He went to Europe to try raising capital for a trading venture to Nootka, but he had no luck and after much wandering he died in Cairo in 1789. He should have looked closer home. His pamphlet and Cook's own account of his North American discoveries, published five years after his death, had aroused the interest of some keen merchants in Boston. In 1787 they sent two ships under captains Kendrick and Gray to find some of this hairy gold in the Pacific.

The ships, *Columbia* and *Lady Washington*, rounded Cape Horn and sighted the coast of California in the summer of 1788. The speedier *Lady Washington* made straight for Nootka, where she found three British ships at anchor. On the shore near the Indian village stood a trading post, a flagstaff flying the British flag, and a small shipyard, where British captains John Meares and William Douglas were busy launching a schooner for the fur trade up the coast. It was the first ship built on the Pacific coast north of Mexico and they named her *North West America*. The Britons invited the Americans to join them in toasting this portentous event. Meares had bought Nootka from the Indian chief for some copper and a brace of pistols, and the flag betokened a British possession, but there was no international jealousy. They were traders all and there seemed room for everyone.

The British had done some exploring. Meares had looked for the rumored Great River of the West and had not found it. He mentioned seeing a great toss of breakers in what he called Deception Bay and he had named the nearby headland Cape Disappointment. (It was to deceive and disappoint many British hopes in the time to come.) But he and Captain Barclay of the *Imperial Eagle* had found the elusive Strait of Juan de Fuca and marked it on their charts.

In September Captain Meares sailed for China with a cargo of furs. The other ships remained to trade, including the *Columbia*, which had now joined her consort, and by the following May all had a cargo. The *Columbia* was preparing to sail for China when another visitor arrived. This one was Spanish and he had not come for furs.

The Spanish officials on the west coast of Mexico had shown some interest in Oregon between 1774 and 1779, when three of their captains ventured as far as the island on which Nootka stood. Since then they had done little or nothing; but when rumor of the British activities reached them in the spring of 1789 they sent their Captain Martinez to investigate with two armed ships. It did not take him long to perceive that a nest of the wandering British had planted themselves in what the Mexican viceroy considered Spanish territory. As the United States had been an ally of Spain in the late war

Martinez treated Kendrick and Gray politely and let them carry on their business. With the British he was rude. He seized their ships, looted their fittings and cargoes, destroyed their post ashore, and set up a battery under Spanish colors to bar the harbor to any further intruders.

The *Columbia* sailed away to China, exchanged her furs at a rich bargain for chests of tea and other Canton produce, and in the autumn of 1790 turned up safely in Boston, where tea was worth as much as furs in China. The profit of her single three-year voyage made a sensation.

In England there was quite another sensation. The news of Spanish insult in the Pacific had reached London in the spring. Captain Meares was a former officer of the Royal Navy and his trading venture at Nootka had the powerful interest of the Honourable East India Company. Therefore the Nootka incident could not be ignored by Parliament — certainly not by William Pitt, who was now in office with all of his father's wide grasp of affairs and all his instinctive hostility to France and Spain.

As it happened, France was shattered by the Revolution and Paris was a chaos. Spain had to stand alone in the face of the English wrath. On May 5, 1790, Pitt arose in the House, related the Nootka affair, and demanded full satisfaction for the Spanish insult to the British flag and the "usurpation" of British property in New Albion. Madrid received this with disdain at first, but it was soon omniously clear that the British meant exactly what they said. Lord Howe was putting the British fleet in readiness for war, and he was doing it to the expensive tune of two millions sterling.

A few British voices were lifted against this headlong rush toward war, but they got small hearing. The former Lord Shelburne, now Marquis of Lansdowne, declared that Spain had a right to the whole western coast of North America and that Captain Meares and the other traders at Nootka were merely "a set of young men of letters seeking for novelties." He was crushed by Pitt's cousin Lord Grenville, who observed that the war measures were proof that British honor and British power had arisen from the depths of 1783 where Lansdowne had left them.

All of this was not a matter of territory so much as a point of national touchiness where the British were concerned, because the aggressor happened to be the old Spanish bogey and the incident kindled all the old Elizabethan fire. For the future Canadian nation it was highly fortunate. Spain backed down, promised to surrender Nootka, make full compensation, and offer no further objections to British subjects settling on the unoccupied coast north of the Spanish settlements — i.e. north of San Francisco Bay. To make sure of these matters the British Government sent Cook's onetime midshipman, now Captain George Vancouver, to accept the Spanish surrender of Nootka and to explore the "unoccupied coast."

Vancouver's warships *Discovery* and *Chatham* sailed from Falmouth on April 1, 1791. As they made their way out into the Atlantic, the British Government returned its attention to the Act making separate provinces of Upper and Lower Canada, an early and quite unconscious demonstration of British interests in North America from sea to sea.

Vancouver made his Pacific landfall on the coast of California, followed it north, and sighted Meares's Deception Bay and Cape Disappointment, which lived up to their names. Although Vancouver noted the telltale color of the water coming out of the bay, the line of breakers marking a great bar seemed to him proof that this fresh water could not come from one strong river but a number of small streams.

Meanwhile Captain Robert Gray in the *Columbia* had returned to the Pacific for another cargo of furs, and came on the California coast two weeks behind Vancouver. He sailed into Deception Bay, saw the wall of discolored waves on the bar, and guessed the truth — that it marked the meeting of a mighty river and the mightier Pacific. He sailed over the bar, found himself in the long-sought "Oregon" at last, and named it Columbia after his ship.

Vancouver, sailing on, explored Puget Sound (which he named after his second lieutenant), turned up the Strait of Georgia, missed the mouth of the Fraser, rounded the north tip of the island which now bears his name, and dropped anchor in Nootka Sound. It was now the summer of 1792.

During the past three years the Spaniards had seized several more British ships and sent them as prizes to Mexico. To solidify their claim they explored and charted the east side of Vancouver Island and the mainland opposite. Their captain Quimper had examined the harbors of Esquimalt (which he called "Valdes") and Victoria ("Cordoba"). Captain Narváez had seen the mouth of the Fraser River ("Boca de Florida Blanca") without suspecting the great stream behind it. Unfortunately for all these efforts Spain had signed the Nootka Convention in October 1790, renouncing her claim to all of this part of the coast.

Imperial word from Madrid finally reached Mexico, and when Vancouver came to Nootka he found a Spanish officer, Quadra, waiting to hand over the captured ships and the ruins of Meares's "fort." Quadra's instructions were not clear. He was willing to make formal surrender of nothing ashore but the "fort" and the patch of land on which it stood, a radius of not more than a hundred yards. Finally Vancouver sailed down to Monterey, California, to settle the matter with Quadra's superior. On the way he looked inside Deception Bay and found what Gray had found before him, the Columbia River. Afterward he denied Gray's claim, but that was foolish, for Gray had even charted the estuary roughly for thirty miles above the bar.

Obviously the discovery was of immense importance. The Columbia mouth formed the only deep-water harbor between San Francisco and the Strait of Juan de Fuca, a coastal stretch of eight hundred miles. The river itself was the largest flowing into the Pacific from the North American continent, twelve hundred miles long, with twice the average flow of the Nile. Nobody was to know for years how long the Columbia was or whence it came, flowing as it did in a vast crazy fishhook among the mountains, with its shank reaching up into the north, not the east.

With his Monterey conference finished Vancouver turned his mind to the unfinished task left by his old commander, Cook. For the next two years he remained on the coast, charting it from California to Alaska, and sailing away to the warmth of Hawaii in the winter months to rest his crews. Among other matters he penetrated the screen of islands off the British Columbia-Alaska coast and explored the long fiords that Cook had missed, proving one after another to be merely a salt sleeve in the mountains and not a passage to the Arctic nor to Hudson Bay.

He was ill, indeed dying of tuberculosis when he sailed for England finally in October 1794, but he could look back on his task with honest satisfaction. Apart from his charts, the work that lay closest to his seaman's heart, he had wrung from the Spanish authorities of Mexico a full admission of British rights on the northerly coast. A seaman could do no more. It was up to landsmen now.

CHAPTER 22

1793

Alexander Mackenzie's journey to the Pacific

IF MACKENZIE'S RIVER had made small impression on the pragmatic minds in Beaver Hall, the experience of discovery meant a good deal to the young *bourgeois* of Fort Chipewyan. For one thing he had learned that a man moving through such distances needed the art of navigation as much as a sailor on the ocean. It was one thing to follow a river to its end and quite another to strike off into the blue as Samuel Hearne had done, rivers or no rivers, putting his faith in the compass and in the old sea quadrant, the bottle of mercury and the reflecting pan in his knapsack. And Mackenzie was keen now to enter the blue toward the west where the mountains loomed.

He obtained leave to visit Britain for a study of navigation and astronomy, and reached London in the autumn of 1791. People were eager for his tales of the Canadian Northwest and there was much for him to hear. The French Revolution was now well set on its furious course. Pitt, having shaken a successful fist at Spain over the Nootka affair, was now shaking another at Russia over her designs on Turkey. Some of the excitement of the Nootka incident still hung in the London air, and George Vancouver was well on his way to the scene. Cook's discoveries had been published and the general position and trend of the west coast of Canada were known.

Mackenzie took ship back to Montreal in the spring of 1792 and found that the chief Nor'westers had caught a rich scent of profit on the far Pacific coast. They had no thought of sending ships around the world. They were curious to know what lay between their farthest western outpost and the ocean of Cook's charts.

Mackenzie left at once for Fort Chipewyan, a summer's journey in itself, and there he determined to go on toward the mountains while the autumn weather held. In October his chosen party set out from Lake Athabaska in canoes and followed up the Peace River, a course that took them far southwest through the prairie country of what is now Alberta and into the foothills of the Rockies. Six miles above a fork where the Smoky River fell into the Peace they halted, built a log hut, and spent the winter.

In the spring they made a canoe big and strong enough to hold ten men with four months' provisions (mostly pemmican) and some trade goods for the good will of the savages beyond the mountains. On May 9, 1793, they set out; Mackenzie, Alexander Mackay, six French-Canadian *voyageurs*, and a pair of Indians. A week's hard paddling and poling up a stream swollen by melting snows in the mountains brought them to a place where the Peace lost all resemblance to its name, a wild torrent hurtling through a slit in the mountain wall. They tried to drag the laden canoe by ropes, scrambling like goats along the dizzy ledges, but at last they had to haul canoe and stores up the rock face and hack a path through the woods along the crest. This rugged carry-place, nine miles long, famous afterward among the Nor'westers as the Rocky Mountain Portage, was in fact the first of several.

The Rockies were not a single barrier. They stood in ranges one behind the other like waves of a giant sea frozen at a height of storm, and the rivers that drained them ran in the troughs for long distances before leaping through some canyon toward the east or west. When Mackenzie arrived at the upper forks of the Peace he found them forming a huge T, with the Finlay branch flowing in from the northwest and the Parsnip from the southeast. His true course lay at a dead right angle to these streams.

A chance-met party of Indians directed him up the Parsnip. At the head of it he would find a small lake, and from there he could carry his canoe over a steep ridge to another stream that went toward the west. Mackenzie arrived at the small lake on June 3, after a terrific struggle up the stream among towering mountains and the winds from their snowy peaks. A half-mile portage over a rocky shoulder brought the party to another small lake whose waters tumbled away toward the west. They had crossed the divide. But their greatest troubles lay ahead. What they had struck was a feeder torrent of the Fraser River, which gathered many such streams and rushed through a series of terrific gorges in the Pacific slope, growing in size and violence as it went.

The voyagers launched their canoe and went down. As if the river itself were not bad enough, strange Indians shot arrows at them as they passed and the mountain Indian guide deserted them. Mackenzie's own crew became mutinous. After days and many dangerous miles he came upon a puzzle that was to baffle one Canadian explorer after another. The Fraser described a great bend and then roared away toward the south. The Pacific lay west. The truth was that a crazy pattern of streams wandered in the wrinkled face of the Pacific slope and the two giants, the Fraser and Columbia, ran southward for an immense distance before curving toward the sea. When the map was finished after many years, the two great streams lay well apart but roughly parallel, like a pair of long fish-hooks laid one within the other.

After a mad ride down the Fraser as far as what is now Alexandria, British Columbia, Mackenzie halted. The river was still going south and getting worse by the mile. An Indian made signs that the river was impassable below, that they must return upstream and follow a tributary that came in from the west. On June 21 they turned back, and after a hard upstream toil of sixty miles they reached the fork where the Blackwater River tumbles into the Fraser. This they followed back through steep forested walls until July 4, when they came to an Indian trail leading off through the woods. Here in a drenching mountain drizzle they left the canoe, cached some of their stores, and tramped away toward the west, each man burdened with a ninety-pound pack together with his musket. That night and each night thereafter Mackenzie slept next to the Indian guide lest he slip away.

After some days they came on a river (the Dean) clattering through the woods across their path. They waded across and went on. Finally they came to another (the Bella Coola) where they found a small camp of Indians who had in their hands such significant things as a metal spearhead and European beads. Mackenzie and his men had now been two weeks afoot. With trade goods they bought dugout canoes from these people and paddled down the river. On July 20 it brought them to the head of a long salt-water fiord, one of those tantalizing sea canals, winding for leagues through the steep forest, which Vancouver was now exploring hopefully in quest of the Northwest Passage.

On they went, seeing on either hand a forest of trees bigger than anything even imagined in the East. Near the mouth of Burke Channel they saw at last the broad gleam of the Pacific. Mackenzie's quadrant and some calculation told him his distance north of the equator. (Without a chronometer he could not fix his longitude.) Among his few trade staples he carried the usual packets of powdered vermilion which the Indians bought for face paint. He mixed a paste of this rouge and daubed an inscription on a large rock by the waterside:

Alexander Mackenzie, from Canada by land, the twenty-second of July, one thousand seven hundred and ninety three. Lat. 52 20 48 N.

The journey from their winter camp had taken seventy-four days of continual struggle and risk. Since leaving, their tough buck-skin shirts and leggings had gone to shreds and their feet were almost bare. An old savage emerged from the woods and demanded gifts, making signs that white men had been there lately and had fired a shot at him. Vancouver's sailors had been here barely two months before, charting and naming the long channels and the very head-land where Mackenzie's party stood.

Mackenzie now turned back, and toward the end of August reached the crude log hut on the Peace. This journey, the second and last of his achievements, he had made at the age of twenty-nine. In the next year he traveled east to report at Montreal, pausing at Niagara to chat with Lieutenant Governor Simcoe. At that time Simcoe was still hot with the Maumee affair. The Pacific was another world.

Mackenzie went on to Britain. His savings and his Nor'west shares had made him independent and, unlike most explorers, he was wise enough to quit the wilderness before his youth and strength began to fail. He bought a home in Scotland, and when he published an account of his journeys and observations in 1801 he received a knighthood from the King.

His journeys had proved two things to the Nor'westers; that the easiest route of travel in the western wilderness ran merely to the empty shore of the Arctic Sea; and that the worst lay over the mountains to the Pacific. This posed a problem. In less than ten years their hard-driving men had stretched the Nor'west empire across the continent as far as the Rocky foothills, but at that point the time and cost of transportation from Montreal made their goods expensive. To drag the stuff over the mountains meant another heavy cost, and on the farther side they would have to meet the competition of sea traders bargaining along the coast.

The Nor'westers had always despised the Hudson's Bay Company as a seabound concern. But they were riverbound themselves and they clung to the methods that had taken them so far. The profits in the Pacific trade were tempting, a veritable pot of gold at the end of a rainbow arching across the continent from Montreal. Somewhere in that jumble of mountains there must be a way for the canoe. The Great River of the West perhaps, which cropped out in so many Indian tales. It was some time before they knew that anyone had found it.

CHAPTER 23

1792 — 1807

*Napoleon's dream of Canada — Nova Scotia privateers on
the Spanish Main — Lower and Upper Canada at the turn
of the century*

A T THE close of the eighteenth century the world seemed to
be hurrying dangerously toward an unknown destination, like
Mackenzie's canoe in a mountain gorge. In 1799 Napoleon
Bonaparte made himself the dictator of France, and the struggle
"to save the Revolution" was now to become a war of ambition and
conquest that would souse all Europe in blood and set other men in
conflict half around the world.

In this year, too, George Washington died, removing a powerful
conservative influence from American politics at the very time when
Jefferson with his radical and expansionist views was moving toward
power. President John Adams was near the end of his term and now
Philadelphia had ceased to be the capital of the United States. In
the autumn of 1800, driving up from Philadelphia to Washington,
the Adams' coachman missed his way and was lost for two hours in
the woods. The new capital was no more than a few imposing but
unfinished buildings rising above a swamp, yet this ambitious creation
was a token of the rising power and confidence of the new American
nation.

The country wrested from the Indians below the Great Lakes was
already crawling with settlers. Almost half a million Americans were
living west of the Alleghenies. In Ohio there were fair-sized towns
and already some of the inhabitants were wealthy men. One of them,
Aaron Burr, had built a luxurious home in the style of a Persian
pavilion on an island in the Ohio River, where he lived in the midst
of lawns and gardens and dreamed magnificent dreams. He and

Jefferson were about to part company in a matter of politics. After that, Burr would evolve his scheme for seizing Louisiana, marching like a new Cortes into Mexico, and making himself emperor of an independent state that would include all the continent south and west of the Mississippi. Such vast dreams were not peculiar to Burr. They were a symptom of the times. Other men were fascinated by the mass of the continent, unoccupied except by Indians, who did not count. Jefferson was as ambitious and as ruthless in his dreams as Burr, although his ambitions were for the United States and not himself. Even Napoleon had his American dream.

France had given over to Spain the whole vague sprawl of the country west of the Mississippi (all known as "Louisiana") when she withdrew from the North American scene in 1763. In 1800 Napoleon took it all back in the secret treaty of San Ildefonso. His mind reached in all directions and in their brief American phase his ambitions were as magnificent as Burr's. To guard his approach to the Gulf of Mexico he sent a large fleet and army to reoccupy Haiti, the rich and strategically valuable French colony which had been seized by the rebellious blacks of Toussaint L'Ouverture. When that was done the army would move on to Louisiana and make firm the French possession up the whole west bank of the Mississippi. Finally, striking from a point far up the river, his favorite general, Bernadotte, would lead an expedition to drive the British out of Canada.

This airy castle was tumbled by the black man Toussaint and his ally the Haitian mosquito, which killed sixty thousand French soldiers in two years. Napoleon's brief armistice with Britain, the so-called Peace of Amiens, came to an end in 1803, and with the British fleet once more prowling the West Indies the last hope vanished. Napoleon abruptly recognized the fact by selling "Louisiana" to the United States on April 30, 1803. For a little over $27,000,000 (including interest) the Americans gained title to all the lands between the Mississippi and the Rocky Mountains and extending south to Mexico. Nothing was said of the lands beyond the mountains, where Spain still had large claims as far as Oregon — and Thomas Jefferson had his own ideas about Oregon.

In the year 1800 the chief effect of the French war on the Canadian provinces was a steep rise in the cost of manufactured goods, almost all of which had to come from Britain. Only Nova Scotia was touched by the war itself. The port of Halifax, playing its role in naval strategy, was buzzing with troops and warships, and French and Spanish prizes were blowing into the port on almost every wind. For six years the Duke of Kent had pursued his fantasy of a coming French invasion, pouring out money for the defenses, and when he left finally for England in the summer of 1800 Halifax was the most powerful fortress outside Europe. All of which made the war a profitable affair for the Halifax merchants.

The provincial merchants of Nova Scotia had less to be pleased about. Since the war began in '93, their ships in the West Indian trade had been under attack by French and Spanish privateers; many had been lost; hundreds of Nova Scotia seamen were languishing in the fever-haunted prisons of those parts. By May 1798 the marine-insurance rate on a cargo from Nova Scotia to Jamaica had risen to 33⅓ per cent. Under these ruinous conditions there was only one thing to do — to join in the war under official letters of marque. Within a few months a small fleet of Nova Scotia privateers were sailing down the 65th meridian to attack French and Spanish shipping in the Caribbean Sea. The naval rules were strict. All prizes and their cargoes had to be sailed north (a gauntlet of two thousand miles) and condemned in proceedings of the Halifax vice-admiralty court, and the owners were placed under heavy bonds for the correct behavior of their crews.

This kind of sea adventure was not new to the Nova Scotians. They had taken it up for the same reason in the American Revolution. And in the course of the West Indian trade they had come to know the southern islands and the ports of the Spanish Main as well as they knew their own. A book might be written about their exploits on the Spanish Main alone — that old hunting ground of the Elizabethans.

One Nova Scotian privateer, the brig *Rover* with sixteen small guns and forty-five men and boys, ran into a trap at Puerto Cabello, where she was beset by a Spanish squadron in September 1800. The Spanish flagship was larger in size and crew, and with heavier guns, and her consorts were three large gun galleys rowed by slaves and manned by Spanish soldiers. Captain Alexander Codfrey of the *Rover* refused a demand to surrender. By quick maneuvering and deadly gunnery he shattered the gunboats one after another, turned on the flagship, boarded and captured her, and sailed her home to Nova Scotia as a prize.

The Canadian Navy is sometimes said to have its origin in the

Provincial Marine, established on Lake Ontario during the American Revolution. But the Provincial Marine was engaged in transporting troops and supplies on inland waters, it was built by British Government funds and operated by an army department. The far-faring and hard-hitting Nova Scotia privateers were the first warships built, financed, manned, and commanded on the high seas entirely by Canadians.

By 1800 the alarm of invasion from Vermont had subsided in Lower Canada, and tales of the Terror, carried to Canada by fifty refugee French priests, killed any illusions the *habitants* might have had about the new regime in Paris. At the news of Nelson's victory at the Nile, Bishop Denaut of Quebec ordered a public thanksgiving, and Bishop Plessis in the course of a sermon asked his flock, "Alas where should we be, brethen, if this country by an unfortunate reverse should return to its former masters?"

This warm and sincere attitude toward the British rulers might have gone far to remove the *habitant* suspicion of *les anglais;* but as usual a group of *les anglais* were more interested in removing the *habitant* faith and language. The Anglican bishop Mountain, with amazing stupidity, insisted that schools with English Protestant teachers should be set up in every parish so that the *habitant* children could be led "to embrace by degrees the Protestant Religion."

In this he was supported by Lieutenant Governor Milnes. Milnes, in the name of the Crown, had taken possession of the ownerless Jesuit Estates when the last of the old Jesuit priests, Père Casot, died in 1800. It was now proposed that the estates be used to support the Mountain system of education, and as a first step the Royal Institution for the Advancement of Learning came into existence. The directors and advisers of the Institution were all drawn from the English merchant and official class — the "Château Clique" — and its only French-Canadian support came from members of the old *élite*, busy fighting a rear-guard action against the land hunger of the *habitants* and the rising influence of the village lawyers.

As a result, when the bill setting up the Institution passed the assembly in 1801, the French-Canadian majority in that body carefully inserted paragraphs to safeguard church schools, and to require the consent of a majority of the people in any parish before the Institution put a school in their midst. Nothing more was heard of the Institution for a long time.

Such attempts, always with the same purpose, were bound to arouse a stubborn reaction in the French Catholic clergy and people. Nor could the *canadiens* regard with anything but contempt the other activities of the Château Clique and their money-making friends. The successive governors, whatever their own honesty, were willing to condone all sorts of jobbery, including a flagrant speculation in public lands, on the ground that friends of the regime must be rewarded for their loyalty to His Majesty. Nobody but the French Canadians seems to have questioned the value of loyalty bought in this manner.

As the new Parliament of Lower Canada opened in 1792 the French-Canadian members discussed the matter of loyalty with eloquence and point. One of the first proposals of the English-speaking minority was that their language alone must be used in the assembly as a sign of loyalty to the Crown.

"Ridiculous!" cried Pierre Bedard. "Is it not ridiculous to make the loyalty of a people consist only in its tongue?" Chartier de Lotbinière sharpened the point, especially for those of Anglo-American origin, with embarrassing detail. "Remember the year 1775! Those Canadians who spoke nothing but French showed their attachment to their sovereign . . . they helped to defend this province. You saw them join with faithful subjects of His Majesty and repel attacks made on this city by people who spoke very good English! It is not, you see, a uniformity of language that makes people more faithful or more united."

Meanwhile the province of Lower Canada went on with its business in the old peaceful fashion. There was a continual increase in the *habitant* population, and because the *habitant* liked to see his family about him there was little attempt to open new lands for settlement. Instead there was a continual slicing and reslicing of the narrow farms, and the cultivated strips running down to the St. Lawrence came to resemble more and more the legendary grid on which the great saint perished. There was a small but healthy ship-building industry. In 1800 there were only twenty-one Quebec-built ships on the local register. By 1810 there were fifty-four. In the next generation hundreds of ocean-going vessels were to be launched in yards along the St. Lawrence.

Quebec was still the main seaport. Montreal was growing as a clearing house for goods passing up and down the river and the Great Lakes, and for the money transactions in connection with them. This business included a considerable amount of American goods and money, for traders in upper New York State and Ohio found it cheaper to move their goods by water via Montreal, just as the upstate Vermonters used the convenient passage of Lake Champlain and the Richelieu. Moreover Montreal was headquarters of the North West Company, the root of that immense and tough commercial vine whose tendrils reached to Great Slave Lake, to the Rocky Mountains, to Nebraska and Dakota. Other fur traders had branches in Montreal, notably John Jacob Astor, the enterprising German who had landed at Baltimore in 1784 with twenty-five dollars and seven flutes as the sole basis of his fortune. His Montreal agent was Henry Brevoort, an American from Albany and a friend of Washington Irving.

In 1803 Irving visited Brevoort in Montreal and feasted in Beaver Hall at the invitation of the veteran magnates of the North West Company. Irving was enraptured with their tales of the West, he never lost his interest in the fur trade; and long after, when he was a world-famous author and Astor had his own fur empire, Irving wrote the story of Astoria.

In Upper Canada, as in the lower province, there was much speculation in public lands by men in favor at London. As early as 1791, the year of the Canada Act, Sir William Pullency was able to obtain 1,500,000 acres for one shilling an acre and to sell half of the huge grant soon afterwards for eight times that price. He was probably the worst offender, but many were busy at this game of land-grabbing and holding and selling, and the settler finally paid the cost.

Simcoe's "metropolis" on the Thames was still a dream. His actual creation, York, was the capital of Upper Canada with neat wooden parliament buildings and a few rows of stores and houses. His careful building regulations had been forgotten. Most of the houses were of logs, squared or round; the rest were of frame and clapboard in the common American style. Even the residence of the lieutenant governor was "formed of wood in the figure of a half square, one story in height, with galleries in the centre . . . sufficiently commodious for the present state of the province."

The town was little more than a pioneer camp in the edge of the forest. (Bay Street is said to have been called Bear Street in the early days because the judge's horses attacked and killed a bear in their pasture there.) At the close of 1803 the town plot of York measured

420 acres and the population was hardly more than one man, woman, or child per acre. A traveler who saw it in 1798 described it as "a dreary dismal place, not even possessing the characteristics of a village. There is no church, schoolhouse, nor in fact any of the signs of civilization. There is no inn, and those travellers who have no friends to go to pitch a tent and live there."

Simcoe's "Dundas Street" had never been finished and some parts through the woods had begun to disappear in new growth. In 1798 Asa Danforth, an American settler, offered to cut a new road around the Lake Ontario shore between Kingston and York. The provincial government made a contract with him and in 1801 the road was complete, though very rough with stumps and boulders, and with "corduroy" thrown down in the swampy stretches.

American settlers were still flocking into the Ontario peninsula; but there were others, Scots, Germans, even a hopeful company of French Royalists, exiles from the Revolution, who settled in a patch of woods on "Yonge Street." These poor gentlemen were quite unfitted for a life in the wilderness and after a few years of struggle most of them made their peace with Napoleon and went back to France.

The restlessness of the times brought all sorts of odd characters to the Canadian provinces. One was a mysterious "Mr. Edwards" who came to Halifax in 1808 and sought a private interview with the governor and admiral. "Mr. Edwards" turned out to be Aaron Burr, the dashing hero of the American Revolution, the onetime Vice-President of the United States, the man who had killed Alexander Hamilton in a duel and had plotted to set up a private empire in the Southwest. He was now disgraced and in flight and his fantastic ideas had taken another turn, a scheme for a British seizure of Florida and other Spanish territory on the Gulf of Mexico, which had not been included in Napoleon's Louisiana transactions. The details of his scheme remain a mystery, for Governor Wentworth bundled him off to London with a letter of introduction to the great Castlereagh, and if his ideas were ever committed to paper, that paper is lost.

There was Stephen Burroughs, the Yankee Casanova, privateersman, schoolteacher, and coiner. His coins were not good enough, and he had been in and out of jails and pillories all over the eastern states when he crossed into Canadian territory in 1800 to try the coining there. Repentance came upon him finally in Three Rivers, where he put aside his old tricks and his old admiration for Voltaire, Rollin, and Hume, became a convert to the Roman Catholic religion, taught school, and eventually died devoutly at a ripe old age.

There was La Rochefoucauld, the aristocratic refugee from the French Revolution, wandering about the Canadian settlements, peering, questioning, noting everything carefully, from the dress of the *habitants* to the exact state and strength of the Provincial Marine on Lake Ontario, and finally drifting back to France in 1799.

There was the Connecticut Yankee, Lorenzo Dow — "Crazy Dow" — the self-appointed prophet and saviour of sinners in the wilderness, tall, red-bearded, hollow-cheeked, with a mop of red hair brushing the shoulders of his cloak. A voice from the sky told him to convert the Papists of Quebec, and he and his wife Peggy paddled a leaky canoe through the Champlain pass "to sound the alarm to the fallen race of Adam." Like Bishop Mountain he found them inconvertible and he and his partner sailed away to try their luck in Dublin.

In contrast to Dow, but with the same fanatic sense of a mission, came a cold, ambitious, and levelheaded Scotsman, John Strachan, who turned up in Kingston in December 1799 hoping to teach in the "university" there. He found that the Kingston college was merely one of former Lieutenant Governor Simcoe's unfulfilled dreams. However he started a private school there for the sons of gentry. He soon found that the Presbyterian way of thought in which he had been educated "was not much in demand, while the Church of England on the contrary had good prizes in possession and splendid ones in remainder." In 1813 he was ordained a deacon in that Church. Meanwhile he taught his pupils at Kingston the three Rs, much Latin and Greek, and the divine right of sons of the gentry to rule the country in which they were born or in which they found themselves.

Several of his pupils became men of mark in the provinces of Upper and Lower Canada. One of them, John Beverly Robinson, became chief justice of Upper Canada and Strachan's right-hand man in the operation of the so-called Family Compact, which ruled that province for many years. Another, Robert Baldwin, became the Compact's greatest enemy and eventually its conqueror.

Tom Moore, the Irish poet, arrived in Canada in 1804 on his way home from a year's boredom in Bermuda, taking a roundabout route in order to see something of North America. He spent "a delightful fortnight" at Niagara, the guest of Lieutenant Colonel Isaac Brock of the 49th Regiment, and he paid for this hospitality with song, to his own accompaniment on the piano. He called at Kingston and went on down the St. Lawrence by *bateau*. The songs of the French-Canadian boatmen charmed him, and later on he wrote his own *Canadian Boat Song*, which charmed the world.

A very different Irishman drifted into Upper Canada at the turn of the century in the person of Thomas Talbot, who had served on Simcoe's staff there in 1792. In the spring of 1801 he returned as a civilian, made his way along the Erie shore to the woods near the present Port Stanley, cleared a small patch for a cabin, and named it Skittiewaaba, the Chippewa word for "fire-water," his favorite beverage. His ambition was to live as a backwoods baron, commanding many acres and choosing settler-tenants to whom every irascible word he spoke was law.

He had influence in England and by 1803 he had secured five thousand acres, which spread by degrees to sixty-five thousand acres. On this huge estate he built a manorial dwelling of logs which he called Castle Malahide after his old home in Ireland, and gradually he admitted settlers, each of whom was required to open a roadway, put up a log house, and clear five acres during his first year. None were permitted to live in his immediate vicinity. At Malahide he lived and worked as hard as his own gang of servants, white and black, in an establishment self-contained even to a cobbler's hut and a whiskey distillery.

The typical new settler in Upper Canada, however, was the independent stump farmer, usually an American, clearing his patch, cultivating a few acres, fishing and hunting in his spare time to vary the diet, cutting a path to the next trace of chimney smoke in the woods for human company. Thus the farms grew, and the rude backwoods roads, for they were getting away from the lake shores now. And now the lumber industry was becoming something more than a small watermill for local supply. In 1790 Samuel Sherwood floated the first raft of mast timber from Lake Ontario to Quebec. In 1807 Philemon Wright drove the first logs down the Ottawa. For the next century Ontario loggers were to be busy slashing down the great stands of white pine; and in their wake, wherever the sunlight fell among the stumps, the farmers came.

CHAPTER 24

1789 — 1811

*Travel from Upper Canada toward the West — The origin
of the* métis *— The Russians in Alaska — The search for the
Columbia*

UNTIL about 1789 the only portage road past the Niagara
cataract lay on the American side of the gorge, but then the
Canadians opened a road of their own from Queenston to
Fort Erie. It was not used much until United States troops replaced
the British garrison in Fort Niagara in 1796 and set up a customs
post on the portage. By 1800 as many as fifty wagons a day were
passing over the Canadian road, and most of the traffic was to and
from the new settlements on the Canadian shore of Erie.

In their own traffic the busy Nor'westers preferred the northerly
canoe route between Montreal and the upper lakes, by-passing the
Ontario peninsula altogether. However their costs were increasing
as the French war grew in violence, and they turned to the cheaper
bulk carriage of schooners on the lakes. The long detour at Niagara
and through Erie troubled them, and in 1799 they voted twelve
thousand pounds to improve the old Toronto portage (Simcoe's
"Yonge Street") to Lake Huron.

At the head of Lake Superior in 1803 they built their famous Fort
William, a range of big frame warehouses and living quarters, two
stories high, with tall pitched roofs to shed the winter snows. A
watchtower stood above the landing place, and one building housed
the long hall where the rough barons of the trade ate, drank, and
made merry through the winter months.

From Fort William a chain of streams, lakes, and portage trails
brought the westward *voyageurs* to Lake of the Woods, whose wide
glitter was broken by scores of picturesque islands, some of them
haunted by spirits, according to the savages. From here a powerful
river flowed through the forest to Lake Winnipeg, whose long
trough spilled northward into Hudson Bay. This, too, was haunted;

the whole landscape here was haunted; its very name, Manitoba, meant "Where the Great Spirit Speaks"; and it was easy to believe anything in this place where the shade of forest gave way suddenly to a naked sky and a sea of buffalo grass that flowed all the way to the Rockies and most of the way to Mexico.

This was the country explored by Pierre de la Vérendrye and his two sons between 1731 and 1743 and many a *canadien* had followed in their tracks, enchanted by the wild free life in the sea of grass. The Indians were hospitable and a giggling young squaw could be purchased for a handful of hawk bells or a twist of tobacco. A man could buy as many girls as he liked and exchange them as he pleased, a privilege not to be had in the prim villages along the St. Lawrence, where instead there were farms to be worked and taxes and tithes to be paid. For years these careless adventurers from Lower Canada had been disappearing into the West, reinforced by another stream, also French-Canadian in origin, coming up the Mississippi from St. Louis.

The horse, introduced into Mexico by the Spaniards, was now wild and common through the plains, so that the prairie tribes were not tied to the rivers like the canoe-faring Indians of the North and East. They moved on their shaggy ponies where they pleased, and the white adventurers rambled with them. How many Canadians chose this life will never be known. There must have been thousands. They left name traces everywhere from the Great Lakes to the Rockies, and the Canadian River in Texas and Oklahoma still marks a fringe where these prairie rovers met a similar scatter of wanderers coming up from Mexico. Young Francis Parkman, traveling the American plains from Missouri to Wyoming in the 1840s, found "Canadians" everywhere he went, most of them with evident traces of Indian blood, and speaking a *patois* of French, Indian, and English.

On the United States side of the northern boundary this widespread Canadian strain lost its identity soon afterward, disappearing in the flood of westward-moving Americans. On the Canadian side there was no corresponding movement across the prairies for many years, and the *métis* race throve and remained distinct, a human by-product of the old fur business. In the year 1800 the Nor'westers employed nearly thirteen hundred men between Lake Superior and the Rockies, the majority French-Canadian and the rest mostly Scots. Attached to them were hundreds of Indian women and half-breed children, maintained at the company's expense. A considerable group of these men worked as hunters in the plains below Lake Winnipeg, killing buffalo, slashing the meat into strips and drying it to make pemmican, the basic food of all the trading posts through the North and West. (The company employees who worked east of Fort William were known derisively as "lard eaters" because their ration was salt pork.)

Pemmican made an ideal journey ration. On the strength of it the Nor'westers made their long thrusts across the map. After Mackenzie's march to the Pacific they went on probing at the Rocky barrier, entering the mountains by Mackenzie's route up the Peace River and searching vainly for a good canoe route on the other side. The British sea traders on the Pacific coast were content with their foothold about Vancouver Island, sharing the fur trade companionably with a few American ships coming around the Horn. The Russians were much more acquisitive.

During the last years of the eighteenth century the greed and brutality of the Siberian adventurers in Alaska aroused a native revolt in which many Russians were slain and their posts destroyed, and in 1799 the Russian Government put its American empire on a more businesslike footing, following the example of the British in India by forming a semi-official corporation, the Russian-America Company, to rule the country and enjoy a monopoly of its trade.

Aleksandr Baranov, who had been trading in Alaska since 1790, became the company's first resident governor. In 1805 he shifted his headquarters from Kodiak Island to Sitka, a significant move that placed him closer to the southward run of the American coast. This was the year of Trafalgar, when Nelson shattered the naval power of Spain and France. From this time the old Spanish empire in North and South America crumbled rapidly, and Baranov soon had posts along the coast of California. Unless the Canadians could do something overland within the next few years, the Russians would grip the whole coast from Alaska to Mexico except for a small British enclave about Vancouver Island.

In the spring of 1799 the Nor'westers had an able trader-surveyor named David Thompson working in the Alberta foothills, and they ordered him to look for a pass in the Rockies well to the south of the rugged one traveled by Mackenzie. The position of the Columbia mouth was known by this time and obviously the main stream must be sought closer to that latitude.

Accordingly Thompson and his party journeyed up the South

Saskatchewan River and followed its Bow River tributary into the mountains. On the way they met a party of mounted Indians, a wandering band of Piegans, who said they were only ten days' journey from the Missouri River. This was important news, although Thompson failed to see the point. If horsemen could reach these foothills so easily from the Missouri, it was possible for American traders or explorers on that river to ride into the mountains straight toward the Columbia mouth.

In the late summer of 1799 Thompson and Duncan McGillivray went up the Bow Valley past the site of the city of Calgary. Winter came early in the mountains and snow was falling when they explored the Banff region and turned back. From what they had seen and heard from the local Indians, this was the approach to a pass through the Rockies. In the next year Thompson sent a party of *voyageurs* up the North Saskatchewan to examine another pass, which he named after Joseph Howse, a Nor'west factor. Both of these passes were obviously difficult. There seemed to be no easy way to the Pacific or to the Columbia River in any part of the Rockies so far known to the Nor'westers, and for the next several years Thompson was employed in mapping the branches of the Saskatchewan and the upper valley of the Peace.

And now the Americans entered the picture with the famous Louisiana Purchase. Although the Purchase had a definite western limit at the line of the Rocky Mountains, President Jefferson immediately turned his mind to Oregon. In this he was inspired by Gray's discovery of the Columbia mouth years before, but undoubtedly he was moved also by the example of Mackenzie, who had published in 1801 a full account of the Canadian march to the Pacific. He determined to send across the continent, not a canoe crew of buckskinned traders, but a squad of American regular soldiers, with orders to show the United States flag and uniform all the way to the Columbia mouth. There would be much for them to discover, but whatever they discovered, the mere fact of their journey was the main thing. It was to show that the United States could and would reach an arm overland to the Pacific whenever it suited the national purpose.

In the summer of 1803, months before the Stars and Stripes were hoisted officially at the Mississippi mouth, the American officers Lewis and Clark and a picked squad of soldiers were on their way to the upper waters. They wintered at St. Louis, the old Canadian settlement of pre-Revolution days, since swelled by a rush of settlers from Ohio. (Of ten thousand people in the region about St. Louis in 1804, no less than four thousand were of French-Canadian origin).

Just above St. Louis the Mississippi River was joined by the Missouri, an immense brown flood pouring out of the mysterious Northwest. Lewis and Clark had built a river barge during the winter, and on May 14, 1804, they "hoisted Sail and Set out in high Spirits for the Western Expedition." They reached North Dakota when the snow came, and after a winter among the Indians there, they followed a branch of the Missouri through Montana toward its source in the Bitter Root Mountains. Here they obtained horses and an Indian guide and rode on through the successive ranges of the Rockies to the Pacific slope. On a branch of the Columbia they changed to canoes, reaching the river mouth finally on November 15, 1805. In all it was a magnificent achievement, and when they returned east in 1806 President Jefferson lost no time in conveying their careful report to the Senate and Congress.

Lewis and Clark had traversed only the lower hook of the Columbia. Its long main stream remained a north-reaching mystery among the mountains, and in the huge wild jumble of the mountains the Canadians went on looking for it. In 1805 Simon Fraser entered the Rockies by Mackenzie's old route and built fur-trading posts in the high valley of the Parsnip stream. In 1806 he pushed the Nor'west empire further into the mountains, building fur posts at the head of the wild river which Mackenzie had ridden for many perilous miles in '93. Eventually it was to bear Fraser's name, but in 1806 he and every other trader in the mountains believed it to be the Columbia.

In the spring of 1807 Fraser sent Jules Quesnel with a canoe party to take the winter's furs east to Fort Chipewyan for transport to Montreal. When Quesnel returned in the autumn with supplies he had some surprising news. Some Americans had crossed the continent by way of the Missouri River and the mountains and had reached the Columbia mouth! Fraser realized that now or never something must be done to establish a Nor'west claim to the Columbia Valley. With the first snow falling in the mountains he could only build a hut on the Nechako River where it joined the Fraser, ready for a descent of that fierce torrent in the spring.

Fraser was on the wrong river, of course; but the search for the Columbia was getting warm. David Thompson traveled over the

Banff pass in 1807, found a stream which he called (from the fruit on its banks) the "Blaeberry," and followed it down to a larger stream which the Indians called Kootenai. He was now actually on a branch of the Columbia, but its true identity was to baffle him for years.

In May 1808 Simon Fraser left his winter quarters and launched down his own big river. Anyone who sees the Fraser canyon and rapids today can appreciate the desperate dangers of his journey. He had to abandon his canoes at last and follow the torrent by the bank. At the mouth, where the city of Vancouver sprawls today, he was disappointed. Peering at the sun through his quadrant, he found that he was in Latitude 49°. The mouth of the Great River of the West was known to be in Latitude 46° 20′. He wrote wearily, "This river therefore is not the Columbia. If I had been convinced of this when I left my canoes I would certainly have returned." He was standing on ground that in another century would be worth a handsome price; but seeing nothing of value in an outrageous river that entered the Pacific in the wrong place, he clambered back to his post on the Nechako.

While Fraser's party were making this glum discovery at the risk of their lives, Thompson's party had been busy in the mountain valleys farther east, with no better result. In April 1808 they traced the Kootenai upstream to its source in what is now known as Upper Columbia Lake. The river remained a puzzle. Actually the Kootenai rises in the British Columbian Rockies, flows south into Idaho and Montana, and then with a long loop turns north into British Columbia again and flows into Kootenai Lake, a trough seventy-five miles long whose tip lies within fifty miles of Thompson's starting point. Midway along this gutter in the hills, the outlet pours away to the southwest and becomes the Columbia, flowing into the state of Washington. After a summer's wandering in this watery maze Thompson knew no more than when he started, and he withdrew across the ranges to winter on the North Saskatchewan.

In 1809 he tried again, and spent an arduous but fruitless summer following the Kootenai and its meandering branches in Montana and Idaho. In 1810 he traveled east across the continent to show his maps and report his puzzle to the Nor'west board of strategy at Fort William. This was an important year, for again the Americans were planning a move on the Columbia mouth, this time a commercial one.

In 1810 John Jacob Astor formed the Pacific Fur Company and enlisted a number of experienced Nor'westers. He had studied the findings of Lewis and Clark and the profitable ventures of the Boston ships in the Nootka-China trade. From his Montreal branch he had been able to see the separate ruts in which the Canadian fur traders had set their minds. The Hudson's Bay Company clung to the coast and hinterland of the bay itself, making the best advantage of sea transport for their goods, but apparently blind to the fact that their ships could sail around the world and trade in a richer field. The Nor'westers used sailing vessels on the Great Lakes, but their minds were still governed by the canoe, as if the long rivers and sweating portages of the West were the only decent means of getting anywhere.

Both the Baymen and the Nor'westers were facing financial trouble due to the Napoleonic wars. Someday the war must end; but in the long view their best move was to bury their old rivalry and unite their genius for moving goods by river and sea. In 1808 the Hudson's Bay Company showed no profit at all. By 1810 the Nor'westers were in no better case.

The shrewd Astor was able to profit by Canadian mistakes. His Pacific Fur Company (an offshoot of his American Fur Company) was to be amphibious in the widest sense. To this end he sent a party (most of them Canadians) to travel overland from Lake Michigan to the Columbia mouth. At the same time (1810) he sent the ship *Tonquin* around the Horn. The land party would look for fur-trading sites along the way. The ship, carrying the stores, would establish a post at the Columbia mouth, engage in the sea-otter fur trade at Nootka, and carry the furs to China.

In Canada the Nor'westers, deserted by some of their best factors and *voyageurs*, were soon aware of Astor's plans. In conference at Fort William they decided that the mysterious Columbia Valley must be found and claimed; otherwise Astor's men would soon be doing it the easy way, following it up from the mouth. And there at the board sat David Thompson, fresh from his experiences on the Kootenai, brushing the very edge of the mystery.

They sent off Thompson at once. It was autumn when he reached the Alberta foothills by way of Fort Chipewyan, and winter when he reached the headwaters of the Athabaska in the mountains. On New Year's Day, 1811, he and his party on snowshoes, with their supplies lashed to the backs of four Indian ponies and two dogs, were struggling through the Athabaska Pass. Thompson's thermometer showed twenty-four degrees below zero. He reached the Blaeberry stream toward the end of January, built a hut, and waited out the rest of the fierce mountain winter.

In the spring he pressed on to the Kootenai and again followed its course into Montana; but this time, at the end of its great hairpin loop, he struck off across the hills toward the known position of the lower Columbia. In June he came to the Spokane River, followed it down, and came to a mighty stream that was the Columbia beyond doubt.

By July 9, 1811, he reached the fork where the Snake River comes up from Idaho to join the Columbia. Here he set up a pole and a British flag, and nailed to the pole a few scrawled lines claiming the country for Britain and the North West Company. When his canoe slid around a bend of the lower Columbia at noon on July 15 he saw that he was too late. There stood "Astoria," the new log fort of the Pacific Fur Company. In their own long effort to find and follow the Great River of the West, the Canadians had been trying to capture an elusive serpent by the tail. Astor had seized the head, which is always the better way. But could he hold it? That remained to be seen.

Thompson stayed a week at Astoria and returned up the Columbia to his base on the Kootenai. He had been the first white man on the upper waters and he was the first to survey and map its whole curious course.

CHAPTER 25

1805 — 1812

Origins of the War of 1812 — The "Chesapeake" affair
— Tecumseh and the Prophet

IN 1812 Canada became the chief battlefield of a second war between Britain and the United States. It was a strange war, and neither nation had much reason for pride in it taken as a whole on land and sea, hence contemporary historians gave it a spotty cover in their national story.

For the Canadians naturally the war was an epic. The fighting took place largely on their soil, their farms and towns were destroyed, their own men bled in battle. They could not have survived a month without the force of British arms on land and sea, even though that force at times was perilously small; yet the war showed the Canadians their own fighting abilities and gave them a consciousness that they had a land worth fighting for. Thomas Jefferson had once remarked that a certain amount of bloodshed now and then was necessary to refresh the tree of liberty. For Canadians 1812 provided the bloodshed. The tree they chose for their national emblem in later years still shows the tinge of that refreshment every fall, and on their great national day Canadian school children still chant *The Maple Leaf For Ever*, with its reminder that "at Queenston Heights and Lundy's Lane our brave fathers side by side . . . firmly stood and nobly died." Such small but desperate battles as these constitute the Canadian's Bunker Hill, Saratoga, and Yorktown; sacred names to be recited every first of July, as the American celebrates the fourth.

The cause of the war went back to the Revolution. In the United States the old animosity against the British had never died except among the Federalist party, and many Americans regarded the conquest of Canada as a piece of unfinished business left over from 1783. The excuse was provided by the British themselves. After the

ruin of French and Spanish sea power at Trafalgar, Britannia ruled
the waves with an iron fist, and when Napoleon shut her trade out
of Europe by his Berlin Decree in 1806 she retorted with her famous
orders in council forbidding all foreign trade with the continent
under French rule.

In the United States the Federalist party took the British ban
calmly, seeing that American seaboard merchants and shipowners
were doing a booming business in food and other war supplies to
Britain, and reasoning that any enemy of the French dictator was
a champion of the rights of man.

Jefferson's party, whose strength was in the South and the inland
states and territories, were determined to stand on the rights of
American men. They pointed out that the British were not only
interfering with the American right of free ocean trade. The Royal
Navy was impressing American seamen on the high seas (claiming
them as deserters) and forcing them to serve in His Majesty's ships.

This lawless habit sprang from an old evil in the British sea
service. There was no adequate system to provide recruits for the
fleet. The shorthanded captain of a man-o'-war by custom was allowed to ransack the jails and to send his press gang through the
streets and taverns of every British (and British colonial) seaport
in which he dropped anchor. These efforts gathered a poor crop of
criminals and other misfits who were seldom good sailors. With the
growth of the Napoleonic wars and of the British fleet, it was found
easier and more practical to take men out of merchant ships at sea,
and after 1803 not only British merchantmen but the ships of neutral nations became victims of the press.

The harsh conditions of the lower deck led many British seamen
to desert when the chance came, and in search of a job they were
attracted by the good food and pay in American ships, naval and
merchant. The result was that British warships made a practice
of stopping any American ship that came their way, searching
its crew for deserters, and in the same practice taking any man
who spoke with a British accent and looked like a good seaman.
This habit led to an act of supreme folly in 1807, when the British
frigate *Leopard* fired a broadside into the unprepared United States
frigate *Chesapeake* a few miles off the American coast, killed or
wounded several of her crew, and took out of her by force a few
alleged deserters. The *Leopard* carried these men into Halifax, where
one man only was found to be British. He was defiant, a court-

martial convicted him of "mutiny, desertion and contempt," and he was hanged at the yardarm in full sight of the mustered British crews and the staring people of the Halifax waterfront.

This piece of brutal arrogance gave the United States the best of reasons for declaring war at once, but Thomas Jefferson took a cooler view. He was in his second term as President. His old suspicion of standing armies and navies had been deepened by the spectacle of France in the hands of a military adventurer, and during his time in office he had kept the armed forces of the United States at a cautious minimum. It was no time to go to war.

There was every reason to believe that Napoleon, now master of Europe, would bring the British down at last, and the longer it took, the more certain the ruin of both. Jefferson's answer to the *Leopard-Chesapeake* affair was an Embargo Act which forbade American commerce with any foreign nation. As Britannia got most of the American supplies this was a blow at her stomach, where it would hurt most. But the blow fell equally upon the Americans of the seaboard states north of the Potomac, who were profitably engaged in the business of British supply—and whose politics naturally were opposed to Jefferson's.

The Federalist merchants turned to various ways of smuggling goods to Britain. A popular way was to load supplies in a New England port, ostensibly for the American coastal trade, and to transfer the cargo (sometimes ship and cargo) to British hands at sea. The seafaring Nova Scotians just across the Bay of Fundy were willing partners in this game, and energetic shipowners like Enos Collins (who died the richest man in Canada) made a very profitable business of it. In this way the existing cause for an American war with Britain was denied by a large body of Americans in the states supposedly most abused by the British practices.

It was the people of the South and West, the land-faring Americans, who really wanted war and eventually got their way. With them Free Trade and Sailors' Rights were a good excuse, but the real issue was something else. Their frontiersmen were again encroaching on Indian lands in the West. Since their victory at Fallen Timbers the tide of American settlement had reached the base of the Michigan peninsula, whence it followed the line of the Wabash River to the Ohio and thence to the Mississippi. The white population had grown quickly on this captured ground. Kentucky was admitted a state of the Union in 1792, Tennessee in 1796, Ohio in 1803. Since then another wave of white expansion had been gathering.

The frontiersmen were eager to cross the line of the Wabash, and there was the familiar pattern of backwoods brawls, with white intruders murdered here, Indians murdered there, and the whole situation developing into another outright war. Some of the Indians were armed with guns. The cry arose once more that the British in Canada were arming and stirring up the Indians, and every American south of the Potomac and west of the Alleghenies believed it. John Randolph of Virginia put a cold finger on the truth. Speaking in Congress he demanded proof of the westerners' accusations, and he went on to say, "It is mere surmise and suspicion. It is our own thirst for territory that has driven these sons of Nature to desperation."

The British in Canada, for the safety of their fur trade and of their own back settlements, made a firm policy of friendship with the Indians at large. It was also in their interest, in case of future war with the United States, to keep the tribes quiet and intact until the war came. At this time a supply of arms to the tribes below the Great Lakes was beyond their means even if they wished it. Since 1793 Britain had been engrossed in the struggle with France, sending every possible musket to the Portuguese, the Spaniards, and other nations opposed to the French ambitions, while striving to furnish the demands of her own army and fleet. The supply of arms to Canada was barely enough for the garrison and the militia. Under the orders of Sir James Craig (governor general of Canada 1807–11) the agents of the Indian Department were forbidden to supply muskets or ammunition to the savages on the frontier, and the ban was repeated by Sir George Prevost when he took office in 1811.

This combination of British friendship and British military poverty on the Great Lakes was the ruin of the Indians, as Tecumseh and his people found, and their struggle for the Wabash lands led directly toward the second attack on Canada by the United States.

The man whose name meant Shooting Star (*Tekumtha* in the Shawnee dialect) had the characteristics of his race; pride, courage, cunning, and a touchy temper. He was tall and handsome, with an eloquent tongue. His brother, the Prophet, was scrawny, ugly, blind in one eye, subject to epileptic fits, and more than a little mad. These qualities led the Prophet into the profession of a tribal wizard or medicine man, in which his looks and fits were an asset. The savages, seeing him lie stretched and rigid for hours, as if dead, believed him touched by the Great Spirit; and the Prophet increased this awe by revealing in the mysterious shadows of his lodge such powerful medicine as a torch lit by sacred fire, and a belt of sewn beans which had, he said, grown out of his own flesh and made him safe from any human harm.

The Shawnee sire of these strangely different brothers had been slain by Virginian frontiersmen in a fight on the Ohio in 1774. In manhood both had fought the Long Knives at Fallen Timbers. Both refused to recognize the subsequent Treaty of Greenville, in which some of the defeated chiefs had signed away the Ohio lands. Both had an abiding hatred and distrust of the Long Knives and of the flag spangled with what they took to be the Long Knives' council fires.

The Prophet's reputation as a wizard spread among the Shawnees, Wyandots, Potawatomies, Delawares, Miamis, Senecas, and other tribes and remnants of tribes ruined in past clashes with the west-ward-marching Americans. In 1808, with a large following of various tribes, the brothers built a sprawling town of huts and tepees on the Tippecanoe River, a tributary of the Wabash, about halfway between Fort Wayne and the present city of Chicago. All this region was now coveted by the frontiersmen, and in 1809 William Henry Harrison, the governor of Indiana Territory, was able to make a bargain with certain petty chiefs for a huge tract of land extending nearly one hundred miles on each side of the Wabash River. In effect it was a surrender of all Indian rights between Lake Michigan and the Mississippi, including the rights of Tecumseh's people, who had not been consulted.

Tecumseh now sought the counsel of the British on the Detroit River. The British were in the old invidious position of 1794. Relations between Britain and the United States were again twanging dangerously at a time when the garrison of Canada could expect little support from across the sea. They would need their Indian friends. The difficulty was the old one, to keep the Indians quiet until an actual outbreak of war. There was every danger that they would fly to arms and be ruined by a swift American blow like the Fallen Timbers affair in '94.

At Amherstburg the agents of the Indian Department, breaking the governor's rule, supplied Tecumseh and his thirty destitute followers with guns and hatchets as well as food and clothing. They urged him to avoid a fight with the Long Knives at all costs, and to move among the tribes of the Middle West preaching unity. All this gave a faint color of truth to the old canard of the frontiersmen, without actually furnishing the tribes with the weapons they needed to stand off an American attack. Harrison knew better. He was determined to have the Wabash lands and he sent the Prophet a warning: "Do not deceive yourselves; do not believe that all the nations of the Indians are able to resist the force of the Seventeen Fires." (There were now seventeen stars in the United States flag.) He added, "Do not think the redcoats can protect you; they are not able to protect themselves. They do not think of going to war with us. If they did you would in a few moons see our flag wave over all the forts of Canada."

In the autumn of 1811, while Tecumseh was absent on his mission among the western tribes, Harrison marched on Tippecanoe with a thousand riflemen. The Prophet, screaming magic incantations, induced his credulous warriors to rush out and do battle in the open prairie. The end was certain. After a wild struggle the Indians were beaten with great slaughter and the survivors fled. With them went the Prophet, not trusting his bean belt. His influence was gone. Tecumseh returned from the Southwest to find nothing but the ashes of the Indian town and the scalped bodies of the dead warriors lying on the plain. After a lean winter in the forest he and a few followers headed for the British post on the Detroit. A new war was in the wind. At the end of April, Governor Jonathan Return Meigs of Ohio was mustering a large force of frontier militia and United States regulars at Dayton. The command was given to Governor Hull of the Michigan Territory with the rank of brigadier general. Four weeks before the official declaration of war at Washington he and other officers announced in speeches to the troops that they were bound for Canada, and that they would conquer Canada or die.

Tecumseh's party slipped across the Detroit River on a day in early June; and in the presence of Colonel Matthew Elliot, the agent of the Indian Department at Amherstburg, the Shawnee chief pledged his allegiance to King George.

On June 12, 1812, Hull's columns marched out of their Ohio camp, passing under an arch of evergreens and flowers and a banner inscribed *Tippecanoe—Glory*, and headed for the Canadian frontier.

CHAPTER 26

1812

The American "War Hawks" — The Canadian as a fighting man — Material interests in 1812

THE declaration of war on Britain was a triumph for an influential group of young politicians within the Jeffersonian party, all from the South and West, all fanatic believers in national expansion. John Randolph, who opposed the war, called them the War Hawks. Foremost among them was the small but strong-voiced Henry Clay, an energetic Kentucky lawyer who had long breathed war in the air of the Midwest. Clay and the other War Hawks glided into power on the wind of anti-Indian and anti-British feeling that expressed itself in the elections of November 1811, when Harrison was on the march to Tippecanoe.

One War Hawk was elected speaker of the House, another became chairman of the Naval Committee, three more controlled the Foreign Relations Committee. President Madison himself was against an invasion of Canada, but in the end he fell in with the War Hawk demand, calling out the militia of the various states and territories on April 10, 1812, and declaring war on Britain on June 18. The decision was strongly opposed by representatives of the coastal states from Maine to Delaware, and the Federalists always called it "Mister Madison's war."

To the War Hawks the year 1812 was an opportunity not to be missed. Harrison had crushed the western Indians and so cleared the flank for a march into Upper Canada. Britain was neck-deep in the Napoleonic flood, her only field army committed to the defense of Portugal, while the French stood victorious in almost the whole of Europe. Only the Russians remained their own masters on the continent, and Napoleon was about to tackle them.

Canada and its garrison could look for small help across the sea, and the white population of the whole country was barely half a million, the majority French. The population of the United States was eight millions, of whom nearly three millions lived in the states actually bordering on Canadian lands and waters. Farther inland, but within a few days' march, lived more than four hundred thousand people in Henry Clay's warlike state of Kentucky alone. Within the grip of the western states, like a thumb in a vise, lay the peninsula of Upper Canada. It was not even necessary to cross the lakes. Two approaches at Niagara and Detroit lay under American guns. The British regular garrison was known to be small and believed to be weak. Under the rule of Sir James Craig the discontent of the French Canadians had become notorious, and most of the Upper Canadians were settlers of American birth or parentage.

Dr. Eustis, the United States Secretary of War, declared; "We can take the Canadas without soldiers; we have only to send officers into the provinces and the people, disaffected towards their own government, will rally round our standard." Henry Clay said on the floor of Congress, "It is absurd to suppose that we will not succeed in our enterprise against the enemy's provinces. We have the Canadas as much at our command as Great Britain has the ocean ... I am not for stopping at Quebec or anywhere else, but I would take the whole continent from them and ask no favors. I wish never to see peace until we do."

These confident assumptions overlooked several important facts. The United States Army had not fought a battle, except against Indians, since 1781; and its generals were relics of the Revolution or politicians given army rank because they thirsted for glory in a quick campaign. On the other hand the British Army had come a long way since Bunker Hill and Saratoga. For almost twenty years their regiments had been in action against the tough and expert soldiers of the French and learning some sharp lessons at their hands. This training and the constant shift of garrison reliefs about the world had placed in Canada a force of self-reliant officers and men not to be dismayed by opposing numbers or by the isolation of their posts.

Moreover the Canadian farmer and backwoodsman had learned from childhood the shooting skill and the other frontier knowledge that made the Kentuckian so adept in warfare. The Canadian's fighting experience had been small, for he had managed to get along with Indians; but on his own ground, in his own clearings, with his own farm and property at stake, he was deadly in defense and with training and actual battle experience he became formidable in attack.

Had the invasion been made from the start by a sufficient force of trained and well-led American troops, the British garrisons must have been overwhelmed, and a rigid care for private property might have induced the Canadian countryman to shrug his shoulders and accept the inevitable. Most of the American invaders of 1812 were state militia and frontiersmen accustomed to Indian warfare, in which the prime object was to scatter the hostile tribe with a few well-aimed volleys and then destroy its village and crops. The first looting and burning of Canadian farms raised the hackles of every man and woman in the country, whatever their national origin. The first clash of the war, in which an American army was captured entire, showed that the defense of Canada, far from hopeless, had a sporting chance of success.

A few hundred Upper Canadians of American birth or sympathy joined the invading forces, and throughout the war the Americans found useful spies and informers in the population; but these were an exception that proved a rule of fierce resistance. The French Canadians, whatever their dislike of British governors, proved equally ready to fight against American ones. Even the American settlers of Lower Canada (there were nine thousand, mostly Vermonters, in the Eastern Townships) raised several battalions of militia for the defense of their adopted country. None of this sprang entirely from patriotic sentiment. There was a strong material interest.

Until 1806 the Canadian trade with Britain had been small; but in that year Napoleon closed the ports of Europe against the British and in 1807 Jefferson closed the ports of the United States. In spite of busy smuggling by American merchants the British were desperate for supplies, especially food and timber, and by 1808 the Canadians were doing a rich business. The demand for masts and ship timber in the Royal Navy alone was tremendous; all the wood supply formerly drawn from the Baltic countries had to come from Canada. A stream of gold flowed westward across the Atlantic in the wake of British purchasing agents, private and official.

In 1809 the British Government announced a fixed customs preference for Canadian timber, a permanent policy, war or no war. With this guarantee the lumbering industry became a major

Canadian enterprise, a position it was to hold for generations. Quebec, the chief shipping point, became a hustling place of timber rafts and cargo ships.

The new prosperity soon affected communications. In 1807 Fulton's *Clermont*, the first American steamship, made a trip up the Hudson River. By 1809 the Montreal brewer John Molson had launched his *Accommodation*, the first steamship on the St. Lawrence. In 1811 he had another, the *Swiftsure*. Meanwhile roads were improving and spreading. In 1808 stagecoaches began to run between Montreal and Kingston. There had long been a stagecoach line between Quebec and Montreal, and by 1811 there was a coach route from Quebec to Boston.

Such signs of the new bustle were apparent to provincial woodsman, farmer, and shipbuilder, who also knew that it came from the British connection. In their 1812 manifestoes urging the Canadians to receive the invading armies as liberators the Americans were asking them to cast away something solid, the British guinea, for the doubtful shadow of the dollar, which the old men of '76 could remember all too well.

But beneath all this, at the very heart of the Canadian attitude, lay something very much more important. The Americans were right in their belief that most Canadians disliked the rigid imperial rule from across the sea. The discontent sprang from various grievances and it affected in quite different ways the Bluenoses of the coast, the French Canadians and the backwoods farmers of Upper Canada; but a yearning for self-government was there, articulate in English and in French, although the voice was still a grumble, not a shout.

What the Americans could not see was that Canadian thought moved slowly but inevitably toward complete home rule, and home rule was not to be had by swapping a government in London for one in Washington. The expansionist demands of the Jeffersonian party in the United States spelled domination to the Canadian as clearly as the supercilious and dictatorial manner of the British officials sent overseas to govern him. The difference was in the distance. John Bull was at least three thousand miles away. Brother Jonathan was peering right over the fence. When it came to a choice of imperialisms, the broad Atlantic distance lent enchantment. A few Americans recognized this. Most did not. Even after the plain

disclosures of the War of 1812 the doctrine of Manifest Destiny
was still popular, and there were recurrent demands and threats and
cloaked military excursions toward the Canadian border for another sixty years. But 1812 was the Canadians' year of decision.
If the war showed clearly their military dependence on Britain
and set back the vague dreams of home rule for more than thirty
years, it also set hard their determination to live apart from the
United States.

CHAPTER 27

1812

Preparations for war

THE small Navy of the United States entered the war in a high state of efficiency. President Jefferson's policy had kept their funds low, and the naval staff had concentrated on frigates and brigs, each more than a match in size, speed and gun power for British warships in the same class. With these ships and a host of privateers, which could be armed quickly among idle merchant craft kept home by the embargo, the Americans made British sea trade a costly business while the main British battle fleet was engaged in the blockade of Europe; and in ship-to-ship encounters they gave a stinging account of themselves against British warships.

The war on salt water is no part of Canadian history except the activities of the Royal Navy out of Halifax and the tit for tat of Canadian and American privateers on the adjoining coasts, a lively enough tale. The United States Navy, having judged their sea problem accurately long before the war, were also awake to the situation on the Great Lakes. In 1808 the first party of naval officers, seamen, and carpenters arrived on the American shore of Lake Ontario, among them James Fenimore Cooper, then a midshipman of nineteen, not even dreaming about novels of the backwoods and the sea. The detachment built a brig of sixteen guns, the *Oneida*, and later on Cooper and his comrade, Lieutenant Woolsey, made a leisurely inspection of the lake shore from Niagara to the Thousand Islands, where the St. Lawrence pours away toward the sea. The vigilant Loyalist merchant Cartwright at Kingston reported to army headquarters at York, "It is known that there were aboard a small American schooner which put in here a few days ago, under pretence of being driven in by stress of weather, two officers of the American Navy, who came for the express purpose of informing themselves of the different entrances of the port."

About the Great Lakes, where the chief fighting of the war was about to take place, the attitude of the armed forces on each side was strangely reversed. The United States Navy staff were alert and laying plans not only for Lake Ontario but Lakes Champlain and Erie, although lack of funds prevented them from doing much until the first fighting season had passed. The United States Army staff were overconfident and lax, nursing the dream that a few thousand state militia with a backing of regular troops could over-run Canada with no trouble.

On the British side the Provincial Marine was badly maintained and weakly manned. The Royal Navy took no interest in the lakes at all, no plan existed, and when need became urgent the naval effort was a blind makeshift that dwelt mainly on Lake Ontario and contented itself with the winds of chance on Erie and Champlain. On the other hand the British Army forces, though small, were enterprising and alert, and those of Upper Canada were commanded by General Isaac Brock, who had served against the French in Portugal and Spain, had seen amphibious warfare with Nelson's expedition to Copenhagen, and for six years had been studying the Great Lakes country.

In one respect only was there parity in the opposing forces and it lay at the top. If Secretary Eustis of the United States War Department was a hopeless incompetent, so was the British commander in chief in Canada, Sir George Prevost. Craig, his predecessor, had been a sound enough soldier but a bad governor. In four years at Quebec he had offended the French Canadians in every possible way. In 1811 the British Government were glad to replace him, and politically their choice was a wise one. George Prevost was a British officer of Swiss blood, speaking French fluently, a diplomat to the finger tips. In winning the good will and support of the *canadiens* he was more successful than any previous governor except Murray.

As a soldier he was a failure. His military experience had not fitted him for high command, especially in the huge Canadian scene, where bold decision and swift action alone could win the frontier battles and where the frontier battles had to be won if the country was to be saved. Prevost's fighting service had been mostly in the West Indies, in small joint operations among the islands in which the Royal Navy was always his more powerful partner. He had been made a baronet for defending Dominica in a brief French siege in 1805, and this small affair had given him also a military rank far beyond his abilities. At forty-four he made a fine figure in his gold-laced scarlet frock coat, tight white breeches, ebony-polished wellingtons and spurs; but the size of the Canadian defense problem bewildered him, and when war came to the Canadian lakes the absence of a large fleet always at his left hand frightened him.

The appointment of such a commander in chief on the eve of 1812 was an invitation to disaster. Fortunately for the Canadian defense, this well-meaning but timid and rattled man could not be everywhere at once. Wherever they were free from interference his officers in the field were able to act promptly with the forces in their hands.

The classic pattern for the invasion of Canada from the south had not been changed by time. Lacking a battle fleet, the Americans could not make the classic descent on Quebec by sea, and this time there was no bold Arnold with an army of tough Yankee adventurers to make the attempt by land. There remained the other classic moves, the frontal thrust through the Champlain pass, the left-hook movement by way of Lake Ontario and the upper St. Lawrence, both designed to capture Montreal. With Montreal in the invader's hands, the way was open for the attack on Quebec by land. At the same time the defending forces on the Great Lakes would be left in air, and one winter without munitions and supplies would ruin them.

The agile mind of Benjamin Franklin at the Paris peace table in 1783 had given his people a perfect setup for a future conquest on these lines. The boundary had been so contrived that the Canadian lifeline along the St. Lawrence and the Great Lakes was exposed to attack at all the vital points. Winter was an American ally, for it froze the whole channel for five months in the year; and the tall thumb of Maine, thrusting up between the Maritime Provinces and Lower Canada, enabled an American force to cut the precarious overland trail between Quebec and the ice-free ports of St. John and Halifax.

The treaty had placed the entire Champlain pass in American hands, with border posts less than forty miles from Montreal. It had planted the state of New York on the St. Lawrence itself for more than a hundred miles, enabling American forces to menace the whole stretch from Lake St. Francis to Lake Ontario at the very outbreak of war. Finally it had given to the United States all the key forts along the Great Lakes, enabling their forces to command the gateways of Upper Canada at Niagara and Detroit and to isolate the warlike Indians of the West.

When President Madison called out the state militia in April 1812 it was plain that war was not far off, and Prevost and Brock took steps to guard against surprise. During the past four years of international tension the Canadian militia had been reorganized and trained under British Army officers. Now they were warned for active service, and four regiments (The Canadian Fencibles, Canadian Voltigeurs, Glengarry Highlanders, and Royal Veterans) were put on a regular footing.

The first warning of hostilities reached Halifax on June 22. It came in a letter from the British ambassador at Washington, dated June 15 and sent express by H.M.S. *Tartarus*, saying that the House of Representatives had passed a resolution to declare war and that the Senate probably would pass it. Confirmation arrived in a convincing form on June 27, when the British frigate *Belvidera*, Captain Richard Byron, limped into Halifax badly damaged about the spars and decks and with two men dead and twenty-three wounded. Unaware of the war, Byron had met an American squadron of five ships which promptly attacked him, and he had got away through an accidental explosion in the American flagship and a lucky shift of wind.

At Quebec, Sir George Prevost got word of the declaration of war by a private channel, an express letter overland to the North West Fur Company from their agent in New York. It was passed to him on June 24. His warning to Brock did not reach Niagara until July 3, but by that time Brock was aware. John Jacob Astor had sent a courier from Albany to one of his fur agents in Upper Canada, Thomas Clark of Niagara Falls, who passed the news downriver to Fort George. The fur business knew no boundaries.

General Hull had announced at Dayton, Ohio, nearly a month before the official declaration at Washington, that he and his troops were bound for Canada. Such news travels on the wind, and it was obvious that his main point of attack would be the Detroit River, with a probable side stroke from Mackinac against the small British post on St. Joseph Island, which guarded the outlet of Lake Superior.

If there was any doubt about Hull's plans, they were revealed fully on the morning of July 2, when an American schooner slipped into the Detroit River from Lake Erie on her way to Fort Detroit. The British guns in Fort Malden near the river mouth halted her, and Lieutenant Rolette of the Provincial Marine searched her with a boarding party from the *Hunter*. They found on board a cargo of army stores and the campaign baggage of General Hull, with letters and documents setting forth in detail the strength and intentions of his force. Moving toward Detroit by easy marches, Hull had sent this impedimenta forward by water, assuming that the British could not learn of the actual declaration of war before he did.

On this note began the War of 1812, a comedy of errors.

CHAPTER 28

1812

The Detroit front — the fiasco of General Hull

WHEN the war began there were 4450 British and Canadian regular soldiers in the whole of Canada from the coast of Nova Scotia to the head of Lake Huron. Of these, less than 1500 were posted above Montreal. In theory all male civilians between the ages of sixteen and sixty were subject to a militia muster in time of war, but most of these could not move far or stay long away from their farms, where planting and reaping had to be done if their families were not to starve in the long Canadian winters.

In practice the militia could only form and train in the larger towns and villages, and according to their age and fitness they were divided into two groups, the Embodied and the Sedentary forces. During the full course of the war the Embodied Force provided about ten thousand men of the best physique, trained and equipped well enough to fight beside regular troops in the field. The Sedentary Force provided about the same number from first to last. These sometimes engaged in the fighting but were usually employed as military labor and in guarding the lines of communication. Nothing like these numbers could be mustered at one time or place, and only a small proportion could be held in service during the spring and autumn months. With these variable supports the regular troops in Canada had 1300 miles of frontier to watch and guard.

General Hull with 2500 men arrived on the American bank of the Detroit River on July 5. On the Canadian side were 150 British regulars, 300 militia, and 150 Indians gathered by Tecumseh. The American troops camped about Fort Detroit. The British were grouped chiefly about Fort Malden and the village of Amherstburg near the river mouth. The site of the Canadian city of Windsor at this time was a stretch of pleasant meadows, part of Colonel Baby's farm; and here, on the undefended upper reach of the river,

Hull chose to cross, setting up his headquarters in Baby's house and addressing a proclamation to "the Inhabitants of Canada."

He declared that he had come to free the Canadians from the tyranny of Britain and promised protection to their persons, property and rights. "Raise not your hands against your brethren . . . the arrival of an army of friends must be hailed by you with a cordial welcome . . . Had I any doubt of eventual success I might ask your assistance but I do not . . . I have a force which will look down all opposition, and that force is but the vanguard of a much greater. No white man found fighting beside an Indian will be taken prisoner . . . instant destruction will be his lot. The United States offers you Peace Liberty and Security. Your choice lies between these and War Slavery and Destruction."

With this announcement the venerable general (he was a veteran of the Revolution) sent patrols down the bank but otherwise made no move against Fort Malden. His only enterprise was in a direction where there were no British troops at all. As he scrawled his name on the proclamation, a foraging column under his orders rode sixty miles up the Thames Valley, plundering farms and village stores.

In these preoccupations Hull neglected the small American garrisons at Mackinac and Fort Dearborn (Chicago) in the watery distance to the north and west. The British officer at St. Joseph Island, Captain Roberts, had only 45 redcoats in his post, but he enlisted 180 Canadians and 400 Indians and set off for Mackinac on July 16 in a flotilla of *bateaux* and canoes. He had fifty miles to go, but on the following morning he landed on Mackinac Island and slung a cannon up the cliffs. The sixty blue-coated regulars of the American garrison at once surrendered the famous old fort with its seven cannon and stores.

As St. Joseph guarded the approach to Lake Superior, so Fort Mackinac guarded the entrance to Lake Michigan. With both in British hands, the tribes of the West were free to join Tecumseh or to attack the posts of the Long Knives in Illinois and Indiana. The Indians at the foot of Lake Michigan, eager to avenge Tippecanoe, promptly fell upon Fort Dearborn and slaughtered half the unfortunate garrison in their retreat.

General Hull deplored the fall of Mackinac, predicting correctly that it would be "the opening of the hive." To the Indians of the West the lone defiant figure of Tecumseh was now a symbol of all their hopes for the recovery of their lands. Warriors eager for a

place in his band traveled hundreds of miles to join him on the
Detroit. When the first shots were fired on the frontier he had only
150. In a few weeks he had 600, and still they came.

Meanwhile Hull sat inert on the Canadian side of the river opposite Fort Detroit. Seeing this, Tecumseh and his feathered and
painted company slipped over the river and ambushed 200 American
soldiers escorting army mail toward Ohio. His presence there disturbed Hull even more than the loss of his dispatches and he sent
a regiment of regulars to clear the road. After a confused fight, in
which British troops took part, both sides withdrew; but soon
Tecumseh and some redcoats crossed again.

Hull was alarmed. He knew by this time that the Canadian militia,
far from receiving the invaders as brethren, were out to fight them.
The combination of sharpshooting frontiersmen with the bayonets
of veteran British regulars was formidable and the addition of a
gathering swarm of Indians under Tecumseh was frightening. Wild
rumors and speculations went about the American camp and Hull
was ready to believe them all. On August 11, after a whole month
of worried idleness, he retreated across the river to Fort Detroit.
Actually his most dangerous enemy was his own imagination. His
army still outnumbered the British force (including Indians) two
to one. But now came a British reinforcement powerful indeed.
It contained no more than three hundred men, most of them
Canadian militia from the Lake Erie shore, but with them came
Brock himself.

Until now Brock had been detained at York, busy with government affairs and reports from the frontier posts. In reply to
Hull's proclamation he had issued one of his own, and so had Allan
Maclean, speaker of the House of Assembly. Bombast was not
a purely American failing. Brock (as he admitted) "spoke loud"
to impress the worried people of the countryside; and Maclean
spoke louder still. The pompous documents with their high-flown
language make amusing reading now. (Maclean declared to the
Canadians; "You are defeating the most formidable conspiracy
against the civilization of man that ever was contrived.") Both
shrewdly linked the American invasion with Napoleon's grand
scheme for the conquest of the world; and Brock especially played
on the Upper Canadians' undying suspicion of a French design
to recover the country, pointing out that "This restitution of Canada

to the empire of France was the stipulated reward for the aid afforded to the revolted colonies, now the United States; the debt is still due." This slant of thought and the news of Hull's looting in the Thames Valley stiffened the backs of the Canadian settlers of Yankee birth as much as the native born.

Of Brock's two danger points the Niagara River was the more important, and this single fact governed the whole defense of Upper Canada throughout the war. A lot of ground could be yielded behind the Detroit River before the American pressure became dangerous. The Niagara peninsula was vital, for with that in American hands the Detroit line was cut off, York was indefensible, and the British must fall back on Kingston, abandoning everything to the west.

American troops had been mustering on the Niagara since June, but so far they had not ventured across the river. In his perilous situation Brock had to juggle the chances and he tossed the Niagara chance into the air for a start. On August 5 he sailed from York to Burlington Bay, crossed overland to Lake Erie, and there embarked in boats with his small party of troops. They had a stormy passage but arrived safely at Amherstburg on the night of the thirteenth.

Although the hour was past midnight, Brock summoned the garrison staff at once, and Tecumseh and a group of lesser chiefs came over from their camp on Bois Blanc Island in the Detroit River. The meeting between Brock and the great Shawnee took place by lamplight in a chamber of Fort Malden. They made a striking pair, about the same age (Brock was forty-three) the British officer an auburn-haired man with a keen blue gaze, standing tall in a scarlet frock coat with bullion epaulettes. One of the officers present described the Shawnee thus:

"Tecumseh was very prepossessing, his figure light and finely proportioned, his age I imagined to be about five-and-thirty [Tecumseh actually was about forty-four], his height five feet nine or ten inches, his complexion light copper, his countenance oval, with bright hazel eyes beaming cheerfulness, energy and decision. Three small crowns or coronets were suspended from the lower cartilage of his nose; a large silver medallion . . . was attached to a mixed coloured wampum string which hung about his neck. His dress consisted of a plain neat uniform, a tanned deerskin jacket with long trousers of the same material, the seams of both being covered with neatly cut fringe, and he had on his feet leather moccasins much ornamented with dyed quills of the porcupine."

On the table for Brock's inspection lay the documents captured with Hull's baggage in the schooner *Cuyahoga*, together with his dispatches and other American letters taken in Tecumseh's raids across the river. They betrayed Hull's flustered mind; his own soldiers poured out their distrust in his ability; all imagined themselves cut off, with a horde of savages between them and Ohio, and with a powerful British force gathering at Amherstburg for their destruction. To Brock all this indicated one course—a prompt all-out attack.

His officers were dubious. Hull's strength was known in detail, and against his 2500 horse, foot, and artillery the British could muster no more than 700 infantry (of whom 400 were country militia) and Tecumseh's 600 Indians. To cross a wide river and attack a fortified position against odds of almost two to one seemed to them folly. The discussion went on until four in the morning when Brock made an end of it, announcing crisply that he would attack. Tecumseh turned to the other chiefs with a loud "Ho!" and pointing a finger at Brock cried his memorable "This is a man!"

Two days later, after careful preparation, the curiously mixed British force was at Sandwich, opposite Fort Detroit. Brock sent his personal aides Captain Glegg and Colonel John Macdonell (the peacetime attorney general of Upper Canada) across the river under a white flag. They bore a written demand for Hull's surrender that played adroitly on his fears by mention of the Indians and the difficulty of controlling them if the British stormed the fort. Hull was defiant however and when Brock's aides returned, the rival batteries opened fire on each other across the water.

After dark Tecumseh's warriors crossed by canoe below Detroit. It was now the early morning of August 16 and Brock followed in boats with his whole force, including a field battery. They landed at Spring Wells and marched through the farms for Detroit in the first light of day. At the same time the British guns at Sandwich and the armed schooner *Queen Charlotte* opened another bombardment on the fort. One of their mortar shells exploded in the midst of Hull's staff, killing three officers and wounding several others.

In this moment of confusion Hull saw British troops coming through the fields and up the Ohio road where he had marched himself six weeks before. At the head of them Brock and Tecumseh rode their horses side by side, a deliberate bit of bravado. And now came a sudden hullabaloo of shots and yells from the Indians concealed in the woods behind the fort and village. One Indian could make an astounding noise. Six hundred frightened a shaky old man who had done well enough as a young soldier in the Revolution. Many of his officers had brought along their wives to see the triumphant march into Canada, and Hull had with him his son, his married daughter, and two small grandchildren. The shells from Sandwich continued to explode inside the fort. From the rampart Hull could see the redcoats and their frontier militia forming into three columns for the assault. In a few minutes the storm would come. In those minutes he was lost. He ordered a white flag and a parley, and within half an hour surrendered his army and the fort. Apart from the prisoners, the British were given intact thirty-three cannon, all the stores and equipment, the horses of the supply train and of two troops of Ohio cavalry, the Detroit shipyard, and the newly built brig *Adams*, which they renamed *Detroit* and added to their little squadron on Lake Erie.

Under the terms of surrender the American militia were allowed to go home on their oath not to serve again in the war. The United States regulars were sent east to Quebec as prisoners of war. Thither went Hull and his officers with the rest, often passing in sight of the American shore, so long and precarious was the Canadian line. In their passage they were the object of interest to troops and people alike, and at the sight of them the Canadians had a new surge of confidence. The Americans could be beaten.

After the surrender of Detroit, with one of his instinctive gestures Brock slipped off his richly tasseled scarlet sash and fastened it about Tecumseh in the presence of the troops and Indians. The Shawnee accepted the compliment gravely and in turn presented Brock with the gaudy arrow-patterned Indian sash about his own waist. On the following morning Brock noticed Tecumseh without his gift and asked him why. The great chief answered simply, "I have given it to Round Head of the Wyandots, who is older and a more valiant chief."

Round Head remained valiant to his death, but within a year the Wyandots deserted Tecumseh in his darkest hour. Brock's time was shorter. His bullet came within two months, and he was wearing the sash of Tecumseh when he died.

CHAPTER 29

1812

British troops in Ohio — The Niagara front —
The battle of Queenston Heights

HAVING juggled the Detroit ball successfully, Brock hastened back to catch the one tossed up at Niagara. In the plan of the American commander in chief, General Dearborn, the strokes at Detroit and Niagara would destroy the whole British garrison in Upper Canada and compel Sir George Prevost to send troops in that direction from the St. Lawrence Valley. Dearborn himself with the main army of invasion would then spring from the Champlain pass into Montreal.

The Detroit affair had miscarried, and as a result General Stephen Van Rensselaer was so slow in making up his mind to cross the Niagara that late in September Dearborn reminded him sharply of the plan. In the meantime the British supreme command did some fumbling of their own.

In a belated attempt to patch up a peace with the United States, London had offered to cancel the notorious orders in council affecting American trade with Napoleon's Europe, and in the same slow Atlantic mail Sir George Prevost was told to ask the Americans for a military armistice at once.

Prevost, only too eager, sent off his Adjutant General Bayne to Dearborn's headquarters at Albany, and on August 6 the two officers signed a formal cease-fire agreement. Dearborn's signature was subject to confirmation from Washington, and he insisted that he had no authority over the American forces on the Great Lakes; therefore the armistice would not apply to them.

Sir George Prevost agreed to this. Moreover he ordered Brock to take only defensive action in Upper Canada. The order came when Brock was in a position to cross the Niagara, taking advantage of Van Rensselaer's muddle, and to repeat the vigorous action of Detroit. Whatever he thought of it privately, Brock passed the word to Colonel Procter on the right wing, where Ohio was wide open — where in fact a large force of Indians and a core of red-coats under Captain Muir already were moving on Fort Wayne.

The result might have been foreseen by anyone but Sir George. Van Rensselaer was able to collect his forces and build up stores from Oswego, unmolested by the Canadian warships on Lake Ontario. In the West Muir's troops and Indians halted short of Fort Wayne (where seventy uneasy militia made the whole American garrison), while American General Winchester mustered an army to drive them off. All the advantage from the capture of Hull's whole army had been thrown away. The Indians were amazed and suspicious, for on the march to Fort Wayne they had passed the old battlefield of Fallen Timbers with its unhappy ghosts. They could never forget or forgive that occasion when a company of red-coats had stood aside and watched the Long Knives slaughter their people.

President Madison and his Cabinet ordered Dearborn to end the armistice on August 29. The war must go on. When the British troops in the West received word of this the whole situation there was changed. Fort Wayne had been strengthened and Winchester was marching with two thousand men against Muir's mixed force on the Maumee. Behind these loomed the able figure of William Henry Harrison, calling up troops by forced marches from Kentucky, Virginia, and Pennsylvania. The news of Hull's disaster had startled the War Hawk country all the way from Michigan to Tennessee, and Harrison had taken over the western command.

When Muir began to retire before Winchester's troops, every backward step brought him closer to the ill-omened field of Fallen Timbers, and the specter of the past was too much for his allies. Three quarters of them vanished, leaving him no choice but a quick return to Detroit. While Muir and Procter had these troubles and exasperations at the upper end of Lake Erie, Brock had a problem below. The Niagara River ran thirty miles between the lakes and apart from the whirling rapids in the gorge below the falls it was easy to cross. To watch the whole stream he had 1500 regulars and militia and about 250 Indians. Fort George at the river mouth was a small work built after the Americans took over Fort Niagara on the other side. At the upper end of the river was the partly built Fort Erie, sheltering a British outpost on that lake and nothing more.

So far there had been no worry about American forces crossing the lakes. Although the United States Navy had the *Oneida* and was arming some merchant ships on Lake Ontario, the Provincial Marine had been able to guard the Ontario shore and to take an active part in the operations at Detroit. The Marine had some good officers and men, but in general these fresh-water sailors were doubtful stuff, inexperienced in war, accustomed to harbor every night, to navigating by landmark, and to long months of indolence in the winter season. If it came to naval warfare on the Great Lakes, these men would be no match for disciplined tars from the seaboard. And such a time was very close, for six hundred American sailors had arrived on Lake Ontario from Baltimore. With them were Commodore Chauncey, until now superintendent of the New York Navy Yard, and Henry Eckford, one of the master shipwrights of America.

By this time General Van Rensselaer had 6300 troops on the Niagara. They could see redcoats moving up and down the Canadian bank, but they knew that most of Brock's force was concentrated about Fort George. On October 10 an American spy returned from the Canadian side with a rumor that Brock, again taking a long chance, had moved off to Lake Erie with a large part of his force, apparently heading for the Maumee.

Van Rensselaer decided now to put a force across the river at the Canadian village of Queenston. The river here was little more than two hundred yards wide, but the current was swift and his first try in the dark wet morning of October 11 failed in a bungle of boats. Brock had posted 350 men at Queenston with three guns. These reported the American attempt, but Brock regarded it as a feint.

Before dawn on the thirteenth the Americans crossed at Queenston in earnest, their general's own nephew Colonel Solomon Van Rensselaer in the lead, with 225 men. They were discovered landing above the village, but, although wounded, Van Rensselaer led a gallant rush up the scarp to the crest of the Queenston heights. There they met part of the Queenston garrison under Captain Williams, guarding a small earthwork and a single cannon, and they were driven back to the river. In spite of the British fire from Queenston village and from the heights above the landing place, the American boats continued to dash back and forth, carrying infantry to the foot of the scarp, where they were sheltered to some extent but could not face the open climb.

The thudding of guns at Queenston had aroused the British troops at Fort George. Brock dressed quickly, slipping on the gaudy sash of Tecumseh as the final touch. He mounted his big stallion Alfred and rode away up the road with his aides Glegg and Macdonell, leaving orders for General Sheaffe to march with all the available troops. This is the picture of Brock familiar to every Canadian, the gallant figure in black cloak, scarlet frock coat, and tall cocked hat, galloping past the Niagara farms at sunrise and shouting the alarm to every man along the way. He came in great haste and made a hasty error of judgment on the crest of Queenston Heights, where a busy gun crew and Williams' redcoats and militia still kept the Americans pinned to the foot of the scarp.

Brock saw American boats crossing from Lewiston with more troops and ordered Williams' men to go down and support Captain Dennis' company in Queenston village, leaving a few men to serve the gun on the crest. Brock thought the heights inaccessible so long as the two companies in Queenston kept the open scarp under fire. He was mistaken.

Colonel Van Rensselaer had with him a civilian from Lewiston familiar with the Canadian side of the river, especially a smugglers' path hidden in trees and shrubbery that led around to the back of the knoll on which Brock stood. He sent Captain Wool with two hundred men to follow the path and seize the height. They almost caught Brock, who suspected nothing until a rush of bluecoats came out of the trees behind him. He and his party managed to get away, but they left the gun to the enemy.

General Sheaffe was now well on the road to Queenston with a thousand men, but in his impetuous way Brock determined to recapture the heights and the lost gun at once. He ordered up Captain Williams' company from the river again and with these alone (about a hundred men), he led the way up the slope against the Americans. It was a splendid little scene; the "dark October day" of the song, the wet grass of the slope, the trees in autumn color, the Niagara surging below: the American regulars on the crest in their blue jackets, white trousers, and black fire-bucket shakos: the British regulars in their sun-faded scarlet jackets, gray trousers, white shoulder belts and tall black stovepipe shakos, each with its leather sun visor and colored tuft, its glittering brass regimental badge and chain strap: the Canadian and American militiamen alike in the plain dress of the woods and farms, buckskin or gray homespun or a mixture of both, and rough boots of beefhide sewn like moccasins.

As on many another occasion, the little British charge was magnificent but quite mad and nobody asked the reason why. Undoubtedly Brock felt that he must drive Wool's soldiers off the crest before any more got up there; but he must have seen the odds and these Americans were not the nervous militia of Detroit.

In the open field the British regular's uniform made him a perfect target for American riflemen. The scarlet tunic marked him out clearly against any background and the pipe-clayed shoulder belts crossing on the breast made an exact point of aim. As an officer, Brock wore no crossbelts but a double row of brass buttons glittered down the front of his coat. One of the American riflemen aimed for the customary point and his bullet struck exactly between the button rows near the heart. Brock fell and died. (The coat he wore, with its deadly bullet hole, may be seen in the Archives of Canada at Ottawa, a memento of a very gallant gentleman and a tribute to American markmanship.)

His men dragged the dying general away with the rest of their wounded and hurried down the hill. While Williams was rallying them Colonel John Macdonell appeared with two companies of militia. Again they charged up to the crest, this time two hundred strong; again the American riflemen shot down the leading officers and men as soon as they came within range (among others Macdonell and Williams both fell wounded, Macdonell mortally) and again the rest dropped back. Obviously Wool's marksmen could go on doing this all day. Captain Dennis now came up from the river with his own company of redcoats and militia, took charge of the rest, and sensibly fell back on Vrooman's Point, toward Fort George. The American troops were now scrambling up the scarp in hundreds and the crest of Queenston Heights was a blue mass.

Meanwhile Sheaffe spattered along the muddy river road with a mixed force of regular and militia infantry, an artillery section and a few mounted volunteers who called themselves the Niagara Dragoons. With them came fifty Indians, who appeared on the American flank first. Although their small wild rush was beaten off, the sound of the war whoop in the wet October woods had its old effect on the American militia, some of whom had crossed the river with the bluecoats. Every tree, every quivering bush, became a savage thirsting for their blood.

Sheaffe wisely avoided the steep and open fields where Brock and his men had been such easy targets. He made his way around by woods to the right and moved unseen through the trees toward the crest. The first notice of his presence was an attack on the American outposts by a mixed company of redcoats, militia, and Indians. Almost at once the whole British force broke into the open, close to the crest and with bayonets fixed for the assault.

Brigadier Wadsworth had taken command of the American troops on the heights and he had nearly a thousand men, mostly regular soldiers. About seventeen hundred state militia remained on the American side of the river, where the sudden uproar of musketry and Indian yells gave notice that Wadsworth was in trouble. They refused to cross, arguing that they had enlisted for the defense of New York State, not for adventures in Canada. In the words of an American gunner in the Lewiston battery, "The name of Indian or the Devil or something else petrified them. Not a regiment, not a company, scarcely a man would go." Wadsworth was marooned beyond the river.

His force there was equal in number to Sheaffe's; but as Wellington had noted in Spain, a soldier with a musket could not fight without ammunition — and in an average two hours' fighting he spent all the ammunition he could carry. When the British bayonets sprang out of the woods the American position was hopeless. Some men scrambled down the two-hundred-foot scarp to the river, but the boatmen had fled to the American side and few could swim the Niagara.

On the crest a young American officer, Winfield Scott, tore a white cravat from a dandified officer beside him, tied it to his sword tip and held it aloft. Scott stood six feet four inches and the white fabric fluttering caught the eye of the leading British officers. They ordered the attack to cease at once — just in time, for the Indians were darting through their ranks howling for scalps. The rest did not take long. Wadsworth surrendered with 73 officers and 885 men. About two hundred others had been killed or wounded. The British killed and wounded (including Indians) were less by half, most of them suffered in the rash attacks of Brock and Macdonell.

CHAPTER 30

1812

The fighting seasons ends on the Niagara —
All quiet in the Champlain pass — The war at sea

GENERAL VAN RENSSELAER resigned in disgrace, and a regular officer, General Smyth, took command of the American army on the Niagara. He decided to shift the attack to the easier stretch of the river above Niagara Falls, where the banks were fairly low. He marched 4500 men to Black Rock, opposite Fort Erie, and a naval party collected boats for a crossing there. His strategy was sound. Lacking troops to defend the Niagara bank in force the British had to keep their main strength at Fort George, to guard their marine base and the water line to Kingston. They could not risk that place until they were sure that any American attack above was the real thing and not a feint — and Fort Erie was a hard thirty-mile march away.

The autumn season was far gone and the hardwood leaves had fallen when Smyth addressed his men with eve-of-battle eloquence on November 17:

"Companions in arms, the time is at hand when you will cross the stream at Niagara to conquer Canada and secure the peace of the American frontier. You will enter a country that is to be one of the United States. You will arrive among a people who are to become your fellow citizens. Soldiers, you are amply provided for war. You are superior in numbers to the enemy. Your personal strength and activity are greater. Your weapons are longer. The regular soldiers of the enemy are generally old men whose best years have been spent in the sickly climate of the West Indies. They will not be able to stand before you. And when you attack the enemy's batteries let your rallying cry be *The cannon lost at Detroit or death!*"

Along the Canadian shore of the upper river lay a mixed force of redcoats and militia about a thousand strong, scattered in various posts from Lake Erie to Niagara Falls and commanded by Colonel Bisshop at Chippewa. Of these, four hundred were in the chosen area of Smyth's attack, a five-mile stretch of farms and woods. Two or three hours after the windy midnight of November 28 the American troops came across the water, striking at various points to prevent a British concentration. The defense was alert and there followed a wild tussle in the dark, in squalls of sleet and snow. The Americans stormed a four-gun battery and the vital bridge over Frenchman's Creek, by which any British supports must come, but in a short time they abandoned these intact. About daylight, after a ten-mile march from Chippewa in the miserable weather, Bisshop arrived with a few companies of militia, bringing his force on the scene to about six hundred men. In the face of these, Smyth gave up his isolated footholds along the Canadian bank and went back across the river. The British had suffered eighty-three casualties. Smyth was vague about his. Both sides had taken a few prisoners. For the powder burned in the stormy dark it was a thin result all round.

On the evening of December 1 Smyth ordered another attempt. His troops began to enter the boats with a band playing martial music on the shore. (The tune of "Yankee Doodle" was to be the signal for the dash across the river.) About fifteen hundred men had embarked when a regiment of Pennsylvania volunteers raised the cry of the New York militia at Lewiston, that they had enlisted for defense, not foreign service. The infection spread rapidly among the troops and their officers decided that the campaign must be abandoned for the season. The regular troops marched away to winter quarters, the militia and volunteers went home, and Smyth followed Hull and Van Rensselaer into official disgrace.

So ended the operations of 1812 in Upper Canada.

In Lower Canada there was the same general note of comic opera. General Dearborn had mustered ten thousand troops in the Champlain pass at Plattsburg, ready for the blow at Montreal. To defend the whole province Sir George Prevost had three thousand British regulars, three Canadian regular regiments (Glengarries, Fencibles and Voltigeurs), and a wide scatter of local militia companies, in all perhaps equal to Dearborn's army at Plattsburg. A sufficient garrison had to be kept in the key fortress of Quebec (the British had never forgotten Arnold's dash), with a chain of detachments all along the frontier to Kingston. The immediate danger points were Montreal and Kingston, and until Dearborn revealed his choice the

British could only spread their men and rely on a quick concentration when it came. To bar the direct approach from Lake Champlain to Montreal General Prevost had about twenty-five hundred regulars and militia.

General Dearborn clung to his rigid plan, in which the American invasions at Niagara and Detroit were to draw off the British reserves before he struck at Montreal. The summer and autumn passed in a few light raids on the upper St. Lawrence. At the end of November, when the Upper Canadian affairs had failed, and with winter already white on the Adirondack peaks, a single regiment of regulars under Colonel Zebulon Pike (the discoverer of Pike's Peak) made a brief venture into Canadian territory, rushed a Canadian outpost, and then retired. Like Van Rensselaer and Smyth on the Niagara, General Dearborn had found his militia reluctant to enter Canada and he did not consider his five thousand regulars enough. After Pike's raid, therefore, he marched his regulars away to winter quarters on Lake Champlain and sent the militia home, without once making contact with the main British defense.

On all three fronts the American lesson was plain. The conquest of Canada required better troops and much better generals.

The story of 1812 on the sea was a very different tale. In single actions, ship to ship, the United States Navy won a quick and formidable reputation with the startled British — and with the folk at home, where the captures of the British warships *Guerrière*, *Frolic*, *Macedonia*, and *Java* made a happy offset to the sorry news from Canada.

Apart from their Navy, American privateers were scouring the Atlantic almost from the day war was declared. Unescorted British merchantmen were snapped up with ridiculous ease. As in the Revolution, the coast of Nova Scotia became a haunt of bold Yankee privateers, who did not hesitate to take ships at the very entrance to Halifax harbor and under the nose of the British admiral on the station.

Preoccupied wtih their blockade of Napoleon's continent, which was now squeezing him to an act of desperation — the great assault on Russia — the British could spare few ships for the North American station. Privateering was anybody's game however. With a few gun ports cut in the bulwarks, any merchant ship could be changed to a private ship of war, and during the long Napoleonic struggle the Nova Scotians had learned the fine points of this chancy trade in their Caribbean raids. Sir John Sherbrooke at Halifax urged them to turn their talent now against the Americans, promising that the Royal Navy would lend all the necessary cannon, small arms, and other warlike stores.

Within two months the first Nova Scotia privateer of 1812, a swift little schooner called *Liverpool Packet*, put forth to harry the American coastal trade. She had only five cannon and forty-five men, but in her first twelve months she took more than thirty ships. In 1813 she was captured herself, served for a time as a Yankee privateer, was recaptured, and sailed again under her old name and flag. In all she seized about one hundred American ships. Some of these were sailing with supplies under secret license from the British authorities and she had to let them go. Others were too small or their cargoes not worth the trouble of a prize crew. Still other captures, heading for Halifax under prize crews (seldom more than four or five men), were retaken by American privateers hovering off the Nova Scotia coast. From first to last the *Liverpool Packet* got forty-four prizes home and earned £52,800 in prize money for her owners and crews.

In all, 37 private ships of war sailed out from Nova Scotia and New Brunswick in the period 1812–14, ranging in size from a fishing sloop to the 300-ton brig *Sir John Sherbrooke* which carried 18 cannon and 150 men. These ships played a lively part in the blockade of the United States coast, and the cargoes they captured were manna to the Canadian commissariat at a time when food supplies especially were hard to come by. Indeed the provisions, cannon, ammunition, and specie brought into Halifax by the privateers and the increasingly effective ships of the Royal Navy enabled Lieutenant Governor Sherbrooke to send half his army stores and ordnance to the St. Lawrence, and to furnish Prevost at Quebec with useful sums for the Canadian war chest.

The war at sea was a game many-sided and curious. Some American merchants fitted their ships as privateers, seeing the fat profit to be made in preying on British commerce. Others preferred the profit to be made in smuggling supplies to the British, a game played before the war in defiance of Jefferson's Embargo Act and now in defiance of the Non-Intercourse Act. With the advent of "Mister Madison's war" the game became more complicated.

As a concession to the eastern states the Non-Intercourse Act permitted American ships to trade with any nation but Britain or

France. Suddenly and oddly there was a vast demand for American supplies in Spain. The usual customs clearance read "Cádiz." Actually some of these supplies were for Wellington's army in Portugal, just around the corner; but "Cádiz" was a general term for British purposes and if supplies were needed for the forces in Canada they could be switched to Halifax (or Quebec in summer) by a simple pen endorsement. The arrangements were made in secret correspondence between merchants in Halifax and merchants in American ports, and the trade was so brisk that printed forms called "Import Licenses" were freely issued, signed by Sherbrooke, to protect these ships and cargoes from interference by prize-hunting British warships and privateers. One typical license of this kind, still preserved, bears the following bold pen endorsement:

> *This license is appropriated to the Schooner* Rebecca *of New York, of the burthen of 86* (etc) *tons. Capt. Garnett Vaughan cleared out from the Custom House of New York this day — ostensibly bound for the port of Cadiz but actually bound to the Port of Halifax Nova Scotia with a cargo of flour.*
>
> *New York, 15th June, 1813*

The United States Government could not fail to discover such amiable conspiracies, but the game went on throughout the war in various disguises and by varying routes. In one period the neutral island of Saint Bartholemew in the West Indies (then owned by Sweden) became a distributing point for American supplies, some bound for Britain, some for Wellington's army, some for the British forces in Canada. Nova Scotia ships furnished with special papers and often a neutral flag (to ward off interference by American and British privateers alike) sailed to the Caribbean and back again to get the necessary stores to the north.

The strangest part of all this was that the northeastern states, which opposed the war in the first place and furnished these British supplies throughout, raised hundreds of bold and skillful seamen for the fighting at sea and for the naval struggle on the Great Lakes. These contradictions made sense to a large and shrewd part of the American people, to whom the British Navy was the only culprit in the quarrel and Canada a friendly neighbor and in any case not worth the trouble of conquest.

CHAPTER 31

1813

Naval preparations on the Great Lakes — The Detroit Front
— Fighting at Frenchtown, Fort Meigs, and Fort Stephenson

AS THE year 1813 opened on the cold white Canadian scene
all the signs of war pointed to rougher weather. John Armstrong, one of Jefferson's men, replaced the muddling dentist
Eustis as Secretary of War. General Dearborn commanded a growing Army of the North. Winfield Scott, the able young Virginian
regular officer, (captured at Queenston Heights and since exchanged) was giving a stiffer training to the troops on the Niagara
frontier. In the West General Harrison was already on the move
in the freezing weather toward Detroit. At Sackets Harbor on
Lake Ontario Commodore Chauncey was creating a formidable
squadron, and in February young Captain Oliver Perry U.S.N. set
off through the snow to create another on Lake Erie.

On the American political scene the Federalists still vehemently
opposed the war, taking as their cue the speech of a forthright
Yankee, Josiah Quincy, who on the floor of Congress had denounced the invasion of Canada as a "cruel, wanton, senseless and
wicked attack, in which neither plunder nor glory was to be at-
tained upon an unoffending people bound to us by ties of blood
and good neighborhood, undertaken for the punishment over their
shoulders of another people three thousand miles away by young
politicians fluttering and cackling on the floor of the House, half-
hatched, the shell still on their heads and their pin-feathers not yet
shed — politicians to whom reason, justice, pity, were nothing,
revenge everything."

But the War Hawks remained in power, half hatched or not, and
the ruling spirit at Washington was still theirs. The United States
Army had been authorized to raise and train sixty thousand regulars.
The border and western states were calling up fresh drafts of militia.
A bright new weapon was in the forge and it must be used.

The prospect was grim in Canada. From Detroit to the sea there were not more than seven thousand regular troops, including six British and six Canadian regiments (Glengarries, Voltigeurs, Fencibles, Royal Newfoundland, Royal New Brunswick, and Nova Scotia Fencibles). General Sheaffe, who had stepped into Brock's boots at Niagara, was a stiff martinent with none of Brock's daring imagination nor his gift of inspiring the militia and Indians. Colonel Henry Procter in the West was an energetic young officer and he had the daring Tecumseh at his right hand, but his force was small and how long they could maintain themselves against Harrison's gathering army was a matter of grave doubt.

The lack of a British naval plan for the Great Lakes was now hard felt. With American warships on the inland waters, the weak Provincial Marine could no longer guarantee the transport route from Kingston to the West. Sir George Prevost had written urgently to London asking that the Royal Navy take over the Provincial Marine; meanwhile he passed his alarm to Admiral Warren, commanding the North American squadron at Halifax. Warren had his own problems on the seaboard. The best he could do in the winter of 1812-13 was to send Captains Barclay, Pring, and Finnis with six lieutenants and a few sailors overland by sleigh and snowshoe. Barclay took charge of the Provincial Marine squadron on Lake Ontario and drove the work on new ships in the yards at Kingston and York, while the others under his command tried to improve the existing ships and crews.

These were meager expedients in view of the coming storm. The only ray of sunshine came from the farther side of the Atlantic. Napoleon's ferocious genius had led him into a fatal mistake at last. At the very moment when General Hull was directing the first American thrust into Canada, the "Little Corporal" had invaded Russia; but his operations in the summer of 1812 had failed to destroy the Russian armies, and in the retreat from Moscow his own *Grande Armée* had perished in the snows. While he was thus engaged the French army in Spain had been roughly handled by the British; Wellington had fought his way to Madrid, and now he was back in his old winter lines preparing a decisive stroke for 1813. These campaigns, one at each end of Europe, had shot away the legend of French invincibility after years of allied struggle and defeat. The Spaniards, Germans, Austrians, and other conquered peoples were on their feet and fighting again. Britain no longer stood alone.

In these circumstances London could send a little help across the Atlantic. It could never be much until Napoleon was crushed, but by chance or by some uncanny genius lurking in its thickets of red tape, the British War Office during the next eighteen months was able to feed the Canadian fighting line with a trickle of men and materials measured exactly to stave off disaster and keep the defense alive. After traveling nearly four thousand miles by sea, by river, by snowshoe or merely by foot over the wretched Canadian back-woods roads, again and again the arrival of one or two red-coated battalions or a few companies of recruits were just enough to turn a doubtful fight into a success or to patch a gap after a defeat.

And now the British Admiralty agreed to take a hand on the Great Lakes. On May 5, 1813, Sir James Yeo, one of Nelson's former officers, arrived at Quebec with 448 seamen, gunners, and marines. Eleven days later Yeo reached Kingston. The situation there was ominous. Chauncey's American seamen and carpenters had not wasted a moment in their seven months at Sackets Harbor. An American squadron was afloat on Lake Ontario and the Provincial Marine had nothing afloat to match it. In a few more months the same thing would be true of Lake Erie.

The campaign of 1813 began early in the West, where Harrison had been clearing his Indiana flank by a systematic destruction of the Indian villages and their food supplies. At the beginning of the year he had mustered near the west end of Lake Erie about three thousand troops. Early in January, as the swamps and rivers began to freeze hard, he ordered his advanced force under General Winchester to build a camp of huts on the Maumee River as if they intended wintering there. This was to deceive the British intelligence. As soon as the ice on the Detroit River was thick enough to bear the passage of troops, Winchester was to make straight for it, moving his supplies by horse and sled. He was to ignore the captured Fort Detroit up the river for the moment. His force was to cross the ice and strike at the British army and shipping base at Amherstburg near the mouth.

Colonel Henry Procter, the senior British officer on the Detroit, was only twenty-six years old, an active young Welshman with a shrewd understanding of the Indians and of his American opponents. At Amherstburg he had 500 British and Canadian troops and 450 Indians. Of these, a militia company with one field gun lay on the

American side of the lower river, watching the Ohio road from a post at Frenchtown, a hamlet of log huts standing in a few fields and surrounded by woods. A stream called the Raisin flowed through the village on its way to join the Detroit. It was the site of the present city of Monroe, Michigan.

On January 18 Winchester drove the Canadian outpost from the village and his one thousand troops halted there for the night. They felt secure and their sentries huddled in shelter against the bitter weather, a fatal error. Colonel Procter crossed the Detroit with his whole force and made an attack by night. Although surprised, the Americans fought stoutly for a time, but Procter's bayonets drove them out of the village and into the woods across the stream, where the Indians were waiting. Winchester himself was caught in bed and surrendered in his nightshirt, and old Round Head of the Wyandots put on the general's uniform and pranced about the village. Some of the American soldiers surrendered to the British troops, others fled away in the darkness toward the Maumee.

It had been a savage little battle. The British had lost 182 killed and wounded. For the Americans it was the bloodiest defeat of the war. Of Winchester's 966 men, only 33 escaped; 536 were prisoners in British hands, the rest perished in the fighting or in the flight through the woods, where the Indians tracked them down and slaughtered them in the snow. Tecumseh's firm and merciful hand was missing—he was away, ill, in one of the Indian villages. On this occasion the leader was Round Head, whose small quality of mercy had not been improved by Harrison's scorched-earth tactics in the previous months. Nearly four hundred scalps dangled from the Indians' belts. One of them belonged to Captain Hart, a brother-in-law of Henry Clay.

At the news of this disaster General Harrison held the rest of his army on the Maumee River near what is now the city of Toledo, Ohio. His thirteen hundred men threw up strong ramparts of logs and earth, mounting eighteen cannon and enclosing eight acres of ground, calling this entrenched camp Fort Meigs in honor of the governor of Ohio.

Procter's obvious move was to follow up the Frenchtown affair and strike at Harrison before his Kentucky reinforcements arrived for the summer campaign. But Fort Meigs was too strong for an open attack and cannon could not be moved to the Maumee (a distance of fifty miles) except by Lake Erie, whose shores were gripped in ice. It was April before he was able to embark his field artillery and stores and part of his troops (the rest marched through the swamps) for the attempt. His little flotilla of ships and *bateaux* anchored in the mouth of the Maumee twelve miles below Fort Meigs, and the troops and guns passed up the river in the *bateaux*. The timing was close, for the Americans also had been watching the weather and General Clay was on the march to Harrison's post with another twelve hundred men.

Tecumseh had recovered from his illness and his couriers had gathered more than a thousand warriors from the angry tribes of Indiana and Michigan. Procter had scraped up five hundred redcoats and four hundred Canadian militia. This mingled host coming up the stream would have appalled a man like Hull. The cool and patient man inside Fort Meigs declined Procter's invitation to surrender and awaited the attack with confidence.

When Procter's artillerymen wheeled up their guns and opened fire, one reason for Harrison's confidence was plain. No cannon light enough to be floated up the Maumee in *bateaux* could damage in any way the log-and-earth walls of Fort Meigs. The alternative was to take it by storm. Against a fortified camp containing thirteen hundred frontier marksmen, eighteen cannon, and William Henry Harrison, that was madness, although the Indians argued that the redcoats should try it. Procter refused. For five days the British guns tapped away. Then the second reason for Harrison's confidence appeared in the persons of General Green Clay and twelve hundred Kentuckians, moving down the Maumee and taking part of Procter's force in the rear. Clay quickly captured one of the British batteries. Harrison made a sortie and captured another. The siege of Fort Meigs was at an end.

A fight in the woods outside the ramparts however was quite another thing. Procter and Tecumseh turned and struck fiercely, first at Clay and then at Harrison's sortie. Clay was utterly defeated, and he and the survivors of his force were lucky to scramble inside the fort with Harrison's men. The Indian loss was slight. The British had 101 killed and wounded. The Americans lost 836, of whom 627 were prisoners. But this very success outside the walls of Fort Meigs ruined all further hope for Procter's expedition. The Indians were laden with the loot of the battlefield, including hundreds of muskets and the prized Kentucky rifles, together with other equipment and Clay's own baggage. To linger outside an impregnable fort with such a treasure in their hands was not in the Indian temperament. Ignoring all Tecumseh's pleas the feathered swarm drifted away. At the same time the Canadian militia, most of them farmers, drifted home for the spring plowing and planting. In five days Procter found himself with his redcoats and twenty Indians (including Tecumseh himself) trying to hold a siege of about three times their number of Americans.

On May 9 Procter put his guns and stores into the boats and retired toward Detroit. Harrison made little attempt at pursuit beyond the Maumee rapids. He could afford to wait and let Procter try again. The situation in the West was now a matter of simple mathematics. Every day the busy American carpenters far down the Erie shore at Presque Isle brought Captain Perry's warships nearer to completion and shortened the time in which Procter could make these amphibious raids; and with a superior American squadron on the lake Procter himself would be the target, cut off from all effective military supply from Niagara and exposed to a superior American army landing anywhere they chose on his flank and rear.

Procter could only try to stave off the evil day by hitting out repeatedly, harassing the various parts of Harrison's force before they could join against him. In this cut-and-thrust warfare Harrison could easily replace his losses, for he had the whole midwestern American population behind him. Procter could not. He drew his militia from the scattered population along the Canadian side of Erie and the Detroit. His Indians were too foot-loose for the grind of a steady campaign—success, no less than defeat, could scatter them like feathers on a wind. His few companies of British infantry were irreplaceable. Again and again he wrote to Sir George Prevost, pleading for more troops and for an adequate naval force to secure his Erie flank. Much was promised him, little done. Prevost's main concern was the defense of the St. Lawrence. The few army reinforcements he released to Upper Canada were retained almost entirely on the Niagara front, where the British were hard pressed. Yeo on Lake Ontario held greedily to his naval personnel and stores. In a modern term, Procter and Tecumseh were expendable. Procter summed it up in a letter to General Sheaffe in January 1813—"Witih my inadequate means the Game will be a difficult one, however I will do my best."

In July a few hundred Indians straggled back to Tecumseh's

camp on the Detroit. Memory of the loot outside Fort Meigs was in their minds and they were eager to try that fruitful place again. Procter was doubtful, knowing that the fort was beyond his strength, but Tecumseh had a romantic plan. This time the Indians would stage a mock battle in the woods behind the fort while Procter's troops waited below. The Americans would assume that a supply column was under attack, they would sally forth to help their comrades, and once again the redcoats and Indians would catch them in the open and destroy them.

Whatever Procter thought of this naïve proposal any movement was better than sitting idle by the Detroit, and in the latter part of July he appeared on the familiar Maumee scene with four hundred redcoats and Tecumseh's warriors. With so small a force the game was risky, for there was still a strong garrison in Fort Meigs and a day's ride away on the Sandusky River lay Harrison himself with twelve hundred men. Tecumseh stole to the woods east of the fort and staged his play with a great clamor of yells and musketry, but the garrison were not deceived. The yowling and the shots died away in a downpour of rain and the British soldiers regarded once more the Stars and Stripes hanging soggily but imperturbably over the fort.

Procter had a few light cannon with him but there was no point in going through all that again. The Indians now proposed another target. Near the mouth of the Sandusky, farther east along the Lake Erie shore, was a small American post called Fort Stephenson, three log blockhouses joined by a stockade and surrounded by a ditch. Surely Procter and his redcoats could take that?

If the Fort Meigs venture was risky, this one was wild, for one of Harrison's outposts was only nine miles up the river and in two days he could concentrate his detachments and be on the scene. Nevertheless Procter passed down the Lake Erie shore in his boats and on August 1 appeared at Fort Stephenson. He made the customary demand for surrender, and the youthful American commander, Major Croghan, made the customary refusal. Procter's artillerymen wheeled up their fieldpieces and opened fire, but again these popguns had no effect on solid logs. By the next day there was no more time to waste. The Indians were disgruntled and drifting away. The agents of the Indian Department with Procter told him warmly that the British soldiers must storm the fort or lose face forever with their allies. Procter had no choice but to swallow his own cool judgment and agree. In the broad light of an Ohio afternoon the redcoats attacked in two columns, one at the front and one at the rear of the fort. At close range the "ditch" was found to be twelve feet wide and eight feet deep. The stockade beyond was more than twice the height of a tall man. The soldiers leaped into the moat and with a variety of old axes from the boats tried to hack their way through the tough paling of the stockade, while Croghan's rifles blazed at them from the loopholes and his cannon from a corner blockhouse shot a blast of grapeshot along the ditch. It was a desperate and hopeless business. In a few minutes Colonel Short of the 41st Regiment was killed and nearly a hundred others lay dead or wounded at the foot of the stockade. The rest stumbled back, bringing some of the wounded but leaving nineteen others in the ditch. None of the Indians had joined in the attack. With Harrison's troops approaching, Procter trundled his cannon and his wounded back to the boats and returned up the lake to Amherstburg.

This was the last of the adventures by which he had disturbed and pinned down in Ohio the forces that Harrison was slowly gathering to crush him. In September Captain Perry was ready to do battle for the waters of Lake Erie. Procter's naval partner, Captain Barclay, was not. Thereby hung a tragedy for him, for Procter, and Tecumseh. To understand what happened one must look back to the command of the Royal Navy on the Great Lakes.

CHAPTER 32

1813

Sir James Yeo — Captain Robert Barclay — The Battle of Lake Erie

WHEN Sir James Yeo arrived on Lake Ontario with his officers and seamen he came straight from a court-martial dealing with the loss of his ship on a West Indian reef. The court acquitted him of negligence, and so he happened to be available for duty in Canada just when Admiral Warren wanted an officer of the proper seniority to take charge of the naval forces on the Great Lakes. Yeo was thirty, a dark-haired intense man with a lantern jaw and a willful mouth, subject to recurring fits of a tropical fever suffered on his previous station. He was by nature lonely and morose, and these ills of body and soul shut him off from his officers and men and gave rise to his characteristic baffling behavior in Canada, alternating, like the lake winds, between dull hesitation and sudden irritable energy.

Warren had given him a free hand in this novel environment; nevertheless Yeo was subject to the orders of Sir George Prevost as commander in chief of all His Majesty's forces in Canada. One experience of Prevost's incompetence, a bungled attack on Sackets Harbor, robbed him of anything but a frigid politeness to that nervous man. Yet one feature of Prevost's mind struck him favorably because it enabled Yeo to indulge his own sense of importance. That was the commander in chief's fear of an American army thrusting down the St. Lawrence from Lake Ontario at the same time that their Plattsburg army struck down the Richelieu from Lake Champlain. Prevost's fear and Yeo's own egotism combined to warp his judgment on everything else about the Canadian campaign. He saw his ships on Lake Ontario as the supreme factor in the war, a fleet to be increased and nourished by every possible means but never risked in battle—an attitude strangely different from that of his onetime commander, Horatio Nelson.

Yeo's first act was to clear out brusquely most of the Provincial Marine personnel on Lake Ontario, the good with the bad, thereby depriving himself of nearly everyone who knew the lakes and the peculiarities of fresh-water naval operations. His second act was to get rid of the sea officers sent up from Halifax in the past winter, among others ordering Barclay to Lake Erie and Pring to Lake Champlain. From that time Lake Ontario was strictly Yeo's show, and he was able to secure for his show practically all of the naval men and materials sent out from Britain for the war in the Canadian interior. He was right in his belief that Ontario was the most important of the lakes and that the east end of it was more important than the west. He and Prevost were wrong in making it an obsession. At a time when risks had to be taken over the whole scene, the small British squadrons on Lakes Erie and Champlain were starved of men and equipment while Yeo on Lake Ontario at tremendous cost built up a fleet fit for a deep-sea battle. The obsession reached its height in 1814 when Yeo hoisted his flag in the newly launched *Saint Lawrence*, a ship of three decks and 102 guns, requiring a crew of at least 700 officers and men. It was bigger and more powerful than Nelson's *Victory*—and it never fired a shot in battle.

Yeo's American opponent, Commodore Chauncey, also saw the importance of Lake Ontario, and having come straight from the command of the New York Navy Yard he was quite in his element when Yeo undertook a shipbuilding contest. Shipwrights in Canada were few. Chauncey could draw on the whole American seaboard, where the British blockade had thrown thousands of seamen and carpenters out of work. By 1814 the British actually were cutting and shaping the complete frames of frigates in English dockyards, shipping the parts across the sea to Canada, dragging them laboriously up the St. Lawrence rapids, and assembling them at Kingston —in the heart of a forest. Indeed one of these ships (the *Psyche*) seems to have been fashioned in England from Canadian timber, which thus crossed the Atlantic twice.

In all their operations Yeo and Chauncey were devoted to the theory of a fleet "in being," which is to say the importance of keeping one's own fleet intact as a constant threat to the other but never chancing an outright battle. The result was an endless and largely bloodless war of carpenters and riggers on both sides of Lake Ontario, building more and bigger ships with heavier guns and larger crews all through 1813 and 1814, while the two fleets performed a stately minuet on those pallid green waters, one sailing to the east end of the lake while the other went west (or west while the other went east), now advancing, now retreating, brushing sometimes in passing but never coming to the embarrassing point of a downright collision. There was plenty of room. Lake Ontario was fifty miles wide and nearly two hundred long, a magnificent floor for the dance.

At the war's end Yeo flattered himself that his policy had enabled Prevost to keep alive the British army along the Niagara. But with equal justice Chauncey could say that he had guarded the American water line between Niagara and Oswego (the lake shipping point for army supplies from the Hudson Valley), enabling American troops to invade the Niagara peninsula and twice to capture York, the capital of Upper Canada. In the final analysis another result was clear. Building his ships in the careful and even finicky method of the royal dockyards in England, Yeo had created on Lake Ontario a squadron fit for a royal inspection. The Americans, more concerned with utility, had built ships just as big and just as effective for fleet-in-being purposes on Lake Ontario, without neglecting for an hour their fighting needs on Lakes Erie and Champlain. There lay a vital difference. Yeo's obsession was the ruin of the British naval forces on the other lakes.

Captain Robert Barclay of the Royal Navy was thirty-two, a capable young officer who had fought at Trafalgar and had lost an arm in the service, when he arrived on Lake Erie with nineteen seamen (all that Yeo would give him) in the early summer of 1813. He found there five small ships of the Provincial Marine and another under construction in the Amherstburg shipyard. In size and armament they ranged from the veteran schooner *Queen Charlotte* of nine guns to the midget *Chippewa*, which carried one. Their Canadian crews totaled about a hundred officers and men, enough to handle the ships under sail but not to man the guns. Excepting the *Queen Charlotte* and *Hunter* at the brief siege of Detroit, the ships had seen action only as transports moving Procter's troops and supplies in his raids on Fort Meigs and Fort Stephenson. There had been nothing on the lake to fight.

On the American shore of Erie Captain Perry had been busy at Presque Isle Harbor (now the city of Erie, Pennsylvania), where his carpenters had finished three warships and had two more on the ways. At Black Rock, a nook in the Lake Erie end of the Niagara River, lay five other American ships, ordinary lake sloops and schooners armed for war; but these were bottled up there by the British guns in Fort Erie. Perry had another sort of bottleneck at Presque Isle. This harbor had been chosen because it was well sheltered, with a good local timber supply and a passable road by which guns and naval stores could be brought up from Philadelphia by way of Pittsburg; but it had an awkward defect. Ordinary lake craft could pass over the bar at the entrance, but the two twenty-gun brigs that Perry was building as his main fighting ships could not get over it with the weight of their cannon on board. They would have to be floated over it unarmed or eased over it slowly with barges lashed alongside to buoy them up. Either way they would be helpless targets if British warships lay outside.

This became known to Barclay, who set up a blockade off Presque Isle. It was this situation that enabled Colonel Procter to continue his amphibious raids at the other end of Lake Erie. Two things upset this convenient state of affairs. In May a new American invasion of the Niagara peninsula forced the British gunners out of Fort Erie and the five ships bottled up at Black Rock were free to sail into the lake. This was bad enough; but at the beginning of August Barclay relaxed his close watch at Presque Isle, and Captain Perry by prompt and ingenious efforts got his big brigs over the bar and brought the whole squadron together.

Why did Barclay leave his post outside the Presque Isle bar? This is one of history's puzzles, and there is no answer in the official accounts. The people of Port Dover, on the Canadian side of the lake, told a story afterward that may explain it. One of Procter's officers at Amhertsburg had died, leaving a young and charming widow. The lady was anxious to return to York; she had met Barcley at social affairs in Amherstburg, and that gallant officer had promised to take her down the lake as far as Port Dover, where she could take carriage over the cross-country road to Lake Ontario. Accordingly on the promised date Barclay sailed to Amherstburg, embarked the lady and her baggage, and carried her to Port Dover. Moreover he escorted her to the home of Dr. Rolph, where she was to stay until the road arrangements could be made, and the Rolphs invited the obliging captain to stay over and have dinner with them the next day. In all Barclay was absent from the watch off Presque Isle from July 30 to August 4, and when he arrived off that place he found Perry's ships outside the bar is what seemed to him "a most formidable state of preparation."

The story may or may not be true. This much is certain. Lake Erie is shallow and a strong wind blowing continuously for a few hours has a remarkable effect on the depth, which may increase by several feet on the lee side while shrinking by the same amount on the windward side. It is known that the wind was southerly, and that on the day when Perry began to work his ships out of Presque Isle the depth on the bar had shrunk from five feet to four. It seems logical that Barclay, certain that the Americans could not navigate the bar in the prevailing wind, took advantage of an opportunity to run up to Amherstburg and thence down to Port Dover, the British supply base, which he had to visit from time to time in any case, lady or no lady.

Whatever the cause, the effect was plain. No genie popping out of a jar in the *Arabian Nights* could have wrought a more magical change. In a stroke the Americans were sailing the lake with ships and guns that far outmatched Barclay's and placed the British forces on the Detroit in a most dangerous position.

When Barclay reported that the American ships had come up the lake to Put-In-Bay, the British general (he had been promoted for his Frenchtown victory) took a grim view of it. Put-In-Bay was off the mouth of the Sandusky River, and a few miles up that stream lay General Harrison with 4500 men. The combination spelt a waterborne invasion, landing anywhere they chose. A few reinforcements had reached Procter from the Niagara front, but he still had less than 1200 troops to hold the line of the Detroit. Tecumseh had mustered another swarm of Indians, but in defensive warfare against a superior force their value was doubtful. Even if Harrison did not move his troops, the mere presence of Perry's ships in the west end of Lake Erie meant that Procter's supply ships could not escape capture.

In the face of this arithmetic there was one immediate thing to do. Barclay must seek battle with Perry and try to destroy or capture the American ships. If the British sat still they were lost. This had been Brock's philosophy and Procter had adopted it and carried it out in all weathers and at all risks. Barclay would have to do the same. Procter's view and its outcome made him later the victim of critics, beginning with Sir George Prevost, who had done so little to support his lonely campaign in the West.

It is easy to understand Barclay's complaints as well. Secret informers on both sides of the lake had kept the two naval commanders well posted on each other's ships, their armament and the number and quality of their crews. Barclay was a brave man, but his own experience of naval warfare told him what was likely to happen if he tackled Perry. Still he accepted the hazard, and all that remained was to make the best of a doubtful job. There was not much time. Barclay's new flagship *Detroit* was just completing at the Amherstburg shipyard, but the guns ordered for her equipment were still held at Kingston, Yeo's base on Lake Ontario. To arm the ship for battle Procter had to strip Fort Malden of its guns, a medley of various age, weight, and caliber never intended for naval use. (They were not equipped with the flintlocks and lanyards necessary for the quick and exact timing of a ship's broadside; even the ignition tubes and matches supplied from the army magazine at Amherstburg proved defective, and in the actual battle Barclay's men had to fire the guns by snapping a pistol at each touchhole.)

There was also the matter of crews. The Canadian personnel were enough to handle the ships but not enough to fight them. Barclay had written to Prevost in June, "it will require at least from 250 to 300 seamen to render His Majesty's Squadron perfectly effective." By September he still had only his 100 Canadians and the 19 seamen he had brought with him from Kingston. Three days before the battle he received 36 seamen who had just made an arduous journey of 800 miles from Quebec. At the last moment Procter had to send aboard 250 of his soldiers to fill out Barclay's complement for action. With this odd collection of ships, guns, and men Barclay sailed from Amherstburg on September 9. By the following morning he was off Put-In-Bay, and as soon as he appeared the Americans came out to fight.

There was a light shower of rain and then the weather cleared. Perry had named his flagship after gallant Lawrence of the *Chesapeake*, and from one of her mastheads he flew a large banner bearing Lawrence's last words, *Don't give up the ship*. In all Perry had 9 ships, Barclay 6. Perry had 55 guns, Barclay 65, but on the average the American guns were of larger caliber, so that in close action Perry could blast the British ships with 936 pounds of shot at each discharge, while Barclay could return only 459. In the actual maneuvering of the ships not all of these guns could be used on either side, but those in action fired shot in about that proportion. Barclay's crews amounted to 407 officers and men, of whom only 55 were experienced naval seamen. Perry had shipped some volunteers and Kentucky riflemen, but 60 per cent of his 532 officers and men were naval personnel from the Atlantic coast, including some veteran gunners from the famous frigate *Constitution*.

The British had a single advantage. With their higher proportion of long guns they could hit the American ships harder at a distance than the Americans could hit them. The advantage would vanish as soon as Perry closed to carronade range, and then the Americans would have a two-to-one advantage in weight of shot. Perry, like many other American naval officers, was a student of Nelson's tactics, and at his last conference with his officers before going into battle he offered them Nelson's instructions at Trafalgar—"If you lay your enemy close alongside you cannot be out of place."

So the fight on Lake Erie was a Trafalgar seen through the wrong end of the spyglass, a battle of toys in a bathtub, in which the "battleships" had at most twenty guns and the "frigates" were lake schooners armed with one or two; but the battle was none the less furious for that. The two squadrons sailed toward each other in column. In their order of size and armament they were as follows:

American	*British*
Lawrence (flagship)	Detroit (flagship)
Niagara	Queen Charlotte
Caledonia	Lady Prevost
Ariel	Hunter
Scorpion	Chippewa
Somers	Little Belt
Porcupine	
Tigress	
Trippe	

Of these, Perry's *Lawrence* and *Niagara* and Barclay's *Detroit* and *Queen Charlotte* were far the largest and best armed. Perry's eagerness to close the range led him into a headlong attack, and at long range the *Detroit* and *Queen Charlotte* were able to shatter his flagship at the head of the American line. The ships then drew together in three struggling groups, all moving slowly in a light northeast wind. In the center were the two flagships, hammering each other with every gun they could bring to bear and suffering the fire of other ships, British and American. The *Lawrence* had been hard hit before she closed with the *Detroit*. Both crews worked their guns with determination, but by two o'clock in the afternoon the American flagship was a ruin, a large part of her crew were casualties, and all of her guns on the engaged side had been knocked down by the British shot.

Captain Perry's middle name was Hazard and he lived up to it. He removed his *Don't Give Up The Ship* banner and had a boat's crew take him through the flying shot to hoist it in her sister ship, the twenty-gun brig *Niagara*, which so far had taken little part in the action. As soon as he left the *Lawrence* the first lieutenant of that ship hauled down the Stars and Stripes in surrender. Aboard the *Detroit* Captain Barclay lay terribly wounded and his first lieutenant was dead. The ship was in charge of Lieutenant Inglis. He saw that the *Lawrence* had struck her flag, but his own boats were smashed and he could not send a party aboard to take possession. And now, in what seemed a miraculous moment of victory, disaster came. The *Detroit* was badly damaged about the spars and rigging. So was her consort *Queen Charlotte*, which also had lost her captain and first lieutenant. The two ships with their torn rigging and the severe casualties among their crews were only partly manageable.

The undamaged *Niagara*, with Perry on board, now closed in to renew the fight. Seeing this, the *Detroit* and *Queen Charlotte* made an effort to turn and meet the new attack. In doing so they fell foul of each other and remained with their spars locked, unable to move. Here was a rich opportunity and Perry seized it. Sailing toward these shackled targets, he steered between the four smaller British ships, all busily engaged, and smashed them with both broadsides as he passed. He now approached the entangled *Detroit* and *Queen Charlotte* from the bows, where their broadside cannon were of no use, swung smartly, and at close range blasted the whole length of their decks with grapeshot. And now came the opportunity of the Kentucky riflemen, firing at a distance of not more than twenty yards. At the same time the *Caledonia* and other American schooners drew in for the kill. It did not take long. The survivors on the British decks ended the slaughter by hauling down their two flags.

With Barclay's flagship and her consort gone there was no

hope for the rest. The *Lady Prevost* and *Hunter*, crippled and unable to escape, surrendered. The *Chippewa* and *Little Belt* made a run for it, but Perry chased them with swifter craft and they were taken also. His victory was complete. When the gray fog of powder smoke drifted away to the Ohio shore the autumn sunshine revealed a huddle of silent ships, their sides starred and scored by shot, their cordage a tangle, their spars tottering, their sails a beggar's wardrobe of slits and shotholes. The battle had lasted three hours. The British had lost forty-one killed and ninety-four wounded, about one of every three men aboard. The Americans had lost twenty-seven killed and ninety-six wounded, about one of every four.

CHAPTER 33

1813

The Detroit front—Procter and Tecumseh—Retreat
and disaster on the Thames

ON SEPTEMBER 12, 1813, William Henry Harrison opened a note in his headquarters on the Sandusky. It was scrawled on the back of an old letter and it said:

We have met the enemy and they are ours; two ships, two brigs, one schooner and one sloop. Yours with great esteem and respect,

O. H. PERRY

A curt statement of fact, not a boast, it gave notice that General Harrison could now put his careful plans into effect. This time the victor of Tippecanoe left nothing to chance—there were to be no more Detroits or Frenchtowns. The attack would be made by resolute troops in overwhelming force. The inhabitants on the American side of the Detroit had kept Harrison informed about the state of the British defense. The 250 soldiers lost with Barclay's squadron had reduced Procter's regulars to 877 men, of whom a hundred were sick. His Canadian militia were away harvesting their crops. His chief numerical strength was in Tecumseh's 1200 Indians, and Harrison drew his plans accordingly.

Harrison had never lost sight of the War Hawks' twofold object in this war, to destroy the last trace of Indian fighting power in the lake country and to drive the British out of Canada, and for him the first was far the more important. He could finish now what he had begun at Tippecanoe. As a young captain at Fallen Timbers he had seen how easily a force of daredevil mounted riflemen could defeat any number of Indians, even in a wooded position. For his new campaign he had mustered a brigade of Kentucky cavalry under Colonel Richard Johnson, and he sent them now by road toward Detroit. His 4500 infantry he moved in Perry's ships to

The Detroit-Lake Erie front in the War of 1812

an island halfway between Put-In-Bay and Amherstburg. Here he could choose his landing place while the horsemen closed up to Detroit.

The western tip of the Ontario peninsula ends in a thumb forty miles long with the nail along the Detroit River. General Procter's troops lay along the nail, with a detachment in Fort Detroit on the American side of the river and the main force at Amherstburg twenty miles downstream on the Canadian side. American infantry landed at the base of the thumb could march across it in four or five hours, horsemen in half the time. Strangely, Harrison neglected to do this. Instead he waited a week and then landed his troops at the mouth of the Detroit near Fort Malden. Fortunately for the main American purpose the British general had delayed his retreat from the peninsula.

Procter's danger was plain from the moment of Barclay's defeat and he saw it, but he hesitated to tell Tecumseh, and even when Tecumseh knew the whole unhappy truth he refused to believe it. Thereby hung disaster. After the fiasco at Fort Stephenson the Shawnee had exerted himself in gathering another horde of warriors from the dispossessed Ohio tribes. On the promise of British supplies his messengers had drawn twelve hundred Indians to Amherstburg, and these had brought their women and children to join in His Majesty's bounty. This huge and hungry swarm made a heavy drain on Procter's commissariat. Perry had cut off all the regular supply from Niagara and it would be some weeks yet before the farmers along the Detroit bank and up the Thames Valley could thresh and grind their grain.

Thus the very presence of the Indians made a grave food problem. Their sentiment was another. Nearly all of these people had their hearts in the lost lands of Indiana and Ohio, for which they were eager to fight. A defensive war in the strange Canadian countryside was not to their fancy, even on British rations. Procter had not dared to tell Tecumseh of the British defeat on the lake, and even when the truth was out none of the Indians understood that the mysterious disaster of "Our-father-of-the-one-arm" (Barclay) meant disaster to all unless they got away quickly from the Detroit peninsula.

Tecumseh was angry and contemptuous on September 18 when Procter ordered his outpost in Detroit to burn the fort buildings and come over the river as the first step in a general retreat. The

Shawnee gathered his feathered and buckskinned multitude and addressed the British general in their presence, recalling all the British promises of the past. He could not resist taunting the young officer with British failures as well; how at the time of the American Revolution they had asked the Indians to fight for them, and how in their defeat they had shaken hands with the Long Knives and left their Indian friends helpless; how after the battle of Fallen Timbers many years later, the redcoats had shut the gate of their Maumee fort and refused to give the fleeing Indians shelter or to fire a shot in their defense. He admitted naïvely that in the recent affairs at Fort Meigs and Fort Stephenson the Indians had refused to risk their skins against the American ramparts—"It is hard to fight against a people who live like ground-hogs"—but he observed sourly that the redcoats now were about to quit their own ramparts without even waiting to see the enemy. "We must compare our father [Procter] to a fat dog who carries his tail on his back but drops it between his legs and runs away when he is afraid." Finally, scornfully, he invited the redcoats to give the Indians their muskets and run away if they wished. "Our lives are in the hands of the Great Spirit. We are determined to fight for our own lands even if we leave our bones there."

The Shawnee's spirit was admirable, but this bilious outpour damaged himself as much as Procter. All the Indians' old suspicions were aroused, and many of the petty chiefs began to play with the notion that it might be better to change sides. Procter was in an evil fix. He could not expect his militia to muster after the harvest merely for a retreat into the back country, leaving their homes and families exposed to the wild American frontiersmen. He saw that retreat now, while Tecumseh's rage was still hot in their ears, meant losing the Indians also. As a compromise he delayed again.

On September 24 (two weeks after Perry's victory) he would wait no more. Fort Malden, robbed of its guns for Barclay's use, was useless to defend the river mouth. The British troops set fire to the fort buildings and to the Amherstburg barracks and shipyard, and began their retreat through Sandwich. Three days later General Harrison landed his infantry below Malden. By the twenty-ninth he was in Sandwich, and on the following day, with a neat piece of timing, Colonel Johnson's mounted brigade rode into Detroit.

Procter's only line of escape lay up the valley of the Thames, which flowed into Lake St. Clair at the base of the Detroit thumb. The river was fantastically crooked, wriggling over the valley floor like an attempt at a straight line drawn by a palsied hand; and by a quirk of geography the valley itself stretched a great part of its length parallel with the shore of Lake Erie and seldom more than twenty miles from it. Harrison could land troops almost anywhere along that shore and in a few hours' hard marching cut off the British retreat. As things turned out he had no need.

About seventy miles by crow flight up the Thames Valley was the site of Governor Simcoe's unbuilt "metropolis" (London), toward which the old military track called Dundas Street ran through the woods from Burlington (Hamilton) on Lake Ontario. Some distance downstream a rough road led off toward the Mohawk settlement on Grand River. The summer's news from that direction had been grave. The Americans had driven General Vincent's army far back from the Niagara. At one time their troops had been in sight of Burlington, and although Vincent had since defeated them the Americans still had an army on the Canadian side of the Niagara.

Procter's object was a retreat to the upper waters of the Thames. Every step in that direction brought him closer to Lake Ontario and Vincent's army; each step in pursuit carried Harrison farther from his supply base at Detroit. The American general would have to reduce his force the farther he advanced, and somewhere toward the head of the long valley the British and Indians could hope to make a stand on even terms. Such indeed was Procter's only chance, and with three days' start from the Detroit it seemed possible to get well up the Thames before giving battle. He was encumbered with a hundred sick men, with the wives and children of his soldiers (including his own wife and child) and of Tecumseh's warriors, and with the stores and baggage necessary to maintain his fighting force. Part of this impedimenta moved in boats through Lake St. Clair and up the Thames, the rest crawled up the river road in a long procession of wagons. To watch the rear and destroy the bridges after the people and troops had passed, Procter assigned Tecumseh with a force of Indians and his only mounted men, fifty militia dragoons.

Perry's ships ferried the American cavalry across the Detroit River while General Harrison selected from his infantry the men best fitted for a swift march, 140 regulars and 1900 frontiersmen. With

Johnson's horsemen these made up a force of 3500. And they were unencumbered, for Perry's sailors boated all their supplies (and part of the troops) through Lake St. Clair and up the Thames.

Johnson's Kentucky horsemen were in their element, for the river valley was a level country of rich farm land patched with open woods of beech and other hardwoods in autumn leaf, easily passable, with forage to be had at every farm. They left the Detroit on October 2 and soon overtook the British rear guard, capturing a dozen provincial dragoons trying to destroy a bridge at one place and scattering Tecumseh's Indians at another. Pressing on at a speed and with a force beyond all Procter's calculations the Americans caught his troops on the march, or rather on the river, for many of the redcoats were laboring at the oars of boats and scows, toiling to get the artillery and stores up the fantastic windings of the stream. The rearmost craft were overtaken by horsemen galloping across the bends, or by American boats in the hands of Perry's expert seamen, and captured one after another. In some cases the British soldiers were able to set their craft on fire and escape into the woods; others had no choice but surrender.

In this way Harrison snapped up Procter's heaviest field guns, a great quantity of muskets, all the reserve ammunition, and 174 of his soldiers. Apart from these losses, Tecumseh's discontented followers drifted away by hundreds and some of the chiefs with their warriors went over to the Americans.

On October 1, the day before Harrison set out from Sandwich in pursuit, General Procter had reached the village of Chatham. His progress had been slow, but he was confident in the gap between the two armies and now his personal concerns intruded and laid him open to the critics later on. His child was ill and his wife distressed. He ordered Colonel Warburton to take command of the troops while he escorted Mrs. Procter and the girl to the Indian mission of Moraviantown about twenty miles upstream. He was absent for three days. During that time the Americans caught up with the British rear guard and scattered it. Tecumseh was eager to make a stand with the British troops at Chatham, and at his insistence Warburton delayed there a full day. On the following morning Indian scouts dashed in with alarming news of the size and speed of the American force, and most of the Indians with their women and children began to hurry away up the river or into the forest. Warburton resumed the retreat at once, not even giving his soldiers time to eat the meager ration on which they had been existing for the past month.

Six miles beyond Chatham General Procter rejoined his ragged and starving little army and at nightfall he gave the order to halt, five miles below Moraviantown. Tecumseh had been wounded in the rear-guard fighting and he was in a desperate mood. His own fighting men had dwindled to five hundred and he refused to go farther without an all-out battle, arguing that it was better to risk everything in one chance than to straggle on and see his whole band drift away.

Above Moraviantown the valley highway ran through woods for thirty-five miles, a rough stretch known as the Wilderness Road, where the troops and Indians could at least delay the American advance. There was little hope of a successful stand below it. However, refusing to abandon Tecumseh, Procter agreed to stand with him before the shabby little Indian village. At this point the valley road ran two hundred yards from the river, passing through a beech wood. Procter posted his soldiers in two thin lines, extending from the river through the beeches to a cedar swamp, and Tecumseh placed his Indians in the swamp. To defend a ford in the Thames two miles at his rear against a probable American encircling movement, Procter posted some infantry with five of his six remaining field guns. The other gun he placed in his line to cover the road.

His effective force facing Harrison's advance consisted of 356 redcoats, 38 provincial dragoons and Tecumseh's 500 Indians, altogether 894 harried and starving men with no ammunition but what they carried in their cartridge pouches. Behind them in Moraviantown's church and Indian hovels lay their sick and wounded together with their women and children and what remained of their baggage. Just before the Americans attacked, Tecumseh put aside his anger and despair and shook Procter's hand for the last time, saying simply, "Father, have a big heart."

What followed was a sorry anticlimax. The odds were hopeless and the so-called Battle of the Thames was no battle at all. General Harrison had intended to attack with his infantry, resting his cavalry horses for the final pursuit and slaughter. But when his scouts reported the British infantry stretched thinly through the beech wood he changed his plan, formed the horsemen into two columns, and sent them forward at a gallop. He wrote afterward, "American backwoodsmen ride better in the woods than any other people. I was persuaded, too, that the enemy would be quite unprepared for the shock and that they could not resist it."

His persuasion was right. The shock of the horsemen was swift and overwhelming. The lone British cannon covering the road was overrun before it could fire a shot. The beeches stood tall, with no undergrowth to impede horse or man. Plain to be seen under their yellow foliage stood the open lines of men in patched and faded scarlet, armed with "Brown Bess," the standard smoothbore musket of the British Army, which could not kill or wound seriously with aimed fire at much over one hundred yards. The redcoats barely had time to shoot, reload, and shoot once more at the swift figures weaving toward them through the trees when the mass of horsemen was upon them. It was all over in a few minutes; forty-eight officers and men were shot or cut down, including Warburton and the gray-haired Major Muir; some on the flanks managed to escape, the rest dropped their empty muskets and surrendered to the cavalry milling all about them.

For more than fourteen months the little British army on the Detroit, thousands of miles from home, had marched and fought in the wilderness against crazy odds and in every extreme of weather. In that time, with the variable aid of the Indians, they had killed, wounded or captured more than four thousand Americans, mostly on American soil, and by all these exertions staved off the invasion of Canada from the West. It was a sorry end to a brave campaign.

With the collapse of the British force Harrison turned his cavalry on the Indians. There the tale was just as brief, although in their swampy thickets, where horsemen could not follow, most of the Indians were able to get away. Some escaped upstream and eventually reached Burlington by circling through the woods, bringing with them a number of the British soldiers. Tecumseh by his own fierce example held a few together at the front of the wood, but they were overrun and the Shawnee was killed. In the quick shift and confusion of the fight some of his band seized a chance to drag the body into the thickets, where they scooped a shallow grave and buried it, concealing the traces. When darkness came they slipped away, never to return. So ended *Tekumtha*, the Shooting Star, and with him the last hope of Indian unity in the West. His grave was never found.

The Kentucky riders included some of the wildest spirits of the West and as soon as the scuffle was over there was a brisk hunt for

Indian scalps. The hair crop was poor. Most of the Indians had fled at the appearance of the dreaded horsemen and less than three dozen bodies were found to mutilate. The keenest search was for the body of Tecumseh. The Kentuckians found a corpse in buckskins and wearing some rich ornaments which they assumed to be that of the famous Shawnee. They sliced away the scalp and carefully flayed the lean body itself. Some of these strips of tough brown skin they later fashioned into souvenir "razorstrops" for presentation to western members of the Congress, and Henry Clay is said to have boasted of one of these grisly possessions.

When Procter saw the collapse of his little force he barely had time to gather up his wife and child, salvage the colors of the 41st Regiment from the baggage wagons, and make off with a handful of survivors through the Wilderness Road. The American cavalry chased him for some distance and Procter was obliged to abandon his carriage with all his private and military papers. General Harrison halted his advance at the river ford above Moraviantown, where he found the rest of the British guns abandoned and silent. Some of his wilder men mistreated the Indian women and children brutally and then burned the village to the ground, church and all. Yet their victory had been so quick and complete that little blood was spilled among the fighting men on either side. Of the British, 12 were killed, 36 wounded, and 477 taken prisoner. A diligent search found only 33 Indian bodies — the frontiersmen, as a principle, took no Indian prisoners. The American loss was trifling; 15 killed and 30 wounded.

With Procter's rout and Tecumseh's death General Harrison's main objects were achieved. So long as the American naval squadron rode Lake Erie (and they held it unchallenged for the rest of the war), the British could not restore the Detroit wing of what their army documents called the Right Division — the garrison of the Ontario peninsula. The overland route from Lake Ontario was too long and rough to supply any useful body of troops. Partly for the same reason, mostly because he was satisfied, Harrison did not follow up his victory by striking at General Vincent's rear. Instead he retired down the Thames, left a garrison in Detroit, shipped thirteen hundred men to join the American army on the Niagara, and went home with the rest.

Meanwhile General Procter arrived at the village of Ancaster on Burlington Heights to face another battle against odds, but of a different kind. His scalp was sought now by his own superior and a number of other critics. He was blamed for Barclay's defeat as well as his own. He was blamed for Tecumseh's death. Comfortable gentlemen in staff offices declared that he should have died with the Shawnee, and complained that instead he had let his own soldiers surrender and then fled from the battlefield, leaving the Indians to fight on hopelessly to the end.

The facts reveal small justice in these charges. If, when all was lost, the young general had run sword in hand against the victorious American army he might have gone down to history as a hero to the last — but as a fool. His spur-of-the-moment choice was to salvage what he could from the wreck (eventually 246 officers and men reached Burlington), and if he saved his wife and child in the process that was an instinct surely human. However Sir George Prevost in a general order to the army condemned Procter's failure with the Right Division — "its well earned laurels tarnished and its conduct calling loudly for reproach and censure" — and in the meantime Procter was sent to command the little garrison of York ("it being a post of little importance at present"), awaiting the further pleasure of his commander in chief.

The sequel was a court-martial in the cold white city of Montreal at the end of 1814, when Prevost's own conduct at Plattsburg was calling much more loudly for censure and reproach. The court cleared Procter of any reproach to his courage. Instead it found "that he did not take the proper measures for conducting the retreat; that he had in many instances during the retreat and in the disposition of the forces under his command been erroneous in judgment, and in some ways deficient in those energetic and active exertions which the extraordinary difficulties of his situation so particularly required." With this ponderous language he was sentenced to suspension from pay and rank for six months. At that moment, far across the sea in Belgium, the British and American peace commissions were about to end the war. So at the very close of the struggle Procter was condemned to history in disgrace. He deserved a better farewell. Canadians owed him much.

CHAPTER 34

1813

*The Americans raid York — British defeat at Fort George
— The British raid Sackets Harbor — American defeat at
Stony Creek and Beaver Dam — The burning of Newark
— British reprisals*

WHILE Procter and Tecumseh were traveling their lonely
road from triumph to defeat, the campaign of 1813 had
been crackling busily all along the Canadian line. In the
garrison of Upper Canada the troops of General Procter had formed
the gaunt right arm. General Sheaffe's in the Niagara peninsula
formed the stronger left. At the beginning of the campaign season
Sheaffe had along the Niagara River (including a few Indians) about
three thousand men. His responsibilities included the defense of
York, the little capital, where he kept barely more than a corporal's
guard. York with its population of nine hundred lay isolated by
the muddy spring roads, one hundred miles from Niagara and nearly
twice that from Kingston. Water communication was in American
hands, for in the previous autumn Commodore Chauncey had struck
at the wretched Provincial Marine squadron on Lake Ontario, driving one damaged ship into York and the rest into Kingston, where
they had lain through the winter undergoing slow repair.

When spring melted the ice along the shores of Lake Ontario
Sir James Yeo and his British naval detachment had yet to arrive on
the scene, but Chauncey scented danger in the port and shipyard of
Kingston at the lake's outlet toward Montreal. He was anxious for
the American army to capture the place before the British could
equip a squadron there to match his own. His view was shared by
the War Department, and Secretary Armstrong's broad scheme for
the Canadian campaign of 1813 began with the seizure of Kingston
in February, when American troops could cross the lake end on the
ice.

This was sound planning. Unhappily for sound plans General Dearborn remained in command of the Army of the North, an old man resolute in nothing but his wrangles with Armstrong and his own subordinates, and so fat that he could travel only in a carriage built to his design. (It was a comfortable vehicle much copied in later years by American farmers, who called it "the Dearborn".) Dearborn found various excuses for inaction until the winter had gone, and with it the last chance to catch Kingston exposed to an army afoot. Chauncey then turned his attention to York. One of the Provincial Marine ships had wintered in Toronto Bay after the scuffle on the lake last fall, and the York shipyard was known to be building another. Also known was the weakness of York's defenses.

For such a target Dearborn was willing to spare troops and on April 25 he and his aide, General Zebulon Pike, with seventeen hundred men left Sackets Harbor in eight of Chauncey's ships. The voyage made Dearborn ill and General Pike conducted the landing. Most of the troops were United States regulars, but they had with them two battalions of frontier riflemen under Major Forsyth and Colonel McClure. There was no opposition on the lake. The Provincial Marine was still patching its old ships and building two new ones, including a fine twenty-four-gun ship on the stocks at York.

The American squadron entered Toronto Bay in the dark early hours of April 27 and at daylight the troops began to land under cover of a brisk bombardment from the ships. General Sheaffe, hibernating amid the simple winter comforts of Niagara, had not concerned himself with such an attack, and he was still unconcerned when he moved his household up to York in the spring. There were some old guns mounted in two small batteries. A blockhouse and a trench guarded what York townsmen called "the Garrison," meaning the barracks and magazine. The guns for the new ship were still lying in the mud of the foreshore, where they had been tipped from the boats that brought them from Kingston last fall.

By chance two companies of redcoats had just halted at York on the long muddy tramp from Kingston to Niagara. With these, Sheaffe had 510 regulars, 250 York militia, and 40 Indians as his entire garrison. The Americans landed west of the town at what is now called Sunnyside Beach, brushing aside the handful of Indians and pushing through the woods toward the western battery. Sheaffe rashly ordered his men into the woods for a bayonet attack. The

American riflemen handled them roughly, and after a bloody half hour they came back, dragging their wounded to the western battery, which was on the site of the present Toronto Exhibition grounds. Disaster walked with them. The artillerymen in this makeshift work had been firing back at the American ships and in the scurry someone had left open the ammunition store. As Sheaffe's beaten men staggered inside the battery the store exploded, killing or wounding 40 men and throwing the guns off their carriages. With this blast Sheaffe's casualties amounted to 200; of these 50 were among the York militia, who were now badly shaken and flitting away to their homes. The Indians had vanished. Sheaffe managed to escape from the town with 180 redcoats, many of whom were wounded; but first he sent men to set fire to the new warship in the yard and to the main magazine at the barracks.

The Americans moved into the abandoned garrison quarters. Many of their soldiers were rambling about the barracks and General Pike was questioning a captured British sergeant when the magazine exploded. It contained 500 barrels of gunpowder and a large store of shells and solid shot which flew in all directions together with chunks of stone and broken masonry. The blast killed 52 American soldiers and injured 180 others, as well as various British soldiers and York civilians. Sheaffe's aide-de-camp, Captain Loring, was struck, and the horse he was riding was killed. General Pike was hit in the back by a piece of flying stone and died in an hour.

General Dearborn came ashore and held a victory parade of the American army through the muddy streets. He then ordered his regular troops away to the garrison barracks, leaving the town itself in the hands of Forsyth and McClure and their undisciplined riflemen. For the next four days these wild frontiersmen and some of Chauncey's sailors amused themselves in pillaging the shops and homes. They freed the tenants of the York jail and invited these and other furtive characters of the town to help themselves. In the looting these native robbers outstole the Americans, knowing exactly where to seek. Some merchants and officials removed their cash and valuable papers to farms up the Don River and elsewhere, but these too were hunted down by roving gangs of riflemen guided by local thieves. Others robbed Saint James' Church and stole many books from the town library, a curious sort of loot, which Commodore Chauncey recovered and sent back to York. These adventures led to something else, the looting and burning of the parliament houses of Upper Canada. Thereby hangs an odd tale.

In his dispatch to the Secretary of the Navy the American commodore mentioned that "a British standard, accompanied with the mace, over which hung a human scalp, were taken from the parliament house by one of my officers and presented to me." The only "scalp" likely to be hanging anywhere near the mace, that symbol of parliamentary dignity, was the speaker's wig, which was certainly carried off by the Americans but which Chauncey's officer surely would have recognized. According to Robert Gourlay, a writer well able to learn the truth from contemporary witnesses, there was indeed a human scalp in the building. It had been obtained from the Indians long before by a British officer and sent to his friend the clerk of the House as a curiosity of the backwoods. That worthy had tossed it into a drawer, where it lay forgotten until the American sailors found it. There was a common belief in the United States that the British Government paid the Indians a regular bounty for American scalps. To the looters this was proof.

It may have been the reason (if indeed there was any reason) why the looters set fire to the parliament buildings with their library and law-court offices and all the records of both Houses of Assembly. Whatever the motive it was a bonfire with far-reaching flames. The British blamed this destruction on the American general, which was unjust, for although his laxness was responsible he had not ordered it. The sequel came in the following year, when a British expedition entered Washington and (as if one folly excused another) burned the Capitol and other public buildings in revenge.

With York and its Toronto Bay anchorage in his hands, and with Chauncey's ships unchallenged on Lake Ontario, General Dearborn was in a remarkable position. In one inexpensive thrust he had cut off the entire British forces in the Ontario peninsula, and just at the end of a winter season when they would be short of every kind of supply. He had only to post a strong garrison at York for the next few months and he could deal with the British on the Niagara at his leisure while Harrison dealt with those on the Detroit. Instead he regarded the capture of York as a successful raid and nothing more. He waited for Chauncey's sailors to repair and hoist sail on the captured Provincial Marine ship *Duke of Gloucester*, to stow in Chauncey's ships as much of the captured stuff as they could carry (including the town fire engine), and then, having fired the block-house, the barracks, and the government storehouses, he embarked his troops and sailed off to attack the British army on the Niagara.

Head winds delayed the ships, but on May 8 the American troops landed some distance from Fort George on the shore road to Burlington. Transports with troops, artillery and stores arrived from Sackets Harbor during the next three weeks. By May 26 Dearborn had an army of six thousand on Canadian soil. Fortunately for his men, at this point the aged blunderer fell ill again, and Colonel Winfield Scott drew up the plan of attack. The troops would move in Chauncey's ships and boats, landing close to Fort George and moving swiftly to trap General Vincent's army there. At the same time a troop of cavalry, waiting on the American side of the river at Lewiston, would be ferried across to Queenston to cut off any British soldiers who might try to escape up the Canadian bank.

To oppose all this General John Vincent had 1350 regulars and militia and 50 Indians, concentrated mainly about Fort George but with a field battery guarding the river crossing at Queenston and other detachments watching the upper river. Colonel Scott chose his landing place shrewdly at a point where the houses of Newark shielded his troops from the guns in Fort George. A party of Canadian militia with two cannon guarded this blind spot, but they were driven from their guns by a hot fire from the American ships. At the same time Fort George itself was under bombardment from the ships and from Fort Niagara across the river. Shot heated red in a furnace at Fort Niagara soon set all the wooden buildings in Fort George aflame, and some of the houses in Newark began to smoke and then to burn.

The American troops landed in an early morning mist on May 27. The British force attacked them, but as brigade after brigade poured ashore under the covering fire of the ships the end was certain. After a tussle of more than three hours (in which they lost 458 men) Vincent's force was driven beyond Newark. Fort George was untenable and Vincent ordered the garrison to spike the guns, blow up the magazine, and join his retreat up the river. At the same time he sent word at a gallop to Colonel Bisshop, commanding at Chippewa, ordering him to quit the posts on the upper river, including Fort Erie, and retire inland to the village of Beaver Dam. The battery at Queenston had kept the American cavalry from crossing there and Bisshop's movement was made in time and good order.

Vincent himself retired on Beaver Dam, gathering up a few odd detachments on the way, including a party of sailors under Captain Robert Barclay, who were on their way all unconsciously to a bloody rendezvous with Perry at Put-In-Bay.

The triumphant American soldiers entered the ruins of Fort George, over which the British flag was still flying, nailed to the staff, and Colonel Scott and another officer seized axes and hacked it down to secure a memento of their success. The Americans had lost only 150 men, a small price for the whole Canadian bank of the Niagara. The abandonment of Fort Erie enabled five American ships cooped up in Black Rock Creek to sail into Lake Erie and join Perry's new squadron, and from Fort George General Dearborn could now thrust inland with the surety of a solid line of communication with American territory. If he had held York he might have used that place as the anvil for his Niagara hammer. As things were, Vincent was able to retire through Beaver Dam to Burlington, where he was in touch with Procter's force in the West, and where he could still get supplies and reinforcements from Kingston over the long shore road through York.

Where was the Provincial Marine squadron all this time? Sir James Yeo had arrived at Kingston with his naval detachment in mid-May, about two weeks after Chauncey and Dearborn raided York. With Royal Navy energy Sir James hurried the last repairs and adjustments, and toward the end of the month he was ready to sail. However he did not sail for the other end of Lake Ontario where he knew Chauncey to be, and where in consequence the small British force on the Niagara was facing a water-borne invasion. Instead Yeo chose a combined army-and-naval attack on Sackets Harbor, Chauncey's base at the east end. Sir George Prevost, always more concerned with the East than the West, decided to lead this attack in person. This alone was a warrant of failure.

At Kingston 750 British and Canadian redcoats went aboard the ships and a war party of Indians came along in canoes. Yeo sailed on May 27 (the day that Chauncey's ships landed the American army at Niagara) and arrived off Sackets Harbor the next morning. The soldiers scrambled into the boats and were starting for the shore when Prevost called them back on board. He was alarmed by the sudden appearance of nineteen boats filled with American soldiers. Actually these were some cavalrymen (without horses) on their way to join Dearborn's army at Niagara. Far from formidable on the water they were quite as alarmed as Prevost; they made for the shore at once, and the Indians and an armed boat party from the British ships were able to dash in and capture twelve of the boats with their discomfited horsemen. But then, to the surprise of his officers, the British commander in chief ordered Yeo to stand off the shore for the rest of the day and through the following night.

By the time Prevost was in a mood to land on the morning of May 29, the able officer commanding at Sackets Harbor, General Jacob Brown, had collected thirteen hundred regulars and militia to oppose the landing. Once ashore, the British troops attacked with vigor, and although Brown's regulars fought stoutly his New York militia broke and ran. Convinced that all was lost, the American officer in charge of the naval base set fire to the barracks, storehouses, and workshops, to the captured *Duke of Gloucester* and the unfinished warship *General Pike* on the stocks. At this moment General Prevost called his troops back to the boats. His officers were indignant. Major Drummond of the 104th (New Brunswick) Regiment pleaded to go on. But Sir George was never so stubborn as when his own courage had gone cold. Back to the ships went his troops. In Sackets Harbor the American sailors hastily doused the flames in their ships but were too late to save the barracks and stores, and half a million dollars' worth of government property went up in smoke as Yeo's ships sailed away. In the brief fighting the American marksmanship had again been notable. The British lost 261 men, the Americans 167, and Jacob Brown rightly claimed a victory.

General Dearborn (using Scott's brains) also had won a victory, although, as Secretary Armstrong coldly reminded him, "Battles are not gained when an inferior and broken enemy is not destroyed." Heavy rains followed the capture of Fort George. Dearborn sheltered his army in camp for five days while the British, inferior and beaten but far from broken (Vincent's united force was now sixteen hundred strong), trudged away under the downpour toward the western tip of Lake Ontario. There they were in touch with General Procter, still undefeated on the Detroit, and soon Dearborn had a false report that Procter's force was on the march to join them. It startled him out of his sodden tents, for obviously Vincent must be destroyed at Burlington before Procter got there. He sent off two brigades under Generals Winder and Chandler, who marched along the shore road to Stony Creek, within seven miles of Vincent's camp.

The American brigadiers had a well-rounded force of two thousand infantry, cavalry and artillery, and on the way a troop of Canadian volunteer cavalry watched and reported their movement. A British scouting patrol in the evening light saw that the Americans had camped for the night, that their tent lines were long and straggling, that their artillery was badly posted, and that a sudden attack could crush their forward troops before the rest got up to help them. Vincent wasted no time. Shortly before midnight on June 6 a picked force of redcoats began to move through the dark woods and farms. At two o'clock in the morning they rushed an American field battery and stormed into the camp itself. The American soldiers fought fiercely (and shot with their usual accuracy at the British musket flashes), but both their generals were soon prisoners and by dawn their whole force was in confusion.

Vincent might have gambled everything on one final effort, but the attack had cost 214 men and he deemed it wise to retire before full daylight showed his weakness. General Winder had surrendered to a British sergeant and General Chandler was found lying wounded under one of the captured guns. With these officers and 123 other prisoners the British moved back to their Burlington lines, taking with them two of the guns as souvenirs of the night's work.

The American casualties, including prisoners, were only 180. They could afford the loss and were still able to follow Vincent and attack him in their turn, but after a hasty conference they withdrew from Stony Creek, leaving their tents standing and their dead unburied. At Forty Mile Creek on the road to Fort George they met a reinforcement of four hundred infantry and halted; and here on the next day they were joined by Generals Lewis and Boyd with further troops and supplies. Lewis took command and prepared to do battle with the advancing British; but at this point a quaint new factor came on the scene.

The dance of the rival naval forces on Lake Ontario had come to another of their stately sweeps in opposite directions. Chauncey having sailed back to Sackets Harbor at the east end of the lake, Sir James Yeo left Kingston on June 3 for the Niagara peninsula, bringing with him stores and three hundred soldiers for Vincent's army. When his lookouts reported American tents at Forty Mile Creek he sent in two of his smaller ships to bombard them, at the same time sending ashore the routine demand for surrender. The bluff met the routine reception, but Lewis suspected a large body of troops on board the British ships. He pictured himself cut off by a British landing in his rear and then crushed between them and Vincent's hard-hitting redcoats. Yeo's ships had appeared at daylight on June 8. By midmorning the American army was in full retreat to Fort George, harried all the way by the Canadian militia and Indians.

In addition to the small replacements carried in Yeo's ships, General Vincent was now joined by the hard-marching 104th (New Brunswick) Regiment. This tough Canadian regular battalion had left Fredericton in midwinter, marching on snowshoes four hundred miles through the bleak forest to Quebec, and losing only one of its six hundred men on the way. As soon as the ice went out of the St. Lawrence it had moved up by ship and *bateaux* to Kingston, paused there to take part in the abortive raid on Sackets Harbor, and then traveled another five hundred miles to join Vincent's army. It was a famous journey, and the trail blazed through the eastern forest enabled the British to move other regiments from the seacoast to the fighting front whenever the St. Lawrence was frozen shut.

General Vincent now moved up toward the Niagara, sending a few infantry companies to occupy the village of Beaver Dam on his right flank, within striking distance of Queenston. General Dearborn saw the threat to his posts on the upper river, and on June 23 he sent Colonel Boerstler with 570 men and two guns to make a night attack on Beaver Dam. The American column sweated up the river road to Queenston and rested there in the cool of the evening until darkness came. Boerstler was a loud-voiced blustering man, a bad example to his juniors, who talked freely of their mission. Some of their chatter was overheard in the farmhouse of James Secord, a militiaman wounded in the fight at Queenston Heights the previous year. Secord was still disabled, but his wife Laura slipped away to warn the British at Beaver Dam.

It is one of the best Canadian stories of the war; how the devoted young woman walked past the American sentries, barefooted and carrying a stool as if she were going to the cow pasture for the evening milking; how she vanished into the woods and traveled through the darkness with her news; how a party of Indians leaped from the shadows and how she cried out that the Long Knives were coming; how at last, footsore and tattered, she came on a British patrol under Lieutenant Fitzgibbon and told them also. But in fact her courageous journey turned out to be needless. The Indians were aware of Boerstler's movement; they were preparing an ambush when she happened upon them and by the time she reached Fitz-gibbon the American force had walked straight into it.

At daylight Colonel Boerstler found himself in a wooded glen that rang suddenly with shots and Indian yells. The savages were a mixed party of Mohawks and Caughnawagas, about two hundred altogether, but they made the glen frightful with their noise and after a blind skirmish of two hours Boerstler decided to retreat. At this point fifteen Canadian militiamen appeared in the road at Boerstler's rear, fired on his men, and slipped back into cover. Then Fitzgibbon arrived on the scene with his company of unshaven redcoats. Major de Haren was close behind with 220 more.

Boerstler, convinced that he was gripped by a host of savages, and with an unknown number of Canadian sharpshooters gathering on his road back to Queenston, greeted the appearance of Fitzgibbon almost with relief, and lost no time in surrendering his whole force. Fitzgibbon wrote afterward with honesty but some inaccuracy; ". . . not a shot was fired on our side by any but the Indians. They beat the American detachment into a state of terror, and the only share I claim is taking advantage of a favourable moment to offer them protection from the tomahawk and scalping knife." It was indeed a coup for the Indians, with an honorable mark to Laura Secord and to the adventurous party of Canadians.

General Vincent now moved up in strength. Dearborn, shaken by the disasters at Stony Creek and Beaver Dam, drew back to the lower reach of the Niagara between Queenston and Fort George, abandon-ing the Canadian bank above. British troops reoccupied Fort Erie and promptly began a series of raids across the upper river. On the lower reach the Americans were held close to their remaining strip of Canadian territory and the Indians prowled between the lines. Toward the end of July an American officer (General Porter) wrote angrily and mistakenly, "We have had an army at Fort George for two months past . . . panic-struck, shut up and whipped in by a few hundred miserable savages, leaving the whole of this frontier, except the mile in extent which they occupy, exposed to the inroads and depredations of the enemy."

The only other American activity at this end of Lake Ontario for the rest of the summer was another raid by Commodore Chaun-cey, this time with fourteen ships and three hundred troops under Winfield Scott. By chance or design they steered first into Burling-ton Bay, where Vincent's supply depot was guarded by a single company of Canadian regulars. Word of the American sails reached York not far away, and the only troops in the capital, a few files of the Glengarry Regiment, set off hotfoot for Burlington. The Americans landed some troops at Burlington but they did not attack the depot. Instead, when the Glengarries were well on the road, they boarded their ships again and sailed around the corner to York, catching the town without a single soldier to defend it. This time the loot was poor. The seat of government had been removed to Kingston. The invaders again liberated the inmates of the town jail, demanded a formal parole from the sick soldiers in the army hospital, carried off some barreled flour from the shops, set fire to a newly built barrack and other army structures on Gibraltar Point, and left on August 2 for Niagara.

The rival fleets on Lake Ontario now staged a few of the more intricate movements of their formal dance. Sir James Yeo appeared off Niagara on August 7 while Chauncey was there, and for three days they tacked back and forth, always threatening a general battle but never coming to grips. When the American commander turned away to Sackets Harbor on August 11 he had lost four of his smaller ships. Two of these, tacking at the wrong time, had found themselves in the midst of the British squadron and surrendered. The others had foundered in a squall. Sir James, who had made no missteps, could claim the honors.

A month later there was a return performance, this time below York, where the honors were Chauncey's. In a brief exchange of gunfire Yeo's flagship *Wolfe* lost her main topmast and main yard and turned away into the safety of Burlington Bay, shielded by the skirts of her consorts, while Chauncey went off to pick up a few redcoats sailing in unarmed sloops to York. British army officers watching these graceful sweeps and curvettings of both squadrons referred to them cheerfully as "the Burlington races."

By this time General Dearborn had been replaced by James Wilkinson, an Armstrong man, and in line with Armstrong's plan the main American effort was concentrated against Kingston and Montreal. Although delayed, the plan was going well. By October 5 General Harrison had destroyed the remnant of Procter's army on the Thames, and although Dearborn's brigadiers had bungled things beyond the Niagara they still had a good bridgehead on the Canadian side about Fort George. Indeed things were going far better than Armstrong realized.

On October 9 Vincent heard the ill news from the Thames and it seemed likely that Harrison's cavalry would cross the peninsula to strike at his rear. Therefore he pulled the British troops back to Burlington, where he was joined by Procter with the tatters of his force. When Sir George Prevost heard of Procter's rout he, too, assumed that Harrison's army would march across to Lake Ontario, and he had no confidence in Vincent's ability to stand off the combined American armies of the Niagara and the Detroit. Also the new American moves against Montreal were now developing. Sir George advised Vincent to retire on Kingston, giving up the whole of the Great Lakes country without another shot. For the Americans this would have been victory indeed, whether they took Montreal or not.

Vincent chose to stand on his position at the west tip of Lake Ontario. His choice was not so mad as it seemed to Sir George. The American troops in the West were now entirely on Canadian ground and among a people quick to notice and report every move they made. It was not long before Vincent knew that General Harrison, satisfied with his success, had gone back to Detroit and sent most of his hard-riding Kentuckians home. That danger was gone. On the other hand he learned that most of the American regulars in the Niagara peninsula had been withdrawn for the drive on Montreal, and their places had been filled with three thousand New York militia and frontier volunteers commanded by General Mc-Clure, one of the looters of York.

This was a tempting prospect, but Vincent could expect no reinforcements and few supplies until the American movements against Montreal had been defeated, and he had to bide his time. Thus for nearly three months the Niagara peninsula remained in the hands of McClure's men, whose chief interest was plunder. They were joined by a renegade Irish Canadian named Willcox and a band of other outcasts who called themselves the Canadian Volunteers. The peninsula settlements and those of the Lake Erie shore were now at the mercy of wandering groups of McClure's men, of the Canadian renegades, and of every sort of frontier ruffian drawn to the prospect of easy loot, all in the name and under the flag of the United States.

This behavior brought an angry reaction. Like his American counterpart (they came of the same stock), the Canadian farmer and backwoodsman was used to self-reliance and his eye over a gun barrel was deadly. Men in the afflicted area began to form secret or open "associations" to resist the plunderers and to take revenge whenever possible. As the approach of winter clouded the Ontario sky, so the Canadian hatred of McClure's men darkened behind his lines. Foraging parties mysteriously disappeared. Stragglers perished. In one case the Canadians shot up a party of plunderers, conducted eight survivors to the British lines at Ancaster, and saw them tried, convicted, and hanged.

McClure had other troubles with his undisciplined troops. Many of his volunteers were at the end of their short enlistments. His militia felt themselves insecure in this hostile country. By the end of November he knew that the American drive on Montreal had failed utterly, and that in a few more weeks the British force at Burlington might be strong enough to attack. Indeed when General Vincent made an experimental prick at him with less than five hundred men he abandoned the whole countryside and pulled his troops back to Fort George.

This led to an outrage that disgraced American arms more than any military defeat of the war. In the previous spring when Winfield Scott's regulars captured Fort George they had made their approach behind the neighboring houses of Newark, which shielded them from the fort's cannon. McClure now feared that the British might do the same, and with canny foresight he had obtained from Secretary Armstrong a written permission to destroy the village as a military necessity. Armstrong had pointed out carefully; "You are hereby directed to apprise the inhabitants of this circumstance and invite them to remove themselves and their effects to some place of greater safety." This was in October when the days were still warm and the snows a month away.

McClure held his hand until the frigid month of December, when he decided to abandon Fort George and get back to the safety of Fort Niagara on the home side of the river. To cover his movement he awaited a snowstorm, and it came on December 12, 1813. Just as darkness fell he notified the inhabitants of Newark that their homes were to be destroyed, giving them two hours to get out with their household goods. During these two hours he passed most of his troops and stores across the river. At the end of that time his rear guard blew up their magazine in Fort George, tumbled the guns into the ditch, and set every building in Newark afire. Some of the able-bodied men of Newark were away on service with the British Army; others were now carried across the river and locked up in

Fort Niagara. The old and infirm, and four hundred women and children, were driven into a wild night of wind and snow to watch their homes making a torch for the American retreat.

Colonel Murray, commanding the British advanced posts, saw the glare and moved in too late to catch the American rear guard in retreat or to save the village. Newark was aflame and Fort George empty, with the tents of the American army still standing all about it. But the season was not too late for reprisal.

The American campaign against Montreal had collapsed. As soon as Sir George Prevost was sure that the American armies on that front had gone into winter quarters, he released some of his troops for action on the Niagara, and he sent with them two fire-eating general officers. Vincent, who had borne the British burden in the Niagara peninsula for so many anxious months, was sent on sick leave. It was a distinct loss, for Vincent knew the country and the troops of both sides better than any British soldier in the West except Procter, and the British mistakes of 1814 on the Niagara front might have been avoided if his exact mixture of caution and enterprise had been in charge. He was replaced by Lieutenant General Gordon Drummond, who brought with him as his right-hand man Major General Riall. They reached Fort George just after McClure's flight across the river. Drummond, Canadian born, was a British regular officer of energy and dashing experience in the wars against the French in Egypt and Holland. Phineas Riall had served in small affairs in the West Indies, like Sir George Prevost. He had arrived at his present rank chiefly by cash purchase in the peculiar system of those days, a short burly man of much courage but only routine ability, and without a warm drop of humanity in dealing with his own troops or with the enemy.

The black ruins of Newark and the tales of maltreatment of the Canadian inhabitants all along the Niagara enraged the British army. Drummond was hot for action at once, and on the night of December 18 he sent Colonel Murray across the river with 550 men. Carrying axes and scaling ladders they crept upon Fort Niagara in three assault groups. The orders were strict: To ensure surprise not a shot was to be fired. The fort must be taken with the bayonet alone.

A small party under Lieutenant Dawson killed the American pickets outside the main gate, found the gate unfastened, and dashed inside. They were followed quickly by Murray with the rest. The American main guard turned out valiantly but they went down in a stabbing rush of bayonets. A few riflemen held out for a time in the mess quarters and then all was over. Of the garrison only 20 men escaped to carry the news to McClure, far up the river at Buffalo. The redcoats had bayoneted 79 and taken 344 prisoners. They captured also the stores and equipment left there by McClure in a naïve belief that the campaign was over for the winter, including 3000 muskets and large quantities of wagons, harness, clothing, blankets, shoes, and ammunition. Murray's force had lost 11 men, a bargain price for the famous old fort with its 27 cannon, which remained in British hands until the war's end.

When Murray's men attacked Fort Niagara, General Riall was waiting up the river at Queenston with 500 troops and 500 Indians. The thud of a signal gun from Fort Niagara told the story there, and Riall sent the Indians across the river, following with his redcoats. The American militia guard at Lewiston fired a few shots and disappeared into the night. A party of renegade "Canadian Volunteers" under a "Major" Mallory offered the only resistance to the British troops, who killed eight or ten of them before they ran. At the sound of Indian yells the people of Lewiston and other villages along the American bank of the Niagara joined the militia in their flight. Drummond had given strict orders that the Indians were not to do any damage or violence to the inhabitants; but now with an indifference as guilty as McClure's deliberate act, General Riall allowed his wild allies to loot and burn every house and barn from Fort Niagara to Tonawanda Creek, a distance of twenty-five miles, as if this could in any way compensate the sufferings of Newark.

At Buffalo the egregious McClure assured the people that their town was safe, but by Christmas he had vanished, dropping the command of the American forces like a hot potato into the hands of Colonel Amos Hall. On the frosty night of December 29 General Riall crossed the upper end of the Niagara and attacked the fortified post at Black Rock, which covered the town of Buffalo. His fifteen hundred men, mostly British regulars, had little trouble in taking the place, scattering Hall's two thousand militia, and pushing on to take Buffalo, two or three miles away. In Black Rock Creek they found laid up for the winter two of Captain Perry's ships, *Ariel* and *Trippe*, also two of the prizes taken from Barclay, *Chippewa* and *Little Belt*. All of these they burned. Then their torches passed on to every building in Black Rock and Buffalo. With this final witless destruction the whole American side of the Niagara from Lake Erie to Lake Ontario was a desert of burned homes and abandoned farms.

So ended the campaign of 1813 in Upper Canada, with the Americans victorious on the Detroit front and the British on the Niagara. For simple humanity on both sides there was nothing but defeat. The war had taken an evil turn.

CHAPTER 35

1813

*Naval operations on Lake Champlain — The American
campaign against Montreal — Chrysler's Farm*

THE defenders of Lower Canada had spent an anxious but
anticlimactic year. Here the population was large compared
to that of Upper Canada, with greater resources in men and
supplies. Sir George Prevost, whatever his failings as a general, was
a governor whose mild conciliatory qualities had won the friendship
of the French-Canadian people and of their Church. When they
compared the truculence of American spokesmen like Henry Clay
with the almost timid deference of Prevost there was no doubt in
their minds about which government they preferred or on which side
they would fight.

During the past twenty years the Duke of Kent (Prince Edward),
always a close friend of the Canadian *élite*, had been diligent in
getting commissions and promotions in the British Army for sons
of French-Canadian families such as the De Salaberrys. These had
distinguished themselves in the wars against Napoleon. (Edouard de
Salaberry died gallantly in Wellington's storming of Badajoz, that
famous Spanish fortress, in April 1812. A short distance away in the
bloody moat lay the body of Frank Simcoe, the boy brought up at
Niagara and York, son of Upper Canada's first governor. It was the
first mingling of English and French-Canadian blood on a foreign
battlefield.) Colonel Charles de Salaberry had returned to Canada
and raised the first regiment of French-Canadian regular troops, the
Voltigeurs. His influence and example in the province were a powerful aid to Prevost. When the governor general called out six thousand
militia for the defense of Lower Canada the men came forward
quickly. Many others were ready to follow.

Apart from the militia actually under arms, Prevost had about
four thousand regular soldiers in the St. Lawrence Valley for the
campaign of 1813, and he was able to call on the Navy for detach-

ments of sailors and marines. The most tender spot in his defenses was the old one, the Richelieu Valley, where an American army coming through the Champlain pass could thrust at Montreal only forty miles away. British troops had thrown up fieldworks and batteries on Ile aux Noix (Nut Island), the cork in the Richeleiu River neck, and on both banks of the stream.

The Americans commanded Lake Champlain, for it lay entirely in their territory and they had the only warships on it. The famous old water pass to Canada, 125 miles long and at most 12 miles wide, made a natural canal for the movement of American troops, guns, and supplies toward the border. The other American approach to Montreal, by way of the upper St. Lawrence, was a disputed passage for much of its length, with British outposts along one bank and American outposts on the other. The British guarded the outlet of Lake Ontario with their fortified naval base at Kingston, and just across the nipple of the lake the Americans had created a similar base at Sackets Harbor.

In February 1813 General Dearborn had four thousand troops at Sackets Harbor, idle except for the necessary shoveling of snow about their barracks. According to Secretary Armstrong's plan for 1813, these troops were supposed to cross the frozen nipple of Lake Ontario and capture Kingston while the ice was strong enough to bear their passage. Dearborn shoveled and shuffled and the winter passed without an attack. The only ice crossings of the upper St. Lawrence were made by light forces, British and American, raiding each other's posts at Brockville and Ogdensburg. (At Ogdensburg the British found among the captured American cannon a pair of field guns taken from Burgoyne at Saratoga thirty-six years before, an odd little restoration.) After these raids the St. Lawrence remained quiet until autumn.

The only action of the summer came in the Champlain pass. Since his failure of the previous year Dearborn had kept an army with headquarters at Burlington, Vermont, halfway down the eastern side of Lake Champlain; and he had built barracks and stores at Plattsburg, Swanton and Champlain, all jumping-off places for the attack on Montreal. Commodore Macdonough also was at Burlington with a detachment of the United States Navy, fitting sloops and schooners to carry the American army up the lake and down the neck of the Richelieu when the proper moment came. The only warships on these waters were the United States sloops *Growler* and

Eagle, each of eleven guns and fifty or sixty men. The British at Ile aux Noix had nothing but three open barges, each armed with a single heavy cannon in the bow.

Early in June Macdonough sent both of his warships to test the British defenses of the upper Richelieu. This was a mistake. Once the ships left the open lake and dropped down the river they were open to attack from either bank if the British were alert — and they were. Sir James Yeo, in clearing out the former personnel of the squadron on Lake Ontario, had sent Captain Pring to command the three crude "gunboats" at Ile aux Noix. When scouts reported American warships coming down the river Pring took up a position to challenge them. At the same time Major Taylor of the Ile aux Noix garrison sent his redcoats to lie in wait on both banks. The *Growler* and *Eagle* found themselves in an awkward part of the river where it was impossible to swing and use their broadside cannon, while Pring's boats, low in the water and hard to hit, were able to shoot at the American hulls near the water line. The *Eagle* was soon badly holed, her crew had to run her aground, and both ships came under a pelter of musket balls. After three hours they surrendered.

Thus by the fortune of war, always fickle and often ridiculous, the British obtained the only warships in the Champlain pass and with them command of the lake. Sir James Yeo, busy with his own concerns on Lake Ontario, would spare neither men nor equipment for Pring on Lake Champlain. However H.M.S. *Wasp* lay at Quebec and her Captain Everard was curious to see naval action on a lake in the midst of the forest. He came to Ile aux Noix with some officers and men and found Pring busy repairing the captured ships. Pring had changed their names whimsically from *Growler* to *Chubb* and from *Eagle* to *Finch*, in keeping with their size and armament, and by the end of July he was ready for action. He and Everard sailed into Lake Champlain with these sloops, the three gunboats, and nine hundred British infantry in *bateaux*. At Plattsburg the garrison of state militia under General Mooers promptly vanished into the woods. The redcoats landed, burned the barracks, the blockhouse and the military storehouses, and carried away a large stock of supplies and ammunition. They did much the same at Saranac, Champlain and Swanton. Everard went on down the lake with the *Chubb* and *Finch*. General Hampton, commanding the army at Burlington, and Commodore Macdonough and his sailors, had to stand by helplessly while Everard seized and destroyed the sailing craft which were to convey the American force to the frontier for the attack on Montreal.

In the orthodox military mind, always comparing the ease of water transport with the sweat and difficulty of a backwoods march, there was a strong tendency to lean on the mast instead of the musket. Both Sir George Prevost and Wade Hampton were victims of this delusion. In this case Hampton refused to move a soldier until an American squadron rode the lake again. Yet the British force at Ile aux Noix was too small to attempt anything more than a raid, and an American march by backwoods tracks to the head of the Richelieu would have forced Pring off the lake altogether. Hampton did nothing and the summer passed without a blow at Montreal.

By that time there was a change in the American army command, for General Dearborn was now thoroughly discredited. On July 6 Secretary Armstrong invited General James Wilkinson to leave his post at New Orleans and take charge of the invasion of Canada. ("Why should you remain in your land of cypress when patriotism and ambition equally invite you to one where grows the laurel?") It was a strange choice, for Wilkinson's career had been one long record of incompetence and fraud, beginning with theft of army funds during the War of the Revolution and including a period as a Spanish spy and a plotter with Aaron Burr in the long years since. Why Secretary Armstrong chose this shady adventurer for the northern command in 1813 remains one of the mysteries of the war.

Another was his choice of Wade Hampton to lead Wilkinson's right wing from Lake Champlain. Hampton also was a relic of the Revolution, in which his only fighting experience had been with a band of swamp guerillas harrying the southern Loyalists and the British communication lines in Carolina. Since then he had risen by slow degrees to the rank of brigadier in the regular army, and he was serving in Virginia when Armstrong posted him to Lake Champlain in July 1813. Hampton was not merely incompetent, he had a sour jealousy of Wilkinson as commander in chief. If the British themselves had been allowed to pick the leaders of the forces moving against Lower Canada they could not have chosen a pair more certain to bring about an American defeat.

The summer had almost gone when General Wilkinson, after a leisurely journey from the deep South, arrived to take over the campaign against Montreal. He reached Sackets Harbor on August

12 and Secretary Armstrong arrived there in person in September to hurry the invasion and see Montreal doomed before the cold weather came. The boldness and success of Pring and Everard on Lake Champlain had convinced Armstrong that the British force on the Richelieu was too strong for a direct attack on Montreal. He now took a leaf from the British army book of 1760, when Jeffrey Amherst had the same problem in the invasion of French Canada. In that ancient campaign Amherst had made his main attack with a wide left hook by way of Lake Ontario and the upper St. Lawrence. The only difficulty now was that the British also knew the book. A new touch was required.

Therefore the main American army, led by Wilkinson in person, would first threaten Kingston in combination with Commodore Chauncey's squadron, as if the whole purpose were to seize that place and strangle the British supply line to Upper Canada before the winter set in. This would compel Sir George Prevost to send troops to Kingston at the expense of Montreal. The American army would then turn away swifty and dive down the St. Lawrence. At the same time General Hampton would quit Lake Champlain and side-step westward through the woods to the Indian village of St. Régis on the St. Lawrence. There the two American armies would unite and descend on Montreal's back door while Sir George Prevost still awaited the main attack in the Richelieu Valley. In October the plan was set afoot and afloat.

Wilkinson's movement from Sackets Harbor was delayed by a damaging storm, but by October 29 his army was on Grenadier Island, four miles from the outpour of Lake Ontario and in easy striking distance of Kingston. Chauncey's ships were there blockading Kingston and preparing to move the American army's guns and supplies down the St. Lawrence as far as Prescott, where the rapids began. Sir James Yeo did not challenge Chauncey's squadron, although some small armed craft got out of Kingston and harried the American transports. Meanwhile ten inches of snow had fallen, an early and ominous taste of winter. Secretary Armstrong, having seen the troops off, left Sackets Harbor at once for the more congenial climate of Washington.

At dawn on November 5 General Wilkinson turned away down the St. Lawrence with 8000 infantry, two regiments of cavalry, 38 field guns and 20 siege guns. All of the troops were embarked in a fleet of 300 boats and scows, especially built for the descent of the

St. Lawrence rapids, an imposing array passing among the Thousand Islands and down the broad stream below. So far all looked well, but the feint at Kingston had failed in its purpose. Sir George Prevost, far from sending troops from Montreal, had recalled from Kingston several companies of Canadian militia under Colonel Macdonell. The British commander at Kingston had only two weak battalions of regulars, one of which had come from the Niagara front a few days before. As soon as Wilkinson's intention was clear, Colonel J. W. Morrison with 560 soldiers picked from these battalions embarked in boats and followed the American army down the St. Lawrence.

There were British observation posts along the Canadian bank, each manned by a few militia, but the only fortified place was Prescott, where Fort Wellington's guns commanded a stretch of the stream opposite the American village of Ogdensburg. Wilkinson decided to by-pass this battery rather than waste time in its capture. He landed his troops and marched them four miles down the American bank, while his crews ran the boats past the British guns in the dark of a long November night. This was done with finesse. By November 8 the American army was camped at a place called the White House, eighteen miles below Ogdensburg and roughly halfway between Lake Ontario and Montreal. So far all had gone well. There was no word from General Hampton, but there was no reason to suppose that he had met any serious difficulty on his march through the woods from Plattsburg.

On that day (November 8) the British force from Kingston reached Prescott, where they picked up several companies of regulars and militia, bringing the total to about eight hundred men. They were now at the head of the St. Lawrence rapids. The American army was moving down the rapids cautiously and Wilkinson had placed Brigadier Boyd with a brigade of all arms on the Canadian bank to guard against attack. At the same time he sent General Jacob Brown down the Canadian bank to secure the passage as far as the foot of the dangerous Long Sault Rapids, where his scouts reported a large British force.

The only British troops at that spot were three hundred militia and a few Indians gathered by Captain Dennis of the 49th Regiment, who had distinguished himself at Queenston Heights. Dennis destroyed the lone bridge over a creek that Brown's troops had to cross and concealed his men along the wooded bank. At the approach of the Americans they shot at every head that showed and the Indians made their customary noise, so that Brown felt obliged to deploy his troops and bring up artillery for a formal attack. This took several hours of November 10, and having gained that much valuable delay Dennis was able to slip away intact, removing the military stores from Cornwall as he went.

By this time General Wilkinson was aware of Morrison's redcoats and militia coming down the river behind him. The thudding of Brown's guns argued a strong British force ahead of him as well. His blood, thinned by the Louisiana climate, did not take kindly to the bleak Canadian weather, and in notes headed "From My Bed" he advised Brown of his situation and ordered Brigadier Boyd to watch the British at his rear and if necessary "turn about and beat them." All through a rainy night he awaited news from below. At mid-morning on November 11 he learned that Brown had reached the foot of the Long Sault safely and he set the rest of his boats and troops in motion down the rapids to join them. Just then Boyd found that the British behind him were no longer a floating shadow. They were ashore, in plain sight, close to his camp and ready to pounce as soon as he tried to go on down the rapids. He turned about to beat them as his orders prescribed. The scene was a strip of fields between the St. Lawrence and an ash swamp, the farm of one John Chrysler.

Chrysler's farm lay on a bend in the river and the Montreal-Kingston highway wound around the shore. The American boats were drawn up below the curve and they had pitched their tents on the inner side of the road. The British troops were posted about Chrysler's farmhouse and along a rough lane between the river road and the swamp. Colonel Morrison had a mixed force of British and Canadian regulars, militia and Indians, in all 830 men with 3 guns. Brigadier Boyd had 1800 regular infantry and cavalry with 6 guns. Under a capable commander these troops could have destroyed Morrison's force in one shock where it stood, in the manner of Procter's rout on the Thames less than a month before.

Instead Boyd tossed his infantry units piecemeal toward the British muskets. The redcoats were able to beat off one attack and, turning smartly, to shatter another and another. He used his cavalry just as badly, and General Covington, conspicuous on a white charger, was among the slain. The weather was cold, with flurries of snow and squalls of sleet, so that at times the battlefield was covered with a slippery white slush. It was a miserable day and a strange affair — strange because Boyd's regiments were not the uncertain American troops of the previous year but trained soldiers with brave and skillful officers. (After the battle Morrison sent a note across the river asking the name of the colonel commanding the 25th U. S. Infantry, which had been handled admirably, and expressing a hope of meeting him in friendship when the war ended.)

As the British themselves were to learn in another year, the finest troops can be defeated by their own general, no matter how favorable the odds. So Boyd's brigade was defeated, indeed driven from Chrysler's pastures by a final rush of British bayonets. Only the approach of fresh troops from Wilkinson's reserve saved them from destruction. As it was they got over the river to the American side leaving 100 prisoners in Morrison's hands. Their battle casualties had been 339. The British had lost 181.

To Wilkinson, still spending most of his time in bed and complaining of his ills, the affair at Chrysler's farm was a mere rear-guard action and the loss of no account. But as he went on down the St. Lawrence he had the specter of a small but hard-hitting British force always at his heels, while the country militia turned out to harry his flanks along the way. (His dispatches complained of "the universal hostility of the male inhabitants of the country.") However he was now well on the way to Montreal and close to his rendezvous with Wade Hampton. Before him the river widened into Lake St. Francis, where on the south bank the army from Plattsburg would be waiting to join in the final stroke.

CHAPTER 36

1813

The fight at Chateauguay — Peace overtures

WADE HAMPTON had left his New York militia to defend the Champlain pass and set off on October 21 with
four thousand regular infantry, a squadron of cavalry and
ten guns. The air distance from Plattsburg to the St. Lawrence at
Lake St. Francis was only seventy miles, and although the country
was rough and thickly wooded his soldiers at the end of two days
were pitching their tents on Canadian soil beside the Chateauguay
stream. In front of their camp lay seven miles of open farm land,
then a stretch of swamp and forest, and beyond that more farm land
reaching fifteen miles to the St. Lawrence. A country road ran
through the farms and woods, and in the woods Hampton's scouts
discovered men in Canadian uniforms.

The British had been warned beforehand of Hampton's movement, probably from gossip drifting over the frontier from Plattsburg, and Colonel Charles de Salaberry had moved quickly to set
up a defense on the Chateauguay road. His force was largely
French-Canadian, including four companies of his own gray-clad
Voltigeurs. Altogether he had on the spot 800 Canadians and 170
Indians, and he was in a strong position in the forest on the left
bank of the Chateauguay with several shallow ravines across his
front. The only road passed through the woods on that side of the
river, and the stream itself was too deep to cross on foot except
at a ford in De Salaberry's rear.

General Hampton paused to drag up his artillery and take stock
of the situation. He was slow about it. Three days passed before he
made up his mind to attack. In these days De Salaberry's men made
their position formidable. To guard the ford at the rear, they built a
thick log breastwork along the left bank and filled it with riflemen.
They barred the road leading up to their position for a mile by fell-

ing trees across it. Behind each of the ravines they raised a log rampart from which poked the muskets of De Salaberry's regulars. The Indians lay in ambush on the right flank.

On the evening of October 25 Hampton made his battle plan. His scouts had seen the river ford, which seemed the key to the Canadian position, and he sent Colonel Purdy with a regiment of regular infantry to approach it by a night march, circling through the woods. Purdy was to storm across the ford at daybreak, throwing the Canadian rear into alarm and confusion, and at the sound of the firing Hampton would send the rest of his force under General Izard to attack the position from the front.

Nothing went well. Purdy's men became lost in the dark, wandering in cedar swamps far from the river. Daylight came, and as morning grew there was still no firing from the Canadian rear. Izard's regiments moved up until they were confronted by the first of the ravines with its breastwork and menacing muskets on the other side. The trees made it impossible to bring up their cannon, and their own volleys of musketry had little effect on the breastwork or its defenders.

It was well on toward noon of October 26 when Purdy's wandering men came out on the riverbank and moved down to the ford. A blast of aimed musket balls whistled across the stream from the defending Voltigeurs. The American soldiers hesitated. While they were hesitating De Salaberry marched part of Macdonell's militia to support the Voltigeurs at the ford. At the same time he sent a militia company, some Indians, and all his buglers over the river farther down. As so often in this war, a determined front and an impudent bluff on the flank won the trick. Unable to face the deadly shooting at the ford, Purdy's soldiers heard in the woods behind them a hullabaloo of Canadian shouts, Indian yells, and half a dozen bugles sounding the British Army call to advance. They turned and ran. A few swam the Chateauguay at a safe distance from the firing, and these chilled and sodden refugees stumbled into Hampton's headquarters with a tale of redcoats and Indians coming on the scene from the direction of Montreal.

Long gusts of musketry rattled in the woods across the river, where in fact various groups of Purdy's men were firing at each other. The tale seemed true, and Hampton ordered General Izard to draw his troops back on the camp. George Izard was a good soldier, his regiments were in fighting order, and De Salaberry stood fast in his position awaiting the next attack. It never came. At the end of three days Hampton retired up the Chateauguay and the battle was never fought. Four thousand American soldiers had been turned back by 400 resolute French Canadians — for the invaders never got past De Salaberry's first line of defense and half his force was not engaged at all. The Canadians had lost 22 men. The American loss was given as 38, but Canadian scouts picked up 20 prisoners and counted 90 scattered graves along the river-banks.

In the wordy storm that followed this affair, Colonel Purdy swore that Hampton was drunk during the fight and Hampton charged coldly that Purdy's blunders had ruined his battle plan. But there never was any doubt about the blame for the sequel to the "battle" of Chateauguay. That was Hampton's alone.

On November 12, just after General Wilkinson reached the foot of the Long Sault Rapids, within ten miles of the agreed rendezvous, he received a message. He was doubtless glad to see the messenger, Colonel Atkinson, the inspector general of Hampton's army. But there was no cheer in the message that Atkinson, riding fast and far, had carried around De Salaberry's flank posts on the river. It was from Wade Hampton, dated November 11, and it said that he had decided to break off the campaign and he was marching back to Plattsburg for the winter.

Wilkinson called a council of his officers and put Hampton's letter before them. The season was far gone. The snow and sleet of an early winter had stung their faces ever since they left Sackets Harbor. The upriver retreat with its difficult rapids was watched by Morrison's force. Before them at Montreal Sir George Prevost, unmolested by Hampton's vanished army, could now call in every man and musket on the lower river. The council of war decided that the only course was to seek winter quarters on the friendly side of the St. Lawrence, within easy sled journey of Plattsburg for supply, and where the flank march against Montreal could be resumed in the spring.

Wilkinson chose the Salmon River, and at a place then called French Mills (now Fort Covington, New York), he drew up his boats and scows and built a great camp of huts to shelter his troops through the cold weather. When the news reached Armstrong and his War Department they took a dubious view of this, seeing Wilkinson exposed to attack by British troops on snowshoes when full winter came. In January they ordered him to safer ground. He must detach Brown with two thousand men to make their way back across country to protect Sackets Harbor, and with the rest he was to join Hampton at Plattsburg. Early in February Wilkinson set fire to the long ranges of huts, the blockhouses he had built to defend them, the twelve gunboats and the three hundred *bateaux* and scows in which he had descended the St. Lawrence. As the smoke rolled up to the winter sky, he sent off Brown and retired with what supplies and equipment he could drag over the snow toward Lake Champlain.

The British were aware of his retreat at once. Colonel Scott with 1100 troops struck across the ice from Coteau du Lac and harried Wilkinson's rear to within a few miles of Lake Champlain, capturing nearly a hundred sleds laden with baggage and stores.

So, a few weeks past the turn of a new year, the campaign of 1813 against Canada came to a close. On the whole it was a triumph for the defense, but the British had no ground for complacency. Their thin line of redcoats, militia and Indians had fought with skill and audacity, but the germ of American defeat was in the American body. Never before or since in the history of the United States has their formidable strength put forth such feeble fingers or directed them with such fuddled brains. How long could it last?

The American people were still sharply divided over the policy of hammering the Canadians for British sins committed on the high seas. Now that Tecumseh was dead and the British had been driven off Lake Erie and the Detroit River, the people of the western states and territories, the very hatchery of the War Hawks, were inclined to fold their wings if not their tongues. But at the same time American military pride had been stung by the ludicrous defeats in the north, and the Army was determined to vindicate itself. Hard training and the harder knocks of war had begun to produce American officers and men equal to the veteran soldiers of the Canadian defense. Whatever the political divisions in their country, the American soldiers on the Canadian frontier were firm in their belief that victory had to come before any talk of peace.

Honor and vindication are holy words to men-at-arms. Pride and vindictiveness are their shadows, and in the rancor of war the shadow often goes by the shining name. The Americans were not alone in mistaking one for the other. British men-at-arms shared the illusion, not only in Canada but among the powerful formations in Spain and in Britain itself. Letters from British soldiers in Canada describing their lonely struggles had been read with sympathy by their comrades across the sea. Now that the French empire was crumbling, there was a light undercurrent of gossip in the officers' mess tents and even in the War Office, saying that when "Boney" had been knocked off his perch — and before the politicians could disband the Army — there would be a chance to pay off the score with "Brother Jonathan." The Royal Navy, smarting from defeat in many a ship-to-ship duel with the expert and hard-hitting Yankee frigates and brigs, had much the same view; indeed all through 1813 the Royal Navy had been moving ships across the Atlantic for the blockade of the American coast and for a final reckoning when at last the Army came.

Thus revenge, whatever name it went by, burned under the uniforms on both sides. Yet the civilian heads of government were able to see past the irritable jiggle of epaulets. President Madison, despite the jibe of the Federalists, had never wanted the war in North America. Nor had Castlereagh, the man in power in Britain, whose brilliant and fanatical mind was devoted to the downfall of Napoleon and who saw the American war, whatever its rights or wrongs, as a waste of useful powder. Under his harsh drive during the year 1813 the British people had maintained at home and abroad no less than 230,000 soldiers and 140,000 sailors, had poured out huge sums in subsidies to their needy European allies and furnished them with nearly a million muskets and other war material — this in an age when mass production by machine was unknown. For the people of Great Britain it was a marvelous but costly output, and both Napoleon and Castlereagh knew that they could not keep it up indefinitely.

In 1813 these efforts had produced at last a hopeful crop of victories. The continental nations had risen and driven the Little Corporal back to his own borders on the east; Wellington's redcoats had fought their way from Portugal to the French border on the south; a large British home army now threatened to cross the Channel on the north. Nevertheless a cornered Napoleon was still a dangerous enemy, using his agile mind to inspire new French armies, to divide his enemies and delay the final crash.

While all this was going on, a small American peace dove had been fluttering uncertainly in the powder smoke of Europe. In the late summer of 1812 the Czar of Russia, anxious to keep Britain's undivided attention on their common enemy Napoleon, had offered to mediate in the North American war. John Quincy Adams, the American ambassador to Russia, had forwarded the offer to President Madison. Owing to the war-shattered communications of Europe and the long Atlantic passage, the offer did not reach Madison until March 1813. He sent off a commission of two able men, Bayard and Gallatin, who reached Moscow in July with instructions to hold out firmly for an end to the British practice of search and impressment at sea—the official excuse for "Mister Madison's War."

By this time however the Czar had lost all interest in the American war. Napoleon's Russian adventure had perished in the previous autumn, a powerful European alliance was closing in upon the French armies in Germany, and the British themselves had refused to send more than a handful of troops to Canada. For months the American commissioners cooled their heels in Moscow. But in the autumn of 1813 Britain's strong man Castlereagh turned his thoughts to the North American scene. He was a cold man. Simple humanity was not in his heart. He had come to see the age as a duel between Napoleon and himself, and humanity did not matter.

In the past twelve months much had happened on the far side of the Atlantic. For one thing the garrison of Canada had survived. Canadian geography was vague in England, even in the Admiralty and War Office. (Someone in the Admiralty's supply branch had sent Sir James Yeo a large number of water casks, assuming that the Great Lakes must be salt). All that was clearly known was that somehow, in a series of astonishing episodes, the American conquest had broken down in 1812 and again in 1813. Just what logical processes occurred in Castlereagh's mind regarding the American war toward the close of 1813 are difficult to estimate.

How much would a North American peace gain for the final round against Napoleon? The French Navy was insignificant now, and out of its own huge strength the British Navy had been able to send a large fleet to blockade Brother Jonathan. On the other hand the British Army's efforts in Canada, while expensive at such a distance, were only a drop compared to Wellington's busy bucket. An American peace would release ships which Castlereagh did not need; it could not free more than a brigade·or two for the battlefields of Europe. It seems more probable that the British Cabinet saw a chance to end the American war on their own terms before Napoleon fell, thus heading off an expensive war of revenge, the reckoning with Brother Jonathan of which many army and naval officers and a powerful group in Britain itself were talking. Whatever the ultimate motive, on November 4, 1813, sixteen days after Napoleon's defeat at Leipzig, Castlereagh wrote a letter to President Madison suggesting peace talks.

The Atlantic passage was always slow in the teeth of the late autumn gales, and winter had come when President Madison received this out-of-season olive branch. He could now weigh the year's events in Canada; the victories of Perry and Harrison in the West, the Niagara disasters, the shameful farce before Montreal. At home there was a new note of bitterness in the anti-war feeling of the eastern states, with threats of secession in New England — even some wild talk of union with the Canadian provinces. Abroad there was the shadow of Napoleon's impending collapse and of a Britain free to turn elsewhere the powerful fighting machine she had built up in twenty years of war. These things made a sum, even by the War Hawks' arithmetic. When Madison added it up he did not hesitate. His acceptance of a conference sailed across the sea and as the year closed he was choosing his peace commissioners. Meanwhile on both sides the generals and admirals would continue to have their way. The marching and shooting and burning in North America were to go on for another year before the civilians could have theirs.

CHAPTER 37

1814

Preparations for the final campaign — American raids in Ontario — American defeat at Mackinac — Canadian troops in Illinois

A S 1814 opened, Madison's peace commission took definite form. In January the United States Senate confirmed his appointment of John Quincy Adams, J. A. Bayard, Henry Clay and Jonathan Russell. In February the Senate confirmed the appointment of Swiss-born Albert Gallatin, who had been Secretary of the Treasury for the past thirteen years. Gallatin's careful work for a sound currency and government economy had been ruined by the war and he forsaw in this year the utter collapse of American finance, public and private. Henry Clay, most ardent of the War Hawks, had seen his group's chief aim won in the destruction of Tecumseh's power, Canada or no Canada, and his main concern at the peace conference was to insist that the British drop forever their notion of an independent "buffer state" of Indians in the West. Adams, a Yankee of the Yankees with a clear and general view, was chairman and the best mind on the commission.

As Adams, Bayard, and Gallatin made their way from Moscow to London and thence to Ghent, the neutral Belgian site of the peace conference, and as Clay and Russell crossed the sea, the armed forces of both nations prepared for the third and most violent campaign of the war. Among the people of the United States there was still no feeling of danger. Outside of Fort Niagara not a single British soldier stood on United States soil. The regular army of the United States still consisted of no more than twelve thousand trained and battleworthy troops, and nearly all of these were on the Canadian frontier. The defense of the whole Atlantic coast was left to assemblies of raw volunteers and militia. The British blockade, operating from bases at Halifax, Bermuda, and Jamaica, was now very tight. Except on a few raiding warships and the always daring privateers, the Stars and Stripes had vanished from the ocean.

Even American coastal trade, moving close inshore, sailed at a ruinous cost and risk. Traffic between the northern states and those of the South, even on the seaboard, moved largely by land. The chief sign of American distress was a universal groaning of wagon axles; but there were other signs. The scarcity of manufactured goods had led to speculation and a wild rise in prices. For lack of a national bank, and with the drying up of customs receipts and the absence of any form of direct taxation, the United States government was bankrupt. All these things had produced a dissatisfaction with the war that was no longer confined to the northeastern states. As the campaign of 1814 opened there was nothing like the ardent national spirit of '76.

For their part the British War Office had now evolved the bones of a policy for the North American war. While Napoleon survived, the British could not move armies across the Atlantic and for the present they saw no need. The Canadian garrison must be reinforced enough to meet the new American attack; but with sea power in their hands the British had no intention of relying on muskets five hundred or a thousand miles inland, where the Americans had the advantage of large native supplies and reinforcement close to the fighting scene. Instead they would exploit the oak walls of their blockade, landing at various points on the long and vulnerable American coast, keeping the seaboard population in a state of alarm. In its application this policy might defend Montreal by firing shots at Baltimore or Norfolk or New York. It might even fire a few at Washington.

Secretary of War Armstrong also had his plan. He had long recognized Montreal as the main target and Kingston as the key. So far his strategy had been ruined by worthless generals, an antique military organization, and badly trained troops. Now he had scrapped the old framework and now at last he got rid of the bungling generals. The 1814 campaign against Canada was to be directed by capable Jacob Brown, who would also command the attack on Kingston. The hardheaded Carolinian George Izard commanded the army in the Champlain pass and Winfield Scott was in charge on the Niagara. The Detroit front, which the British had not attempted to restore, was now recognized as unimportant, and this alone was left to militia and a second-rate officer in command.

On the Great Lakes the American squadron on Erie still ruled un-challenged. On Lake Ontario, Commodore Chauncey, like his British opponent, was still absorbed in the Alice-in-Wonderland game of building more and bigger ships with less and less intention of battle. On Lake Champlain, Commodore Thomas Macdonough now had a squadron easily capable of beating anything the British had been able to assemble in the upper waters of the Richelieu.

From the Canadian defense viewpoint also the situation was un-changed. Sir George Prevost watched Montreal with his main forces and a nervous eye. On the Niagara front General Drummond and his hotheaded aide Riall held their posts along the Canadian bank, itching for attack and chafing because their forces were still too small. With the Americans commanding Lake Erie, they had to face the strong chance of a slash at the root of their Niagara thumb. For that reason Drummond's defense of the Niagara frontier was like a gate hinged on the twin forts at the river mouth. Under a hard American thrust from the Erie side he would swing back on Lake Ontario, retiring his right wing to Burlington Bay.

The Canadian command also kept a definite view toward the upper lakes. The influence of the alert Nor'westers had much to do with this. Since Perry's victory the adjoining waters of Lake Huron had been at the Americans' command, but they had done nothing about it. To the British their connection with the trading posts in the far West was of great value and, in a military way, so was the ability of their garrison at Mackinac to rouse the western Indians and make disturbing raids into the central American plains. To rebuild the British squadron on Lake Erie was impossible, much as Drum-mond wanted it. American troops raiding from Detroit and Buffalo ravaged the whole Canadian shore, and General Drummond could not spare troops to defend it. Therefore the British sought to restore their old command of the western lakes by another route.

During 1814 they opened a naval base at Penetanguishene (chosen by the foresighted Simcoe long ago) where, dragging everything over the "Yonge Street" track from Toronto Bay, they planned to build a squadron that would dominate Huron and Michigan and secure the passage of goods to Superior and the far West. Had the war lasted into 1815, these slowly mounting activities would have obliged the American squadron on Lake Erie to sail into Huron and do battle or else resign the whole water past Detroit. As it happened, only light forces operated on the western lakes in 1814 and the whole of this immense area was at the mercy of a few armed schooners.

The western campaign of 1814 opened in the frosty month of February, when a small American force from Detroit raided Port Talbot on the Canadian shore of Erie. In May the Americans made a larger raid (there were many petty ones), this time at Port Dover. This village inside Long Point was less than fifty miles from Lake Ontario, and Drummond had posted a cavalry patrol to watch it. When five hundred American regulars under Colonel Campbell landed from naval craft the lone patrol withdrew before them. The Americans burned the settlements of Long Point and Dover and marched on to Ryerse. What happened there was described later by Amelia Ryerse Harris, then a young girl living with her widowed mother on the Ryerse farm, which had among its buildings a mill on which the local settlers depended to grind their flour.

"On the 14th the Americans burnt the village and mills of Dover; on the 15th as my mother and myself were sitting at breakfast the dogs kept up a very unusual barking. I went to the door to discover the cause; when I looked up I saw the hillside and fields as far as the eye could reach covered with American soldiers. Two men stepped from the ranks, selected some large chips, came into the room where we were standing and took coals from the hearth, without speaking a word. My mother knew instinctively what they were going to do. She went out and asked to see the commanding officer. A gentleman rode up to her and said he was the person she asked for. She entreated him to spare her property and said she was a widow with a young family. He answered her civilly and respectfully and expressed regret that his orders were to burn, but that he would spare the house, which he did; and he said as a sort of justification of his burning that the outbuildings were used as a barrack and the mill furnished flour for the British troops. Very soon we saw columns of smoke arise from every building, and of what at early morn had been a prosperous homestead, at noon there remained only smouldering ruins. My father had been dead less than two years. Little remained of all his labours excepting the orchard and cultivated fields."

In August a swarm of American backwoodsmen and Indians descended again on Port Talbot, destroyed the buildings and mills of crusty old Colonel Talbot, pillaged fifty farms, and drove off every horse. This sort of thing was now cruelly familiar to loyal Canadians of the Erie shore all the way from Niagara to Detroit. Not even the settlers who professed American sympathies (many for instance in the Thames Valley) were safe. The Thames farmers had suffered from Hull's raid in 1812 and from Harrison's wild Kentuckians in 1813. In the late autumn of 1814 they were scourged again, this time by 750 mounted riflemen under Colonel McArthur. The horsemen left Detroit on October 22 and for three weeks ravaged the valley and beyond as far as Grand River, where a detachment of redcoats turned them back.

Meanwhile there was a sudden activity on the western lakes, where all had been quiet since the British capture of Mackinac and the Indians' capture of Fort Dearborn (Chicago) in 1812. In the interval Canadian fur traders had been able to carry on business reaching as far as Prairie du Chien on the Mississippi, where there was a settlement of French Canadians and a trading post for the western Indians. In the spring of 1814 a small American force prepared to move up the Mississippi and seize Prairie du Chien. A more ambitious American force at Detroit prepared to recapture Mackinac and seize the Canadian fur posts at the entrance to Lake Superior. The British got wind of these expeditions. They were now making much use of the "Yonge Street" portage as far as Nottawasaga Bay on Lake Huron. As the spring sun rotted the ice about that shore, Colonel Robert McDouall started in boats from the Nottawasaga River with two dozen seamen, a company of Newfoundland regulars, one or two field guns, and a quantity of stores. They reached Mackinac on May 18 after a voyage of three hundred miles.

The Detroit expedition was delayed and nothing hostile appeared at Mackinac for two months. In the interval McDouall learned that the Americans had captured Prairie du Chien. The Mississippi was almost five hundred miles away but McDouall determined to retake the post. Other than his small garrison, he had available a company of the Michigan Fencibles, a frontier unit drawn from the Canadian population about Lake Michigan and commanded by Colonel William McKay, a former Nor'wester. With 150 Fencibles and a picked war party of Green Bay Indians, McKay headed for the Mississippi by way of Green Bay, Lake Winnebago and the Wisconsin River, taking with him a light field cannon. On July 17 he appeared at Prairie du Chien (fifty miles above the present city of Dubuque, Iowa) and with his cannon forced the American gunboat *Governor Clark* to drop down the river. On the next day the small

American garrison surrendered. McKay promptly sent a party down the river to arouse the Indians and attack the *Governor Clark* and other American river craft at Rock Island, Illinois.

The affair, carried out at such a distance, was a feat in itself. Its impact on the War Hawk politicians down the Mississippi and up the Ohio was more remarkable still, for at this very time William Henry Harrison was dictating a new Treaty of Greenville to the tribes formerly led by Tecumseh, in which they promised peace to the United States and declared themselves enemies of their former British friends. The treaty, made on July 22, 1814, was the climax of Harrison's effort for years. He had resigned his army commission after the victory on the Thames and devoted himself to this end. And now, at the moment of his triumph, came news of British bayonets and another feathered swarm whooping in the West. McKay's impudent thrust had served a wider purpose than he dreamed. More than ever now the War Hawks' minds were fixed on their local interests, regardless of what happened in the East. These interests were important far across the sea where their own man Clay sat with his knees under the peace table and his powerful voice across the top.

While this was going on, the American expedition from Detroit floated up Lake Huron with 5 warships and 400 seamen under Commander St. Clair and 750 soldiers under Colonel Croghan, the hero of Fort Stephenson. The British had abandoned their army post on St. Joseph Island for the better one at Mackinac, and Croghan contented himself with burning the shacks of the settlers there and at Sault Ste. Marie, where his soldiers looted and burned the village and the fur post of the North West Company. He now sailed to capture Mackinac, the source of the new British and Indian adventures in the West. Colonel McDouall's garrison had been weakened by the dispatch of McKay's force to the Mississippi and he was able to muster no more than ninety redcoats, fifty backwoodsmen and fifty Indians. With these he slipped out and met Croghan's cautious advance in the woods between the fort and landing place. For a time the outcome was doubtful, but the deadly shooting of his men and the old magic of the Indian yell turned the trick. Croghan's force panicked and fled back to the ships. From this time, Fort Mackinac flew the British flag undisturbed until the war's end.

St. Clair burned a British supply schooner in the mouth of the Nottawasaga River, left the armed schooners *Tigress* and *Scorpion* in

Lake Huron to prevent other supplies from reaching Mackinac, and returned with Croghan's soldiers to Detroit. The last word of this emtpy venture came late in August, when one hundred Canadian soldiers and backwoodsmen under Lieutenant Worsley left Mackinac in boats and in a surprise attack captured both *Tigress* and *Scorpion* off St. Joseph Island.

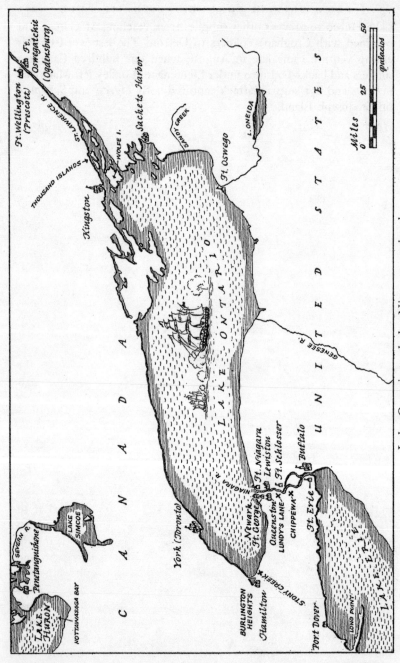

Lake Ontario and the Niagara peninsula
during the War of 1812

CHAPTER 38

1814

*British raid on Oswego — American victory at Chippewa
— The battle of Lundy's Lane*

WHEN General Jacob Brown assumed formal command of
the American army at Sackets Harbor in the spring of
1814 he had firmly in mind Secretary Armstrong's aim to
capture Kingston. So had the British command in Upper Canada.
General Drummond had posted himself there with his small reserve.
In the Kingston yard the naval carpenters hurried work on a pair
of powerful new frigates which were expected to give Sir James
Yeo a clear mastery of Lake Ontario. All of this in turn was
known to the Americans, and Armstrong decided early in the year
that before General Brown made his leap at Kingston, Drummond's
redcoats must be decoyed away to the old battlefields along the
Niagara.

Accordingly he wrote Brown in March: "You will immediately
consult with Commodore Chauncey about the readiness of the fleet
for a descent on Kingston the moment the ice leaves the lake. If he
deems it practicable and you think you have troops enough to carry
it you will attempt the expedition. In such an event you will use
the enclosed as a *ruse de guerre.*"

The *ruse* was a brief paper of false instructions intended for British
eyes: "Public sentiment will no longer tolerate the possession of
Fort Niagara by the enemy. You will therefore move the division
which you have brought from French Mills and invest that post.
General Tompkins will cooperate with you with 500 militia, and
Colonel Scott, who is to be made a brigadier, will join you. You
will receive your instructions at Onondago Hollow."

What followed was the most fantastic of all the blunders that
characterized the War of 1812. Brown misunderstood the words
ruse de guerre. In confusing his orders he had the aid of Commodore Chauncey, who was ailing, cautious, jealous of any dic-

tation by the Army, the perfect counterpart of Yeo on the other side of the lake. Chauncey was just completing two new frigates, *Mohawk* and *Superior*, but to his mind these were not enough, and his sole ambition for 1814 was to confound Yeo's carpenters by building at Sackets Harbor a pair of line-of-battle ships larger than any British ship yet laid down, in fact the biggest warships in the world. He did not consider an attack on the Kingston batteries practicable while Yeo's ships were there, and Brown's two thousand soldiers seemed too few to storm the place while Drummond's men were there. With these fixed ideas he convinced himself and General Brown that Armstrong's first document was the *ruse* and the real intention in the second.

Accordingly Brown's muskets trudged away by the slushy March roads along the south shore of Lake Ontario. He halted at Onondago Hollow for the promised instructions, but none were there. He marched on to the village of Batavia, fifty miles behind the Niagara front, where he camped for a month awaiting them. At last he had word from the Secretary of War explaining the mistake. Apparently Armstrong accepted it philosophically. Now that Brown's troops were at the wrong end of Lake Ontario, they might as well fight there. As Armstrong put it, "If you left the harbor [Sackets] with a competent force for its defence, go on and prosper. Good consequences are sometimes the result of mistakes."

With this blessing Brown moved on to Buffalo and prepared another invasion of the Niagara peninsula. Once more the American blow had been diverted from the Canadian throat to the finger tips.

Drummond and Yeo now had one of the golden chances of the war. Brown's departure had left open to attack not only Sackets Harbor but the busy port of Oswego, through which poured the main stream of American naval and military supplies from the Hudson Valley. Commodore Chauncey, absorbed in his shipyards, was unlikely to sail out and challenge Yeo, and the American garrisons were small. Yeo now had eight ships of war including the new frigates *Prince Regent* of sixty guns and *Princess Charlotte* of forty-four guns, both launched at Kingston in April and completely equipped and manned by the first of May. The other ships had been carefully refitted; Yeo had busied himself in changing their rigs, their armament, and even their names, thus creating a frantic puzzle not only for Chauncey but for generations of naval historians.

Sir George Prevost as usual was shy about offensive action, but Drummond and Yeo won his consent to a raid on Oswego, the weaker place. Drummond marched a thousand troops aboard the ships and arrived off Oswego at noon on May 5. The port was defended by a battery of six guns and three hundred regular soldiers under Colonel Mitchell. Under this meager guard Oswego held an expensive mass of weapons, stores, and equipment destined for Chauncey's new ships and for Brown's wandering army.

A Nelson would have gone in and seized all this before his enemy could organize a real defense or move the stores. Yeo had no spark of his old commander's fire. Cautiously he sent in light craft to reconnoiter, and wasted the rest of the day and night before he deemed it safe to attack. In the twenty hours thus granted Colonel Mitchell had drawn in militia from the countryside, bringing his force to six hundred, and like disturbed and purposeful ants the people of Oswego had removed most of the war supplies to a point eighteen miles up the Oswego River.

At last the British troops got ashore. A wild Highland yell and a bayonet dash of the Glengarries scattered the Oswego militia. The gunners in the battery kept up a tart fire on the ships and landing parties while Drummond's soldiers and marines climbed the bluff on which it stood, but after a ten-minute scuffle there Mitchell and his men slipped away up the river. It was not a glorious affair. The Americans lost 69 men, most of whom were prisoners, and the British lost 95. The spoils were only a fraction of what they might have been, although the expedition found and carried off 2400 barrels of provisions, much ammunition, some heavy cannon (which later made a useful battery for the Kingston defenses), and the scuttled schooner *Growler*, which Yeo's sailors raised and sailed away as a prize.

Yeo was now bold enough to blockade Sackets Harbor, pinching Chauncey where it hurt, for the American commander was anxious to get guns and cables for his new ships and such heavy stuff could only come by water from Oswego. Fenimore Cooper's old comrade, Captain Woolsey of the United States Navy, volunteered to fetch guns and cables for the new frigate *Superior* from the dump at Oswego Falls. He set off from Oswego on the evening of May 28 with 19 large boats, manned by his sailors and guarded by a company of riflemen. The boats moved slowly through the night, burdened with 35 heavy cannon and a dozen mooring cables, and at dawn Yeo sighted them and sent 175 sailors and marines in boats to intercept. Woolsey, also watchful, turned in to the shore and crept up a winding inlet called Big Sandy Creek, where a painful surprise awaited the British tars. Woolsey had arranged for a war party of Oneida Indians to follow him along the shore. These and his riflemen ambushed Yeo's boat party in the narrow wooded creek, and after 68 of the British had been killed or wounded, the rest surrendered. Significantly it was the heaviest loss suffered by Sir James' squadron in the whole course of the war. Woolsey's guns and cables, dragged overland the rest of the way, came safely to Sackets Harbor. In truth the British raid on Oswego had accomplished nothing. The port had to be held firmly to embarrass the American supply line to Sackets Harbor and Niagara, and for that Sir George Prevost would not spare the troops.

Meanwhile the British intelligence had failed to detect the meaning of Brown's strange march away from Sackets Harbor. After the Oswego raid General Drummond remained with his thousand men at Kingston in a belief that Chauncey, as soon as he had equipped his two new frigates, would sail there with the American army. As June passed into July, this left General Riall still guarding the Niagara frontier with his thin spread of redcoats and militia. Riall was not unduly worried. For one thing, like Drummond, he thought that Brown's force was still at Sackets Harbor. For another his brave but blind temper still reckoned one veteran redcoat, British or Canadian, worth two or three Americans — which was no longer true. Under the short blue or gray jacket, the white trousers and the black fire-bucket shako of Brown's regulars marched a new kind of American soldier, steady, alert, well drilled in battle formations and movements, a match for any British regular with the bayonet and usually a better shot.

Secretary Armstrong, thwarted once more in his direct plan, had adjusted it to strike at Kingston by the long way around Lake Ontario. It offered some advantages. The British had only light forces on the Niagara and their strategy was familiar from experience. Therefore General Brown should join his regiments to the well-trained troops of Winfield Scott on the Niagara, cross the eastern tip of Lake Erie where the British were weakest, destroy their force on the upper river at its Chippewa mustering point, and then march along the Niagara scarp to Burlington Heights at the west tip of Lake Ontario, ignoring the twin forts at the Niagara mouth. At Burlington, Commodore Chauncey would meet him with reinforcements and supplies, and the American army would move on Kingston by land and water, leaving the remnant of Riall's troops at the Niagara mouth to wither for lack of supplies.

On July 3, 1814, General Brown shipped his forces from Buffalo and landed them on both sides of the British post at Fort Erie, whose 170 men surrendered tamely at the first cannonade. The way was now open to Chippewa. Once more the quiet fields and orchards of the Niagara peninsula were to know the tramp and jingle of marching regiments and the sharper sounds of battle. The population were to learn something else. This time a greedy mob of Senecas and other American Indians came with the American troops.

When General Riall heard of the new invasion he moved with his usual fierce energy, marching 1500 troops up to Chippewa and calling in 300 militia and 300 Canadian Indians. He had with him a troop of the 19th Dragoons (the only British regular cavalry regiment in Canada), who met and skirmished with the American advance as far as Street's Creek, a small stream flowing into the Niagara a short march from Chippewa Creek, where the British force was encamped. The land between these gullies was an expanse of uncut hayfields belonging to the farms along the riverside. This became a battlefield.

Riall had a good defensive position with Chippewa Creek and its lone log bridge as his front, but he was a thruster by instinct and on the morning of July 5 the tramp of his columns woke the hollow echoes of the bridge. The American army was more than twice the size of his own, but his dragoons had seen only their skirmishers and Indians and he rashly assumed that Fort Erie was still holding out against Brown's main force. Fortunately for him the three American brigades were very loosely joined, and one section of Porter's brigade on their left consisted of three hundred Pennsylvania volunteers and six hundred Indians, who panicked as soon as they were attacked. These white and red men of Porter's did not stop running until they reached the protection of the second American brigade under General Ripley at Street's Creek. The rout happened so quickly that some of the Canadian Indians were able to slip behind Winfield Scott's brigade, where they surprised Scott and his staff sipping coffee at a farmhouse and nearly captured them. So little had the Americans expected Riall's risky leap from his Chippewa defenses that Scott's officers actually were planning a formal parade and dinner as a belated celebration of the Fourth of July.

General Riall now turned to maul Scott's brigade — and caught a Tartar. The accepted color of the American regular's jacket was blue; but after last winter when Scott required fresh uniforms for his men he found that the quartermaster general had run out of blue cloth. The only substitute was gray. Accordingly Scott's regiments wore a color that happened to be the common hue of the homespun made and worn in the backwoods settlements. It was noticed by one of Riall's staff, the dashing Marquis of Tweeddale, who declared the enemy to be nothing more than a body of country militia. Riall (whose own eyesight was poor) promptly ordered a full attack with the bayonet — a painful mistake. Scott's 1300 gray-jackets were veterans of the war and he had trained them hard since the close of the 1813 campaign. His regiments wheeled into line and stood their ground firmly, their field guns were well placed and smartly handled, and together they shattered the waves of reckless scarlet infantry rushing at them through the grass.

After a time, seeing Ripley's blue regiments moving up, Riall admitted defeat. Under cover of a drenching thunderstorm he fell back behind the Chippewa, where a wiser commander would have stayed in the first place. He had lost 515 men. The American troops (including Porter's wild mob) had lost 335 altogether. Scott's brigade, which alone had beaten the British, lost only 275. It was a lesson in the changed arithmetic of the war in Canada. The old bold days of successful British gambling at long odds were gone.

Riall destroyed the Chippewa bridge and stood on the farther side of the creek until July 8, when American troops began to cross in boats beyond his right flank. By that time he knew the size as well as the quality of Brown's army, and he ordered his battered battalions to fold their tents and retreat at a smart pace down the river to Fort George. The Americans chased him as far as Queenston, where they halted and camped in accordance with the set plan of campaign. If Riall's beaten troops chose to shut themselves up in the forts at the Niagara mouth, so much the better. To this point nothing had been seen or heard of Commodore Chauncey's ships, on which so much depended. On July 13 General Brown wrote urgently to that opinionated and service-jealous man.

"All accounts agree that the force of the enemy at Kingston is very light. Meet me on the lake shore north of Fort George with your fleet and we will be able I have no doubt to settle a plan of

operations that will break the power of the enemy in Upper Canada
... at all events let me hear from you. I have looked for your fleet
with the greatest anxiety since the 10th. I do not doubt my ability
to meet the enemy in the field and march in any direction over his
country, your fleet carrying for me the necessary supplies. We can
threaten Forts George and Niagara, and carry Burlington Heights
and York, and proceed to Kingston and carry that place. For God's
sake let me see you. Sir James will not fight. Two of his vessels are
now in the Niagara River. If you conclude to meet me at the head of
the lake have the goodness to bring the guns and troops that I have
ordered from Sackett's Harbour."

Riall had sensed his risk of being cut off by an American march
to Burlington. Like Brown, he had been watching hopefully for a
friendly fleet and reinforcements from the other end of the lake, but
only a pair of Yeo's smaller ships had appeared. At Fort George he
was joined by 650 Canadian troops from York (350 Glengarries and
the rest militia), which replaced his Chippewa loss but still left
him badly outnumbered. Therefore he left garrisons in the Niagara
forts and moved away toward Burlington along the shore road.
After twenty miles he met another marching reinforcement, this
one of British regulars from Burlington, bringing his effective force
to about two thousand. More confident now, he turned inland a few
miles to the farming settlement of Twenty Mile Creek (Saint
Catharines) where he could oppose an American flank march to
Burlington.

Both sides had their scouts and informers. At his Queenston camp
General Brown was well aware of Riall's movements and had a good
estimate of his force. In his own tents he had 2700 regulars and
Porter's potpourri of state militia, frontier volunteers and Indians,
bringing his force to 3700. On the day after he wrote his earnest
appeal to Chauncey he held a staff conference. The opinions of his
officers were divided. Some were for destroying Riall before he
could get help from the other end of the lake. Winfield Scott and
others were for taking the Niagara forts first, to secure a good
anchorage for Chauncey's ships in the mouth of the river.

Brown fell in with Scott, his most experienced officer, and ordered
a march down the river; but on July 21 spies reported that Riall had
been joined by still more troops marching from York. This was not
true, but on the face of it Brown returned to Queenston, the obvious

point for Riall to strike. The American general was a bedeviled man. He had received a bolt of cold sarcasm from Chauncey in reply to his letter of the thirteenth.

"I shall afford every assistance in my power to cooperate with the army whenever it can be done without losing sight of the great object for the attainment of which this fleet has been created — the capture or destruction of the enemy's fleet. But I consider the primary object. We are intended to seek and fight the enemy's fleet and I shall not be diverted from my efforts to effectuate it by any sinister attempt to render us subordinate to, or an appendage of, the army."

Further light came on July 22, when a note from an army friend (General Gaines) at Sackets Harbor told him that Chauncey was a sick man grimly holding the American fleet in port, and that Brown should expect no naval help whatever. So much for Secretary Armstrong's plan of campaign. Meanwhile there was bedevilment in his own camp and in the countryside, arising from the behavior of his irregular troops and Indians.

On July 12 an officer of volunteers with an imposing rank, Brigadier General Swift, had gone foraging with 120 men and clashed with a Canadian militia patrol near the village of St. David's. His men had driven off the patrol but in the clash one of the Canadians shot Swift dead. A week later, giving Swift's "murder" as the excuse, Colonel Stone of the New York militia destroyed every home in St. David's. This affair, indeed the whole conduct of the irregular troops, enraged the United States Army officers.

Major McFarland of the 23rd U. S. Infantry wrote on July 25: "The whole population is against us; not a foraging party but is fired on, and not infrequently returns with missing numbers. This state was to be anticipated. The Indians were sent off some days since, as they were found useless except to plunder. The militia have burned several private dwelling houses, and on the 19th inst. burnt the village of St. David consisting of 30 or 40 houses. This was done within three miles of the camp and my battalion was sent to cover the retreat . . . My God! What a service. I have never witnessed such a scene, and had not the commanding officer of the party, Lieut. Col. Stone, been disgraced and sent out of the army I should have handed in my sheepskin."

So Brown's worries grew. With the warning note from Gaines it was clear that the planned move on Kingston was now impossible, and so long as Chauncey would not risk his ships the British at Kingston were free to send troops up the lake to Riall. Moreover it was now known that some of Wellington's veteran redcoats had arrived in Canada from France, where Napoleon had been deposed at last and sent to Elba; and more were on the way. Brown's problem was no longer one of conquering Upper Canada; it was one of defending himself where he was, in fiercely hostile country at a distance from his Buffalo base. With this in mind he drew back as far as Chippewa, which he reached on the evening of July 24. With his tents pitched in sight of the fresh graves in the fields he awaited grimly the next British move. It was not far away.

Brown's suspicion of an overwhelming British force moving against him was groundless, as he was soon to discover. Sir George Prevost's powerful reinforcements were being concentrated about Montreal for quite another purpose. Upper Canada was General Drummond's nut and he was left to crack it with what troops he had. His subordinate Riall was already on the move, hoping to catch Brown's retreating army by a surprise attack from the flank. His advanced force, which he led in person, was composed almost entirely of veteran Canadian regulars and militia. These troops marched by interior roads toward Niagara Falls through the night of July 24, and soon after daylight they halted to rest on Lundy's Lane, just where that dusty track passed over a small rise in the farm land, close to the famous cataract. They numbered less than a thousand men. The rest of Riall's force, a thousand British regulars and three hundred militia, were in the camp at Twelve Mile Creek (Saint Catharines) with orders to march at dawn on the twenty-fifth. Through some fumbling of the orders, these troops did not set out for Lundy's Lane until noon, giving themselves a long trudge in the afternoon heat.

The information of both sides, usually good and often prompt for that horseback age, was curiously at fault. Neither army knew where the other was and neither could guess the other's intentions. Darkness had covered the march of Riall's Glengarries, New Brunswickers, and other Canadians to Lundy's Lane, and there were no British troops on the river road to keep touch with Brown's retreat. The highway from Queenston to Chippewa ran roughly north to south, separated from the Niagara by a strip of woods and fields half a mile from Lundy's Lane came in from the west, a handy route for Riall on his right-hook march to Niagara Falls. When his Canadians halted on the rise in the fresh morning light they could hear the boom and see the mist of the great waterfall a mile or so away.

The American army stood beside its tents at Chippewa, invisible three miles to the south, watching the river road and unaware of Riall's approach. General Brown had posted a troop of volunteers at Lewiston, some miles down the American side of the Niagara gorge, to watch the Queenston road across the river and report the expected British march. At last it came and the volunteers sent word up the river. But it was not the march of Riall's men.

When General Drummond heard the bad news of the Chippewa battle he knew that Riall faced the main invasion. Yeo's ships were windbound in Kingston harbor. Drummond set off by road for York with the pick of his redcoats, leaving the rest to come on by ship as soon as the wind changed. On the evening of July 24, just as Drummond's marching men arrived there, four of Yeo's ships appeared at York with the rest of the Kingston force. Drummond's troops joined them, and with a good night breeze the ships arrived in the Niagara mouth at daybreak on the twenty-fifth — just as Riall's Canadians reached Lundy's Lane twelve miles up the river.

Colonel Tucker, commanding the fort garrisons at the mouth, could offer only vague news, chiefly that the American army had threatened Fort George and then vanished up the Canadian bank, that Riall was inland somewhere making for Niagara Falls, and that the only American troops on the lower river were a small group at Lewiston. Drummond had been obliged to leave a garrison at Kingston. His own few companies added to the garrisons of Forts George and Niagara made up a force of a thousand, all veteran British regulars. He sent half of them up the American bank with Tucker and the rest along the Canadian side under Colonel Morrison, the hero of Chrysler's Farm. Tucker was to capture or destroy the American troop at Lewiston and then recross the Niagara, joining his force to Morrison's at Queenston on the other side.

All this was done with speed but the two hundred Americans at Lewiston got away, leaving behind a store of tents, baggage, and supplies intended for Brown's army. At Queenston General Drummond rested and fed his united columns after the morning's exertions and sent back a few companies to guard the forts below. With the 850 remaining redcoats he set off along the river road toward the south. The time was well into the afternoon. Unknown to Drummond, the rear half of Riall's force was only now making its way toward Lundy's Lane by the zigzag tracks of the plateau, so that both of these bodies of British troops were moving miles apart in the fierce July heat but heading for the same destination, the road junction near Niagara Falls where Riall's advance guard stood.

The American army was still in the Chippewa camp, an hour's march beyond the junction. Until noon General Brown had no news of the British at all, but then came a message from Lewiston. It said that British ships had arrived at Niagara in the night, that boats were moving up the river, and that redcoats could be seen marching toward Queenston. Soon after this came another hasty report saying that British troops were in Lewiston itself. These were Colonel Tucker's men; but with this scanty information General Brown made a summary of the British movements, partly right and partly wrong — that Drummond had come up the lake to Niagara, joined his troops to Riall's at Queenston, and sent part of his army across to the American bank for a thrust at Brown's communications.

A lesser American soldier, a Hull or a Hampton, would have quit Canadian soil and turned back to the defense of Buffalo. Brown was a fighter and he saw an opportunity. The British army evidently was divided by the river and he had a chance to destroy the force at Queenston before the other got back to support it. He waited for confirming news of a British march up the American bank from Lewiston, but as the afternoon drew on without further word he ordered Scott's brigade to strike at Queenston, ten miles by road below.

Scott moved off between four and five o'clock in the afternoon with his four regiments of infantry, two troops of cavalry, and a pair of field guns, in all 1200 men, the victors of Chippewa and the best troops in Brown's army.

The sun was well down the sky but there was no slacking in the heat. As the head of his column reached the house of a Mrs. Wilson, close to the thunder of the falls, Scott had surprising news. A British force of some strength was moving in from the west and had halted on the gently rising ground at Lundy's Lane, which joined the main highway a mile or so ahead. He sent this word back to General Brown, moved on half a mile, and then swung left off the highway, deploying his troops through the fields and orchards facing Lundy's Lane. The rise was before them, not large or high, a mere swelling in the farm land with the lane across its top.

Riall had with him 390 Canadian regulars, 500 militia, a troop of the 19th Dragoons, and a field battery; altogether 980 men. When he saw the familiar gray jackets of Scott's brigade moving through the woods and pastures he guessed that he had come upon the main American force. There was no sign of his own rear and he had no knowledge of Drummond's whereabouts. The bloody experience of Chippewa was fresh in his mind, and with a prudence quite foreign to his former nature he ordered his troops to quit the knoll and draw away down the main river road. At the same time he sent a galloper to find his distant rear and change its line of march to Queenston.

As the sun dipped toward Lake Erie, three sweating columns of redcoats and militia stirred the dust of the country roads; one retiring toward Queenston on the main highway, another trudging by a side route to Queenston, and the third (Drummond's) hurrying up the road from Queenston to the junction at Lundy's Lane. On the American part, Scott's brigade remained deployed toward Lundy's Lane and the rise; Ripley's brigade was on the march to them, and Porter's militia and volunteers were among the tents at Chippewa, preparing, in their indolent way, to follow the regulars.

The first encounter was between redcoat and redcoat. Drummond on the river road met Riall marching back. Drummond and his men had been on the march since dawn but the general was eager for battle, and on hearing Riall's news he hurried the combined force up to the knoll before the Americans could get there. Together the British now numbered 1800, more than a match for Scott's brigade until Ripley arrived to support him.

Winfield Scott had expected the usual headlong British attack and it had not come. He was puzzled by the disappearance of the redcoats and their lean militia from the sky line ahead, but soon he saw red tunics and stovepipe shakos on the rise once more, extending their lines to the Queenston road, trundling field guns into position on the crest in their center, and pushing some troops into the woods toward his own left flank. These were obviously defensive arrangements and he decided to attack. He chose the British center and left, sending three of his regiments against Drummond's soldiers at the road junction and ordering Major Jessup with the fourth and the brigade cavalry to make his way along the wooded strip between the main road and the river. The attack went forward at 6:30 P.M. At the road junction it met the leveled volleys of a veteran British regiment and a battalion of veteran Canadian militia, while the battery on the rise belched shrapnel and a special detachment fired a stream of Congreve rocket shells. Each of the three gray waves was shattered, each re-formed and came on again gallantly and the fighting was close and fierce, but at last they were thrown back. The loss was heavy. Scott himself was among the wounded. Only Jessup's men escaped damage. Moving behind the screen of orchards and scrub woods between the highway and the Niagara, they were able to place themselves in concealment behind the British left flank. There, for the time, Jessup halted.

Ripley's brigade of bluecoats was now arriving on the scene. It was half past seven, sunset, and the battle had only begun. In the first of the twilight General Brown drew back into his reserve the three torn battalions of Scotts brigade and replaced them in the battle line with Ripley's men. At the same time he ordered Porter's militia and volunteers to move through the woods against the British right flank. These dispositions took time, and night had fallen when the fighting flared up again. Jessup's infantry and horsemen made the first move, springing out of the trees and planting themselves across the road to Queenston at the British rear. Here they captured two noteworthy prisoners; General Riall, badly wounded in the fighting at the junction and riding back in the dark, and Drummond's aide, Captain Loring, carrying a message to the British troops on the flank. But Jessup was in a dangerous position without support, and in a short time a British counterattack hustled him off the road with the loss of one third of his men.

It was full dark now, and although a moon shone fitfully through the smoke, the battle became a blind struggle of regiments and fragments of regiments groping for each other in the bloody angle of the two roads and in the trampled crops and grass on the slope behind. At nine o'clock the long-missing rear of Riall's force tramped up the road from Queenston just as the battle reached a new pitch.

Brown had made a sudden double thrust at the Lundy's Lane knoll. The left attack, made chiefly by Porter's men, shriveled and fell away in a blaze of British musketry and cannon fire. On the right the 21st U. S. Infantry, stealing up behind a creeper-covered fence, were able to see in a patch of moonlight and to shoot down every gunner in the busy British battery at a few yards' range. They leaped forth, dashed past the guns and over the crest. A fierce clash of bayonets and musket butts followed there, but General Brown, close at hand, brought up two field guns and elements of two other regiments to their support and the British were driven back. The road junction, the knoll, and the British battery were all in American hands.

At this moment Riall's rear force came up in a darkness made almost solid by the choking powder smoke. The head of the column plodded straight into the old British position at the junction, where it was roughly handled by Brown's alert infantry. The shock of this reception after their dreary nine-hour march was startling, scores of tired and bewildered redcoats found themselves prisoners, and it was some time before their own officers and Drummond's staff were able to get the rest, with their two field guns, out of trouble and into some kind of order in the changed line of battle. But then, with his whole force assembled after all the various marches of the day and evening, Drummond led them up the slope. The Americans on the crest shot hard at the gleam of crossbelts stumbling at them in the murk, but by that time the British bayonets were close. The survivors fell back to their old line in the trees and fields below the lane. They lost their two cannon but dragged away one of the captured British guns, a blind swap in the hurry.

Drummond now had a grip on the hillock that nothing could shake. For three hours 1800 British troops had borne all of the American attacks, but with the arrival of Riall's belated column Drummond had drawn into the battle 1910 British regulars, 390 Canadian regulars and 800 Canadian militia, a total of 3100 men. Against them Brown had thrown the 2700 regulars of Scott and Ripley, Porter's 1350 New York militia and Pennsylvania volunteers, and 150 "Canadian Volunteers" led by the renegade Willcox. However Porter had done little fighting and the egregious Willcox had devoted his efforts to raiding farmhouses behind the British lines and capturing unwary stragglers. The burden of the American battle was carried first and last by the regulars in gray and blue, and for more than two hours longer these gallant men persisted in attacks up a slope defended by the united British force.

Both sides were now exhausted. Water was not to be found in the fighting zone, and after their marches and struggles in the merciless heat of a Niagara summer day and evening the men were choking for lack of it. Fatigue and thirst finally defeated them all. Toward midnight the battle for a grassy bump on an obscure Canadian country lane came to an end, and as the last shots died away the natural sound of that region could be heard once more — the boom and rush of Niagara Falls in the sudden quiet of the night.

When the British called their rolls in the morning they counted 84 killed, 559 wounded and 235 missing, altogether a loss of 878 men. The Americans reckoned their loss at 171 killed, 572 wounded, and 110 missing, a total of 853. Many of the missing on both sides were prisoners, but after the battle the British found and buried 210 American bodies on the field. The higher proportion of captured British was chiefly due to the misadventure of Riall's second column in the dark. The higher proportion of Americans killed was due to the blasts of shrapnel from the British battery, to the deadly shooting of the redcoats and militia when Scott made his open attack on the road junction, and to the rocket missiles. In the close nature of the fighting not even generals escaped the bullet storm. Drummond had been wounded, Riall was wounded and a prisoner, and on the American side Scott had a severe wound and so had Brown himself.

The pain of Brown's wound forced him off the field toward the last, when he turned over the command to Ripley. According to his dispatches to Washington, he ordered Ripley to march the troops back to the Chippewa camp for food and rest, and to return at daylight to renew the battle if the British were still there. But Ripley failed him. Soon after midnight the American troops left the battlefield. Their dead and severely wounded lay where they had fallen. The British soldiers, as Brown had guessed, were too exhausted to pursue. When the fighting ceased they dropped on the ground and slept where they were.

In the morning Ripley broke his camp, burned the restored Chippewa bridge, tossed some of his supplies and tents into the Niagara, and retired up the river to Fort Erie, setting fire to the mills at Streets Creek as he passed.

CHAPTER 39

1814

*British defeat at Fort Erie — The fight at Cook's Mills
— The American retreat from Upper Canada*

AT THE time of its capture by Brown's army, Fort Erie was a barrack and a pair of blockhouses enclosed in earthworks with one large bastion. It stood about one hundred yards from the shore of Lake Erie where it poured away into the Niagara. American engineers and working parties had prepared to enlarge the old British post, and when Ripley returned with the army he set all his men to work with ax, mattock, and shovel. When Drummond's troops appeared on August 3 the old fort had become part of an elaborate system of log-and-earth ramparts, bastions and redoubts enclosing a camp of fifteen acres. The muzzles of thirteen cannon poked from the embrasures. On the water beyond lay a floating battery in the form of three ships of the Lake Erie squadron anchored in line.

General Pendleton Gaines had taken command of the army until Brown's recovery, and he had in this fortified bridgehead Ripley's and Scott's brigades of regulars, now about two thousand men, and some of Porter's riflemen. Porter, anxious to redeem past failures, was over the water at Buffalo, weeding out his brigade and recruiting and training new men.

General Drummond was not disabled by his wound. He retained command of the British army and his first task after Lundy's Lane was to reorganize it. He sent his worst-mauled regiment of regulars back to Fort George, replacing it with the garrison from that place, and drew a fresh regiment from Kingston. The old drawback of the Canadian militia, the need of harvesting crops, obliged him to part with his "sedentary" personnel for the next month. In all, counting his "embodied" militia and a company of sailors and marines, he had about 3300 men when he closed up to Fort Erie and beheld its new forbidding state. The first enterprise was a naval one. In the autumn of 1812 an American naval party in boats had surprised and captured two British ships lying off Fort Erie. Here was a chance to return the compliment. The American army in retreat had destroyed every boat along the upper part of the Niagara. Boats were found at Frenchman's Creek and Queenston, carried to Lake Erie by relays of sweating seamen and militia, and launched on the night of August 11. Captain Dobbs, R.N., with seventy-five sailors and marines succeeded in boarding and capturing the armed ships *Somers* and *Ohio*, and sailed them down the Niagara to Frenchman's Creek. The *Porcupine*, true to her name, could not be touched. The adventure had no effect on Gaines's water line to Buffalo, for the Americans had other and more powerful ships on Lake Erie.

A cool inspection of the American defenses at Fort Erie (and of his own resources) would have shown a more patient man than General Drummond that his best course was to dig in, hold Gaines's troops immobile in their entrenched camp, and await the march of events elsewhere. During July thousands of Wellington's veterans had arrived at Quebec for the Canadian campaign and they continued to pour ashore all through the month of August. None of these appeared to be moving west of Montreal. Even if Prevost had failed to advise him, Drummond should have known that this powerful British force would strike down the Champlain pass as the major blow at the Americans, and that he could win nothing decisive here on the distant shore of Erie.

But Gordon Drummond was too aggressive an officer to sit still in the presence of an enemy. He could not even wait to drag up adequate siege artillery. On August 12 six British guns opened a feeble fire on the American defenses. Only one was a mortar able to toss shells inside; the rest could not penetrate the bastions and redoubts or the earth-filled log ramparts, seven feet high, which sheltered the American riflemen. Drummond realized this after wasting powder for three days, but then with one of his characteristic snap decisions he ordered his troops to storm the place.

The main points in the American defense were a large new redoubt with five cannon on a knoll called Snake Hill, the old British fort in the center with its added bastions, and a new stone-walled battery at the water's edge. Of these the big redoubt on Snake Hill was the most important, for its cannon could be turned to blast the main enclosure. The Americans, well aware of this, had surrounded it with tall log stockades and posted a strong garrison inside.

Drummond's plan was the old one he had used with such success at Fort Niagara, surprise by a silent night attack with the bayonet alone. Colonel Fischer was to steal up Snake Hill with 1300 men, carrying ladders to get inside the redoubt. To make sure of silence every man of this force was compelled to unscrew and remove his musket flint. As the attack closed in on Snake Hill, another party of 200 redcoats, sailors, and marines would attack the old British fort itself, and 650 men would storm the stone battery at the lake shore.

Fort Erie in its new form and with its present inmates was nothing like old Fort Niagara in the winter of 1813. Drummond here was committing his troops to an open assault on an equal number of veteran American soldiers in shotproof cover and prepared for a quick turnout in the event of a night attack. His staff work was hasty and in one important detail badly at fault. To get Fischer's men over the stockades at Snake Hill his engineers made their ladders sixteen feet long. The stockade turned out to be twenty-five feet high — and ladders must be raised at an angle.

At two o'clock in the morning of August 15 the assault columns crept out of the British lines. The main force under Colonel Fischer contained about three hundred British regulars; the rest were men of his own (the De Watteville) regiment, consisting of Spaniards, Maltese, and Sicilians with Swiss officers and N.C.O.s, recruited in the Mediterranean campaigns against Napoleon and sent off to Canada in the summer of 1813. A swift advance party (as at Fort Niagara) caught the American night picket outside the first stockade, and fifty men were able to pass through the outer gate on their flying heels. However the ladders proved too short to get into the redoubt itself. Elsewhere groups of Fischer's force were trying to climb the stockade, with no better luck. And now, with the American garrison shooting hard at a range of only a few yards, the assault troops had to fumble for their gun flints and re-fix them before they could shoot back. Five times they tried to climb into the redoubt, five times the Americans shot them down. The survivors gave it up, leaving their dead and wounded with the tumbled ladders on the slope of Snake Hill.

Meanwhile the other two British columns had run into a garrison fully awake and shooting. The redcoats attacking the shore battery suffered bloodily and had to turn away. The only success came to the smallest of the British columns, led by Colonel Drummond of the 104th (New Brunswick) Regiment, who got into the main bastion of old Fort Erie and held it against a hasty American counterattack. Many of the redcoats driven off by the shore battery and its riflemen now made their way into the bastion to support this group.

Morning came, and at such close quarters any British movement drew a deadly fire. Colonel Drummond (no relation to the general) was killed with many other officers and men. Nearly five hundred British soldiers had crammed themselves into the old bastion, a force too strong to be thrown out and yet unable to get farther in the pelt of bullets shot at them from three sides. Curiously, no one seems to have thought of the fort magazine, which was directly under their feet. It could be entered through a small stone building still in American hands. Suddenly there was "a jet of flame mingled with fragments of timber, earth, stone and the bodies of men." Nearly all of the men in the crowded bastion were injured or killed outright. The loss in the other attacks had been bad enough. This completed the British defeat. The survivors ran back to the safety of the woods. Of the 2150 men who attacked the American defenses 222 lay dead, 360 (of whom 174 were injured) remained as prisoners in American hands, and 323 other wounded managed to make their way back to the British lines, a total loss of 905. The Americans had lost only 84, one of whom was the Irish-Canadian renegade Willcox, slain at last.

General Gaines made no attempt to leap out upon the shaken British troops however, and as the days passed Drummond settled down to a slow grind at this tantalizing Yankee foothold on Canadian soil. He dragged up more guns from Fort George, added two new siege batteries to his first, and began to dig earthworks for a fourth. To replace part of his loss the reluctant Prevost sent up six hundred veterans of Wellington's army. But now there was other loss. Drummond had to send two badly shattered regiments back to posts on Lake Ontario. Moreover, with the autumn rains splashing about the latrines and cooking huts there was the inevitable epidemic of "camp fever" (typhoid) which smote both sides throughout this war whenever the troops were static for a time.

Gaines had been wounded in the British attack and General Brown, having recovered from his wound, took over the command once more. With it he took over a new problem. The Americans were aware of the veteran British brigades arriving in Canada from France, and it was not long before Brown knew that some of these troops had joined Drummond's force in Upper Canada. He saw himself cornered in Fort Erie and soon to be crushed by a British mass moving up from Montreal. He wrote urgently to Secretary Armstrong and to General Izard at Plattsburg, demanding a strong reinforcement of regular troops and adding ominously; "I consider the fate of this army very doubtful unless speedy relief is afforded."

This led to another of the strange twists of this war, a transfer of American military strength from Lake Champlain to Lake Erie just when Sir George Prevost with his army of Wellington's troops was about to invade the United States at the Champlain pass.

In the latter part of August 1814 the evil star of Secretary Armstrong was still guiding his military path. With a British fleet and army on the way to attack the American heart at Washington (and to burn, among much better things, the Secretary's own offices), with another British force about to pounce on New England and seize the whole territory of Maine east of the Penobscot River, with the third and greatest gathering at Montreal for a thrust toward the Hudson Valley, Armstrong went on dreaming of the conquest of Canada, keeping spread along that frontier almost the entire regular army of the United States and all of the battle-experienced militia and volunteers. His regulars, always too few for the task (they never numbered more than twelve thousand even at the peak of the operations against Canada), were scattered in various garrisons and commands all the way from Lake Champlain to Lake Erie. The largest and best-trained bodies stood at the ends of this long line. General Izard had 5500 at Plattsburg and General Brown had 2000 cooped up with him in Fort Erie.

As Sir George Prevost now mustered a large and dangerous army on the Richelieu, the best American course was to pull their troops out of Upper Canada and send them to Lake Champlain. General Brown was urging them to do the opposite, and he was backed by western politics. The War Hawks still had their potent voice at Washington and their jealous eyes on the western frontier. These eyes magnified the adventures of a few Canadian soldiers in Illinois, their bold presence on the Mississippi and the resultant upsurge of Indian hopes in the West. The spectacle of the only American army in the West cornered and besieged inside a Canadian fort was to them an outrage. All their old fears and ambitions were astir.

As the outcome of all this, on August 29, 1814, General Izard marched away from Lake Champlain with his best troops, heading for the Erie battle front nearly four hundred miles to the west. At this time the graceful naval minuet on Lake Ontario had reached one of its periodical changes of step and tune. It was Commodore Chauncey's turn to glide about the lake while Sir James Yeo fluttered away to the security of Kingston. Chauncey's new frigates *Mohawk* and *Superior* alarmed Sir James. For six weeks he remained inside the Kingston batteries, hurrying the carpenters and riggers working on his own tremendous *Saint Lawrence* and so great was his fear of sabotage by Yankee spies and agents that a regiment of Canadian regulars, the Nova Scotia Fencibles, were detailed to guard the huge ship day and night as it stood on the ways. In these circumstances Commodore Chauncey was in an unusually benign mood toward his country's army and he agreed to ferry part of Izard's force up Lake Ontario while the rest perspired along the shore from Sackets Harbor.

Nevertheless General Izard's change of front took several weeks. In the meantime General Brown struck a stout blow at the bars of his Fort Erie cage. Several warships of the Lake Erie squadron, early in September, ferried over to him from Buffalo the whole of General Porter's remodeled and enlarged brigade of frontier militia and volunteers, so that he now had a stronger force than the British troops outside. Drummond's three active siege batteries stood isolated from each other in the edge of the forest, more than a mile from the British camp and only one third that distance from the American defenses. Each was guarded by a blockhouse and some rude earthworks, and the British army had settled into a routine manning of these works with a small part of their troops while the rest remained in camp. Drummond was one of those impetuous thrusters who have little gift for a waiting game and who regard elaborate defense works as a bad influence on their men. As a result his staff were careless and so were his soldiers in the disjointed siege line.

On September 17 under the veil of a drizzling rain two American columns under Brigadiers Porter and Miller crept out of their entrenchments. Porter's volunteers reached the woods without discovery and followed a roundabout path to the British battery called Number Three. Miller's regulars passed silently along a bushy ravine to Number Two. At a signal 1600 Americans rushed both batteries and captured most of their personnel. Miller moved on to take Number One, but by this time the British camp had turned out, and their regiments stormed into battle with the zest of bored men given a sudden interest. Miller's attack on Number One failed bloodily.

The bayonets of 600 veterans of Wellington's army drove the blue-coats out of Number Two before they could destroy its guns. Porter's men had time to blow up the magazine and shatter the British cannon in Number Three. By three o'clock in the afternoon the Americans were back inside Fort Erie. It had been an expensive afternoon. Brown had lost 510 men. Drummond had lost 609, of whom half were prisoners taken in the first American rush.

This loss following the costly failure of his own attack forced Drummond to a decision that he did not like — an admission of defeat. In less than two months, beginning at Lundy's Lane, he had lost 2400 men in battle, apart from a long sick list. Some of his best regiments were so reduced that their fighting value had vanished. He could not take Fort Erie with his present force, and without a British squadron on Lake Erie he could not prevent the Americans drawing troops and supplies from Buffalo. And now, with fresh American forces marching to the Niagara, there was nothing to prevent them crossing the river and taking him in the rear. At dusk on September 21 he packed up his stores, hitched his guns to the stolid farm horses of the "car brigade," left his camp huts standing (and with fires smoking in their chimneys) to deceive the Americans as long as possible, and plodded away through the night in a downpour of rain. The wisdom of this move was soon apparent. General Izard's troops were moving toward the Niagara just as Drummond's men trudged down the river to the old camp and lines at Chippewa.

By Armstrong's order General Izard was to take command of the whole American army invading Upper Canada. News of a British defeat at Plattsburg had reached him on the way; so had the news of Drummond's retreat from Fort Erie. He was eager to play his part in such fortunate affairs at once, but he had learned something else on the way. The naval dance on Lake Ontario had taken its next turn. Sir James Yeo was sailing on those now chilly autumn waters with the towering *Saint Lawrence* added to his fleet; and Commodore Chauncey, following the unwritten rule of the game, had curtsied away to launch something bigger and better at Sackets Harbor. So it was the British turn to move troops and stores up the lake to Niagara. With this in mind, Izard gave up any notion of crossing the river below Chippewa and marched up the American bank to Black Rock. On October 11 he ferried his troops over to Fort Erie.

He took over his new command in a perplexed state of mind. The 8000 troops at Fort Erie were the largest, best-trained and best-equipped force yet assembled for the conquest of Upper Canada, while Drummond had less than 2500 defending it; but with Yeo's ships riding Lake Ontario unchallenged, the British had an open route to Niagara for that powerful red-coated mass now idling about Montreal. It was no mere nightmare, although Izard might have guessed that a decisive British movement of that kind was unlikely for two human reasons — the mentalities of Sir George Prevost and Sir James Yeo.

Prevost, painfully conscious of his personal fiasco on Lake Champlain and suspecting an uncomfortable reaction at the War Office, was eager to report at least one success in his wide command before the campaign season closed. He now wrote to Drummond, urging him to drive the Americans out of Upper Canada before the winter came. To accomplish this he was sending three regiments, a battery of artillery, and the necessary stores. The absurdity of this small reinforcement in the face of Izard's strength was compounded by the attitude of the man who controlled its movement to Niagara.

The long smoldering quarrel between Prevost and Sir James Yeo had burst into flame with the Lake Champlain affair and it gave them (among other things) entirely opposite views about the proposed autumn campaign on the Niagara. The American squadron on Lake Ontario had gone into winter quarters and Yeo wished to do the same. Like Commodore Chauncey, he regarded army transport demands as a nuisance (some of his and Chauncey's letters on the subject might have been written by the same man) and in the present case he disliked the Niagara anchorage for his big ships and feared the stormy autumn weather for the smaller ones. He could not refuse the commander in chief's demand however, and grudgingly he moved the reinforcements, a few at a time, toward the head of the lake. Some of the troops he landed at York and some at Burlington. Eventually his smaller ships carried some to Niagara direct, returning to Kingston with Drummond's sick and the sorry remnants of several regiments shattered in the summer's fighting.

Meanwhile Izard's army had closed up to Chippewa and discovered the extent and strength of Drummond's new fieldworks along that famous stream. Drummond had learned some painful lessons at Fort Erie and he expected the Americans to pay for them here. But Izard had no intention of a costly frontal attack. Instead he sent General Bissell with 1400 troops to find a way around the British right flank. Drummond promptly sent Colonel Myers with 750 men to stop him.

The two forces fumbled their way toward each other under appalling conditions. The roads had become a porridge under the autumn rains, barely passable for ox wagons. Myers managed to drag along a single field gun and a Congreve rocket apparatus. The Americans, horse and foot, had nothing but the weapons in their hands.

They clashed on October 19 at Cook's Mills, a hamlet in the woods about ten miles from the Niagara. It was a fumbling encounter in which Myers lost nineteen men and Bissel lost sixty seven, mostly from the British rocket shells and the fire of their one cannon. The two forces drew apart cautiously. Bissell was unsure about the size of the British force and its intentions, and he passed his uncertainty to General Izard. Izard drew back warily to a point halfway between Chippewa and Fort Erie. The autumn winds and rains were beating the last leaves off the hardwoods and a Canadian winter gleamed frostily from the next page of the calendar. Whatever happened in the way of battle now, he could not win Upper Canada until another spring. His probe toward Cook's Mills had found a British force apparently moving around his own left flank toward Fort Erie. He knew that Drummond had got some troops from Montreal and he assumed that many more were on the way.

On November 2 American observers on the lower Niagara saw a battery of field guns and a whole battalion of redcoats landing at Fort George. These were the last of Drummond's meager reinforcements, but General Izard could not know that. With everything to lose and nothing to gain by standing fast he made up his mind quickly, and marched his troops away up the muddy Niagara highway to Fort Erie. He had no intention of being cornered there like Brown. On November 5, Guy Fawkes Day, the traditional occasion in England and America for bonfires and fireworks, a British patrol under Captain Fitzgibbon heard a rumble of explosions and saw black smoke pouring up to the cold sky from the direction of the fort. Fitzgibbon rode on curiously and found that the American army had blown up their redoubts and batteries, fired every building inside, and crossed over the water to their winter quarters at Buffalo.

So ended the campaign of 1814 in Upper Canada. Excepting an outpost on the Canadian bank of the Detroit River at Amherstburg, not a single American soldier stood on Canadian soil. Meanwhile strange things had been happening in Lower Canada, especially toward the Champlain pass.

CHAPTER 40

1814

*Wellington's veterans arrive in Canada — British naval defeat
on Lake Champlain — The retreat from Plattsburg*

WHEN Napoleon arrived at his island prison of Elba on
May 5, 1814, a famous British army lay at Toulouse, deep
in the throat of that bearded head which makes the map
of France. Many of the soldiers had not seen Britain in six years, and
after their fighting marches up and down Spain and finally through
the Pyrenees into France (leaving forty thousand of their comrades
buried on the route), they well deserved a furlough at home. The
War Office had another view. A private letter from some gossip in
that mysterious London machine told Wellington's staff that "the
Government have determined to give Jonathan a good drubbing,"
and soon every regimental mess in the army was pondering the
question "Who goes to America?" The answer came late in May,
when sixteen thousand got their orders and began to march by stages
down the long green valley of the Garonne to ships awaiting them
at Bordeaux. General Robert Ross with four thousand of them was
headed for Bermuda. The rest sailed for Canada.

During the months of July and August the people of Quebec saw
these twelve thousand veterans file ashore from various transports
and move up the river by schooner and steamboat to Montreal and
Sorel. They were part of the Iron Duke's invincible army and everyone expected great things of so large a part of it, forgetting that God
seldom fought on the side of big battalions in the War of 1812.

There seems to have been no clear-cut British staff plan for the
use of these veteran brigades. The political notion apparently was to
seize Plattsburg and with it a good part of the Champlain pass, that
dangerous invasion route to Canada, while an expedition from Halifax nipped off the horn of Maine, which almost separated Canada
from the ice-free ports of New Brunswick and Nova Scotia. As
their troops crossed the sea, the British Cabinet knew well that

President Madison's peace commissioners were about to sit down with their own at Ghent. It was important to capture quickly these pieces of territory so vital to Canadian security, and at the same time to harass the long and vulnerable American coast, especially south of New York, and so convince even the War Hawks that it was time to close the adventure of 1812.

The change of affairs pinned upon Sir George Prevost a new and most unhappy responsibility. He had never liked offensive action and in actual field experience he had never commanded more than a few hundred men anywhere. He now found himself expected to lead an army of at least eleven thousand into battle on American soil; and when he looked at the map he could not ignore the fate of Johnnie Burgoyne in the very scene he was about to invade.

A very uneasy commander in chief rode south from Montreal in the bright sunshine of late August with columns of tough red-coated infantry, batteries of war-torn horse artillery, and a long train of baggage and supply wagons. For his second-in-command he had chosen Major General de Rottenburg, a dull man with a long and undistinguished record on the garrison staff in Canada. The matter of naval support for his flank on Lake Champlain he had left naïvely to Sir James Yeo, who was more absorbed than ever with his ship-building fantasies on Lake Ontario. As a result nothing had been done until late in the season to build up the British squadron at the northern entrance to Lake Champlain. The flagship *Confiance* was not even launched until August 25, seventeen days before she sailed into battle with some of the shipyard carpenters still on board. The crews of the squadron had to be filled out hurriedly with officers and seamen plucked from various ships lying in the St. Lawrence. (The crew of the flagship came from ten different ships, together with a party from Lake Ontario, some soldiers of the 39th Regiment, and a few volunteers.)

At the last moment Yeo sent one of his own officers, Captain Downie, to take the squadron into action, placing him over the head of Captain Pring, who had been on the Lake Champlain scene for a year. Downie first saw his new command on September 2, the day after the British army marched over the American border. When he died in action ten days later he was still a stranger to the lake and to his officers and men, and most of the men were strangers to each other.

There had been no action in the Richelieu-Champlain area since

March, when General Wilkinson made a last futile gesture toward Montreal. He had marched over the border with four thousand men. Within seven miles he was halted by Major Handcock with five hundred redcoats and militia posted in a blockhouse and a stone-walled mill at Lacolle, and after a day's inconclusive fighting he had retired to his base at Champlain.

It was now the British turn to muddle and Sir George Prevost did it handsomely; but first came the astounding error of American military judgment which sent General Izard to Niagara with the largest and best part of their army on Lake Champlain. General Alexander Macomb was left with fifteen hundred regulars and a scratched-up force of country militia to meet the whole weight of Prevost's ponderous columns coming down the road from Montreal. Thus all the military cards were in Sir George's favor when he crossed the frontier on September 1, 1814, and headed for the northwest shore of Lake Champlain.

General Macomb had drawn his frontier troops back to Plattsburg, a good day's march. Prevost was suspicious of this voluntary retreat and of Izard's mysterious march toward Lake Ontario, and he followed Macomb with a caution astonishing to his army, especially his brigadiers Power, Brisbane, and Robinson, all accustomed to the rapid and decisive movements of Lord Wellington. In two days Prevost moved a scant five miles. At the end of four days, mending his pace a little, he had covered seventeen. The army crawled in two columns, one along the lake-shore road and the other on a road through the village of Beekmanstown a short way inland. Sir George kept an anxious eye on the lake. From his West Indian days he had never liked to move on any shore without a lot of friendly canvas in the offing.

Captain Downie's squadron had emerged from the Richelieu and followed the shore to Isle La Motte without a sign of the American ships. The British and American squadrons had roughly the same number of craft in various rigs and sizes, about the same number of men (800 British, 850 American) and about the same number of cannon. The main difference was in the type of cannon. In arming their ships, the British as usual had preferred the long gun, with its farther range, over the short carronade with its heavier shot. The Americans, as on Lake Erie, preferred the carronade. In a fight on the open lake Captain Downie would have the advantage of a boxer with the longer reach, and Commodore Macdonough was wise to avoid it. The American's choice was to lie inside Plattsburg Bay and invite a British attack where he would have the advantage of a close fight and the heavier fist.

On September 6 Prevost's patrols found American troops ahead. Macomb had sent General Mooers with a thousand regulars and militia to delay the British advance. Mooers' field guns shot hard at the British infantry as soon as they appeared, but the delay was short. The redcoats, accustomed to much sharper fire from Napoleon's expert artillerymen, did not trouble to deploy but came straight on in column, and at the first musket shots from their advance guard Mooers' militia fled, a frantic mob, leaving his 250 regulars no choice but to follow them back to Plattsburg.

General Macomb had taken a position behind the Saranac River, which curved around Plattsburg town and entered Lake Champlain at a sharp angle, leaving a steep thumb of land between it and the main view of Plattsburg Bay. On this ridge his troops had built a pair of blockhouses and three log-and-earth redoubts, whose cannon commanded the town across the river, the approaches to the two bridges, and on the other side the inner waters of the bay. The river was deep on its lower reach and Macomb had torn up the bridge planking in his retreat. Manned by enough troops, the south side of the Saranac was a strong position. General Macomb had only 1500 regulars and Mooers' 1800 militia, who had shown their quality on the Beekmanstown road. Moreover there was a dangerous weakness on his landward flank. Two miles above the gaping bridge on the Beekmanstown road the river had a shallow ford which the British infantry could (and did) cross with ease.

Lacking troops enough to guard the whole river front, Macomb kept his regulars on the fortified thumb between the town and lake, and to watch the ford on the far left flank he posted Mooers and his gun-shy militia. Plattsburg Bay was formed by Cumberland Head, a long hook of land curving down from the north. Opposite the tip lay Crab Island, on which Macomb had cannon, and a convenient shoal off Crab Island narrowed the channel into the bay. Inside these obstacles lay Macdonough's ships, anchored in line so that their broadsides could fire across the channel through which the British ships must come to attack them. Each of his crews had put out extra anchors with "springs" on the mooring cables, so that regardless of the wind their ships could be swung to fire one broadside or the other. The British squadron would have to sail in, keeping well clear of Crab Island and the shoal, exposing their ships to the Americans' first broadsides while their own crews were still busy with sailing tackle.

Sir George Prevost's duty was plain. His eleven thousand troops with their cannon and rockets were the most powerful force of any kind on the scene. He had only to thrust hard across the ford, scatter or destroy Mooers' militia, and then roll up Macomb's defenses, one after another, along the ridge. The capture of Macomb's batteries would force the American squadron out of the bay or subject them to fire from both sides when the British ships came in. Either way the American ships would have to accept battle at a great disadvantage instead of the shrewd advantage of their position as things stood.

The British commander in chief did none of these things. For five whole days he kept his grumbling veterans at work on the north bank of the river, shoveling earth and cutting timber for siege batteries as if Macomb held a fortress of some powerful and unapproachable kind. And while this was going on he wrote to Captain Downie at Isle La Motte, insisting that the American fleet must be attacked and destroyed as an opening gambit to the movement of his troops. This was putting the cart before the horse with a cosy shift of responsibility. His brigadiers knew better and so did the troops. The cautious approach to Plattsburg had disgusted them. Prevost's hesitation before his present chance amazed them. Most of the British soldiers were of the type made familiar in Wellington's letters from Spain, reckless drinkers and fighters, doomed to hard service far from home, with little sentiment about them. Wellington with a combination of hard driving and good leadership had got the best from them. Prevost was such a different creature that comparison was a joke, and the joke spread through the British tents.

It was no joke to his naval squadron. Captain Downie had been held at Isle La Motte by head winds and a lack of firelocks for the cannon of his still uncompleted flagship, as he explained by letter to the commander in chief. Prevost's reply came late on September 10:

"The troops have been held in readiness since six o'clock this morning to storm the enemy's works at nearly the same time as the naval action begins in the bay. I ascribe the disappointment I have experienced to the unfortunate change of wind, and shall rejoice to learn that my reasonable expectations have been frustrated by no other cause."

Downie noted the promise of joint action and did not fail to appreciate the sarcastic wording, especially the taunt at his courage in the last four words. He snapped to Pring, "I will convince him that the Navy won't be backward!" The wind was shifting to the northeast and he ordered his crews to prepare for battle. On the morning of September 11 a light breeze brought the British ships down the lake and an angry man took them into action. Sir George saw their sails over the low neck of Cumberland Head as they drew toward the entrance, and soon heard a measured thudding of blank cannon shots — the prearranged signal that Downie was going in.

The opposing ships, in their order of size and fighting power, were as follows:

Downie	*Macdonough*
Confiance (flagship)	Saratoga (flagship)
Chubb	Eagle
Linnet	Ticonderoga
Finch	Preble
12 gunboats	10 gunboats

The *Chubb* and *Finch* were former American ships captured by Pring in 1813. The gunboats were open galleys with sails and long oars, each manned by about thirty men and armed with one or two heavy cannon. Only five of the British gunboats fought in the battle, the rest hovered out of gunshot. The *Confiance* and *Saratoga* were far the largest and most powerful ships and the whole outcome of the fight depended on them.

The action began at eight o'clock in the morning and went badly for Downie from the start. The *Confiance*, tacking in toward the *Saratoga* and *Eagle*, received two immediate blasts of shot, one of which smashed her steering wheel and killed Downie and many others on her deck. A similar concentrated blast some time later cut away the *Chubb's* bowsprit, main boom, and cables, so that she could neither steer nor anchor. She drifted, a derelict, into the midst of the American ships and soon surrendered. The *Finch* ran aground on the shoal off Crab Island and became a helpless target for the *Ticonderoga*, a ship with twice her gun power, and for the cannon on the island. A wreck, she too hauled down her flag.

The *Confiance* was under fire from the *Saratoga*, the *Eagle* and several of the American gunboats; but the main fight was a murderous broadside-to-broadside affair between the two flagships. After a time Macdonough's whole starboard battery was knocked down or disabled, but, using his careful arrangement of kedge anchors and warps, he swung his ship smartly and took up the fight again with his undamaged port-side guns. The *Confiance*, also shattered on the engaged side, tried the same maneuver, but she hung with her bows to the wind. The *Saratoga* poured shot into her. The *Eagle* and *Ticonderoga* added their fire. At last the British flagship was in an appalling state. Her sails and rigging hung in shreds, most of her guns had been battered off the carriages, her deck ran with the blood of Downie and nearly half the crew, and water leaking into the splintered hull had risen above the gun-room deck, where the wounded lay in danger of drowning by the inch. Two and a half hours after the action began Lieutenant James Robertson gave the word to strike the flag.

The last British ensign left flying in Plattsburg Bay was that of the *Linnet*, a brig of sixteen guns at the head of the line. Her captain was Daniel Pring, who had built up the squadron under difficulties, only to lose the chief command by Yeo's last-minute change of officers. Now he had seen a year's effort ruined in a morning. Only the five British gunboats, using their oars to get out of the bay, managed to join the seven outside and escape. For fifteen minutes after the *Confiance* struck her colors Pring fought on alone. By that time his hull was so badly shattered that the water was a foot deep on his lower deck. He lowered his own flag then and the battle was over. From first to last it had taken less than three hours. The Americans had lost about two hundred killed and wounded, the British about three hundred, and two hundred unwounded men were prisoners.

Sir George Prevost had promised to storm the American batteries "at nearly the same time as the naval action begins in the bay", and Captain Downie had taken him at his word. Prevost's own interpretation of "nearly" was to hesitate on the north bank of the Saranac during almost the whole time of the mortal struggle in the bay. His batteries smoked away at the American redoubts, his Congreve rockets sailed their course and exploded, his engineers stood ready with ladders to scale the redoubts when the infantry reached the crest of the ridge, and six regiments marched and countermarched above the Saranac bank. Not a man received an order to so much as wet his feet until the ships had been at strife for well over two hours. Then, screwing up his courage and his obligation much too late, Sir George ordered his right brigade to ford the river.

As the redcoats climbed the slope beyond the Saranac there was a loud shout from the redoubts overlooking the bay. The American soldiers had seen the *Confiance* strike her flag. Prevost heard the cheering where he sat his horse across the river, and turning a fearful eye toward the lake he saw the British gunboats rowing hastily to safety. His mind moved quickly now. Away went a galloper to his troops across the stream, commanding them to return to the northern bank. The troops were under scattered American fire and some had been hit, but the loss was trifling and the scarlet ranks were moving steadily toward Mooers' militia when the order came. The British soldiers came back puzzled and angry, and Mooers' men, pouncing on the last company across the river, killed or captured every man.

As Pring fired his last hopeless shots in the *Linnet*, his commander in chief could think of no better command to the British army than a trumpet signal to cook rations and eat dinner. Prevost's cannon went on firing until three o'clock in the afternoon, and Commodore Macdonough, convinced that British bayonets must soon appear in the American batteries, worked hard to get his battered craft out of range, ignoring the silent British ships awaiting his prize crews.

In his camp Sir George faced three angry brigadiers. Brisbane snapped that he could take the ridge, redoubts and all, in twenty minutes. Nothing could change the general's unhappy mind. As the afternoon waned his unease became panic. Having thrown away the ships he now feared the loss of his army, to what phantoms he could not or would not explain. He was only a short way down the lake shore with a well-secured road for his supplies. His army's casualties so far (including the skirmishes on the way from the Canadian border) came to exactly 242 killed, wounded, and missing. General Macomb was satisfied to stay exactly where he was, with his small force on the ridge beyond the Saranac. Commodore Macdonough's ships and crews were in no condition to attempt even a raid toward the Richelieu.

At sunset the fearful British commander in chief declared the army's position hopeless, that its only safety lay in a hurried retreat to Canada, and that the troops must move off as soon as darkness fell. The light airs of the day had given way to a thrashing autumn gale of wind and rain, bad for the roads but, combined with the darkness, a good cover for the withdrawal. All stores and ammunition not easily portable must be destroyed or abandoned. Even the sick and the disabled wounded must be left behind. The astounded Brigadier Robinson declared that a retreat of this kind would lose more men than a battle across the Saranac, but Sir George brushed that aside.

So a retreat began that bore every evidence of a flight, and the loss began at the same time, although not a single American soldier crossed the Saranac. Robinson knew the temper of his own men. The veterans of Portugal and Spain, denied even a glimpse of home after their long campaigns and sent instead to America, were in a touchy mood. Pride in their own past achievements and the habit of discipline had remained with them, but now Sir George had shattered pride and habit in one stroke. It was easy to drop out of a glum column trudging through the wet woods in the dark, and somewhere among the easygoing Americans a man could find a new life after all the hard years on a shilling a day. By the time Prevost reached the Canadian border, not twenty-five miles away, eight hundred of his veterans had slipped away and vanished into the sodden landscape. In less than a fortnight he had lost five hundred sailors and more than a thousand soldiers, for no purpose whatever.

The Americans themselves were amazed. When General Macomb put off in a boat to confer with Macdonough on the morning of September 12, reporting the British retreat, the sailor warned him to be careful. It might be a trick to lure him out of his defenses, although possibly the British (having lost their Lake Champlain squadron) were swinging away to strike at Chauncey's base on Lake Ontario. This was logic, but logic had nothing to do with Prevost's movements. The truth was very different. Leaving an almost mutinous army to settle in winter quarters on the Richelieu, Sir George was back in Montreal writing to London a long explanation of his failure to do anything at all.

Other pens were busy, including those of his brigadiers and Sir James Yeo. Indeed Sir James (scenting a perfect chance to justify his own cautious conduct on Lake Ontario) was laying a formal charge against the commander in chief, declaring that Captain Downie had been sent into battle by a reckless promise and then betrayed in its performance — which was quite true.

So Prevost was recalled in disgrace, a wretched figure suffering from dropsy, of which he died within a year. He had worked well for Canada on the civil side. On the military side he had done his uncertain best; but Canada had been saved by American mistakes and the courage of his own subordinates, not by his own timid exertions, and his final failure was the epitaph of a man with much talent for peace but none for war.

CHAPTER 41

1814

*The war on the Atlantic coast — British troops take
eastern Maine — British attacks on Washington
and Baltimore — The peace signed at Ghent
— The Rush-Bagot Treaty — Effects of the war*

IN THE spring of 1814 Halifax was perhaps the busiest port in
a world at arms. The gathering of the British fleet in the western
Atlantic, the coming and going of merchant conveys, of troop
transports, of privateers and prizes, all made a bustling scene of the
long blue fiord in the wooded hills. As many as a hundred ships of
all kinds could be seen in a single day refitting, victualing, loading,
or discharging. The streets buzzed with soldiers and seamen. Prices
were high but money was plentiful. In their handsome town mansions
or on their suburban estates, Halifax merchants who had become
as rich as rajas with the long wars entertained army and naval
officers with an almost oriental lavishness at suppers, "routs", and
balls. The brothels of Water Street and Barrack Street (known to
the polite as "dancing houses") and more than two hundred dramshops strove lustily to entertain the rank and file. In the background,
in grim barred buildings on Melville Island and at Dartmouth, and
in a growing fleet of dismal hulks anchored in Bedford Basin,
thousands of French and American prisoners of war whiled away
the hours of each day in making trinkets for sale to visitors.

This lively state of affairs, increasing its pace and profit through
the Napoleonic wars, had reached a dizzy height with the addition
of the American war. There seemed no end to the sale of captured
ships and cargoes in noisy auctions at the Split Crow and other
waterside taverns. Regiments from Britain and the West Indies
passed through the port on their way to Quebec, some by ship, some
by the long winter march through the New Brunswick forest. The
townsfolk looked eagerly for news of the fighting in Lower and
Upper Canada, but until 1814 the war as it touched the Maritime

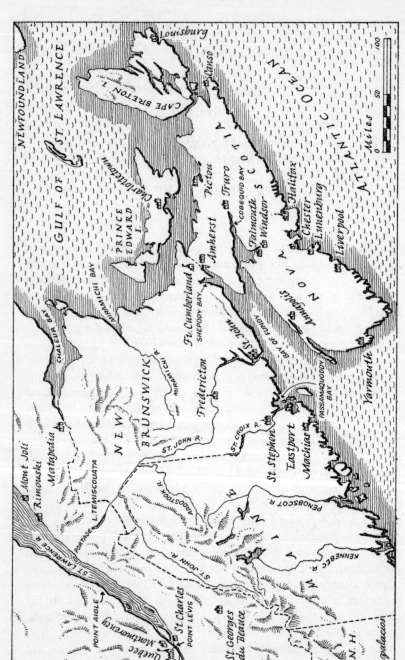

The Maritime Provinces and the vital
Temiscouta portage

Provinces was a purely naval one. They and the adjoining New England states raided each other with privateers as part of the game of war, but ashore their affairs remained on a neighborly live-and-let-live basis and there was a busy trading of American flour and salt meat for British manufactured goods and Nova Scotia gypsum. (Most of the "plaister" for the walls of northeastern America came, then as now, from quarries in the old fourteenth colony.) The clearinghouse for these amiable exchanges was the American village of Eastport, conveniently sited on Passamaquoddy Bay, where the international boundary came down the St. Croix River and wandered among the islands to the sea.

So far in the war nothing had been done to change this comfortable state of affairs, although the 1783 boundary still irritated New Brunswick minds and a glance at the map showed any Canadian the peculiar menace of Maine. In February 1814 a committee of the Nova Scotia legislature declared that some islands in Passamaquoddy Bay were really British territory although the United States had taken possession of them. This was a straw in a wind already blowing from Quebec to London. The Penobscot River had been the ancient fringe of French settlement toward New England, and in the Canadian view it was the natural and proper boundary. There were indications that the present population of eastern Maine would not object strongly to annexation if it could be brought about.

The plan had to wait on the downfall of Napoleon, and on May 21, 1814, a ship arrived at Halifax with the long-awaited news. Early in July a detachment from the Halifax garrison sailed down the Nova Scotia coast to Shelburne, where they rendezvoused with another from Bermuda, convoyed by Nelson's friend Captain Thomas Hardy. Together they sailed across the mouth of Fundy to Eastport in Maine. The only defense of that cheerful smugglers' nest was a small post called Fort Sullivan held by eighty bored blue-coated soldiers. When seven times their number of redcoats splashed ashore with bayonets fixed, the garrison without ado hauled down the Stars and Stripes. The first modest step in the annexation had been made without bloodshed. The prospect for the rest was hopeful but it had to wait on more important British army-navy operations far to the south.

The British attacks on Washington, Alexandria, and Baltimore in the summer of 1814 (unlike the invasion of Maine) had no direct connection with Canada and consequently have no part in Canadian history. As originally conceived, they were to relieve some of the American pressure on Canada, but as carried out by Vice-Admiral Sir Alexander Cochrane, they turned out to be a series of amphibious raids whose chief object was something else. Cochrane was a zealous officer with a personal hatred of Americans which led him to burn the Capitol and other public buildings in Washington, avowedly in revenge for the American destruction at York, Upper Canada, in 1813; but his greed for prize money was well known and Wellington had a poor opinion of him, suspecting that he would use the troops of General Ross to seize places where his seamen could carry off merchant ships and goods regardless of the military object. This proved to be the case. The march of Ross and his 4000 redcoats to Washington was a brilliant affair in which he defeated an American army of 7400 led by General Winder, held the American capital for a night and a day, and withdrew to the ships with the trifling loss of 250 men.

Its chief value to Cochrane was that it diverted American attention from the port of Alexandria on the Potomac, where the admiral made a rich haul of ships, flour, cotton, and tobacco. Getting all this down the Potomac again in the face of American resistance took much valuable time. When Cochrane turned at last to loot Baltimore he found the Americans ready for him, and the gallant Ross lost his life — and Francis Scott Key wrote "The Star Spangled Banner." The summer's adventures were now over, for the hurricane season had begun to stir its ominous breath along the coast. Cochrane divided his fleet and sailed away with most of the troops to Jamaica, where in the winter he planned to loot New Orleans. The rest of the Chesapeake expedition returned to Halifax, bringing with them hundreds of freed slaves from the American plantations (who became an immediate burden on Halifax charity) and the body of General Robert Ross, which was buried with military ceremony in the old town cemetery opposite Government House.

While these diversions were going on, Sir John Sherbrooke, the soldier governor of Nova Scotia, had moved along the Maine coast with a naval squadron and eighteen hundred troops. Entering the mouth of the Penobscot on August 31, he found the defenses weak. A fort at Castine sheltered a few dozen regular soldiers, who destroyed their post and escaped up the river. At Hampden, twenty-five miles upstream, he dispersed with ease a gathering of local militia. The small garrison of Bangor set fire to the frigate *Adams* and another armed vessel lying in the river and then surrendered the town. On September 10 a British detachment occupied the port of Machias.

Eastern Maine was now firmly in British hands. Sherbrooke rebuilt the fort at Castine and gave its name to the whole Maine operation. The people accepted their new ownership cheerfully (many took the oath of allegiance to Britain) and entered busily upon the trade now open to them as British subjects, clearing their ships and paying duties at the Castine customhouse like any other British merchants. Such was the volume of trade in less than a year of British occupation that the customs fund amounted to thirteen thousand pounds, and when the British officials withdrew to Halifax they turned it over to the Nova Scotia treasury in a special account called the Castine Fund. Out of this fund eventually came Dalhousie College, now one of Canada's most famous universities.

The United States forces made no attempt to recover the lost territory in Maine. The British garrison remained in a quiet and even fraternal occupation until, under the terms of the peace treaty, the region became once more a part of the United States.

In the autumn of 1814 the British Government found its people in two minds about the distant war in America. Most of them had heard of it only vaguely. They were tired of the long wars with "Boney" and in no mood for further sacrifices anywhere. In the rich landowning class and among the war contractors, however, there was a strong and belligerent group who were all for attempting a conquest of the United States with the large forces now available. The most prominent (and one of the most vociferous) was the Prince Regent, reigning in the place of his old mad father George III. The grossly fat and dissolute "Prinny" was despised by the British people, who hissed him in the streets, and he and his friends were aware of a deep stir in radical feeling all over the country. This feeling was nothing new; it had been submerged by the general peril of Napoleon; but with that bogey gone a vast popular unrest was coming to the surface. To "Prinny" and his advisers the easiest way to deal with it was the historic one of fixing the popular attention on war abroad, and now that Napoleon was gone (apparently forever) the only visible substitute was Brother

Jonathan across the sea. For a leader these British War Hawks looked to Wellington, the most popular figure in Britain and the very symbol of victory.

The Prince Regent told his government that "nothing should be neglected to induce the Duke of Wellington to accept the chief command in America as soon as possible, as his name alone will reconcile the whole view and opinion of the country, and at the same time be the means of obviating as well as removing many difficulties which may afterwards arise." Castlereagh was in Austria, arranging to mend the tattered affairs of Europe at the forthcoming Congress of Vienna. Wellington was in Paris, doing everything he could to bolster the restored Bourbon regime, but sniffing with his eagle nose a dangerous nostalgia among the French for the glories of the vanished emperor.

When Lord Liverpool approached him on the matter Wellington dutifully murmured that he had "no disinclination to undertake the American concern," but he said flatly that he could not leave France until March 1815 at the earliest. The truth was that he wanted nothing to do with the war across the sea. He doubted the wisdom of sending so many of his best regiments to North America and he was scornful of Admiral Cochrane's raiding schemes. When the War Office consulted him about Cochrane's proposed attack on New Orleans he bluntly declared its object to be "plunder," ran a discerning eye over a map of the Mississippi mouth, and predicted that the British troops were doomed to defeat if Cochrane used them for the purpose — which proved to be the case.

For an opinion on the Canadian field of war he apparently glanced over some of Prevost's and Yeo's glib dispatches (for he saw nothing wrong with those unenterprising men) and declared that the situation wanted nothing but a naval superiority on the lakes. What he did see clearly was that a successful war of defense in North America, and what might have been a successful seizure of strategic points for the future safety of the Canadian border, was now turning to something very different — a war of blind revenge that was bound to fail.

The American War Hawks had led their country into an attack on Canada for which most Americans had no particular desire, and the result was apparent in every defeat on the frontier. But now eight million Americans were under attack themselves; the legendary redcoats of '76 had reappeared on American soil, the flames of

Washington had heated the old hard will to fight, and Francis Key at Baltimore had put the new national spirit into words and found a tune to sing it by.

Moreover there was the country itself, with its enormous distances. Who could conquer that, or even make an impression on it, drawing his troops and supplies three thousand miles across a stormy sea, while a large and warlike race with infinite resources disputed every step? The notion was wildly absurd. Meanwhile Admiral Cochrane was merely squibbing off a few pinches of powder in the rugged face of a whole continent.

These were impressions obvious to any man with a map before him and some knowledge of the art of war. The Iron Duke did not put them in so many words. He made no bones about the situation in North America — Europe was much more important — and in making no bones he went all the way, like so many British officials before and after him who frankly saw nothing in Canada but a wild and frosty wilderness. Of what value were a few miles of that one way or the other? He summed up his military observations in a sentence: "I do not know where you could carry on an operation which would be so injurious to the Americans as to force them to sue for peace." He advised his government to make peace as soon as possible and to forget any notion of annexations.

Wellington was much more anxious about the Napoleonic sentiment in France and a British mustering point in friendly Belgium in case the French became obstreperous again. In the autumn of 1814 he rode along that frontier and surveyed its hinterland, noting various useful places and pausing to inspect a good position for an army at "the entrance of the *fôret de Soignies* by the high road which leads to Brussels from Binch, Charleroi and Namur."

There was a village just beyond called Waterloo.

Forty miles away amid the quaint peaked gables of Ghent the British peace commissioners were still chaffering amiably over peace terms with the Americans. According to Mr. Gallatin's son, who was acting as his father's secretary in his work on the American commission, Wellington took time to scratch a note to Gallatin suggesting much the same thing that he had told his own government — that the Americans come to terms as quickly as possible and end the whole embarrassing business.

In later years as Master General of the Ordnance, with a seat in the British Cabinet, Wellington had much to do with building new and expensive defenses in Canada against a repetition of 1812. However the weakness of the old Canadian border line was beyond his view in the autumn of 1814. After his Belgian survey, his hint to Gallatin and a winter among the fickle flatteries of Paris, he went off to take Castlereagh's place at the Congress of Vienna, while on Elba a deposed emperor counted his little bodyguard and gazed somberly toward France.

The tone of the conference at Ghent had been governed all these months by the shifting state of affairs in Europe and by sea-delayed news of the struggle in North America. On the whole the Americans' news had been bad, starting with Napoleon's collapse soon after they arrived and reaching a painful climax with the tale of British troops in Washington, which came to them late in September. Their spirits rose when they heard of the victory on Lake Champlain, but nothing altered the fact that powerful British forces were now hovering on the Canadian frontier and along the Atlantic coast. As far back as June 27 President Madison had written to the commission telling them that, if necessary, they should agree to a treaty of peace without any mention of impressment at sea — the very thing for which the United States officially had gone to war. It was an admission that the United States had lost the war. It was up to the commissioners now to see that the British did not win the peace.

Lord Gambier, the head of the British commission at Ghent, had no experience in diplomacy. Family influence had got him rapid promotion in the Navy and a title, in spite of a court-martial for neglect of duty in battle in 1808 and in spite of gross incompetence as a member of the Admiralty. London's *Morning Chronicle* wondered why the government had chosen to negotiate the American peace a man who "was a post-captain in 1794 and happened to fight the *Defence* decently in Lord Howe's actions; who slumbered for some time as a junior Lord of the Admiralty; who sang psalms, said prayers, and assisted in the burning of Copenhagen, for which he was made a lord."

The second member of the British commission was Henry Goulburn, thirty years old, an undersecretary for War and the Colonies. The third and last was a Doctor of Civil Law named William Adams, who acted as a legal encyclopedia for the others and took little part in the discussions. Clearly the British Government, in sending these men to Ghent, had saved its most powerful talent for European affairs at the forthcoming Congress of Vienna. Shrewd bald-headed Mr. Gallatin soon took their measure. His son noted carefully, "Father is not impressed with the British delegates — men who have not made any mark and have no influence or weight ... Father feels he is quite capable of dealing with them."

The American commission was larger, better chosen, and stronger in all ways: tall handsome Senator James Bayard of Delaware, an outspoken Federalist whom the British were bound to respect; Jonathan Russell the former *chargé d'affaires* in London; Gallatin with his disarming Swiss accent and his neat mathematical mind; John Quincy Adams, someday to be President of the United States, whose cold manner hid a completely selfless patriotism and a penetrating mind; and Henry Clay the War Hawk, thirty-seven, aggressive, a *bon vivant*, a hearty hater of Indians and Englishmen, one of the finest orators in the United States.

A group of such strong and mixed material could not be entirely harmonious. Adams was at odds continually with the bouncing Clay, and Gallatin was at pains to reconcile their differences. None of the others liked the ascetic Adams and outside of their official duties Adams had little to do with them. "I dined ... at one. The other gentlemen dined together at four. They sit after dinner and drink bad wine and smoke cigars, which neither suits my habits nor my health, and absorbs time which I cannot spare." On another occasion, getting up at five o'clock in the morning for the day's work at his papers, Adams wrote, "I heard Mr. Clay's company retiring from his chamber. I had left them ... at cards. They parted as I was about to rise."

With such labors and frivolities the rival commissions had passed the time since early August in the dull little Belgian town. As the frost began to sparkle over the flat monotonous landscape they drew their minds together on the matter of peace. Within a few weeks they came to an agreement. On Christmas Eve they signed it in the refectory of a Ghent monastery and all the bells of the city rang out on the winter air. On Christmas Day the British commissioners entertained the Americans at dinner, with prime English beef and plum pudding brought across the Channel for the occasion. An orchestra played "God Save the King" and "Yankee Doodle," and there were toasts to The King and to The President. At another feast some days later John Quincy Adams gave a toast himself:

"Ghent, the city of peace. May the gates of the temple of Janus, here closed, not be opened again for a century!"

In the main his wish came true and still is true. But the gates of the temple were not quite closed on Christmas Eve, 1814. They remained ajar. There was no mention of sailors' rights in the treaty nor of the British right of search at sea. Nothing was said of Indian land rights in the West, or American claims in the Canadian sea fishery, or the question of naval forces on the Great Lakes, all of which were put over to future discussion. Each country agreed to give up its conquests and retire to the boundary as it was before the war — this was the coup of the American commission at the peace table. It meant that the Americans would give up the lone Canadian foothold left to them as the fighting closed (their outpost at Amherstburg on the Detroit), while the British gave up the whole eastern district of Maine, Fort Niagara, Fort Mackinac, their posts in the Illinois country, their renewed hold on the Grand Portage at the head of Lake Superior, and eventually (though they did not suspect this at the time of signing) their exclusive possession of Oregon.

The Ghent document was a polite admission that as the Americans had lost their war of conquest, the British might as well forget about theirs — that in fact the whole war had been fought for nothing and therefore all the old awkward questions could be put off to future discussion or ignored. This was ominous for the Canadians with their thin population, their long vulnerable frontier, and their sad experience of London diplomats at table with the astute and destiny-conscious Americans. Although Ghent ended the shooting, it settled nothing and left the Canadian border line to twang with periodic tension for the next two generations.

The pleasant notion of a frontier "undefended since 1814" (a favorite phrase of orators on both sides of the border during the twentieth century) has no root in fact. The frontier was jealously and expensively guarded until the 1870s, when the eagle-screaming doctrine of Manifest Destiny had run its course in the United States and the British sensibly abandoned all but two of their old garrisoned posts in Canada. For almost sixty years after Christmas Eve 1814 both nations built elaborate works with an eye to another war. With the experience of 1812 to guide them the British naturally built most of theirs along the Great Lakes and the St. Lawrence, and with a careful regard for the sea connections; hence, among other things, the existing grim citadels at Halifax and Quebec, the expensive and commercially useless Rideau Canal between Kingston and the Ottawa River, and the fortifications at Kingston itself.

The curious modern visitor seldom realizes that all this massive masonry appeared after, not during or before the War of 1812. With the same experience in mind, the Americans built new defenses at Fort Niagara and on Lake Champlain, and for a time after 1814 they planned a powerful fortress and armed camp on the St. Lawrence above Montreal; but the latter expense was put aside in favor of forts on the Potomac, the Chesapeake, and other waters open to British naval attack. Behind the frontier for many years both nations made roads, dug canals, and laid railways that usually served a sound commercial purpose but seldom lacked a military consideration in the background.

The Ghent treaty had said nothing about disarmament. As a post-war economy the United States Government discharged most of its naval personnel on the inland waters, but in May 1816 the British Navy still had more than a thousand officers and men posted on the Great Lakes, ashore and afloat. This disturbed United States Secretary of State Monroe, who suggested to London the complete dismantling of both naval establishments on the Great Lakes. The British were dubious. In another war the Americans, with a large population and material resources close at hand, could create another fleet on the lakes with ease. The British would have to import carpenters and drag material up the St. Lawrence as they had before, a slow expensive process.

However after some weeks of deliberation Foreign Secretary Castlereagh gave his government's consent. The result was the so-called Rush-Bagot Agreement of 1817. (Richard Rush was Acting Secretary of State for the United States and Sir Charles Bagot was British ambassador at Washington; they confirmed in official documents what Monroe and Castlereagh had decided).

In this agreement Britain and the United States each pledged themselves not to keep more than one armed ship on the Champlain waters, one on Lake Ontario, two on the upper lakes. None of these ships would be larger than one hundred tons. None would carry more than a single eighteen-pounder cannon. Accordingly both nations stripped their inland fleets, which were chiefly on Lake Ontario. It was done in an air of mutual suspicion. Both removed their guns, spars, and rigging to storage ashore under the care of permanent dockyard staffs. Both guarded their ships' decks against the rot of weather by erecting huge peaked roofs from stem to stern. One of the phenomena of Lake Ontario for a whole generation was the sight of these strange marine monsters with roofs instead of masts and sails, browsing at moorings in Kingston or Sackets Harbor or standing unfinished on the slips, all perishing slowly of senile decay.

The British Government ceased spending money on the Kingston ships about 1831 and most of them vanished from the Royal Navy list soon after. By 1837 all of their great wooden fighting machines on Lake Ontario had been sold or scuttled in Dead Man Bay. The mighty *Saint Lawrence*, Yeo's pride, had cost five hundred thousand pounds. In 1832 she was sold to furnish timbers for a Kingston distillery's wharf, at a junk price of thirty-two pounds. True to her history she failed to serve even in this useful function, for she went adrift and foundered in a gale. Most of Commodore Chauncey's ships had been junked before this, but one of the great three-deckers he was building in 1815 (the *New Orleans*, a ship of 2800 tons designed for 120 guns) remained on the list of the United States Navy until 1882.

The most significant relic of a war in which powerful fleets sailed on their own drinking water is still to be seen at Holland Landing, Ontario, on the old cross-country portage from Lake Ontario to Lake Huron. Here in the snowy early months of 1815 came a team of oxen dragging a two-ton anchor on a sled, bound from Kingston to the new British naval base at Penetanguishene. When the teamsters heard the news of peace they drank stout drams at the village inn and happily dumped their burden in a wayside field. There it remains in the heart of the Ontario countryside, an object for the cameras of tourists and the wonder of children still, the perfect symbol of an Alice-in-Wonderland war.

The war that was fought on the wrong side of the looking glass had left a tragic human expense account, not to mention the material waste and damages. Officially the British and Canadian troops, regular and militia, lost in battle along the frontier 8600 killed, wounded, captured or missing men. The Americans in battle against them lost 11,300. On both sides the actual loss was much more, for the casualty lists, especially among the militia, were badly kept and there was no record of the men who suffered death or wounds in small patrol clashes or at the hands of hidden sharpshooters along the lines of communication, a day-by-day friction that went on unceasingly for two and a half years. Nor was there any account of the toll by disease, more fatal than bullet or bayonet, which struck men down by companies and whole battalions in the fetid camps and forts and reached its long arm back along the lines of communication. What the Indians suffered was never known. In actual battle their loss was small, for, after their habit, they invariably fought from the cover of the woods or of darkness, melting away into the landscape at the first sign of defeat; they had learned well the bitter lessons of Fallen Timbers and Tippecanoe. But they were easy victims of the white man's diseases, and in the great flocks of men, women, and children who gathered about Tecumseh in the unsanitary camps along the Detroit River there was little chance of immunity. The tribes of the Middle West were never again a numerous or a formidable people and the last flicker of their spirit perished in Black Hawk's pitiful rebellion against the Americans in 1832.

In Canada the deepest scar remained in the Upper Canadian mind, for their countryside had been the real battlefield of the war and in all ways they suffered more than anybody else. Hatred of "the Yankee," carried as a seed by the Loyalist refugees of 1783, came to full growth and a nightshade blossom in Ontario with the invasions of 1812–1814. This had its effect on Canadian politics in the time to come. The accident of geography had placed the Ontarians at the heart of a future Canadian nation, and before the end of the century they were the largest and most powerful group in it.

Manitoba and the Red River Valley

CHAPTER 42

1811 — 1813

The Pacific coast — The Canadians gain Astoria — Lord Selkirk moves Scots to eastern Canada

IN THE noisy rattle of war to the east, certain affairs in the western prairie and on the Pacific coast had passed unnoticed. The little company financed by John Jacob Astor had built their trading post (Astoria) at the mouth of the Columbia River in March 1811. Their main party, including several veteran Nor'westers and thirteen seasick Canadian rivermen, had sailed around stormy Cape Horn in the ship *Tonquin* while the other group, also composed largely of Canadians in Astor's pay, made their way overland from Lake Michigan. After building the small log post and leaving a few men in Astoria, the *Tonquin* sailed north to trade with the Indians at Vancouver Island. Her skipper was a rough old salt with no experience in dealing with Indians and for that reason Astor had sent with him Alexander Mackay, the Nor'wester who crossed the Rockies with Mackenzie in 1793.

One day in a fit of rage Captain Thorn struck a wheedling old chief of the Clayoquots and tossed him over the rail of his ship. The next day a crowd of Indians came off the shore in canoes to trade, and at the first bellow from Thorn they drew knives concealed in their furs and fell upon him and his crew. Mackay perished with the captain and most of the others. Lewis, the ship's clerk, mortally hurt with a stab in the back, made his way below. Four of the sailors got away in a boat and eventually told the grim story. Its end was a clap of thunder in the bay. Lewis had crawled into the ship's magazine and destroyed the ship, the savages, and himself in one spout of smoking timbers and flesh.

This affair marooned the small group at Astoria. The overland party reached them, starved and exhausted, in January 1812. Several had perished on the way. All through 1812 and much of 1813, living hand to mouth, they awaited help from Astor; but war gripped the East and even Astor, with his international connections, could do nothing for the unfortunate Pacific Fur Company. The Nor'westers of Canada were in a much better position.

In 1813 the Nor'westers saw a chance to gain a post at the Columbia mouth and with it (they had secured the upper reaches already) the whole Oregon trade. In that year a Nor'west party came down the Columbia by David Thompson's well-mapped route to bargain with the unhappy survivors of the Pacific Fur Company. When they were told of the war between Britain and the United States it did not take the Astorians long to realize that a British warship could turn up at any time and capture what they still had a chance to sell. Most of them were Canadians, former Nor'westers eager to see their old company take charge with its reliable system of pay and supply. The rest was a foregone conclusion.

In October 1813 the Astorians sold out their interests on the Columbia to the North West Company, who hoisted the British flag and renamed the post Fort George. Thus through the activity of their sea traders about Vancouver Island and of the Nor'westers working through the mountains, the British now held the west coast and its hinterland from the Columbia mouth northward to the Skeena River. Above and below them the Russians dotted the coast line with trading posts as far south as San Francisco Bay, where the Spanish settlements began. The flag of the United States was not to be seen.

The Treaty of Ghent had made no mention of the Columbia River or its huge and complicated watershed. (All this region was known as "Oregon" — the present state of that name was only part of it.) Soon after the peace, however, the government of the United States declared that Oregon had fallen into British hands by threat of capture and therefore remained part of their territory under the terms of the peace treaty. The British considered the country theirs by prior discovery going all the way back to Drake and confirmed by the Nootka Convention with Spain in 1790. The Louisiana Purchase gave the United States no land west of the Rocky Mountain chain, but the Americans advanced the claim of Captain Gray's discovery of the Columbia mouth in 1792 and the journey of Lewis and Clark along the lower reach in 1805.

The wisdom of the American commission in deferring all awkward questions at the Peace of Ghent was now apparent. The Czar of

Russia had moved into the vacuum left by Napoleon; Europe was faced with another tyranny, and Britain no longer held her commanding position of 1814. The result was a compromise, in which the London diplomats agreed to declare the vaguely defined region of "Oregon" open to trade and settlement by American as well as British people. This was in 1818 when the Canadians had been trading and settling in Oregon for five years, and except for a few hunters wandering into the foothills of the Rockies not a single American stood west of Nebraska. The agreement was for ten years. In 1827, before it expired, the agreement was renewed for an indefinite time, but with a provision — at American insistence — that either nation might end it at twelve months' notice. There were still no American settlers in Oregon, but eventually they were bound to come and to outnumber the Canadians in the country. The stage was set for the final move, a United States claim for exclusive possession of the whole region, including what is now known as British Columbia.

Meanwhile there was a strange new stir of life in the Canadian prairie country, where all this time the only human inhabitants had been roving bands of Indians, fur traders, and their half-breed offspring.

In 1813 the Nor'westers were at the crest of their power. In what Canada's governor general knew vaguely as the "Indian Territories" — the whole sprawl of the continent from Lake Superior to the Pacific and from Minnesota to the Arctic outfall of Mackenzie's river — no rule or law existed but that of the North West Company. In the region about Lake Winnipeg they tolerated some outposts of the Hudson's Bay Company, but the trade was mainly in their hands and their rule went with the trade. Although the Nor'westers flew the British flag and gave a loyal toast to His Majesty at all their feasts, in operation theirs was an independent Canadian empire. For thirty years they had been thrusting to the Arctic and the Pacific, mapping the country as they went and regarding it as their own.

Formal direction of the empire came from the senior partners at Montreal, with active headquarters at Fort William. Many a Nor'wester never returned east of Lake Superior. He became a part of the enormous West. For his white or *métis* sons (some of whom he taught to read and write) a job of any sort with the company was the most desirable thing in life, and for nearly all of them Fort William was at the eastern limit of the known world.

Five thousand men, white and half-breed, ranging the country all the way to the Pacific, looked to Fort William for their pay in the company's service. To take care of all this the village of Fort William had a permanent staff of clerks and "forwarding men" working under the eyes of the "wintering partners," a group of tough strategists, most of them Scots, who seldom or never went down the lakes to Montreal. But in the East these men had a powerful influence. Their Montreal directors' mansions were the finest and most luxuriously furnished in that city; they kept the best horses, the most expensive carriages and *carioles*, and gave the most elaborate dinners. The Nor'west headquarters in Montreal dealt with larger funds, controlled far more territory and ruled it more efficiently than the parliaments of Lower and Upper Canada or the governor general's own staff at Quebec.

Money makes useful friends and the Nor'westers had them everywhere, even in such a quiet backwater as York, the sleepy capital of Upper Canada. There lived the Anglican clergyman John Strachan, who married the widow of a Nor'west partner and thenceforth saw things from a Nor'west point of view in the terrestrial sphere. Strachan eventually achieved great power and firmly believed himself to be the vicar of both God and Caesar in the democratic wilderness of Upper Canada. And there in York and at Kingston lived the other men who became notorious as the Family Compact, of which Strachan was the head, a small but able and ruthless coterie determined to rule Upper Canada as their friends the Nor'westers ruled everything beyond.

The Nor'westers' influence did not stop at York or Montreal. It crossed the sea to Britain itself, where some wealthy partners and friends of the company now lived, among them Sir Alexander Mackenzie, with the honors of his Arctic and Pacific journeys still upon him, and his fellow Scot Edward Ellice, a member of Parliament for the English town of Coventry. With such advocates at the heart of the British empire, the power of the North West Company stretched all the way from London to the mouth of the Columbia.

The irony of this was that the great Nor'west machine, which sucked in furs at one end and poured out guineas at the other, had begun to falter at the cash end just when the fur intake had gained its farthest reach and its toughest efficiency. This was due to Napoleon's decree of 1806, which closed the European continent (the largest and most lucrative fur market) to British trade. The London value of furs had shriveled, and with it the profits of the Nor'westers and of the Hudson's Bay Company. They could only wait grimly for an end to Napoleon's power, meanwhile conducting their Canadian enterprises with the greatest skill and economy, stuffing their warehouses with unsold furs after selling what they could in the British market, and subtracting the annual loss from their capital.

The Hudson's Bay Company had among their papers a charter signed by King Charles II which granted them proprietary rights over all the country drained by rivers running into the great Bay. It was drawn in 1670 when no one knew what rivers there were and whence they came. The Hudson's Bay Company had made small effort to find out; but others, especially the Nor'westers, had found that the bay received through Lake Winnipeg the waters of the Red and Saskatchewan rivers, which drained most of what are now the Dakotas and Minnesota and a vast stretch of the Canadian prairies reaching all the way to the Rockies. This was the huge empire in which the Nor'westers had so firmly established themselves; yet in fact their possession was merely a squatter's right covering a few yards about each of their posts, while the Bay Company held an actual royal charter to the lands.

The man who peered with a candle into this sleeping gunpowder was a Scot named Thomas Douglas, fifth Earl of Selkirk.

Selkirk was born in 1771, a son of the laird of St. Mary's Isle on the southwest coast of Scotland. He became a graduate of the University of Edinburgh, a friend of Robert Burns and Sir Walter Scott, and in 1799 he inherited the Selkirk title and fortune. He was then a handsome young man with auburn hair, wide-set gray eyes, an intellectual brow, a bold aquiline nose and the mouth of a dreamy poet. His future vicissitudes sprang from that brow, that nose, and that mouth.

It was a time of distress in the Highlands of Scotland, where (unlike Selkirk) most of the great landlords were still carrying out the infamous "clearances" — driving their poor tenants from the fields and hills to make way for more profitable herds of sheep. Selkirk pitied the homeless crofters and dreamed of moving thousands of them to the broad spaces of Canada, where they would find lands and a good living that no one ever could take away. In 1803 he made a start, sailing with eight hundred people to Prince Edward Island in the Gulf of St. Lawrence. He went on to a personal tour of Canada and the United States, and on his way through the Great Lakes he bought a tract of wild meadows near the mouth of the Thames river. In 1804 he conducted another party of Highland folk to that spot, which he called Baldoon Farm. Returning homeward, he paused in Montreal to dine and talk with the leading merchants, including the jovial barons of the North West Company. His ideas of settlement so far ranged no farther than the Ontario peninsula and with these beginnings he was satisfied. Naturally so were they.

After Selkirk's second expedition his mind was taken up by marriage, by his duties as lord lieutenant of Kirkcudbright, and by the urgent problem of Britain's defense against a French invasion; for after 1803 the great war with Napoleon entered its second and more dangerous phase. The distress in the Highlands continued and in 1811 Selkirk turned his whole mind to the settlement of Scots in Canada. His colonies in Prince Edward Island and Ontario were struggling to exist, for their lands were poor. The best soil in eastern Canada had been taken up by others before them or (especially in Upper Canada) set aside as Crown and Clergy reserves or for speculation by friends of the government. Selkirk had read Sir Alexander Mackenzie's book on the Canadian West; he had heard tales of the Nor'westers about the deep black earth of Manitoba; and when he looked at the map it showed that immigrants from Britain could approach the country in ships by way of Hudson Bay, avoiding much of the long and expensive travel inland from Quebec.

Selkirk was no mere dreamer, he was prepared to risk a fortune on his dream, and in considering the risk he had the canny quality of the Scot. The war-born difficulties of the great Canadian fur companies were now plain to everyone. Shares of the Hudson's Bay Company had fallen to a low price on the London stock exchange. Shares of the North West Company were closely held in their peculiar partnership system, but their value, too, was low. In planning a large settlement in Manitoba, Selkirk came upon the curious fact that the Bay company had the only legal right of possession there. To make sure, he had lawyers examine the company's charter. With that confirmed he and his friends began to buy Hudson's Bay Company shares at the market price and before long they had about one third of the stock in their control. Selkirk then asked the company's directors for a large grant of land in Manitoba and for permission to carry emigrants across the sea in the company's supply ships.

Word of all this reached the sharp ears of Ellice and Mackenzie, who saw at once the threat to the whole Nor'west structure beyond Lake Superior. For years the Nor'westers had got their main supply of pemmican in the buffalo plains below Lake Winnipeg where the Red River flowed — and where Selkirk now proposed to settle his people and create a new province. More than this the Red River's western tributary, the Assiniboine, was the Nor'westers' canoe route toward the Saskatchewan, the great river whose twin branches offered a convenient passage all the way to the Rockies. And now a colony of farmers, with a governor of their own, and under the patronage of the Hudson's Bay Company, was to be planted in that vital corridor!

Mackenzie quickly bought some Hudson's Bay shares himself, and at the company's annual meeting in London in May 1811 he arose as a shareholder to make strong objections to Lord Selkirk's request. He was backed by some others, but most of the Bay shareholders knew a Nor'wester when they saw one and guessed his motive. The customary show of hands gave Selkirk's proposal an overwhelming approval. On the strength of it Selkirk received, for the sum of ten shillings, a grant of no less than 116,000 square miles, about half in what is now called Manitoba and half in what later became the states of Minnesota and North Dakota. (At this time the United States had no defined boundary beyond Lake of the Woods, and under the ancient royal charter the Hudson's Bay Company claimed the Red River watershed all the way to its end near the present cities of Minneapolis–St. Paul.)

Most of those present at the London meeting regarded Selkirk as a well-meaning visionary who would probably waste his fortune in the Canadian wilderness, and one of them told him so. No doubt Mackenzie thought the same, but he wrote the partners in Montreal advising them of this new and possibly dangerous development. The Nor'westers in Canada were not alarmed at first, seeing the whole thing as a piece of Utopian nonsense that would come to nothing, but they remained watchful.

To gather and lead people into this promised land, Selkirk sent for

Captain Miles MacDonell, a veteran Loyalist who had settled at Glengarry in Upper Canada. The Highland crofters were dubious and held aloof, unwilling to chance their lives on the cold northerly passage to Hudson Bay and then in the heart of a savage continent hundreds of miles from the nearest Canadian settlement. When three ships of the Bay Company sailed on their annual voyage from Britain in July 1811 they carried no more than 105 Scots and Irish men and women gathered all the way from Galway to the Orkneys, including a considerable group of Glasgow townsmen of the poorest class.

CHAPTER 43

1811 — 1821

*Scots in Manitoba — The quarrel of the Nor'westers —
Massacre at Seven Oaks — Selkirk restores his colony
— The Nor'westers sell out to Hudson's Bay*

AFTER a rough passage MacDonell and his settlers landed on the southwest edge of Hudson Bay on September 24, 1811. It was too late in the short northern season to go on to the Manitoba plains and they had to build log huts and winter on the lower reach of the Nelson River. MacDonell found them a fractious company and in the spring he had to weed out some of the Glasgow men and the Irish and send them back to Britain. With the rest he set out in boats built on the spot, toiling up the Hayes River, a rugged journey with many portages but an easier route to Lake Winnipeg than the more violent flood of the Nelson. It took them most of the summer. On August 30, 1812, they drew up their boats on a bend in the Red River forty miles below Lake Winnipeg. They called it Point Douglas in honor of Selkirk's family and built a small cluster of huts.

Two miles farther up the Red River, just where it was joined by the Assiniboine, stood a small Nor'west post with an imposing name, Fort Gibraltar. Just as the real Gibraltar guarded the entrance to an enclosed and valuable Mediterranean, so this rude structure of logs and sods watched the Canadian gateway into the continental plains. It was one of several Nor'west posts in the plains below Lake Winnipeg and Lake Manitoba, chiefly engaged in gathering buffalo robes and bales of pemmican for the use of posts in the more barren parts of the North. About Fort Gibraltar camped a small band of *Boisbrûlé* (Burnt Wood) Indians, and with them lived a large number of *métis* who dressed and looked exactly like them.

Selkirk's settlers were greeted by a pony-borne rabble of these hangers-on, naked to leather clouts and moccasins, their cheeks daubed with vermilion, their long hair plaited and skewered with eagle feathers, and with dyed lovelocks glued to their temples. They rode up brandishing lances, tomahawks, and a few guns, shouting threats in *patois*. However they made no attempt to molest the new-comers, for Captain MacDonell had in the boats half a dozen swivel-mounted blunderbusses, each a miniature cannon capable of firing a dangerous blast of nails or buckshot.

Selkirk had given Miles MacDonell the title of Governor of As-siniboia, and on September 4, 1811, the governor marshalled an awkward squad of musketeers (most of the settlers had never handled a gun before in their lives), hoisted the British flag on a pole, and read aloud his commission. On his invitation the audience included some of the picturesque ruffians from Fort Gibraltar, but whatever their impressions they had nothing more to say. Indeed they were confident that the intruders would perish of cold and starvation in the first prairie winter.

This was a distinct possibility, for the settlers had brought few supplies and when MacDonell tried to buy a winter's supply of pemmican at Fort Gibraltar the canny *bourgeois* set an exhorbitant price, knowing that the immigrants could not pay. The *métis* re-mained hostile but the pureblood Indians, unlike the brown hybrids who wore their dress and aped their customs, were friendly to Mac-Donell, an old Indian hand from his Mohawk Valley days. Under their guidance the settlers moved south along the Red River Valley, following the winter retreat of the buffalo, and returned in the spring to till their fields at Point Douglas. In this way with much hardship they survived the first two years, while far to the east of them the War of 1812 raged on, a struggle in another world.

The Nor'west crew at Fort Gibraltar with their flock of wild retainers continued each year to hunt and kill buffalo, to cut the meat into strips and dry it in the sun, to pound and shred the dried meat, to mix it with berries for taste and melted fat for moisture and body, to mold it into cakes, to press the cakes into bales of buffalo hide, and to send tons of the baled pemmican up the Assiniboine for the supply of posts in the North and West. It was the established routine for the company going back decades into the past and without it the more remote posts would have found it hard to exist in the winter months.

Governor MacDonell took a sour view of the business, seeing winter after winter the hardships of his own people while the

Nor'westers lived in plenty. When the deep cold gripped the prairie country in January 1814 he resolved to make an end of it, and dispatched over his frosty domain a notice forbidding anyone in the fur trade to send food out of the Red River plains. In his own view it was a measure necessary for the life of his colony. In another view it was a calculated slash at the throat of the Nor'west supply system by a representative of the Hudson's Bay Company, and when the news reached the fur barons at Fort William they saw it in that light. Meanwhile MacDonell sent a party of armed men to Souris, a Nor'west post up the Assiniboine River, seized six hundred bales of pemmican en route to the North, and stored the captured meat in Brandon House, a rival post of the Hudson's Bay Company not far away. A worse provocation to the fierce Nor'westers could not have been contrived.

In the summer of 1814 another party of Highland men, women, and children came to Red River by way of Hudson Bay. At about the same time the active partners of the North West Company sat down in their hall at Fort William to consider current problems. It was an annual meeting in which great men from Montreal mingled with the "wintering partners" and with various traders and explorers bringing news from the farthest outposts. Behind the head of the council table, like a listening idol, stood a bust of Simon McTavish, the patriarch of the Nor'westers. Portraits of George III, of Admiral Nelson, of the fat Prince Regent and other British worthies looked down from the walls; and there, too, hung a great painting of the Battle of the Nile, and what was most significant to the men at the board, a map showing the Nor'west empire all the way to the Pacific, made by David Thompson himself.

The Montreal partners and the "Spring brigade" with supplies for the West had traveled with some risk owing to the war. A strong American army was poised on the Niagara for a new invasion of Upper Canada and an American squadron was in Lake Huron for an attack on Mackinac and Sault Ste. Marie. In spite of all this the formidable men gathered about the board at Fort William had quite another war on their minds. One of the wintering partners, Alexander MacDonell, who had come in from the Assiniboine country, wrote to a friend in Montreal, "Nothing but a complete downfall of the colony will satisfy some, by fair means or foul — so here is at them with all my heart and energy."

At the close of the meeting Alexander MacDonell and Duncan

Cameron left the council hall for the West. In Assiniboia they went about their plans carefully and with enormous patience. Cameron had been serving as a captain of Canadian riflemen attached to the British garrison at Mackinac. He appeared in the Red River settlement wearing the full uniform of a British officer and he nailed to the gate of Fort Gibraltar his written commission as a captain in the service of His Majesty. These postures were impressive in the wilderness.

Captain Cameron put a pleasant face on his activities, moving easily among the gaunt settlers at Point Douglas, chatting in their own familiar Gaelic, sympathizing with their hardships, hinting sauvely at Selkirk's neglect of them, calling up pictures of a better life among people in the more civilized parts of Canada or the joy of going back to Scotland. Alexander MacDonell (no relation to Governor Miles MacDonell except by name) and other Nor'west agents appeared among the Indians on the plains and in the forest between Red River and Lake Superior, inciting them against the white intruders and anyone who might try to communicate with them from Hudson Bay or from the Great Lakes. But here they found the Indians as canny as themselves. The Manitoba country was the only region where the Hudson's Bay Company competed directly with the Nor'westers for furs, and in the competition the Indians got a better price. Stolidly they refused to join in an obvious squabble between two rival groups of traders, and the Nor'westers began to realize that their best tools were the *métis*, bound to them by ties of blood and of easy fosterhood about their posts.

At the close of the year 1814 the Nor'westers began to realize something else. The long wars with France had come to an end, and soon a rush of hopeful poor from the British Isles would pour into Canada. At any time now the Red River settlers would be joined by others, with an increasing flow each year, displacing and burying the fur interests on the plains as their rude plows buried the buffalo grass.

During the hard winter of that year Duncan Cameron won over many of Selkirk's settlers, promising them free transportation to the north end of Lake Winnipeg, whence they could make their way down to Hudson Bay and take ship for eastern Canada or for home. His chief dupe was George Campbell, a man of some weight in the little community, who had quarreled with the strong-willed Miles MacDonell. In the spring of 1815, while the governor was still absent in the winter grounds of the buffalo, Campbell and others stole the six small swivel cannon which guarded the settlement and carried them off by pony sled to Fort Gibraltar.

Governor MacDonell returned to find his people divided and the loyal ones at the mercy of the *métis*. He soon found himself a prisoner charged with stealing the pemmican at Souris, and packed off under guard to Montreal, where the Nor'westers had a heavy hand in the courts. Of the Selkirk people about 150 left the settlement, traveling in canoes to Jack River at the northern tip of Lake Winnipeg. Here they would winter in log huts, ready for next spring's journey down to Hudson Bay. About fifty others remained hopefully at Point Douglas; but after a time, dismayed by the increasing mischief of the *métis* and by the lack of any word from Lord Selkirk, nearly all of them joined the others at Jack River. When they had gone the *métis* came over from Fort Gibraltar and burned the village to the ground. One shack survived, and that only because it was defended by three resolute Hudson's Bay men and the lone remaining settler, Hugh McLean. But on the face of things the Nor'westers had won and Selkirk's dream was just a drift of ashes on the prairie wind.

Into this almost deserted scene soon afterward paddled the canoes of Colin Robertson and a party of *voyageurs* bringing Selkirk's promised supplies from eastern Canada. They found McLean and his companions warily tending the abandoned grain and potato crops about the ruined village, and with a tale to tell. At the end of it Robertson sent his *voyageurs* to fetch the people back from Jack River. There was no interference from Fort Gibraltar. Duncan Cameron had gone to report his success in Montreal and to bear witness against Governor MacDonell in the courts.

Under Robertson's vigorous leadership the settlers rebuilt their cabins and in September harvested a good crop of grain. In another month they were joined by ninety more Highland folk sent out by way of Hudson Bay. These included an elder of the Church of Scotland with authority to baptize and marry, and a new official, Robert Semple, a former officer in the British Army. At Selkirk's urging the Hudson's Bay Company had made Semple the governor not merely of Assiniboia but of all their territory in the West, an appointment ominous to the Nor'westers.

Governor Semple's first act was to send an armed party to recover the guns stolen from Point Douglas. They got them from Fort

Gibraltar without trouble. Duncan Cameron had returned, but again he was content to bide his time. During the winter of 1815-16 the colonists again moved south in pursuit of the buffalo, for the summer's crops were not enough to feed the increased population at Point Douglas. When they came back in the spring they found the *métis* in a bad mood.

In the wry phrase of the plains the *métis* were half French, half Indian, and half devil. Although they lived like savages they were always conscious of their white blood. Most of them had sprung from the loins of Nor'west *engagés* and they inherited the Nor'west hatred of everyone and everything that came to the plains by way of Hudson Bay. It was eighty years since the first French Canadians set foot in Manitoba and now a whole race of mixed blood rode the plains, intermarrying freely with the whites, with the Indians, and with each other. They outnumbered the whites by far and they probably outnumbered the Indians, for the prairie tribes habitually slaughtered each other whenever their hunting parties met. By 1815 the *métis* were calling themselves the New Nation, a name and a problem that were to convulse the Canadian West before the century was out.

With the whispers of the Nor'westers in their ears the New Nation saw the continued trickle of settlers to Manitoba as a dangerous portent, an unwelcome foot inside the tepee door, with worse to follow. Thus the air prickled in the Red River valley in the spring of 1816 when Governor Semple, a stubborn and ungifted man, determined to show the Nor'westers and their wild following that he was absolute ruler of the country. In April he sent the fearless Colin Robertson to arrest Duncan Cameron on a charge of burning the village of Point Douglas in the previous summer. Robertson and his group of armed *voyageurs* thrust their way past the rude gate of Fort Gibraltar and seized their man. Semple then ordered them to tear down the fort itself, a job they performed with a will, floating some of the timbers down the river to make a palisade about Semple's house — henceforth to be known as "Fort Douglas." With that done, Robertson and his men set off with Duncan Cameron as their prisoner, not to Montreal (justice there was tainted by the influence of Beaver Hall), but to York Factory on Hudson Bay, where in the next navigation season he could be shipped for trial in England.

The fat — the buffalo fat of the plains — was now in the prairie fire. Alexander MacDonell was up the Assiniboine River at Fort

Qu'Appelle, a Nor'west post. With Cuthbert Grant, a Scotch-Indian leader of the *métis*, he gathered a war party and captured some Bay men taking furs and pemmican down the river in boats to Fort Douglas. They went on to seize and loot Brandon House, and thence to Portage La Prairie, a key point on the canoe route to the West.

In the meantime the Nor'westers in Montreal had been using all their wiles to confound Lord Selkirk and his colony in the West. Sir Gordon Drummond, the gallant but none too perceptive soldier of Lundy's Lane and Fort Erie, was now serving a brief term as governor general of Canada. Since the close of the war most of the British troops had been discharged in Canada or sent home, and Drummond insisted that his military responsibilities ended at the head of Lake Huron, where he had a small post on Drummond Island. The squabble on the plains was a private one as far as he could see — and he could never see very far.

Lord Selkirk prodded the Colonial Office in London and the Colonial Office vainly prodded Drummond, asking him to look into the quarrel at Red River. Drummond was quitting office in the spring of 1816 and he was quite happy to leave the matter to his successor. Unsatisfied, Lord Selkirk sailed from Britain with his wife and family late in 1815, landed at New York in November, and made a rough and chilly journey through the Champlain pass to Montreal. However his personal prodding had no more effect on Drummond than the letters of the Colonial Office. The governor general's only response was a polite shuffling that in effect left the Nor'westers a free hand in the West. All that Selkirk secured in a long winter and spring at Montreal was the freedom of his former governor, Miles MacDonell. This alone was a miracle and he could hardly expect more. Sherbrooke, the incoming governor general, a soldier like Drummond, was bound to be slow in seeing anything beyond the views of his predecessor.

Selkirk, still determined, wrote letters to Red River promising help in the coming summer — help that he would bring himself. The Nor'westers waylaid his messenger in the woods beyond Lake Superior, read the letters over their own council table at Fort William, and decided on prompt action. They sent off to the West a company of well-armed Nor'west retainers under Archibald Macleod, and they armed Macleod with a commission as magistrate for the Indian Territories, which had a much longer range than the guns in the canoes. They had in mind the pliant courts in Montreal — and as it happened the muskets were unnecessary. Their agents in Manitoba had taken care of all the shooting.

On June 19, 1816, a troop of seventy armed Nor'westers and *métis* rode down the Red River bank opposite Fort Douglas. Governor Semple in his hothead way crossed over to demand their business, taking with him about thirty of the settlers, most of them unarmed. The two groups met where seven oak trees cast a pool of shade on the prairie grass and there was a brief passage of angry words between Semple and a spokesman of the Nor'westers. Then the wild men on the ponies closed in with a rush. A few musket shots, a busy flash of knives and tomahawks, and all was over. Semple and twenty-two of his men lay dead. Two were held alive as prisoners who might be useful later on. Only six escaped across the river with the tale.

Cuthbert Grant, leader of the savage horsemen, sent one of the prisoners with a demand for the surrender of Fort Douglas, where the widows and children of the slain men were rending the air with Gaelic lamentations. Colin Robertson was away. There was no word from Lord Selkirk, no sign of soldiers from the East, no hope at all. Grant offered to let the settlers depart unmolested with all their portable property, and on this promise they admitted him and his wild men to the "fort" — the palisaded house of the murdered Semple. The *métis* promptly looted the whole settlement. The people, about two hundred men, women, and children, were allowed to leave in canoes for Lake Winnipeg. As they paddled their doleful way down the Red River, the refugees met Magistrate Macleod and his hundred Nor'westers from Fort William. The magistrate gave their tale no sympathy. He dismissed it as a pack of lies, carried off with him the five settlers who seemed the most dangerous witnesses, and told the rest to get on their way.

Far away in the East Lord Selkirk had engaged a band of *voyageurs* and sent them off for Red River as an advance guard under Miles MacDonell. In Montreal and Kingston he enlisted and armed about a hundred veterans of the late war, chiefly Swiss soldiers of the DeMeuron Regiment. He left Montreal on June 16 and by the end of July he had reached the Sault Ste. Marie rapids between Lakes Superior and Huron. Here his little army met Miles MacDonell, who had traveled at speed to Lake Winnipeg, heard the tale of massacre at Seven Oaks, and turned back to warn his chief. Selkirk's first reaction was to accost the local magistrates at Drummond Island and Sault Ste. Marie, demanding that they go with him to Red River and see justice done. These backwoods dignitaries, both under Nor'west influence, refused to budge.

Selkirk now took the law into his own hands, an expensive gesture, as he found out later in the Canadian courts. The Nor'westers at Fort William were soon aware of Selkirk's approach, but they assumed he would by-pass their headquarters and hurry on into the West. Not all of the partners had been in favor of Alexander Mac-Donell's "fair or foul means" and now that the deed was done there was doubt in the cooler heads as to the wisdom of their agents on the plains. The council at Fort William at this time included men of high intelligence and ability like Simon Fraser, the explorer of British Columbia; Doctor John McLoughlin, afterwards the famous "father of Oregon"; and handsome William McGillivray, for whom the post was named.

These and the other Nor'westers in the lake-head village were in an awkward position when Selkirk appeared and pitched his tents on the river nearby. The best of their own armed retainers had gone to the Red River with Archibald Macleod. They could still muster a rabble of *métis* and Indians, the typical loafers about every Nor'west post, but Selkirk's company were impressive with their military snap and glitter. Nothing like this had ever been seen in the West. The wise heads in Fort William decided to fall back on their most potent weapon, the law as dispensed in Montreal, where all legal matters pertaining to the Indian Territories had to be tried.

They offered no resistance when Selkirk's soldiers thrust their way through the rabble at the fort gate, and nine of the partners (including Fraser, McLoughlin, and McGillivray) submitted quietly to arrest. Selkirk sent them eastward under guard to be charged with complicity in the Red River crime. He had found his own letters in McGillivray's office, clear proof that the Nor'westers had robbed his messenger and learned his plans; but there was no other proof and his legal case was slim — too slim for a court in the shadow of Beaver Hall.

The traveling season was now far gone for the long route through the forest to Lake Winnipeg. Selkirk and his troop settled down in possession of Fort William for the winter. In the spring of 1817 they set off for Red River. Word of their presence and intentions in the West had gone before them. The Nor'westers on the distant plains were astounded by the capture of Fort William and the news of its great men sent east for trial like common criminals. It began to dawn upon them that the old era was past. A new power, of which Selkirk was only the forerunner, had begun to move into the West. The villains of the Red River tragedy slipped away into the safer reaches of the plains and when Selkirk arrived on the scene there was no one to oppose him.

Once more canoes passed up Lake Winnipeg to fetch the bedeviled settlers back from their camp at Jack River. Selkirk, already marked down by tuberculosis, which had killed all his brothers before him, set to work with febrile energy laying out the lines of a new village, allotting lands to his Swiss soldiers, setting apart space for a church and school. He decreed that the parish should be called Kildonan, quite unaware that some day a great city called Winnipeg would sprawl over Kildonan and all the land in sight.

And now at long last British troops appeared, a very small party sent into the West by Sir John Sherbrooke at the urgent demand of the Colonial Office. They found nothing to do. The *métis* had withdrawn, the Red River settlers tilled their lands in peace. The redcoats returned east in the autumn of 1817 and the governor general wrote smugly to London that "a degree of tranquillity" had been established in the Indian Territories. So it had — by Selkirk's personal exertion and at his cost. The Nor'westers, confining their battle now to the Montreal courts, won heavy damages for Selkirk's seizure of Fort William and the arrest and detention of their "wintering partners." But they were fighting for the last time. The long wars had left their company almost bankrupt; the cost of their long overland communication system had gone up steeply with the wages of wartime, it had come down little since, and in the postwar wreckage of Europe there was no immediate hope for the fur business. Moreover it was known generally now that their old exclusive possession of the West had been blown away on the cold legal wind from Hudson Bay. The Montreal courts could fine Selkirk but they could not upset a charter signed by Charles II.

In 1818 Lord Selkirk left Canada, conscious that his main battle was won but sick in body and bitter in mind. His health, never good, had been spent with most of his fortune in these transatlantic ventures. His doctors sent him to France in the hope of keeping life in his wasting body, but he died at Pau in the foothills of the Pyrenees on April 8, 1820. Less than a month before, far away in Scotland,

Sir Alexander Mackenzie had breathed his last at Pitlochry. The passing of the two old enemies, as far apart in death as they had been in life and thought, in a curious way summarized the long quarrel of the companies they represented. For that, too, was coming to an end.

The Hudson's Bay Company, with its ownership of the West confirmed and demonstrated by Selkirk's enterprise, could raise new capital to exploit it. By the same token the Nor'westers could raise none. The Bay Company, with a bulk shipping route to the very fringe of the North and to the heart of the West, could keep its costs at a reasonable level, and similarly, by shipping direct to the Pacific coast, it could operate cheaply beyond the mountains. In 1821 the Nor'westers merged their interests with those of the old rival, surrendering their name along with everything else. Henceforth every post from Labrador to the Columbia was to bear the H.B.C. sign — "Here Before Christ" to the irreverent — while the grim barons of Beaver Hall, too old to adopt a new loyalty like the younger Nor'westers, turned their minds and their money to banks and suchlike interests in Montreal.

CHAPTER 44

1815 — 1825

A decade of peace — The Erie Canal — Canadian banks
— Colleges — Canals — New search for the North
West Passage — Russian and American claims
on the Pacific coast

NAPOLEON'S escape from Elba and the swift sequence of
Waterloo and his final banishment to St. Helena came as an
anticlimax to the Canadians in the summer of 1815, for in the
meantime peace had settled on North America. The great wars
now were truly at an end. There was to be much civil strife in the
time to come, and war between nations here and there, but not
another world war for a century. All unconsciously the human race
was entering upon a century of progress such as it had never known.
The steam engine, finding use in all directions, was about to change
the face of civilization, and the painful but steady advance of general education was about to change its mind.

While steam power had been slowly developing during the long
reign of George III the British people had hit upon a means of
cheap transportation in the canal, which was well adapted to their
landscape. By 1801 Britain had more than three thousand miles of
improved or artificial inland waterways and speculation in canal
shares had become a national pastime. Apart from the well-popu-
lated flat lands below Lake Ontario, the rugged terrain and empty
distances of North America made such a widespread canal system
impossible. Until the coming of the railways the main transportation resource was in the natural flow of the rivers. The Canadians
had a problem which could only be solved by canals in by-passing
the rapids and falls that obstructed water traffic on the St. Lawrence
and the Great Lakes. They had begun in a small way at Lachine and
on the first rapids above Montreal, and the Nor'westers had dug a
crude little boat canal at Sault Ste. Marie on the passage between

Lakes Huron and Superior, but a real tackling of the problem demanded an outlay of capital far beyond Canadian means or dreams.

On the other hand the Americans with their ever-growing capital resources, their swarming population, and their constructive genius, soon seized upon the chance for a canal to draw the rich trade of the Great Lakes region away to the sea through their own territory. De Witt Clinton had surveyed a route between Lake Erie and the Hudson River as early as 1810. The War of 1812 had forced the scheme aside, but in the effort to get military materials to the battle front, the Americans had seen the commercial as well as the strategic value of easy transportation between their own coast and the lakes. Prodded by Clinton, the state of New York began to dig the Erie Canal in 1817. When it was finished in 1825 a loaded barge could leave Buffalo and arrive at New York in a week. Meanwhile (in 1822) another canal had joined Lake Champlain to the Hudson River; and in 1828 the Oswego canal linked Lake Ontario with the Erie system to the Hudson. Through these channels New York became almost overnight the chief port and metropolis of the United States (and a good deal of Upper Canada), while the old Montreal monopoly of the Great Lakes "forwarding trade" became a shadow.

The Canadians were now face to face with the problem of their environment, which was to trouble and challenge them for generations. In their failure to keep pace with the Americans on the south they were often accused of a lack of energy and enterprise, but this was hardly true. The Canadians had thrust their way across the continent and created a busy mercantile empire extending to the Arctic and Pacific while the Americans were still hesitating and squabbling with Indians in the region east of the Mississippi. But as the nineteenth century passed into its second quarter the Canadians found that human daring and endurance were no longer enough.

Their people were few, the Americans many. To the average European, Canada and Siberia were synonyms for all that was cold, infertile and savage, and as a result most of the emigrants pouring out of Europe went to the United States. Money followed the same course. Even British capitalists, making money fast in the new industrial age, preferred to invest their surplus funds in the more promising fields below the Canadian border. And there was a heavy political handicap. The Americans had an increasingly powerful central government — a heart in their own body — and a mind

afire with the creed of Manifest Destiny. The Canadians remained
a coterie of provinces sharply divided by language and religion
(literally divided, for the French-Catholic mass of Lower Canada
stood for hundreds of miles between the English-speaking Protestants of the Maritime Provinces and those of Upper Canada) and
all remained under the rigid rule of the Colonial Office in London,
whose limited imagination had to spread itself over the wide scatter
of British possessions in every part of the world.

The manufacturing and shipping interests of Britain naturally
regarded the colonies purely as feeders to their industries. For them
all imperial roads led to British countinghouses. The empire existed
for their benefit, just as the common people of Britain itself existed to
dig their coal, to sweat in their new potteries and foundries and
textile mills, to stoke their newfangled steam engines, or to spread
their sails about the seas. The great material march of the nineteenth
century, which made Britain the world's greatest industrial and trading nation before it ended, had small concern with British humanity
at home or abroad. Humanity stirred, of course. It had a long and
bitter struggle and eventually it won. In the meantime (to look at
only one facet of the struggle) the Canadians had to wrestle with
an absentee government concerned chiefly with its own commercial interests; and it was difficult to accomplish anything at all with
large and petty divisions among themselves, a pinching lack of
funds and credit, and the harsh facts of their geography and climate.

At the end of the War of 1812 there were barely half a million
Canadians, most of whom lived east of Lake Ontario. The war
brought into the country a good deal of British money, but that
flow ended with the war and the money itself settled inevitably in
the coffers of merchants in Halifax, Quebec and Montreal. Of these,
only the Montreal men had any interest in the country to the west.
The merchants of Halifax and Quebec stood with their backs to
the continent, looking for trading opportunities across the Atlantic
or southward to the West Indies. Even in Montreal in 1815 the
typical merchant was the old Nor'wester, wealthy personally but
well aware that the Nor'west empire was on its last financial legs.
For the development of the West under Canadian auspices there was
hardly a shilling available.

Figuratively and geographically Canada formed the huge mysterious attic of the continent, dimly lit and cluttered with strange
obstacles, where like a small boy the Canadian moved with a lonely

curiosity, conscious always of the snow on the roof above his head, while downstairs the large and exuberant family of the Americans surged with confidence through the warmer chambers of the house, throwing up the blinds one after another and installing everything from churns to chandeliers.

The year 1820 forms a rough milestone in Canadian history. It happened to be marked by the deaths of four men; the Duke of Kent, poor old George III, Alexander Mackenzie, and Lord Selkirk, each of whom in his own way had something to do with the making of Canada. An era had passed.

In the following year the Hudson's Bay Company took over the Nor'west empire, and the old rule of Montreal over the western plains and mountains was gone. From this time until 1869 the whole region from Lake Superior to the Arctic and to the Pacific was to be governed from the Bay Company's offices in London, a domain flying the British flag like the Canadian provinces to the east, but as independent of them as if they did not exist.

The struggling finance of the country took its first step toward orderly progress by the creation of banks. In 1820 the Bank of New Brunswick was incorporated, the first bank in British North America to conduct its business under a proper charter of rights and obligations. John Molson, Peter McGill, and others had formed in 1817 what was known as "the Montreal bank," carrying on a limited-liability business in the old stronghold of the Nor'westers but without a legal act of incorporation. In 1821 it was incorporated as the Bank of Montreal. In that year also two other banks in Lower Canada and one in Upper Canada opened with legal charters of the same kind.

Until 1820 the only institution of higher learning in the Canadian provinces was King's College, founded in Nova Scotia in 1789. The Earl of Dalhousie, coming to Nova Scotia as lieutenant governor after the War of 1812, discovered that King's College had become a jealous preserve of the Church of England, barring students who would not accept the doctrine of the Thirty-Nine Articles. This was very different from the fresh and vigorous atmosphere of the open Scottish universities which he had known at home. In 1818 he set apart money from the useful Castine Fund to create a public institution, and in 1820 the new building of Dalhousie College in downtown Halifax opened its doors to students of all faiths. In

1813 old James McGill had died in Montreal leaving funds for a similar purpose in Lower Canada, but thirty years were to pass before McGill University opened its doors. However in 1819 the little hospital in Craig Street began the organized teaching of medicine, a branch of education for which Montreal was to become famous.

In spite of small means and long distances, the Canadians were struggling to improve their roads and other means of transportation. The physical geography of the land south of the St. Lawrence waterway, which enabled the Americans to dig their useful Erie-Ontario-Champlain canal system, had no counterpart on the Canadian side of the border. Niagara Falls and the St. Lawrence rapids could not be by-passed except at tremendous cost. In 1821 the Montrealers began to dig a modest barge canal around the Lachine Rapids, which they finished in 1825. But in that year the Americans completed the Erie Canal and by-passed the whole St. Lawrence system.

Plainly such piecemeal Canadian efforts were not enough; yet the job was too much for private capital. Soon after 1820 William Merritt of St. Catharines, Upper Canada, determined to realize the ancient Canadian dream of a canal and locks to pass small vessels around Niagara Falls. With his own and the capital of some friends he set to work on the first Welland Canal. Before long he had to beg financial aid from the government of Upper Canada, which in turn borrowed funds at a costly rate of interest from shrewd London bankers. The provincial government was nearly bankrupt when the Welland Canal was finished in 1830, but Merritt's ardent mind leaped on regardless, seeing a series of canals and locks to by-pass the St. Lawrence rapids and make a clear waterway for small sailing vessels or steamers from the Great Lakes to the sea. There were many delays and financial pains. Lower Canada would do little to help until the British Government forced a political union (and common tax funds) with the definitely bankrupt Upper Canadians in 1840. Even when Merritt's dream came true in 1849 only vessels drawing less than eight feet of water could pass from Quebec to the head of Lake Huron.

Quite apart from these ventures, the British Government itself built a notable canal in Upper Canada. The opening of the Cham-

plain and Erie canals disturbed the imperial strategists in the War
Office, seeing that the Americans could now move troops and munitions to the Great Lakes and to the head of the Champlain pass with
the greatest ease, while the defense of Upper Canada still depended
on the upper St. Lawrence and the road along its bank, menaced by
American gun sites on the right bank all the way from Lake St.
Peter to Lake Ontario. Wellington had become Master General of
the Ordnance, and with Napoleon moldering in the grave, the victor
of Waterloo at last could see Canadian defense problems with an eye
unclouded by the closer dangers of Europe.

Something had to be done to secure military communications
between Montreal and Lake Ontario. The Ottawa River offered a
route part of the way and its Rideau tributary dangled a chain of
lakes down the map toward Kingston — the obvious site for a
canal. In 1826 Colonel By of the Royal Engineers began to dig the
ditch and build the necessary locks. The work went on slowly and
painstakingly in the British Army fashion and in 1832 the Rideau
Canal was open for barge traffic. It had little or no commercial use,
but although there was never again a war with the United States,
the future held repeated threats of one, and until the coming of the
railways the Rideau had a military insurance value in its mere existence. Something unexpected sprang from it. A small hamlet called
By Town sprang up about the canal's Ottawa entrance, one day to
become the capital of all Canada.

The 1820 milestone had other significance in the matter of
Canadian transportation, for in that year enterprising Mr. Molson
had eight or ten steamers shuttling between Quebec and Montreal.
His first two had been valuable in moving troops and supplies to
Montreal from the transports at Quebec during the War of 1812.
In 1816 a Kingston company launched the *Frontenac*, the first
steamship on the Great Lakes, plying between Prescott, Kingston,
York, and Niagara; and in 1819 the first steamer appeared on the
Ottawa River.

Although farming remained the mainstay of the Canadian population, the logging industry was growing fast, sawmills were springing up on every stream (even on the far Columbia where John
McLoughlin, now a faithful servant of the Hudson's Bay Company,
built the first Pacific sawmill about 1821) and in 1823 more than

three hundred great rafts of timber floated down the Ottawa. Other industries were' forming, among them the first iron foundry in Upper Canada, built in 1820 by Joseph Van Norman.

The great rush of European immigration had yet to come, but people were moving into the vacant lands of Ontario. In 1824 the population of Upper Canada was 150,000, almost entirely rural. Kingston was still the largest town with 2400 people, Toronto (still known as Little York) had less than 1500, but more than 12,000 people were living on farms in old Colonel Talbot's Erie domain alone.

Perhaps the most dramatic incident of the year 1820 was a rural conference of Canadian and American Methodists at the little red meetinghouse on Lundy's Lane, called to heal the breach created by the War of 1812. There on the battlefield twenty ministers were ordained, some of whom had fought on opposite sides a few years before.

In Lower Canada the French-Canadian population was growing rapidly, although enterprise in their largely agricultural economy was not keeping pace with it. In 1826 Andrew Stuart reported that the population living on the old seigneuries had increased four times since 1784, but that the number of cattle had only doubled, and the land area cleared and plowed had only increased one third. Montreal, having failed with a system of wooden pipes, provided itself with a water supply through iron pipes in 1819. Mr. Molson's steamboats, overcoming the St. Mary current with ease, already forecast a time when ocean shipping would pass Quebec and throng the docks of Montreal, but strangely the first permanent city wharf, 200 feet long, did not appear until 1824 when the population had reached 22,000.

The Maritime Provinces were in the doldrums. The prosperity of the long wars had vanished with the troops and fleets, and in the pinch of postwar economy the British Government had closed even the Halifax dockyard, an important industry in the town since 1758. It was difficult to pick up the bits and pieces of a peacetime trade that hardly anyone could remember. The tight clutch of the leading merchants, made wealthy by the wars, kept all specie out of sight. People were drifting away to Upper Canada or the United States. In Halifax grass grew in some of the residential lanes, where empty houses stood cheek by jowl, even in bawdy Barrack Street.

While the Canadians were thus preoccupied in provincial worries

and money-starved enterprises, something else was going on far to
the north. In 1818 the British Government offered a reward of
20 thousand pounds to the first ship to navigate the Northwest
Passage — assuming that there was such a passage, the old dream of
the Elizabethans. The Admiralty set the example by sending off
Captains Buchan and Franklin to travel by land to the Canadian
Arctic and explore the shores; for at this time the mouth of Hearne's
Coppermine River and the dreary delta of the Mackenzie were the
only known parts of the whole frigid coast between Hudson Bay
and Alaska. At the same time Captain Ross and Lieutenant Parry
sought the passage by sea in the neighborhood of Baffin Bay. In
1819 Parry with a new expedition sailed through Hudson Strait and
wintered on Melville Island. In 1820 Franklin, Back, and Richardson
left York Factory on foot, crossed the barrens, followed the Coppermine to its mouth, and mapped 550 miles of the Arctic coast. Other
British explorers were planning to attempt the passage by way of
Bering Strait, and Franklin had in mind a descent of the Mackenzie
River in order to map the unknown coast toward Alaska.

This busy new interest of the British in the Northwest Passage had
a startling result in the year 1821, when the Czar of Russia issued a
ukase defining his possessions in North America, laying claim to the
whole coast from Bering Strait to Latitude 51° North, close to the
north tip of Vancouver Island, and forbidding the ships of any other
nation to enter those waters. In effect this closed the westerly end
of the passage for which the British were so busily seeking, and it
ignored British claims to much of what is now the coast of British
Columbia.

Typically the British people at this time had no interest in North
America, whatever the Admiralty might be doing in those frosty
regions. That summer they had been absorbed in the coronation of
George IV, who had been Prince Regent ever since his father's
definite madness in 1811. It was an exciting spectacle, with
"Prinny's" estranged wife Caroline going from door to door of
Westminster Abbey, demanding her right to be crowned as his
Queen, and being turned away. The people hated "Prinny" and
sympathized with Caroline, and her sudden death a few weeks later
gave a new and bitter note to the common feeling against their
ruler and the growing revolt against the ruling class, which had
shown itself in the Reform agitations of 1819. With these diversions it was not strange that the British Government made no answer

to the Czar's announcement, for even Castlereagh's strong mind was at the end of its tether — within a year he cut his throat and ended his life's problems in one stroke.

However in 1822 Britain made up her mind to withdraw from the Holy Alliance, which was now dominated by the Czar; and when the Czar proposed to back France in setting up a new despotic government in Spain the British Government was quick to recognize the independence of the old Spanish colonies in South America. It was on this occasion that Canning uttered his memorable "I resolved that if France had Spain, it should not be Spain with the Indies. I called the New World into existence to redress the balance of the Old."

But the Czar's announcement regarding North America did not go unnoticed. Another voice was heard. In 1823 the United States Secretary of State, John Quincy Adams (the man of Ghent), declared, "We should contest the right of Russia to any territorial establishment on this continent, and we should assume distinctly the principle that the American continents are no longer subjects for any new European colonial establishments." This warning flash of political lightning was the forerunner of the famous Monroe Doctrine, of which Adams was really the author. Already Adams had secured from Spain the resignation of all her claims east of the Mississippi (in 1820, after United States troops had occupied Florida by force of arms) and at the same time Spain renounced all claim to the Pacific coast of North America beyond Latitude 42°, the present northern boundary of the state of California.

In 1824 the United States secured from the Czar a treaty in which Russia agreed to lift her restrictions on shipping in North American waters and to make no settlements south of Latitude 54°/40'. The United States in turn renounced all claims to territory north of that line. The American intention was to shut the Russians out as far as possible, but this agreement had an ominous implication for the Canadians. The agreed line of the Russians and Americans lay many miles north of the inlet where the Canadian seaport of Prince Rupert now stands. By inference it challenged every British claim on the Pacific coast. Within twenty years the wilder exponents of Manifest Destiny in the United States were to make the inference a flat statement and a demand, and their famous cry, "Fifty-four-forty or Fight," was to bring the British and Americans again to the edge of war.

CHAPTER 45

1815 — 1836

*Poverty and demand for reform in Britain — Emigration
to North America — The Maritime Provinces
— French-Canadian unrest — The growth
of Montreal*

NAPOLEON had pulled down the rococo monarchies and
aristocracies of Europe one after another, and when he fell
the Holy Alliance set them up again with all the obsolete
political views of their previous existence. Under this crust of reaction the imperishable yeast of the French Revolution remained in
the European masses and set them fizzing more and more dangerously as the memory of Waterloo faded into the past. In Britain
the monarchy had survived in spite of poor mad George and his evil
or merely stupid sons, because there had to be a symbol about which
the British could mold the empire and rally against the armies of the
French, and the crown provided it. The ruling class in Britain, the
aristocracy and the country gentry with their rich landholdings
and their poorly paid tenants and laborers, now sought every means
to bolster the monarchy and themselves as a unit, one and inseparable,
in the political turmoil that was bound to follow the wars.

In this they had the powerful aid of Wellington, himself an
aristrocrat with no love of new ideas, and through Wellington
the power of the Army. The restricted right to vote, the many
"rotten boroughs" and other features of the corrupt British electoral
system had made the House of Commons a preserve of the wealthy
class almost as exclusive as that of the Lords. All this was to be
maintained against the rising demand for reform among the people.
Notable was the so-called Corn Law.

During the Napoleonic wars, when nearly all foreign supplies
were cut off or highly expensive, the landowners had made fat
profits from their monopoly of food. In 1815, seeing the approaching
inrush of cheap food from the opened ports of Europe and America,

they used their control of Parliament to put a stiff tax on grain from abroad. As an imperial gesture the new law granted free entry to Canadian grain only, for at this time it was not enough to matter; otherwise the barrier was tight. The common people of Britain, to whom bread was life, were never to get bread cheaply while the Corn Law remained on the statutes.

The law brought hunger to the poorest class as soon as the post-war slump threw a multitude out of work. The towns were filled with discharged soldiers and sailors, munitions workers, dockyard hands and others, most of whom had known no normal trade since they were old enough to earn a wage. Added to these were the weavers, cotton spinners, hosiers, lacemakers, and other hand labor now being displaced by machinery under the magic power of steam. A rumble of distress sounded all over Britain. In Glasgow in 1819 a mass meeting of forty thousand people gathered to protest against the hard times. Many wanted a petition to the government or to the Prince Regent himself, asking free transportation to Canada, where they could at least grow their own bread. Others insisted that they should be able to live at home, that the solution was a change of laws, and that the means of change was a universal right to vote and an annual parliament which could be thrown out of office quickly if it failed to satisfy the electorate. These sentiments were not merely Glaswegian, they were general.

To the British ruling class all this was downright anarchy, calling up horrid ghosts of the French Revolution, and the government set a harsh face against it. A great public gathering in Manchester in 1819 was attacked and dispersed by dragoons, the celebrated Peter-loo Massacre, which showed how the government intended to deal with the popular unrest. The common man's only hope was in emigration to America. There had been a trickle in that direction ever since the last muskets tramped off the field of Waterloo. After the sabers of Peterloo it became a stream. By 1830 it was a flood. Most of it poured to the United States, but a northerly current drifted to Canada, drawn by the letters of established settlers and by the tales of soldiers and sailors posted there during the War of 1812.

This hegira gave a rich opportunity to greedy shipowners. The poor of the British Isles, ready to sell their last possessions for passage money, made easy victims. They had to provide their own food and bedding on the voyage, and they were eager to believe glib tales of the shipping agents about an easy journey and the prospect of fat lands to be had free anywhere on the Canadian shore. Poorly provisioned, worse clad, these unfortunates were crammed into the dank black holds of ships that were often unseaworthy and always unsanitary, carried away on a voyage that at best took three weeks and at its violent worst might take months, and then dumped ashore at the first landfall. Thousands perished of hardship and illness or by shipwreck on the stormy Canadian coast.

Newfoundland and Nova Scotia made a convenient dumping ground for the shipowners, eager for a quick turnaround and another voyage, and a swarm of men, women and children found themselves in a region where good soil was rare and long since occupied, and where the only lands available to them were patches of rocky forest. The local people were hospitable; but as their churches, charitable societies, and village poor-committees struggled to cope with the increasing inpour of destitutes from overseas, many of them sick, there was at last a cry to the British Government for stricter regulation of the emigrant shipping trade.

The home authorities were slow to interfere with what seemed a cheap and providential means of shifting their burden of unemployed. Every one of these disappearing into the transatlantic forests meant one less voice to shout for the reform of Parliament and an end of upper-class privilege. It was not until the ghastly cholera epidemic among the emigrants in 1832-34 that measures were taken. By that time the sorry accounts written home by earlier arrivals were having their effect, and after 1840 most of the emigrants to Canada traveled past the coastal provinces and joined the others who had made their way up the St. Lawrence.

Most of the Catholic Irish stopped in the ports of Halifax, St. John, Quebec, and Montreal, where they sought work as laborers, and those who could save a little money soon went into business as lumbermen or as the proprietors of small inns and dramshops.

The great body of the incoming people were English-speaking and Protestant, and these traveled past the gleaming tin spires and belfries of the French-Canadian villages to settle in Upper Canada, where people spoke and worshipped as themselves. The Scots among them with the old clan instinct settled in groups. Sometimes these groups were large and organized like those of the Canada Company formed by John Galt, a man of Selkirk's type, more poet than businessman, who obtained a Crown grant of more than a million acres on the Lake Huron side of the Ontario peninsula and founded the towns of Guelph and Goderich.

The English settlers usually drifted into place as individuals, a general diffusion with no particular voice or prejudice except in the case of the "remittance" class. Many of the latter were the families of officers who had served in Canada during the late war, liked the country for its abundant sport with rod and gun, and settled down on their half pay, often deep in the wilderness where the sport was best. Others came as upper-class immigrants with a private income from Britain, a magical possession in a country where coin was precious. On the whole they were people of education and taste who dragged books and even pianos into the forest, regarded their own hardships and the foibles of their backwoods neighbors with a lofty amusement, and sometimes (like Mrs. Moodie and Mrs. Traill) wrote shrewd accounts of both for publication in Britain. Politically this class was an offshoot of the landed gentry in Britain, suspicious of democracy, leaning always to the views of Strachan and his Family Compact, the self-chosen rulers of Upper Canada with their emphasis on Church and flag.

The most notable body among the immigrants in Upper Canada was the large proportion of Protestant Irish, a vigorous and hard-headed folk who carried with them the old fanatic feuds of Ulster against everyone and everything that had to do with "Popery." Pushing into the forest, they hacked out farms for themselves and planted, among much better things, the Orange seed, which in later years made Ontario the home of a harsh and intolerant type of Protestantism that clashed inevitably with the jealous and militant French Catholicism down the St. Lawrence.

Last but not least there was the always useful American immigration, stopped by the War of 1812 but now moving quietly and steadily into the Ontario peninsula by way of Niagara and Detroit. These people, like the English, settled as individuals wherever they could find a patch of good land or what they called a "smart chance" for a sawmill, a store, or some other local enterprise. Their influx was an eddy of the general American tide toward the West, most of which was now moving rapidly by steamboat up the immense waterway of the Mississippi and its branches, and fanning out in the central plains of the continent.

The Canadians and their smaller inpour of new people halted in the Ontario peninsula. Beyond lay a forbidding distance of rocky forest stretching around Lakes Huron and Superior and all the way to Manitoba. There was no means of getting past Fort William except by canoe over five hundred miles of wild rivers or rugged portage paths where everything had to be carried on human backs. Few of the newcomers to Canada were able or willing to reach the prairies by the icy route through Hudson's Bay. Without Selkirk's funds and his passionate interest, the Manitoba settlement languished. The populated area of Canada halted abruptly in the longitude of Ohio, while that of the United States, already large and swelling yearly in the rush from Europe, rolled away on paddle wheels and wagon wheels toward the Rockies and the borders of Mexico.

In the Maritime Provinces the 1820s and 30s were a time of lean toil and small reward. Each of the successive lieutenant governors had his own idea of the way to prosperity. All were soldiers, like those of Lower and Upper Canada. Indeed during these years the Canadian provinces suffered a strange aftermath of Waterloo, for most of their governors were Wellington's generals, given these lucrative colonial posts as a reward for their services. They shared the Iron Duke's view of democracy as an incipient mutiny in the ranks. None of them could understand the complex of mixed nationalities and aspirations which now made up the Canadian people and few of them tried. They drifted naturally in the tight little orbit of the "Family Compact" group in each province, the equivalent of the privileged class at home, to which they belonged themselves.

The Earl of Dalhousie had a better experience in Nova Scotia than he had later on in Quebec. He did not hesitate to flout the Halifax Compact in the matter of a non-denominational college and his other ideas were good but not always practical. Apart from his interest in cultivation of the mind, he believed in a strenuous cultivation of the Nova Scotia soil. To this end he fostered agricultural societies, appeared at plowing matches and autumn fairs, hacked a new road straight as a sword cut through the forest from Halifax to Annapolis and settled whole regiments of ex-soldiers on it. As the postwar stream of immigrants arrived, he packed them off into the woods in the same manner.

Much of Dalhousie's dream perished in the unkind soil of the Atlantic slope. Some of the civilians took root, combining small-

farming with logging or the fishery. The military settlements fell
flat. Nearly all of the soldiers quitted their sorry clearings as soon
as the government ration ceased or their government-issue tools
wore out, drifting into the towns and taking up any trade they could
find. A former sergeant of the Dragoon Guards set up a dramshop
in Halifax with the bird of peace and this doggerel painted above
his door:

> My name is Pat Love at the sign of the Dove.
> I made my money in France and Spain —
> And spent it all on Hammond's Plain.

In the 1820s there were Sergeant Loves in every town of the
Maritime Provinces, in Quebec, Three Rivers, and Montreal, and
all along "the Front" from Kingston to Niagara.

In New Brunswick Lieutenant Governor Douglas busied himself
in Dalhousie's manner with roads and agriculture and education. He
expanded the Fredericton grammar school into a college, got a royal
charter for it, and thus founded the University of New Brunswick.
All his efforts were overshadowed, however, by the smoke of a
tremendous forest fire in 1825, which swept the upper parts of the
province from the St. John River to the Chaleur Bay and the mouth
of the Miramichi. Whole towns and villages were destroyed, hundreds of people perished, thousands were left destitute, and nearly
four million acres of the best timber in the province were turned to a
black desert. Douglas, by appeals to charitable folk in Britain and in
the other colonies managed to raise forty thousand pounds for the
relief of the sufferers, but the province took a long time to recover.

In Nova Scotia Dalhousie was followed by General Kempt, whose
recipe for progress was an elaborate network of roads, ignoring
the fact that most of the population lived on or near the seacoast,
where water transport was easy and cheap. Then came General
Maitland, a stiff and pompous pietist whose remedy for everything
was an ultra-puritan regimen for the colonists' daily life.

Maitland's attitude was an exaggerated reflection of the post-
Regency wave of respectability then sweeping over Britain and
across the sea. It was reflected in all the provinces of Canada in such
matters as feminine dress, especially in the towns where for years
(especially during the Napoleonic wars) the ladies had aped faithfully every extravagance from London. Gone now were the flimsy
peep-bo gowns and all but naked breasts of the Duke of Kent's

romantic days in Canada, gone the turbans, the clinging dresses, the jouncing hips and bosoms, the Wellington jackets, froggings, and epaulets with which the ladies had endeared themselves to the dashing officers of 1812. Stays and tight lacing were back with a vengeance. It became not only proper but chic to wear drawers (hitherto reserved for winter wear) and to wear them in a cascade of ruffles down to the ankles, a sight that would have thrown the semi-nude charmers of Kent's day into hysterics. Over these things, as the years rolled by, the ladies pulled on increasingly numerous and formidable petticoats, gowns, bodices, pelisses, and shawls. By 1835 the female body had gone completely into hiding, not to emerge or even to reveal its shape for half a century.

As for the townsmen of colonial fashion, those vain and contrary creatures were now displaying their manly figures in skintight trousers that strapped under the instep, in snug-waisted frock coats with flaring skirts and padded hips, and balancing on their heads the enormous top hats of the time, which threatened to snuff them like candles at any moment.

Village schools were increasing, especially in the Maritime Provinces and among the people of American origin in Upper Canada, who had inherited the ancient New England passion for education. Higher education was expensive, a privilege for the few. However, that poor man's university the Mechanics' Institute was now springing up all over Britain in the wake of the Reform movement. By 1829 Joseph Howe was urging one upon the citizens of Halifax. It came in 1832 and was busy for the next quarter century with classes and lectures on everything from English literature to comparative anatomy. Not merely "mechanics" but clerks, farmers, and laborers of all kinds crowded the institute to the doors. It was astonishing. And there was much the same experience in the other English-speaking provinces, where for years every town of respectable size supported an institution of this kind, usually with a lending library and a reading room attached.

In all these ways, twenty years after Waterloo, the Canadian provinces with the rest of the British world were well embarked on an age of respectable progress and progressive respectability that needed nothing but a name. This was supplied, curiously enough, by a legitimate daughter of that former Canadian resident the Duke of Kent. She came to the British throne in 1837, bringing with her a strange new cachet of decency and sobriety after the long noisome train of "the wicked uncles," and her name was, of course, Victoria.

The *habitants* of Lower Canada regarded the inpour of English-speaking and largely Protestant immigrants with suspicion during the 1820s and 30s, and were thankful to see it passing up the St. Lawrence. Even the Catholic Irish who settled among them were not welcomed, for they too spoke English. Quebec, the seat of government, held a better-balanced view of things than Montreal, however. The English-speaking merchant group in Quebec was small, with a tradition of courteous co-operation with the French dating back to the regime of Murray, the first British governor; and at Quebec lived an intellectual class of priests and gentry who knew that the world did not begin at Gaspé and end at Montreal. These saw that, whatever happened, French-Canadian rights were firmly secured by the overwhelming *canadien* majority in the legislature and by the very fact that few of the English-speaking strangers were settling in their own province. (The only large English-speaking group outside of Montreal were the long-established settlers in the Eastern Townships bordering on Vermont and New Hampshire, and the Quebec legislature refused to grant them any representation in the assembly until 1829.)

It was in and about Montreal, where the money-making *anglais* of the merchant class (typified by the ruthless Nor'westers) had been at feud with the *canadiens* ever since the conquest, that the friction of language and religion were hottest and intolerance was deemed a virtue on both sides. This was aggravated by a pair of incidents in 1822 when Dalhousie was governor general. In that year the London government received a proposal (instigated by the *anglais* of Montreal) to unite Lower and Upper Canada in one province. At this time Lower Canada had far the greater population and the British immigration into Upper Canada was still too small to change the voting power there. Nevertheless the French Canadians resented this arbitrary attempt to throw them into one bed with the English Protestants of Ontario; so did the wiser element among the *anglais* in the lower province, who saw the squabbles that were bound to arise.

This resentment was sharpened by the second incident of 1822, the discovery that John Caldwell, favored for years with the lucrative post of receiver general in Lower Canada, had stolen one hundred thousand pounds of the provincial funds. This, said the *canadiens*, was the result of the Château Clique giving all the good posts to the *anglais*. Two Lower Canadian representatives crossed the Atlantic to put their case against union. One was John Neilson, editor of the Quebec *Gazette*, the other was a rising French-Canadian politician, Louis Joseph Papineau. Together they convinced the British Whigs, and when the Whigs spoke against the scheme in Parliament the British Government promptly dropped it and went on with its own affairs.

But the real damage of this hasty and self-interested proposal of the Montreal *anglais* had been done. When the tide of British immigration thickened and surged up the St. Lawrence the French Canadians recalled the 1822 proposal and saw it as a monstrous plot to sell them up the river, to link them in a single parliament with the Upper Canadians, and then to flood the upper province with English voters. The more feverish agitators among them, the self-styled *Patriotes*, harped on it year by year as the endless English tide streamed on toward Ontario. When the immigrant ships brought cholera along with their human cargoes in 1832, spreading the plague until every town from Halifax to Niagara was a pesthouse and thousands perished, the agitators did not hesitate to make another charge — that the diseased immigrants had been introduced into the St. Lawrence ports in order to kill off French Canadians.

Indeed no accusation, then or later, was too wild or too absurd to fling at *les sacrés anglais*. The educated French Canadians could smile and dismiss these extravagances with a shrug. They were able to distinguish between their genuine grievances and the froth. The majority of their people lacked this balance. Illiteracy, common enough among the English-speaking poor now flocking into Canada, was almost complete among the *habitants*, who only knew what they were told or what was read to them from the more inflammatory sheets published in the cities. It was a perfect field for the native demagogue and he entered it with the weapon of demagogues everywhere, the dangerous facility given by active jaws and a flaming imagination.

Trade was almost entirely in the hands of *les anglais*, even in the forest, where men like William Price employed large numbers of *canadiens* in cutting logs, hewing them square, and shipping them to sawmills in Britain. Subsistence farming remained the chief source of livelihood and the *habitant* still pursued it with the happy-go-lucky ways of his forefathers, even to dumping the barnyard manure into the river or the nearest swamp instead of spreading it carefully over his fields. The science of cultivation, advanced in Britain by the food needs of the Napoleonic wars and carried to the Maritime Provinces and Upper Canada through the active agricultural societies, made no impression on the *habitant*. In all ways he clung to the past as to a rock in a rising sea. A time was coming when he would know that new ideas, even *anglais* ideas, were not necessarily dangerous, and that he could use them to improve his own scale of living without losing his integrity as a *canadien*; but that day was far in the future. As late as the 1840s he still wore the woolen stocking cap, the linsey shirt, the coarse homespun jacket and trousers, and the cowhide boot sewn like a moccasin which had been the wear of his father and grandfather before him; and his women retained the coarse native linen, the heavy homespun gowns, and the habit of going barefoot except in winter and on the Sunday walk to church. The whole attitude of the *habitant* folk was summed up by Papineau when he rejected any sort of English enterprise in Lower Canada: "Our people do not want English capital nor English people here. They have no ambition beyond their present possessions and never want to go beyond the sound of their own church bells."

The town of Quebec had grown quietly, but in appearance it had changed little since the conquest. Montreal with its mixture of English and French and its busy wharves and stores was a roaring place by 1830. It had burst its old seams long ago. The eighteen-foot ramparts and their gates had been carted away and the small citadel had been razed to make Dalhousie Square. A few traces of the fortifications marked the limits of the old town for the curious and that was all. The Lachine Canal had improved the traffic upriver and the advent of the steam tug made it easy to get ocean-going sailing ships up to the lower wharves. The first ocean-going steamer appeared in 1830. She was the *Royal William*, built at Cape Cove near Quebec under subsidy from the provincial government, which was anxious to get a steamship of at least five hundred tons on the route between Halifax and Quebec. To assist her engines (installed at Montreal) she was rigged with sails on three masts. During 1831 she made successful trips to Halifax and back, but in the next year the cholera epidemic and the quarantine restrictions kept her idle at Quebec. In 1833 she paddled down the gulf to Pictou, Nova Scotia, and thence across the Atlantic to London, the first Canadian steamship to make the ocean passage. (The *Curaçoa*, the first

European ship to cross the Atlantic with steam power alone, had made the long passage from Antwerp to Dutch Guiana as early as 1827.)

A vision of the future was now open to the Montrealers. In 1830 they formed their first harbor commission, gave it four thousand dollars a year to improve the docks, and set up a Canadian branch of Britain's famous Trinity House to chart and mark with lights and buoys the shipping channel from Quebec. In 1832 they incorporated their city and elected a mayor and sixteen councilors by popular vote. Unhappily for the new corporation the future included a prompt visitation of the cholera. Improvements had to wait. Catherine Traill on her way to Upper Canada in 1832 was "struck by the dirty, narrow, ill-paved or unpaved streets of the suburbs, and overpowered by the noisesome vapour arising from a deep open *fosse* that ran along the street behind the wharf. This ditch seemed the receptacle for every abomination and sufficient in itself to infect a whole town with malignant fevers. The cholera had made awful ravages and its devastating effects were to be seen in the darkened dwellings and the mourning habiliments of all classes. In some situations whole streets had been nearly depopulated."

By 1836 the ravages of the plague were a hideous memory and the city was flourishing again. In that year the city installed its first gas lighting and on July 21 there was a mass excursion across the river to see the opening of Canada's first steam railway, fifteen miles long, connecting Laprairie opposite Montreal with St. Jean on the Richelieu. This was the old portage route to Lake Champlain, where American steamers now linked St. Jean with the Hudson canal.

CHAPTER 46

1830-1836

The state of Upper Canada — The Canadians in Oregon

THE emigrant to Upper Canada in the 1830s found a land still largely under forest, although most of the lake fronts were cleared and occupied. The roads into the interior were mere ax-cut slots in the woods, with logs ("corduroy") thrown down in the swampy stretches. Any long journey by cart was a bone-racking experience. There were good houses of brick or frame construction in the towns and on farms along "the Front," but the log cabin was still the common home of the countryman. The new life of the immigrant was a familiar picture in North America: the gathering of cheerful and vigorous neighbors in a "bee" to clear a garden patch and build a cabin; the search for a spring or the digging of a well; the first winter in a cold that was strange and frightening; the return of warm weather; the first planting and the first crop; the gradual extension of the clearing; the first cow; the first horse and wagon; the slowly easing nostalgia for the old country; the sons and daughters growing up caring for nothing but the new.

The birth rate was high among people who married young and lived this hard and vigorous life. The cradles of Upper Canada rocked as busily as those down the St. Lawrence, and every child was welcomed as another recruit in the conquest of the wilderness. In worldly goods the transplanted British weaver or laborer remained as poor as he was across the sea; the great difference was that he could feed all these mouths about him with a plenty unimaginable in the slums of London or Glasgow or in the grim cottage rows about the British coal mines and factories. John Howieson, traveling about the settlements of Ontario as early as 1820, was able to report that "in Upper Canada the people live much better than persons of a similar class in Britain; and to have proof of this it is necessary only to visit almost any hut in the backwoods. The interior of it seldom fails to display many substantial comforts, such as immense loaves of beautiful bread, entire pigs hanging round the chimney, dried venison, trenchers of milk and bags of Indian corn."

Depending on his distance from a sawmill, from a gristmill, and from the easy transportation of Lake Erie or Lake Ontario, the settler's market products were grain, flour, timber, wood ashes (for the production of potash), salt beef or pork, and the furs he caught in his winter traps. He seldom saw money, but all these things could be bartered for his needs at the nearest merchant's store. The free life and its self-sufficiency lifted him out of the old-country attitude toward gentry of birth or money or both and gave him the cool viewpoint of the frontier, where a man was measured by what he was and did himself.

To the thin crust of Upper Canadian society, taking its tone from Archdeacon Strachan, from the British garrison officers and their wives, from the half-pay officers or remittance men and theirs, and from the letters and newspapers of upper-class Britain, all this was an evil circumstance. There was a perpetual sniffing, a tendency to regard the backwoods farmer's independent outlook as "American" — forgetting that it was naturally Canadian and North American — and to see in it something dangerous. The epithet "American," potent since 1812, was applied to every symptom of free thought, precisely as the ruling class in Britain applied the word republican (meaning anarchic French republicanism) to every such symptom in their own working class.

This attitude in what might well be called the Upper-Upper Canadians extended to religion, for most of them regarded the Church of England as a kind of spiritual garrison against the invasion of "American" ideas, precisely as His Majesty's sadly bored redcoats watched the frontier in the flesh. The postwar rush of settlers had brought a strong body of Presbyterians into the country, but Methodism had the popular hold, planted by American settlers long before and still drawing many of its ministers from the United States. For that reason the Upper-Upper people threw the word "American" at all Methodists like a stone, implying disloyalty and perhaps even treason; and consequently British immigrants of the Wesleyan persuasion tended to stand aloof from the other Methodists lest they offer the same target. The fact that in 1828 the Canadian Methodist Church had formally separated from that of the United States (thus creating the first truly Canadian church of any sort) made no difference to those who preferred to throw the stone. The Upper-Upper Canadians, led by Strachan and his Family Compact, went on grimly fighting the War of 1812.

All of this had been exacerbated by the chief justice of England in 1824, when he ruled that any persons who had failed to leave the United States by the end of 1783 were indelibly citizens of that country. They could not possess, obtain, or transmit British citizenship, nor could they inherit real estate in any part of the British empire. In effect this ruling declared that Simcoe's "late Loyalists" and all the other Americans who had settled in Canada during the past forty-one years *and their descendants* had no public or property rights in the country. No attempt was made to enforce this extraordinary decision — it could not be enforced in Upper Canada where a majority of people were of American descent — but it led most of them into the ranks of the Reform party, opposing the Family Compact; and this in turn led the Upper-Upper Canadians to throw the "American" stone at all the friends of Reform.

On the Great Lakes the familiar *bateaux* and Durham boats were disappearing fast and even sailing ships were finding sharp competition from steam. In 1833 steamers were coming and going from Toronto "almost hourly," and a steamer left Prescott every day for Toronto, Hamilton, and Niagara. Upper Canada had 320,000 people, most of whom were securely past the bare struggle to live and could find time now for politics and other diversions.

Amusements were few and crude. In the backwoods settlements the various "bees" and the militia parades, with their accompaniments of fiddling, dancing, horse racing, drinking and fighting, provided the chief outlet for high spirits. In the garrison towns of Kingston, York, Niagara, and Chippewa there were amateur theatricals staged by officers of the British regiments, and groups of strolling players, sometimes English, usually American, made barnstorming journeys about the larger settlements. American circuses also moved about the countryside in summer showing a few wild beasts or performing dogs, pigs, and horses. Niagara Falls was already a popular pleasure resort, and the tone of rustic amusement was demonstrated in 1827 when an old schooner with sheep and other animals aboard was cast adrift above Goat Island and allowed to plunge over the falls. A similar cruel spectacle formed the star attraction of 1829.

Lumbermen were now working a long way up the rivers and lakes, and the production of ax-squared logs for British sawmills was giving way to shipments of plank sawed in local mills. On the Ottawa a great wooden chute passed logs around the Chaudière Falls and the ax was ringing in the stands of virgin pine as far back as Lake Timiskaming. In spring when the log drives came down the river, By Town and other villages along the Ottawa became a bedlam of hard-drinking, hard-playing, hard-fighting lumberjacks, Irish, Scots, French and English. Indeed the whol province was a land of rugged men with rugged ways of passing the idle hour. Kingston and York remained the only places with any pretension to culture. (York with its population of ten thousand incorporated itself as a city in 1834 under the old Indian name, Toronto.) Beyond the towns life had a tang of cruder things, a mingled reek of plowed earth, pine sawdust, wood smoke, candle tallow, rye whiskey, damp wool, manure, and human and animal sweat. It was a frontier smell familiar in America and years were to pass before the scent of finer things crept into it.

West of Lake Huron the forest stood unscarred except for the small clearings about Sault Ste. Marie and Fort William. From there on hunter, *voyageur*, Indian and fur trader were the only inhabitants until the south end of Lake Winnipeg revealed the sweep of prairie and the small settlement of Scots, Irish and *métis* on Red River. Selkirk was dead and almost forgotten. (In 1836 his heirs sold their huge rights in "Assiniboia" back to the Hudson's Bay Company for £84,000.) Westward across the prairies and northward toward the Arctic ran the writ of the great Bay Company, undisputed owner of all its men surveyed.

Soon after the Bay Company absorbed the old empire of the Nor'westers, they sent John McLoughlin from Fort William to take charge of their interests in the Columbia region. Here in the mild climate and rich valleys of "Oregon" (especially the Willamette Valley) the old Nor'wester and his men found an earthly paradise after the purgatory of many years in the bleak North. "Oregon" — or as it was called alternatively "Columbia" — soon became the home of many a Canadian trader and *voyageur* wearied of the northern winters and too long cut off from the East to have any sentimental urge in that direction. It was the beginning of a trend in North America that has since carried millions to the Pacific coast on both sides of the border.

McLoughlin even in old age, when his lean lined face and his long fall of white hair gave him the venerable look of a prophet in the wilderness, was an energetic and inspired man. Like many another Nor'wester he had transferred his whole heart to the service of the Bay Company, and as their chief agent in "Columbia" he was the uncrowned emperor of a region as large as Europe. The canoe and portage route through the Rockies was little used now. Ships came half around the world with supplies and took away the furs. The canoe was still important in reaching the collection posts in certain places, but the horse was better, and horses were plentiful in the Spanish settlements of California. By 1834 McLoughlin's "brigades" (sometimes as many as three hundred horsemen) were moving trade goods as far south as Monterey in California, riding the edges of Utah and Nevada, pushing east into Idaho and Montana, and north into "New Caledonia" or, as it was later known, British Columbia.

A few American hunters had reached the California coast. Farther north between 1831–36 the American Army officer Benjamin Bonneville explored and mapped Utah and the eastern slope of the Rockies. In 1834 the first Americans since Lewis and Clark arrived in Oregon. They were Jason and Daniel Lee, Methodist missionaries. In 1837 Jason Lee returned overland to the eastern states to lecture and raise funds for their little mission to the Indians in the Willamette Valley. He found ready listeners, for in that year Washington Irving published Bonneville's journals and stirred a new and powerful American interest in the Oregon trail. In the following year no less than twenty more American missionaries arrived in Oregon, the vanguard of a movement that in a few years outnumbered the Canadians as the wagon trains found their way through the mountains. Thus in the odor of sanctity came the first faint whiff of gunpowder from the old compromise of 1818.

CHAPTER 47

1828 — 1837

*World unrest — The Reform movement in Canada — The
Family Compact — William Lyon Mackenzie —
Rebellion and persecution in Upper Canada*

A S THE Industrial Revolution began to get up steam in the late
1820s, changing the lives of millions and bringing unease and
pain in the process, it also brought to a head the political
pressure among the European masses that had been gathering for so
long. In the year 1828 the Duke of Wellington, the graven image of
reactionary British politics, became Prime Minister. In the same year
Andrew Jackson, the apostle of a galloping and almost unbridled
theory of democracy, became President of the United States. The
Canadians, governed from London while breathing the North American air, came under these two opposite influences at a time when
Europe's political steam was about to burst the boiler.

The explosion came in France with the revolution of 1830, which
set off similar explosions all through Europe. Britain was not immune.
In southern England crowds of farm laborers rioted over the landscape, burning hayricks and destroying the new threshing machines
which were putting so many of them out of work at harvest time.
Similar riots had occurred in the industrial North, where workers
from time to time gathered to destroy the new weaving frames and
spinning machines. Under Wellington the government put these
riots down with the same harsh force that it had been using since
the first Reform agitations of 1819.

But by 1830 some of the upper class themselves had begun to see a
warning light. A group of liberal aristocrats had arisen, led by Earl
Grey, who declared: "We ought to learn wisdom from what is
passing before our eyes, and when the spirit of liberty is breaking
out all round it is our duty to secure our own institutions by intro-
ducing into them a temperate reform." The word Reform was now
a magic one to the common people of England, seeing the rebirth of
liberty across the Channel, and when the Iron Duke declared himself
utterly against it the whole atmosphere of the island rumbled with
common thunder. No words from any statesman in British history

ever produced such an uproar. Many of his own party were frightened and fell away. His ministry fell and King William IV reluctantly sent for Grey to form a government.

Grey chose his men chiefly from the old Whigs and the Liberals formerly led by Canning, and his Cabinet included two men whose names were to be remembered long in Canada, the Earl of Durham and Mr. Poulett Thomson. His Reform Bill passed the Commons and (after a glum delay) the Lords. The first general election under the new law took place in 1832 and Grey's party triumphed. The old Tory party was shattered. Just as the old Whigs and radicals gathered now under the Liberal banner, so the old Tories began to call themselves Conservatives.

All these matters in Europe had prompt reverberations in Canada, where privilege had been snugly seated for so long. The example of Jackson's frontier democracy was like a fire in prairie grass, not to be stopped by boundary posts. The British immigrants pouring into the country all brought with them the word Reform as a battle cry of the common man. The French Canadians took it up and applied it to themselves, seeing the battle of Reform against Privilege as a new name for the old struggle of *le tout bon canadien* against *les anglais*. Thus there was a wide Canadian unrest with curiously different springs but one common aim, government by the people for the people.

In each of the provinces Reform was opposed by the class which stood to gain most by keeping things as they were. In Upper Canada it was the Family Compact. In Lower Canada it was the Château Clique or Scotch Party, with its ruling circle partly among the old French seigneurial class but mostly in the wealthy Scotch merchant aristocracy of Montreal. In New Brunswick and Nova Scotia it had no special name but it was well recognized, like that of Upper Canada; a tight group of officials, merchants and bankers who kept in their hands the lucrative powers of government appointment and patronage, grouped themselves about the flag and the Church of England, and denounced as "republican" or "American" any move to oust them. In each case the successive British soldier-governors regarded these groups as stout little islands of loyalty in the dangerous North American sea. Their own politics were Wellington's. Their view of Reform in the colonies was precisely his view of Reform at home.

Every human awakening needs a gadfly. In Upper Canada the first appeared as a restless and pugnacious Scot named Robert Gourlay, who arrived in 1817 and set up business as a land agent. His idea was to promote the settlement of the province by people from the British Isles; but when he examined the available lands and the business of getting title to them, he discovered that two sevenths of every township had been set aside for the Crown and Clergy, and that various government officials and their friends were holding other large portions for speculation. None of this land was taxed. The only taxes fell upon bona fide settlers, whose efforts to improve the township roads naturally raised the value of the reserved lands.

In 1818 Gourlay called a convention of settlers at York to air their troubles and discuss remedies. Many came and they approved Gourlay's remedy, a direct petition to Britain over the head of the provincial government. This aroused the immediate hostility of Strachan and the Compact of which he was the mastermind; and Gourlay was bold enough to describe the archdeacon as "a lying little fool of a renegade Presbyterian." From that moment he was doomed, as most gadflies are, but it took some time to crush him.

The "lying little fool" had a face and mind carved out of his native Aberdeen granite. He had the convert's fanaticism for his adopted Church and for the crowned defender of that faith, and he had come to believe that his every act had the sanction of heaven and throne. The so-called Family Compact, which he directed with conspicuous ability, was not a coterie related by blood or marriage. The name popped out in 1828 when Marshall Spring Bidwell mentioned in a letter his plans to "relieve this province from the evils which a family compact have brought upon it." He was using the old sense of the term, common during the War of 1812, in which a general's or a merchant's "family" meant his staff, including servants. The Compact was Strachan's "family" and he wielded a general's authority over it.

Otherwise the members of the Compact were related only in that they loved power and were ready to believe (like Strachan) that all their actions were for the good of the country, whether the country liked it or not. That this sense of duty happened to be a highly profitable one for most of them was not considered a fit subject for public discussion — and the late war had given the Compact a sharp weapon for the restless time that followed. As individuals, many of the privileged class had fought bravely in the defense of Canada, and since the war they had been foremost in raising funds to rebuild the hundreds of farmhouses and mills destroyed by the Americans, and to aid the families of militiamen killed or disabled in the fighting. On the other hand many of their pre-war political opponents, despairing of ousting the group in any other way, had been prepared to welcome an American conquest, and some (like Willcox) had actually joined the American forces. They made a useful scarecrow now.

The first attempts to squelch Gourlay failed. In two trials for libel he was acquitted by sympathetic juries. But there were more ways of crushing a gadfly than by libel cases. The Compact had a powerful ally in the new lieutenant governor, Sir Peregrine Maitland, another of Wellington's Waterloo generals ("Now, Maitland, now's your time!"), and a pious churchman who heard the least whisper of Archdeacon Strachan as the voice of God in the wilderness. Sir Peregrine denounced the farmers' convention called by Gourlay and demanded that such meetings be made illegal. An obedient legislature passed a law to that effect. Gourlay promptly attacked it in the columns of the *Niagara Spectator* with an article headed "Gagged, gagged, by jingo!" The Compact moved as swiftly. Under an obsolete law of 1804 Gourlay was denounced as "an evil-minded and seditious person" and ordered to leave the country. He ignored the order. Before making the arrest the Compact's officials waited until the frosty end of December 1818. Then, like a conspirator in Russia, Gourlay was seized and thrown into the Niagara jail, where he lay through the winter and far into the next summer, without trial, in solitary confinement, in an unheated cell with no light or ventilation except through a small hole in the door.

When his trial came at last in August 1819 the court found in the box what was to be expected, a physical wreck, half mad. John Beverly Robinson, the able attorney general of Upper Canada (a former pupil of Strachan's and a member of the Compact), made his charge a simple one — Gourlay had been ordered to leave the province and he had disobeyed. The wreck was found guilty. Under the 1804 law the sentence was banishment within twenty-four hours and death without benefit of clergy if he was found in Upper Canada after that time. Gourlay greeted it with a burst of maniacal laughter — but he left. In later years a Canadian Parliament declared his sentence "illegal, unconstitutional and without possibility of excuse or palliation."

The Compact had got rid of one gadfly only to find itself stung by another. In 1820 a twenty-five-year-old Scot named William Lyon Mackenzie came to Upper Canada, a wisp of a man, with Gourlay's quick recognition of the selfish power of the Compact and the same wild determination to upset it. In 1824 he began to publish in Queenston a newspaper called the *Colonial Advocate,* in which he wasted neither time nor words in attacking the personalities in and behind the government. In 1825 he moved his newspaper to York, where he could fire his broadsides at closer range. They aroused in York a great deal of anger and amusement, and in the summer of 1826 his press was demolished by a crowd of young men, the sons or friends of the men he was abusing. Among them was Sir Peregrine Maitland's private secretary.

Mackenzie brought legal action against the leading culprits and a York jury awarded him damages of £625, much more than the plant was worth, a sign of the popular feeling against the Compact rather than approval of Mackenzie himself. Many of the Reformers, men of sober judgment, deplored Mackenzie's tactics and suspected his mental balance. This did not disturb him in the least. The Reform movement had begun to lift and roll like a deep swell on Lake Ontario moving in toward the shore; and like a frigate with too much sail and not enough ballast, with hard-hitting guns but no judgment of aim, and with a man in a high fever at the wheel, Mackenzie's bark perched itself on the crest, blazing away right and left.

The movement was made up of many accumulated grievances, not least the Methodist dissatisfaction with the Clergy Reserves. Archdeacon Strachan insisted that "Clergy" meant clergy of the Church of England alone. The Methodists as the chief religious body in the population objected strongly, and their voice was the voice of a capable young minister named Egerton Ryerson. Strachan was quick to hurl the "American" stone, writing to London that most of the dissenting congregations drew their "teachers" from the United States, "where they gather their knowledge and form their sentiments." But the insinuation of disloyalty could not apply to Ryerson, a man of clear Loyalist descent and opinions. Nor could the Compact dismiss other avowed Reformers as mere republican rabble, for they included men of education and worth and not a few of them were veterans of the battles of 1812.

Notable among them stood young Robert Baldwin and his father Dr. William Baldwin, who wrote to the Duke of Wellington in 1829 urging that Upper Canada be given a form of responsible government, although they did not call it that. What they asked was simply a government like that of Britain itself, in which the Cabinet must command a majority in the lower House or quit office. To the stiff Wellington this was suggesting the command of a regiment by vote of the rank and file. He was then in the midst of his own stubborn battle against Reform in Britain and as in 1814 these transatlantic rumbles seemed trifling compared with his dangers closer to home. He ignored the Baldwin document, and when the British Reformers swept Wellington out of office it was forgotten. However Robert Baldwin and his basic idea could not be pigeonholed in Upper Canada, where sober men saw the common sense of a middle way between the privileged road of the Compact and the dizzy and wandering goat path of William Lyon Mackenzie.

In 1829 Mackenzie made pilgrimage to Washington and talked with President Jackson — "Old Hickory" with his lively hate of the British and his contempt for any kind of central government over local interests. In the next year Mackenzie extended his pilgrimage to Britain, where he talked with radical members of the old Whig party. The Whigs were sympathetic, but their minds were on their own struggle for Reform, which was now approaching its climax. Having touched these springs of free thought flowing on both sides of the Atlantic, the fiery little agitator returned to Upper Canada, more convinced than ever that he was the ordained instrument of freedom there, and ready to fly at anyone who crossed his will.

Egerton Ryerson also visited Britain, and when he returned in 1833 he reported in the *Christian Guardian* that the British Tories were a bad lot and the Radicals were atheists and worse. Mackenzie took this as a personal attack and promptly loosed off his guns at Ryerson and the Methodists. This blast drove the Methodists into a position of their own, still insisting on a fair division of the Clergy Reserves and certain other rights withheld from them by Strachan and his group, but holding themselves frigidly aloof from Mackenzie's activities and giving only a qualified support to Baldwin and his moderates. The Compact found immense satisfaction in this rift among their enemies.

When Lieutenant Governor Maitland left to take another post in Nova Scotia he was replaced by another Waterloo soldier, Sir John Colborne (1828-35), who came sternly resolved to be impartial in these strange colonial squabbles but soon drifted into the Compact camp like all the others. The extravagances of Mackenzie and the wild talk of Papineau in Lower Canada had begun to cast an unmistakable shadow of open rebellion by the end of 1835, when Colborne gave up his uneasy post as a diplomatist and took another that was much closer to his heart and capabilities, the command of His Majesty's troops in Canada. Just before leaving for Montreal he signed a bill endowing forty-four Church of England rectories with land from the Clergy Reserves. It was a triumph for Strachan and a stinging slap in the face of the Methodists.

In Colborne's place at Toronto came Sir Francis Bond Head, still another Waterloo soldier with (as he afterward confessed) "a gross ignorance of everything in any way related to the government of our colonies." In a strange way the Iron Duke seemed to have set the stamp of his own features, as well as his attitude toward the rank and file of humanity, upon many of these officers. Thus both Colborne and Head had the typical Wellington face, long and lean, with a tight mouth set between a beak nose and the outthrust chin. Behind this mask however the minds were very different. Colborne's was the mind of a calm, none too intelligent soldier serving in a dull outpost until the time for pension came. Head had the quicker mind, impulsive and self-willed. He regarded the Canadian political scene as a kind of colonial pond, filled with odd creatures, most of them repulsive, the result of stagnation in the backwoods; and he was determined to make a splash.

In England some men in government circles were chuckling over Head's appointment. According to rumor it was made by mistake, a comedy of errors involving two men of the same name. The post in Upper Canada was no plum to the abler men on the government list, who saw it as an exile in the wilds on a salary that seemed to them too small. Lord Glenelg, the Colonial Secretary, casting about for one of the lesser fry who might think it a good thing, had been told to try "young Head." The hint referred to young Edmund Head, a brilliant classical scholar, son of a baronet, with some ambitions for government service. (Long afterward Edmund Head became lieutenant governor of New Brunswick and then governor general of Canada.) Glenelg however thought it referred to Francis Bond Head, a cousin of Edmund, and sent a messenger posthaste into Kent to offer the Upper Canadian post. Francis Head was astonished, but he accepted the job on condition that he be made a baronet. He had served as a subaltern at Waterloo, which was recommendation enough in those days when Wellington's powerful shadow stood over the land. His only knowledge of transatlantic affairs had been a brief disastrous venture into South America as a trade commissioner.

Whether the tale was true or not, Sir Francis Head arrived at Toronto with all his ignorance upon his head, concealed in a fine mop of curly hair of which he was rather vain. The elections of 1834 had placed a majority of Reformers in the Upper Canadian assembly, and Head made the gesture of appointing Robert Baldwin and two other moderate Reformers to the council; but he soon made clear that he intended to rule the province himself, subject only to the Colonial Office in London. The council resigned in a body, for even the older members now could see the coming storm.

A meeting of Reformers in the Toronto city hall sent a delegation to voice their dismay at the lieutenant governor's attitude, and they met an astonishing reception. Sir Francis greeted them with a group of his garrison officers about him as if these quiet civilians were a charge of Napoleon's cuirassiers. With his beautiful locks and his sharp features, a wig on a hatchet, he heard their address in a contemptuous silence. Then he burst into a wild tirade accusing the Reformers of a desire to join the neighboring republic and of plotting to arrange "a foreign invasion" when the time was ripe. He ended by crying, "In the name of every regiment of militia in Upper Canada I publicly promulgate *Let them come if they dare!*"

Not since Simcoe's quixotic words and postures of 1794 had Canadians heard or seen such dramatic nonsense, but they did not laugh. The meaning of this hysteria was much too serious. Sir Francis had come to the Compact view that Reform was another name for rebellion, and if other means failed he intended to crush the movement with musketry. But first he tried the other means. In the spring of 1836 he dissolved the assembly abruptly and called for a new election. In the campaign that followed he took to the platforms himself, crying that the issue was one of continued union with British law and order against separation, republicanism, and anarchy, and he summed it up with the blunt demand; "Are you for me or for the House of Assembly?"

Behind this wordy barrage from His Majesty's representative the Compact party moved with practiced skill, darting every possible appeal or threat at the various political and religious groups in the province. They were careful to link Reform in Upper Canada with the current agitation of the French-Canadian Catholics in the lower province. This was enough to bring to the polls, wielding clubs as well as votes, the whole body of Orangemen in the country, as if Lake Ontario were another Boyne Water. To the Methodists, they offered the twin bogeys of radical atheism and disloyalty to the flag. Egerton Ryerson could forget neither his cloth nor his Loyalist ancestry. Seeing the wild antics of Mackenzie, which seemed to confirm every accusation of Sir Francis and the Compact, he threw his weight and the weight of his people on the Tory side. The result was a triumph for the Compact. The Reformers were badly thrashed by shillelaghs outside the polls and by votes within. A Tory majority marched into the assembly and Sir Francis dashed off a letter to the Colonial Office announcing that he had "saved the Canadas."

From this moment there was only one course open to the frantic little printer of Toronto and he turned his steps that way. A few days after the election he founded another newspaper, the *Constitution*. Its first issue appeared on the Fourth of July with a significance that no one could miss, and its tone was baldly republican. In subsequent issues he made no bones about his own position, writing boldly in one of them; "I am proud of my descent from a rebel race." On the first anniversary of his new sheet he gave an account of the increasing turmoil in Lower Canada, predicted that the French Canadians were about to rise in revolt, and declared that they would win.

The more embittered Reformers in Upper Canada were ready for revolt themselves under the constant agitation of Mackenzie. The melancholy feature of their subsequent misadventure was that their cause was right, and they assumed that all honest men in the province would leap to arms with them. In this they were wrong. Had they been led by a man of different quality, things might have gone well, for they had the sympathy of a great body of people in the countryside if not in Toronto itself. Many a man who had uttered his vote for the Tories in June 1836 experienced a quiet revulsion in the months that followed. But few men were willing to risk life and limb at the command of a jerking bundle of nerves and vituperation whose feet could not reach the floor when it sat on a common chair, whose great head sat on the diminutive body like an absurd rag doll's, whose eyes glared blue fire in every direction but one — for Mackenzie could never look an opponent in the face.

By the summer of 1837 the hot little man was plotting a revolution on the American model, with rustic minutemen springing to arms all over the province and driving the redcoats and Tories into Lake Ontario. He drew up a formal document in the style of the American Declaration of Independence, seeing himself as the Canadian Thomas Jefferson as well as the Canadian Patrick Henry. The difficulty was to find a Canadian Washington. Within his group of plotters the only man of experience in military command was an elderly Dutch settler, Colonel Van Egmond, an unsuccessful Reform candidate in the debacle of 1836, who in younger days had served in the army of Napoleon. His other chosen leaders in the countryside were Captain Anderson of Lloydtown, who had some experience in the militia, and Samuel Lount, a blacksmith of Holland Landing, who had none.

In Toronto the Reformers met openly at Elliott's Tavern, but Mackenzie's inner circle of conspirators held their talks in the yeasty atmosphere of John Doel's brewery, where they debated and adopted his Declaration on the night of July 31. Between these sometimes doubtful, sometimes enthusiastic conferences Mackenzie took horse and raised the dust of the countryside, meeting, persuading, organizing bands of farmers, arranging them in districts, subdistricts, and branches. He told them little of his plans for an armed rebellion but he ordered them to select delegates to be sent to a convention in Toronto at some future date. His maniacal energy never seemed to sleep. As Head put it, "He wrote and then he printed, and then he rode, and then he spoke, stamped, foamed, wiped his seditious little mouth, and then spoke again; and thus like a squirrel in a cage he continued with astounding assiduity the centre of a revolutionary career."

Mackenzie was in touch with Papineau's followers in Lower Canada, who were now drifting obviously into armed revolt. By autumn his own followers began to drill at night in lonely fields, armed with clubs, sticks, fowling pieces, old muskets of 1812, and (about Holland Landing) with pikes made in Samuel Lount's busy forge. Much of this was known to the government, but the landslide election of '36 had shown the strength of any appeal to the flag as opposed to anything that could be tagged republican or "American," and nobody took these drilling boors seriously. Sir Francis Head himself regarded Mackenzie's activities with a cynical indifference, quite willing to let these Reformers hang themselves on the longest possible rope. He raised no objection when Sir John Colborne wanted the British regulars of the Toronto garrison to leave for Kingston, two hundred miles away, in case he needed them for affairs in Lower Canada. There would be plenty of loyal volunteers and militia in Toronto if trouble started there, and Sir Francis had arranged for several thousand muskets and bayonets to be stacked in City Hall. His whole attitude was what he had shouted to the Reform delegates the year before — let them come if they dare.

William Lyon Mackenzie was only too ready to come. He was tempted by the store of arms in City Hall. With the redcoats gone, it seemed easy to muster his men and seize the arms and the government in one stroke. He said so to some of the Toronto Reformers and it startled them, for none but the inner circle had known until this moment how far Mackenzie was prepared to go. One said bluntly, "This is treason." From this time the moderate men drifted aside, wondering how this fanatic could be trusted with the government if he won it, and suspecting that he would fail and involve the whole Reform movement in the crash. The days dragged on until the last of November, when the rebels in Lower Canada came forth in open fight. Already Mackenzie had received a message from them, urging the Upper Canadians to rise and keep the Kingston redcoats occupied if nothing else. On November 24 Mackenzie rode out to muster his "army" in the countryside.

His plans were already betrayed. One James Hogg of Hogg's Hollow (even the names in this largely rural farce were part of the piece) had warned Head of a proposed march on City Hall, even to the exact date, December 7. The rebels, straggling in small companies from various directions, gathered at Montgomery's Tavern, four miles outside Toronto on the Yonge Street highway. Inside the city lean old Colonel Fitzgibbon, the veteran of Beaver Dam in 1813, was busy summoning and arming a swarm of volunteers. Other loyal Tories were on the way from Hamilton and other towns outside. Except a salting of veterans of the old war, none of these men, rebel or loyal, had any military experience beyond the annual militia musters in each district, comic affairs conducted in a single day, a few awkward drill movements performed with old farm guns, broomsticks, even an occasional furled umbrella, and ending always in a spree at the nearest tavern. The well-drilled and armed militia force of 1812 had vanished in the long peace since.

On December 5, without waiting for Colonel Van Egmond and his company from upcountry, Mackenzie marched his strangely armed mob toward the city. At a spot called ominously Gallows

Hill they halted for a parley with a government messenger sent out
to demand their intentions, and there was a long delay while the
rider returned into the city with the rebel ultimatum. In the interval
Mackenzie (as one of his men observed) "went on like a lunatic."
Among other aberrations he dashed into the house of R. C. Horne,
a Toronto bank official, and set it afire with his own hands, for no
apparent reason except that in the true spirit of Jacksonian democracy he hated banks and bankers. In another manifestation he seized
the westerly mail out of Toronto and robbed the letters and packets
of any money they contained, presumably for his war chest.

That night he decided to attack the city. Within a short march his
seven hundred bemused yokels, brandishing their guns, pikes, and
clubs, came upon Sheriff Jarvis of Toronto and twenty-six city
militiamen posted in the semi-rural surroundings of Yonge Street.
It was an absurd affair. The militiamen fired a few wild shots, the
rebels fired a few back, and both ran away from each other as fast
as legs could go. One rebel sprawling dead in the darkness of Yonge
Street marked the spot. The rest did not stop short of Mackenzie's
headquarters in Montgomery's Tavern. Their leader now received
a warning from his friends inside the city, advising him to scatter his
men away to their homes while there was time; the French-Canadian
rebels had suffered a bloody defeat and at this moment in Toronto
Colonel Fitzgibbon had twelve hundred volunteers armed and
ready for battle.

On December 7, the day originally appointed for the rebel march
on Toronto, Colonel Van Egmond arrived faithfully at Montgomery's Tavern. The brave old Dutchman with his memories of
Napoleon must have wondered at his present leader, a frenzied
gnome muffled to the ears in a thick greatcoat, balancing a tall top-
hat on his head, and riding a small white horse. Mackenzie was all for
another "attack" on the city. Van Egmond dismissed this as "stark
madness" and insisted on waiting for reinforcements from the
country. Already two hundred men had slipped away to their
homes. Meanwhile at the house of Archdeacon Strachan in Toronto
— the very heart of the Compact — a government council of war
had decided that the time had come to strike.

On the morning of December 8 the government columns marched,
led by Fitzgibbon and Allan McNab, while Sir Francis Head commanded both from a general position at the rear. His amateur army
with its imposing glitter of muskets and bayonets, with a pair of

field cannon and the martial strains of two bands tootling manfully at their chilly instruments, tramped up Yonge Street past the suburban estates and dairy farms toward Montgomery's Tavern. As they crossed over Gallows Hill, the veteran Van Egmond prepared for battle, arranging his rustic companies in a patch of woods before the tavern. The "battle" was another one-act farce. While McNab made a noisy demonstration from the front with cannon and musketry, Fitzgibbon made a detour, and at the mere appearance of his bayonets on their flank Van Egmond's "army" fled. A few had barricaded themselves in the tavern, but the government artillerymen put a few shots through the walls and windows and these disappeared also. At the end one man lay dead on the scene, an unfortunate German immigrant in the rebel ranks.

Sir Francis, coming forward when the shooting stopped, ordered his men to burn Montgomery's sorry little pothouse to the ground — "to mark and record by some act of vengeance the important victory that had been achieved." To show the magnanimity of power he pardoned a few rebel prisoners on the spot. He showed his larger side afterward by ordering arrests all over the province. Mackenzie's carpetbag had been captured in the tavern, and with it papers betraying the names of every man in the little printer's carefully organized districts and subdistricts.

Mackenzie himself rode at top speed from the scene, fed and bedded by hospitable farmers on the way to Niagara, where, like many others involved in the fiasco, he found refuge on American soil. There followed a rigorous Tory witch hunt all through Upper Canada, but especially in the country between Lake Ontario and Lake Huron where Mackenzie's wild spell had cast its greatest influence. The small bump of Gallows Hill rose suddenly to the proportions of Mont Blanc, throwing its shadow over a whole countryside. Actually the hangings were very few; but thousands of people innocent of any part in the actual rising, guilty of nothing but polling an open vote for Reform in '36, came under a harsh persecution that went on for months and finally forced them to leave the province for the United States. It was the migration of 1783 in reverse, and, like the Loyalists before them, these exiles added a new and bitter element to the tensions of the border.

CHAPTER 48

1828 — 1837

The Reform movement in Lower Canada — Louis Joseph Papineau — Rebellion and persecution in Lower Canada

THE eruption in Lower Canada was a very different affair, for in French Canada there burned much deeper lava fires of race and religion. The thin crust over this molten stuff was a genuine Reform party like that of Upper Canada, seeking change by legal means. It included men of British origin like John Neilson, editor of the Quebec *Gazette* and a member of the legislature; the Irish doctor O'Callaghan, also a member of the legislature and editor of a Montreal newspaper, *The Vindicator;* the English doctor Wolfred Nelson, a general practitioner in the Richelieu countryside; his brother Robert; and Thomas Brown, a hardware merchant of Montreal. These were a minority in the vastly larger crowd of French-Canadian Reformers and above them all towered the remarkable figure of Louis Joseph Papineau.

Here was a man for whom other men were quite willing to fight and die; tall, intelligent, stubborn, passionate, with handsome features and a ready tongue. He was born in the portentous years between the American and the French revolutions, a child of the Canadian soil; he was educated in the Quebec seminary, he had spent the first years of his manhood under the detested regime of Governor General Craig, and at the age of twenty-six he had stood for election and entered the assembly of Lower Canada. The year was 1812. It was no time for party politics. For one thing the mild Prevost had succeeded Craig as governor. For another Canada was about to suffer invasion by American armies. Papineau served his militia duty as an officer on clerical work and he saw no fighting. After the war's close he became speaker of the assembly, a post he was to hold almost continuously until 1837. During these twenty-two years he was the chief voice of the *Patriote* party in its march toward Reform and finally to rebellion.

Papineau's hostility to the British Government as the patron of the Château Clique began with the Clique's petition to London for union with Upper Canada in 1822. He and John Neilson had journeyed to England and squelched that notion through the interest of the British Whigs; but on his return Papineau's tongue ran away with him, accusing the governor, Lord Dalhousie, of complicity in the scheme and for good measure hinting that Dalhousie was involved in the thefts of Receiver-General Caldwell. This was untrue, and Dalhousie's stiff resentment led to a quarrel between the two men that brought the administration of Lower Canada to an impasse. The *Patriotes* persuaded London to recall Dalhousie in 1827, but Papineau was not appeased. He was now the idol of the *Patriotes*, indeed of most French Canadians, whatever their former politics. With his assembly majority he permitted the wheels of government to turn again, but he had tasted the pleasure of worsting a British governor and now he was out for bigger game — full control of the administration of Lower Canada with no British strings attached.

Reform was moving toward triumph in Britain itself, and as British views became more and more liberal, Papineau became less and less reasonable in his demands, forgetting that the British Liberals had to compromise with a Tory king and a rigid conception of imperial rights. Lord Aylmer was governor general in 1830, the year of the second French revolution and the death of George IV. Europe was in an uproar and the British had before them the old nightmares of republicanism and anarchy. However Aylmer persuaded the British Government to offer the Lower Canadians control of all provincial revenue except the income from Crown Lands, with the condition that the assembly must furnish a stated sum for the Civil List of officials appointed by the Colonial Office. This was a genuine concession and the *Patriotes* would have been wise to accept it for the time being. The next King was to be William IV, a crude old man obsessed with his sudden importance, with an autocratic habit (and a blistering vocabulary) acquired in his younger years as a captain in the Navy, and with crabbed eighteenth-century ideas of colonial government.

Papineau induced the assembly of 1831 to reject this good-will offer, and to make matters worse he picked a personal quarrel with Aylmer as he had with Dalhousie. Here began the downward path to bloodshed, for the Colonial Office now stood with a reactionary king on one hand and an increasingly revolutionary Canadian on the other. The Lower Canada constitution of 1791, which Papineau had praised with eloquence in his younger days, he now denounced as something "manufactured by a Tory influenced by the terrors of the French Revolution." His mind leaned toward a republic in which both Houses were controlled by the will of the populace, which in the case of Lower Canada was the will of Louis Papineau. Nothing less would do.

And now events began to move of their own accord, carrying Papineau along with them. In 1832 a by-election in Montreal produced a street riot. It was nothing new. Elections there were always turbulent affairs with an accompaniment of broken heads and bloody noses; but in this case the rioters stoned a party of British troops sent to restore order. The soldiers endured the jeers and bruises for a time and then fired a volley to put an end to them. Most of the shots went over the rioters' heads, but five soldiers took a lower aim. Three men were killed and two wounded. All were French Canadians. The *Patriote* newspapers broke into immediate outcry, calling it a deliberate massacre by the brutal English soldiery — precisely what American newspapers had called a similar affair in Boston many years before. With the authentic blood of patriot martyrs in a Montreal street the Canadian revolution seemed well begun.

At this point, however, Papineau's more moderate followers began to drop away, English and French, seeing the swift rise of racial and religious hate behind his political movement. They included his old and wise companion John Neilson. At the same time many of the Roman Catholic clergy, hitherto favorable to the *Patriotes*, began to regard them uneasily. The Church had unhappy memories of revolution and the recent news from France was hardly reassuring. Under these influences, lay and clerical, the population of Lower Canada began to divide their political attitudes into the same spheres which had been so apparent during the American Revolution; the conservative region about Quebec and the radical region about Montreal and up the Richelieu Valley.

In 1834 Papineau's party carried through the assembly a long and turgid document known as the Ninety-Two Resolutions. It set forth their grievances in a strange jumble of fact and bombast, demanded among other things the impeachment of Lord Aylmer, and made threatening references to the American Revolution. The basic points were real enough and the Reformers now in power at London decided to send out the Earl of Gosford to take Aylmer's place.

They also appointed a board of commissioners, of which Gosford was to be chairman, with generous powers to remedy the troubles in Lower Canada. But now another figure loomed upon Canadian affairs, as self-willed and intransigent as Papineau himself — that of William IV, the so-called Sailor King, an elderly reformed rake (his antics as a young naval officer at Halifax in the 1780s were still remembered by the Nova Scotians) who was impervious to reform of any other kind.

When King William learned of Gosford's mission and instructions he was furious. In the presence of Lord Melbourne's Cabinet he roared at one of the commissioners (Sir George Grey) that he must remember that Lower Canada had been conquered with the sword and he must assert the prerogative of the Crown. A few days later in his famous tops'l-yard voice he informed Gosford, "By God, I will never consent to alienate the Crown lands nor to make the Council elective. Mind, my lord, the Cabinet is not my Cabinet. They had better take all or by God I will have them impeached." The Reform Cabinet were obliged to walk delicately in a Britain that still held a wide opposition eager to invoke the mystical appeal of the throne. To soothe the angry monarch, they weakened Gosford's instructions and doomed his mission to failure.

On the surface Gosford still had some chance of success, for by this time the French Canadians actually had achieved many of the things they had wanted since the conquest. The Quebec Act had been a good start. The constitution of 1791 had been a long forward step, for they had held the speaker's chair and a majority in the assembly ever since. Since then, too, they had acquired a French-Canadian majority in the legislative council as well, although seats in the upper House were still a matter of Crown appointment, not popular election. There was a much larger proportion of French Canadians on the government payroll than before, notably in the judiciary, where there were more French judges than English. But Papineau and the *Patriotes* wanted utter control of the executive council and of the upper as well as the lower House — which meant the power to fill the judiciary and all other government posts with their own party members, with no safeguard for the (largely English-speaking) minority who opposed their politics.

What chiefly concerned London was the demand for an elective upper house. Melbourne's Cabinet did not see how they could grant a principle that the British people themselves did not enjoy at home, and they had to reckon with King William's violent opposition to any such idea at home or abroad. William was still brandishing his prerogative like a sword over their heads. (In the autumn of 1834 he fulfilled his threat and dismissed the Cabinet — the last British monarch to use his prerogative for that purpose.)

Past concessions had only inflamed Papineau's ambition and increased the appetites of the *Patriotes*. All were infuriated in the spring of 1837 when the British Government tried to satisfy both the King and the Canadians with ten resolutions introduced in the House of Commons by Lord John Russell. These repeated Gosford's concessions but refused an elective upper house and withheld from the assembly the full charge of the public purse.

Rebellion was now in the air. The *Patriotes* were in touch with William Lyon Mackenzie in Upper Canada. Papineau, Wolfred Nelson, and others began to hold mass meetings in the Richelieu Valley, that fruitful recruiting ground of *congressiste* battalions in the days of '75. These meetings reached a climax at St. Charles in October 1837, when Papineau and Nelson addressed five or six thousand excited *habitants*. The outdoor stage had been carefully set. Beside the platform stood a wooden post crowned with a red nightcap, the so-called Phrygian cap made popular during the French Revolution. Behind it in irregular ranks stood a company of *habitants* armed with muskets and commanded by a pair of militia officers, both of whom had been dismissed by the governor for seditious behavior.

The meeting passed a number of fiery resolutions, each of which was saluted with a noisy discharge of blank cartridges by the musketeers. Papineau in his speech set forth the *Patriote* cause with less than his customary reckless oratory. He was beginning to feel qualms at the very size and fervor of the passion he had at last aroused. With the reek of gunpowder eddying about the platform, he announced that the time for weapons might never come, adding tamely or cynically that Canadians might bring the British Government to reason simply by refusing to buy British goods. Wolfred Nelson, on the other hand, was in no mood for quibbling. He declared bluntly, "The time has come to melt our spoons into bullets!" As the meeting dismissed, the *habitants* crowded about the liberty post, touching it with their hands and solemnly pledging their lives in the *Patriote* cause.

Although a few parish priests were still enthusiastic in that cause, their Church was now alarmed. Papineau and his English and French lieutenants were strongly influenced by American democracy as demonstrated by Andrew Jackson. Their *habitant* followers rejected American forms however. There was another example unmistakably and authentically French. Liberty poles, liberty caps, the *tricolore* of republican France flying over various houses and taverns along the Richelieu, the armed and organized bands of *fils de la Liberté* drilling in the villages, the singing of the *Marseillaise*, all pointed to the kind of revolution that the *Patriotes* were brewing.

The bishop of Montreal, the heart of the radical *Patriote* area, sent out a pastoral letter to be read in all the churches of his diocese, warning the *habitants* against rebellion as a sin punishable by the laws of their religion. The more devout men in the parishes drew away from the *Patriote* meetings; but these were promptly dubbed *chouayens* and persecuted by the others. Within a few weeks the whole Richelieu region was in a state of anarchy, with parties of *fils de la Liberté* roaming from village to village, threatening, beating, in some cases burning the homes of those who opposed them, French or English, and forcing local magistrates and militia officers to tear up their commissions. By November 6 the violence had spread into Montreal, where disorder was always popular, and bands of *fils de la Liberté* clashed in the streets with equally unruly young men who called themselves the British Legion or Doric Club. Behind Montreal the rural district of Two Mountains boiled with revolt like the parishes on the Richelieu.

Sir John Colborne, commanding the British garrison of Canada, had come to his Quebec post straight from his irritating political experiences with William Lyon Mackenzie. He recognized that the rebellious movement in Lower Canada had much more popular support and was therefore the more dangerous of the two, and the spectacle of the *tricolore* and the newly painted eagles on Richelieu tavern doors aroused all his fighting memories of the Napoleonic war. So far Governor General Gosford had refused any harsh measure against the *Patriotes*. On November 16 the advocates of government force had their way. Warrants went out for the arrest of Papineau, Thomas Brown, O'Callaghan, and twenty-three other known leaders of the *Patriote* movement.

Some in Quebec and Montreal were seized and jailed. Papineau and others slipped away to the Richelieu Valley. And now Colborne made a mistake—the first of several, although this one nominally was the mistake of Gosford, his commander in chief. Instead of acting promptly and in strength, sweeping the Richelieu Valley with a force powerful enough to overawe the rebellious elements without bloodshed, he permitted a small troop of Montreal volunteer cavalry, men of the sort who comprised the Doric Club, to dash through the Richelieu countryside and arrest the *Patriote* leaders at St. Jean. At once the whole region became a hornet's nest. The amateur dragoons of Montreal, armed only with pistols, were ambushed on the road back. After a splutter of shots they managed to escape, leaving their prisoners behind. And now there was blood on the ground (a few men had been wounded on both sides) and on the moon. Up and down the Richelieu flew the word that soldiers had been beaten and prisoners rescued in open fight —an omen of victory for the *Patriote* cause everywhere.

A few days later Colborne learned that Wolfred Nelson was defying arrest with an armed body of *Patriotes* at St. Denis, and that Thomas Brown was with another at St. Charles, a few miles farther up the Richelieu. The general now sent a stronger force, but with no better forethought than the first. Under his orders Colonel Wetherall marched to the old strategic post of Chambly, a day's tramp from Montreal on the road to St. Jean, debouching on the Richelieu River with a regiment of British infantry, a troop of Montreal volunteer cavalry, and two guns. He had posted Colonel Gore at the mouth of the river (Sorel) with half a regiment, another volunteer cavalry troop, and one gun. The plan was simple on Colborne's map. Gore would march up the river and drive the rebels from St. Denis; Wetherall would march down the river and drive them from St. Charles; and the two columns would then come together, sweeping up the fugitives in the pocket between them. But in fact the plan was bad, for these movements were to be made chiefly by night, over country roads deep in mud and without reliable guides. In the main column (Wetherall's) only one man could speak French. Both columns marched without any transport for supplies or wounded, in fact, as one officer complained, "without a dollar, without a loaf of bread, without a commissary and without a spare cartridge." Colborne's old master Wellington would have been sulphurous.

Gore set out on the night of November 22, struggled all through the dark hours in a storm of sleet and snow, and arrived with his sodden and weary troops after daylight on the twenty-third. Before them the church bells of St. Denis were clanging the alarm and armed *habitants* were coming in from all the countryside. The rebels included some veterans of the Voltigeurs of 1812, and under the direction of these men they had erected a strong loopholed stockade of logs and posted some riflemen in a brick house behind it. With them were not only Wolfred Nelson but Dr. O'Callaghan and Papineau himself.

Colonel Gore hesitated to storm the stockade. A halfhearted rush took a lone house on the edge of the village, but that was all. For five hours there was a desultory shooting back and forth in which the British had twenty-four men killed or wounded and the rebels had eighteen. By that time the soldiers had fired away most of their cartridges, they were hungry and cold and dispirited, and Gore decided to retreat. The rebels made no pursuit but Gore abandoned his wounded and his gun, and nearly a hundred of his soldiers had straggled off by the time he got back to Sorel.

The most significant part of the affair, however, was not the retreat of the troops but the flight of Papineau and O'Callaghan. Soon after the shooting began they fled away across country to St. Hyacinthe and thence to the United States, leaving Wolfred Nelson and the courageous *habitants* to fight it out. Papineau afterward declared that he left the scene at Nelson's urging. Nelson indignantly denied it. The truth was that, as in all human upheavals the world over, the Patrick Henrys who cry for liberty or death prefer their personal liberty to a personal place in the firing line. Rebellion must have its gifted agitators no less than its gallant fighters—but they are never the same men.

The British advance from Chambly was larger and better led, though no better organized (by General Colborne) than Gore's march from Sorel. On the same night, in the same weather, and trudging blindly in the same half-frozen mud, the column was still seven miles short of St. Charles when Wetherall got word of Gore's flight down the river. He halted the march and sent back to Chambly for a reserve company of infantry. On November 25 he moved on with his whole force to St. Charles. Here, as at St. Denis, the *Patriotes* had put up a loopholed log barricade and posted marksmen in a commanding house behind it. Here, too, their most eloquent leaders had deserted them at the sight of the British troops. The command fell to Thomas Storrow Brown, the radical iron merchant of Mont-real, who had been savagely beaten in the street riots there before he fled to the Richelieu and was still suffering from his injuries.

Brown had no military knowledge whatever. His garrison con-sisted of two hundred *habitants*, only half of whom had firearms, and these a museum collection of old muskets and fowling pieces. Their outposts under gallant Benjamin Viger made things hot for the troops as they approached, but in an hour it was all over. Colonel Wetherall's cannon drove the villagers from the stockade and his four hundred bayonets stormed over it and through the house. The soldiers lost twenty-one killed and wounded, the rebels seventy, and Brown saved himself by galloping off to St. Denis. The British troops made no pursuit. St. Denis was Colonel Gore's nut and he was left to crack it. Wetherall returned to Montreal in triumph, the caricature of a Roman conqueror, exhibiting to the populace a pitiful thirty prisoners and the captured liberty pole of St. Charles.

Reinforced from Montreal, Colonel Gore marched again from Sorel on December 1. At St. Denis however he found no nut to crack. Papineau's flight and the bloody score at St. Charles had been too much for the villagers. Wolfred Nelson hid himself in the countryside (where he was caught later on) while the *habitants* hid their weapons and watched with apprehensive faces as Gore's soldiers tramped past the empty stockade and along the village street. A guilty secret lay in the shallows of the Richelieu, the body of a British officer bound with cords and shot and hacked to death. He was Lieutenant John Weir, captured while astray from Gore's column in the blind snowy night of November 22. Although his arms were tied, he had attempted to escape during Gore's attack on the village, and in the maniac fury of the moment the villagers had butchered him. An informer told the soldiers where the body was and they dragged it, weighted with stones, from the river. Now the maniac fury was theirs; they took revenge on the village, though not on the people, looting and burning until most of St. Denis was destroyed. And the fury did not end there. As the rebellion ran its course in Lower Canada the cry of "Remember Jack Weir!" arose among the British troops wherever they met armed resistance or found that rebels had been sheltered, and again there was the undisciplined looting and burning and often the desecration and destruction of the village church.

With the captures of St. Charles and St. Denis the rebellion in the

Richelieu Valley was crushed, though far from dead. General Colborne could now turn his full attention to the hotbed of the Two Mountain district northwest of Montreal. Here passions were more deeply stirred than anywhere else, for one of the most ardent apostles of rebellion was a village priest, Abbé Chartier of St. Benoît, whose wild oratory was not to be curbed by his bishop nor by his fellow *curé* Abbé Paquin of St. Eustache nearby. The military leader was a Swiss named Amury Girod, one of several foreign adventurers who appeared from nowhere, drawn to the Canadian troubles like crows to carrion.

Girod's mysterious career had included some service as a cavalry officer in turbulent Mexico and he arrived in Two Mountains in November 1837 with credentials signed by Papineau, took charge of the *Patriotes* in the district, and made his headquarters in the village of St. Eustache. He soon picked a deliberate quarrel with their more moderate leaders, F. C. Scott and Joseph Girouard, and chose as his lieutenant the doctor of St. Eustache, a brave young idealist named J. O. Chenier, who was fired with the desire to fight and die for liberty. Girod was quite cynical about his dupes in general ("It is easier to convince a goose that it should not cackle than to make a Canadian hold his tongue") and in particular ("Chenier is a lazy and foolish fellow — his brother is a drunkard"), but he was able to impose his will upon them and upon the wild-eyed Abbé Chartier.

The Two Mountains region had long been excited by Papineau's speeches and by the *Patriote* press of nearby Montreal. At the news of Gore's defeat at St. Denis it exploded in open revolt against the government. As in the Richelieu Valley, gangs of *Patriotes* went from village to village, forcing local officials to destroy their commissions, terrorizing loyal citizens and those who wished to be neutral — the *chouayens* — and robbing them of any guns they had. The rebels had in their ranks a number of the bellicose log drivers of the Ottawa River, Irish and *canadien*, ready for any excitement. On November 29 Girod and Chenier led two hundred of these, drunk and boisterous, to the Indian mission at Oka, where they looted the Hudson's Bay Company store and obtained among other things some guns and ammunition. Outside the mission house they found an ancient cannon and carried that off as well.

Sir John Colborne made no attempt to deal with the unruly men of Two Mountains until his troops had settled affairs in the Richelieu Valley. In the meantime he was satisfied to post a guard of armed volunteers at the Bord à Plouffe bridge leading to Montreal. As the days went by, Girod and the Abbé Chartier, by threat and persuasion, gathered into their "army" at St. Eustache about a thousand men, a few hundred of whom had guns of various kinds and the rest nothing but pikes and clubs. Girod made no attempt to march on Montreal. He tried without success to train his unruly army, but they would have nothing to do with drill. They passed the December days in lounging about the village, drinking, dancing, stealing, and fighting among themselves.

All this came to an end on December 14, when Sir John Colborne with two thousand troops and eight guns crossed the Rivière des Mille Iles on the ice and marched upon St. Eustache. Three quarters of Girod's army vanished at the mere report. The remaining 250 he posted in the strongest buildings of the village, chiefly in the church, whose thick stone walls were cannonproof, and in the rectory of the indignant Abbé Paquin next door. Having made these arrangements, Amury Girod mounted his horse and disappeared in the countryside. The Abbé Chartier had fled already. Wiser than Girod, he did not stop until he reached the United States.

Colborne's troops and guns made short work of the lesser buildings, but the cannon merely scarred the walls of the church; and J. O. Chenier's men, firing from the windows, killed one soldier and wounded nine others. Finally, however, under cover of the smoke from the burning rectory, a few soldiers managed to set fire to a combustible part of the church at the rear. The flames thickened and spread through the church interior. The rebel garrison began to stagger forth and surrender. More than a hundred had been taken prisoners when someone cried, "Remember Jack Weir!" and after that all discipline vanished. The rest of the rebels, including Chenier, were shot down as they emerged. The troops (who included some rabid Montreal volunteers) went on to loot and burn most of the village. There was strong drink in the loot and drunken soldiers reeled about the streets, one or two wearing vestments stolen from the burning rectory. Seventy rebels had been killed in the shooting and the remains of others were found later in the fire-gutted church.

Colborne's force was now joined by a rabble of volunteers from the Ottawa riverside, many of them victims of persecution in the days when the *Patriotes* were riding high and with a score to pay. These marched with the troops to the nearby village of St. Benoît, the parish of the vanished Abbé Chartier. The villagers came out to meet them carrying white flags, and Colborne halted his troops; but the volunteers rushed into St. Benoît, desecrated the church, and looted and burned the whole village. The British soldiers went on to search the whole region for the surviving rebel leaders. They managed to catch Girouard and others of the lesser sort, but their quest for Girod and Chartier was fruitless. Chartier was safe in the United States; and Amury Girod, finding himself very unsafe in his hiding place near Montreal, put a pistol to his head and blew out the brains of the Two Mountain revolt.

To a casual surface glance the rebellion in both Canadas was now at an end; but in the meantime there had been a significant little affair on the frontier between Lower Canada and Vermont. Many of the leading rebels and some of their followers had fled over the line into that convenient haven, among them Robert Bouchette, a grandson of that daring "Wild Pigeon" who had saved Guy Carleton from capture by the Americans in 1775. The American people in the border country had a strong sympathy for the Canadian rebels, and Bouchette had no trouble in collecting arms and ammunition for another attempt to raise the wind in the Richelieu Valley.

On December 6, 1837, he and two hundred others marched into Canada armed with muskets, two field cannon, and a pair of banners made for them by the admiring ladies of Swanton, Vermont. They did not get far. At Mooers' Corners they met three hundred loyal militia, and after a brief fusillade the rebels fled back across the line, leaving behind their cannon, their banners, and their reserve supply of muskets and ammunition. Bouchette, wounded and a prisoner, was carried to jail in Montreal, where he found several other *Patriote* leaders including Wolfred Nelson, caught in the intensive man hunt after the St. Denis affair.

The significance of this poor little affair was in its point of origin. The rebellions in Upper and Lower Canada were now in the process of changing into something else, a private war nourished and directed from the soil of the United States.

CHAPTER 49

1838

*Robert Nelson — The great conspiracy of the Hunters
— Fighting in Upper and Lower Canada*

THE severity of the rebel hunt in both Canadian provinces was driving a stream of refugees into American territory. In both cases the most ruthless hunters were not the regular troops but a swarm of eager volunteers, and any man of anti-Tory politics was suspect. It was a time for paying off all sorts of grudges. In Lower Canada the volunteers included French Canadians who had been abused by the *Patriotes*, the so-called *chouayens*, who now sought revenge; but largely they were men of the English-speaking minority in the province, typified by Adam Thom of the Montreal *Herald* and his colleagues of the French-hating Catholic-baiting Doric Club of Montreal. The generous Earl of Gosford, who had come to Canada with such hopes, went back to England sickened in body and mind in February 1838, and Sir John Colborne took into his military hands the administration of the province. It was an unfortunate succession for the *habitants* in the rebel districts and for the Reformers of both languages, wherever they were. The early defeat of his troops at the hands of a few poorly armed peasants and idealists had left small room for charity in Colborne's heart, and although many of his officers deplored the savage destruction of the Tory volunteers, hundreds of these partisans were allowed to indulge their bigotry.

All of this played into the hands of the exiled rebel leaders plotting further adventures from the security of the American border states. It was especially useful to Wolfred Nelson's brother Robert, a figure of sudden self-importance, filled with wild schemes for a Canadian republic surpassing those of Papineau. Not that Papineau was idle. Soon after reaching the United States, he and Dr. O'Callaghan got in touch with President Van Buren, asking help for the Canadian rebels, but they had come at a poor time. The great financial panic of 1837 had stunned the business of the whole United States and Van Buren wanted no part of the war in Canada. More than that he suspected that these importunate exiles might try to involve the United States in a war with Britain. On January 5, 1838, he issued a proclamation of strict neutrality in the Canadian troubles, and for their own part the governors of New York and Vermont publicly forbade any aid to the rebels by their citizens.

In the same cold month of January a number of refugee *Patriotes* gathered in the frosty little town of Middlebury, Vermont, where Robert Nelson set forth his aim to raise the Lower Canadian winds again. But with Van Buren's refusal, Papineau's blood had cooled like the blood shed on the snow at St. Denis. He rebuked Nelson, pointing out that further rebellion was hopeless without American help, and that his efforts could only bring new suffering to the *habitants*. From that moment Papineau and the scholarly O'Callaghan drew aside while Robert Nelson, Dr. Cote, and other hotheads traveled the road to a new and larger disaster.

Nelson knew that in spite of Van Buren's decree there was a strong feeling in the border states for the Canadian insurgents, and that even American army officials were ready to assist. Within a few weeks he was able to obtain a thousand U. S. Army muskets and three field guns from the arsenal at Elizabethtown, New York. With these to arm a new uprising, he and Cote and a group of other enthusiasts crossed the border near the tip of Lake Champlain on February 28, 1838. In the first hamlet Nelson issued a manifesto addressed to the inhabitants of Lower Canada, declaring their province an independent republic and styling himself President of the "Provisional Government." The document went on to proclaim a complete separation of Church and State, freedom of the press, a secret ballot at elections, every man a voter including Indians, seizure of the British-American Land Company's properties, seizure of the Crown lands, the equal use of French and English languages in public affairs, cancellation of all the old land rights of the *seigneurs*, and various other matters.

Lower Canada had enjoyed (or suffered) freedom of the press for years, and the equal use of French and English in public affairs had been established firmly by the first Assembly under the constitution of 1791. The reference to seigneurial land rights must have interested Papineau, who owned and cherished a seigneury himself. The most important point was the avowed separation of Church and State. It meant that under President Nelson the Catholic clergy could no longer collect tithes in the parishes, a privilege confirmed to them by the Quebec Act. Some of his other points were sound, but this appeal to *habitants* who grumbled at paying tithes could only stiffen the attitude of the Church, which already had shown itself opposed to rebellion.

The bold declaration of independence failed to mask the utter weakness of Nelson's position as things stood. None of the *habitants* offered to rise in his support. The mere appearance of some loyal militia was enough to send him and his little band hurrying back through the snows to the safety of American territory, where General John Wool, commanding the U. S. Army post at Plattsburg, solemnly took into his possession the incriminating muskets and whisked them out of sight. Nelson was not dismayed. Obviously there must be a better groundwork for establishment of the republic, and it was not long before he and his fellow conspirators hit upon a plan.

During the past fifty years, with the usual drift of frontier populations, thousands of French Canadians had settled in the northern fringes of Maine, New Hampshire, Vermont, and New York, just as thousands of foot-loose Yankees had settled in the Eastern Townships of Lower Canada. The French Canadians on American soil were being increased by the flow of refugees from the Richelieu. Here was a promising source of recruits for a new war across the border. But the prospects below the border were much wider. To many Americans in the border states it was easy to see a parallel between the Canadian rebels and their own ancestors of '76, and it aroused all their old antipathy to the British flag flying just across the frontier.

With all this in mind, and with a shrewd aim at the American weakness for secret societies, with their romantic oaths, initiations, secret signs, and offices of rank, Nelson and his group invented and organized the *Frères Chasseurs* or Brotherhood of Hunters. The society was in its way a curious forerunner of the Ku Klux Klan, with the same Masonic touches and the same disguised military structure. Its hierarchy began with a local Snowshoe who commanded nine Hunters. The scale rose through a Beaver, who commanded five Snowshoes, an Eagle who commanded a varying number of Beavers, and so to the eminence of a Grand Eagle, who commanded a whole region. All of these mysterious officers and brethren were to dedicate themselves by tremendous oaths to work and eventually to fight for the liberation of Canada from British tyranny.

The brotherhood was a runaway success from the start. The idea and the organization spread like measles through the American border states from Maine to Michigan during the spring and summer of 1838. It found a vaccinated flesh in Upper Canada (where the Orange Lodge was all-powerful), but its lodges soon dotted the face of Lower Canada, using French nomenclature from *Aigle* to *Raquette*. By the autumn of 1838 its activities were so widespread and notorious that Sir John Colborne estimated two hundred thousand members in the United States and Canada, with three thousand in the city of Montreal alone. Probably forty thousand in all would have been nearer to the mark, but that number was formidable enough for action and Nelson and his Eagles were ready with a broad plan of campaign.

The Hunters along the American side of the Great Lakes and the upper reach of the St. Lawrence would invade Upper Canada by way of Detroit, Niagara, and Ogdensburg opposite Prescott, at the same time calling upon the anti-Tory groups within the province to rise and join them. The Hunters of the Great Lakes area had met in convention at Cleveland, Ohio, in September 1838 and set up a "Republican Government of Upper Canada." Many were refugees from the witch hunt after Mackenzie's fiasco, but many more were American citizens. They had consulted Mackenzie in exile, but that crabbed little creature, resenting perhaps the success of Nelson's brain child, preferred his own secretive enterprises.

To direct the fighting in Lower Canada, Nelson had picked up in New York a pair of wandering French soldiers of fortune named Hindenlang and Touvrey. The chosen time for both invasions was November, when crops had been harvested and every farmer would feel free to move; but the Upper Canadian affair was to start first in order to pin down the British troops at Kingston and elsewhere. As soon as it was under way Nelson's Hunters would march from Lake Champlain to Montreal, gathering a great army of *habitants* along the way and arming them from stores already collected on the American side of the border. To finance his republic, Nelson proposed to seize the banks, to mulct eighty thousand pounds from wealthy John Molson of Montreal, and to rob and hang every Jew in the province.

Behind all these wild plans and speculations there was a very solid motive. An irruption of this kind, springing from American soil, armed with American weapons and involving many American citizens, was almost certain to bring about a war between Britain and the United States. Whatever happened in the initial fighting, President Nelson could hope to march to power eventually behind the armies of the republic on the south.

The motive was clear to the government of the United States, which now sent General Winfield Scott to take charge of their army posts on the Canadian border, to end the flagrant collusion of certain officials there, and to make sure that the Hunters did not use American soil in their operations. The appointment came a little late. The invasion began before Scott could do much about it on the long border line; but from that point his energy and vigilance cut away the solid base of Nelson's scheme. The result in Canada was another grotesque and sometimes bloody farce. Comparatively few of the Hunters on either side of the frontier proved willing to risk their skins in battle or their necks in capture, in spite of the awesome oaths they had sworn in the lodges. The British garrison in both provinces had been reinforced by regular troops and the Canadian countryside behind the frontier bristled with the muskets and bayonets of organized volunteer companies and battalions.

The invasion by way of Detroit and Niagara amounted to no more than local raids by small armed parties who were easily defeated by the watchful garrisons of those old Canadian battlegrounds. The most serious attempt on Upper Canada was the attack on Prescott, where old Fort Wellington guarded the passage of the St. Lawrence. The invasion here was hatched in the Hunters' lodges at Ogdensburg, Sackets Harbor, Watertown, and Oswego. The "Grand Eagle" was one Bierge, a coward in the pinch, and the active command of the attack fell upon a German Pole named Von Schultz, one of the romantic foreign soldiers drawn to the troubled Canadian scene.

On November 11, 1838, four hundred Hunters embarked at Sackets Harbor and other places on the American shore of Lake Ontario. Their two ships were provided by well-to-do American merchants and they were well armed with muskets, bayonets, pistols, and swords, with a good supply of ammunition, and with a banner. (The banner was a large and expensive flag of silk made by the ladies of Onondaga County, New York, richly ornamented, and with an embroidered star, an eagle, and the words *Liberated by the Onondaga Hunters*.) The ships, a steamer and a schooner, slipped past Kingston by the American channel inside Wolfe Island and headed down the St. Lawrence for Prescott.

The strategy was sound. The capture of Prescott would prevent any quick movement of troops and guns between Upper and Lower Canada — they would have to travel by the Rideau Canal and the Ottawa. But the force was absurdly small and its flesh was weak — Bierge and two hundred others lost their courage and scrambled ashore on the American bank at Ogdensburg. Von Schultz and the rest, a determined band, landed below Prescott in spite of cannon fire from a small British naval steamer and barricaded themselves in a large stone windmill and some adjoining houses.

Their position was hopeless. On November 12 the British naval detachment at Kingston sent two more armed steamers to the scene and on the thirteenth a United States army and naval force arrived from Sackets Harbor and stopped all communications to or from the American bank. Meanwhile various bodies of Canadian militia had surrounded the mill. On the sixteenth some British regulars arrived with three cannon. The combined troops made attempts to get into the mill but were beaten off. However after a few hours' bombardment by the cannon, Von Schultz and the surviving 157 Hunters gave themselves up. They had fought stoutly in their massive little fortress. The British and Canadian troops had lost 76 killed and wounded, the Hunters 37.

In Lower Canada things had gone no better. The Hunters of New York and Vermont had secured for the cause a few cannon, some hundreds of U. S. Army muskets and bayonets, and a supply of ammunition, but none of them offered to march with these things into Canada. On November 3 Robert Nelson entered Canadian territory from Lake Champlain in a boat laden with weapons. With him were a guide, a boatman, and the two French officers Hindenlang and Touvrey. Dr. Cote had gone ahead to muster the *habitants* of Napierville, fifteen miles from the border on the direct road from Plattsburg to Montreal.

On November 4 Nelson and his little party arrived at Napierville, where Cote had raised several hundred *habitants*. Nelson proclaimed himself President of the Republic of Lower Canada and ordered Hindenlang to command the forces with the rank of brigadier general. Word had been passed to all the Lower Canadian lodges of the *Frères Chasseurs* and Nelson confidently expected a general

uprising; but again most of the province remained quiet (even Two
Mountains) and again it was the men of the Richelieu and the region
south of Montreal who gathered to the rebel standard. In three days
Hindenlang found himself in command of about three thousand
habitants, two thirds of whom had nothing but clubs and pikes.

Cote set off with five hundred of them to fetch arms from the
Hunters' supply depot on the American border. On their way back
they were intercepted at Lacolle by a force of loyal militia, and after
a skirmish of half an hour Cote and the greater part of his band fled
away into American territory, leaving a cannon, many muskets and
a number of wounded and unwounded prisoners in the hands of the
government force.

Nelson's venture was now cut off from its American base and
about to face Sir John Colborne, who had crossed over from Montreal and was on the march to Napierville with five thousand regular
and volunteer troops. Other forces of armed volunteers were moving
against the isolated *Patriote* groups at Beauharnois, Chateauguay,
and other villages in the wedge of Canadian territory south of
Montreal. Hindenlang's "army" at Napierville soon dwindled to
about one thousand. Most of these had guns of various kinds and
Hindenlang decided to cut his way back to American soil. At the
Odelltown crossroads, close to the border, stood two hundred loyal
militia strongly posted in and about a Methodist church and supported by the cannon they had taken from Cote. On November 9
Hindenlang drew up to them and ordered an attack. Most of his
raw farmers hung back, crouching and praying in the snow out of
musket range, as he said, like "so many saints carved in stone." The
rest made a desperate assault but they were beaten off with the loss
of a hundred killed and wounded.

There was nothing for it now but to turn back to Napierville. But
all hope was gone there. The *Patriotes* melted away into the countryside. Robert Nelson deserted his dupes and made his way safely over
the border by a roundabout route. Hindenlang remained on the
scene and was taken prisoner by Colborne's advancing troops.

So ended the great conspiracy, and now began the aftermath, a
carnival of revenge in the affected districts south of Montreal, where
columns of eager volunteers set fire to every house known to have
sheltered a rebel. More than 750 rebels had been rounded up and
thrown into jail. Adam Thom in the Montreal *Herald* demanded
that all be hanged. Sir John Colborne suspended trial by jury and

his courts-martial sentenced 99 to death. However in his rigid way he ignored Thom and the ultra-loyal party as much as he ignored the lawyers who spoke for the *Patriotes*. In the end only a dozen of the condemned men went to the gallows, half of them for actual murders committed during the uprising. Of the other six the most notable was Hindenlang, who, in contrast to Nelson and Cote, conducted himself gallantly from first to last.

Of the other condemned men in Lower Canada fifty-eight were transported around the world to the convict settlements in Tasmania, two were merely banished, twenty-seven were freed on their promise of good behavior. In Upper Canada ten captured Hunters, including the brave Von Schultz, were hanged at Kingston. In Toronto two petty leaders of the 1837 revolt, Samuel Lount and Peter Matthews, had gone to the gallows in the spring of '38. From the Kingston jail twenty-nine convicted Hunters traveled in chains to join the melancholy convicts of Lower Canada on their way to Van Diemen's Land.

On the whole the punishments were few in view of the scale of the revolt, especially in Lower Canada, where the hyper-Tories were furious that so many escaped the hang rope. Cooler minds saw little justice in punishing any of these men except those guilty of murder. The rest were merely dupes. Without exception the real culprits had scuttled off to the United States.

CHAPTER 50

1837 — 1841

Lord Durham and his famous report — The union of Lower and Upper Canada — Baldwin and Lafontaine find common ground

BETWEEN the Canadian rebellion of 1837 and its recrudescence a year later the Reform government in London made an earnest effort to deal with the problem. Lord Durham was made governor general of Canada and told to examine the Canadian sores and suggest the remedy. Durham was forty-six, an intellectual with radical ideas, the son of a colliery owner. He was a graduate of Eton and Cambridge, he had served three years in a crack cavalry regiment, made a successful runaway marriage with an heiress, and gone into Whig politics at a time when the Reform movement had begun to stir and march toward its destiny. His name was John George Lambton and he had been given the Durham title for his part in framing the famous Reform Bill of 1832. Nevertheless his ideas were sometimes a little too radical for the more cautious majority of his party (hence his nickname Radical Jack) and he was sent to Canada partly because he had proved himself a shrewd political analyst, party because his liberal outlook would ensure a measure of justice for the liberal underdogs in Canada, and partly to get him out of England for a time.

Durham had an odd mixture of human insight, intellectual snobbery and genuine liberal interest, combined with an incongruous love of personal power and show. He brought with him a staff of clever young Englishmen, chief of whom were Charles Buller and Edward Wakefield. All of them came to Canada with the self-confidence of a team of young doctors moving in upon an interesting plague. As a forerunner Durham sent out a private investigator, Stewart Derbshire, who conferred in New York with the exiled Dr. O'Callaghan and William Lyon Mackenzie before moving on to inquire in Canada itself. Derbishire's report was in many ways the most discerning of all the Durham papers, pointing out with merciless accuracy the virtues, follies and prejudices of both parties in Lower Canada, the chief trouble spot; and he saw what Durham never understood — that French-Canadian nationalism was too strong ever to be subdued and absorbed in the English-speaking body.

Durham landed with an emperor's pomp at Quebec and installed himself and his staff in the Château St. Louis. His first act was to get rid of Sir John Colborne's ultra-Tory council and to seek the knowledge and advice of the leading Canadians, British and French. His next act was ultimately his downfall. He had to deal with the prisoners taken in the rising of '37, a peculiar problem, for any Anglo-Canadian jury would have hanged them and any French-Canadian jury would have freed them, guilty or not. His solution was bold and illegal. He obtained a confession of guilt from Wolfred Nelson and seven other notable rebels and with their own consent exiled them to Bermuda out of harm's way. They were forbidden to return to Canada without proper authority, under pain of death. The same decree of banishment under these terms applied to Papineau, O'Callaghan, Robert Nelson, and thirteen other leaders who already were safe in the United States. Durham then granted a full amnesty to all other prisoners and refugees except six held on charges of murder.

This act of quick common sense fired the highly combustible temper of Adam Thom and the other hang-rope enthusiasts, a sure indication to the French Canadians that Durham was playing no favorites. In Britain, however, Durham's personal enemy Lord Brougham seized a chance to attack him, on the score that deportation and invoking the death penalty without trial were contrary to the laws as well as the instincts of all Englishmen. He persisted until Durham was officially reproved for these "despotic" acts in Canada. By this time Durham had finished his investigation and decided on remedies which, as governor general, he hoped to carry out when Parliament approved them; but his pride was touchy and when the reproof came he threw up his appointment in a sudden pet and left for home. The ship in which he sailed from Quebec in September 1838 was, appropriately, the *Inconstant*.

During his five earnest months in Canada the Brotherhood of Hunters were busy hatching their conspiracy almost under the noses of his bright young men as they moved about the countryside, and when Durham wrote the last word of his famous report in January 1839 the flimsy structures of peace and charity in Canada were again in ruins. He was ill himself with tuberculosis and in little more than another year he was dead. Popular subscription in Britain built a Greek mausoleum over his grave. A much better monument remained in his *Report on the Affairs of British North America*.

The acid Lord Brougham dismissed the report in a quip to Macaulay the historian; "The matter came from a felon [Edward Wakefield, who had once been imprisoned for eloping with a girl of minor age] — the style from a coxcomb [Charles Buller] — and the Dictator furnished only six letters, D-U-R-H-A-M." Like his other attacks on Durham this was only partly true and quite unjust. Undoubtedly Durham had made good use of these men's minds as well as the minds of others, but for all that the report was his and it remains a brilliant study of colonial government.

The report was in four parts, the largest dealing with Lower Canada, the second with Upper Canada, the third with the Maritime Provinces, and the fourth with remedies for their ills. The situation in Lower Canada he put in a famous sentence: "I expected to find a contest between a government and a people; I found two nations warring in the bosom of a single state." He sketched the historical background of the "deadly animosity" he had found between the races, stabbed a sharp pen at the faults of both, and condemned the archaic and blundering machinery of the Colonial Office which had led to "evils which no civilized community can long continue to bear."

The Upper Canadians he described as "hardy farmers and humble mechanics composing a very independent, not very manageable, and sometimes a rather turbulent democracy" — a perfect picture of them — and he observed that such people were not disposed to be "slavish tools of a narrow official clique or a few purse-proud merchants." The Maritime Provinces, where there was strong agitation for responsible government but so far no rebellion, he dismissed in a comparatively short treatise.

In his summary he wrote, "It will be acknowledged by everyone who has observed the progress of Anglo-Saxon civilization in America that sooner or later the English race was sure to predominate even numerically in Lower Canada, as they predominate already by their superior knowledge, energy, enterprise and wealth." This was his cardinal error, and as he saw it the French Canadians for their own ultimate good must be absorbed in the English-speaking race in Canada as the French of Louisiana were melting into the English-speaking race of Americans. What he obviously had in mind for Canada was a modified United States still loyal to the British Crown, with fully responsible government in each of its states or provinces, and all ruled by a federal government that was responsible partly to the Canadian electorate and partly to Westminster. To give them a tangible bond with each other he advocated an "intercolonial" railway to run between the Great Lakes and the Atlantic Ocean.

Nevertheless in regarding the human and geographical obstacles, he found "great practical difficulties" in the way of a complete Canadian federation from the lakes to the sea, observing regretfully, "Such a union would at once decisively settle the question of races; it would enable all the provinces to co-operate for all common purposes; and above all it would form a great and powerful people, possessing the means of securing good and responsible government for itself, and which under the protection of the British Empire might in some measure counterbalance the preponderant and increasing influence of the United States on the American continent . . . it can only be done by raising up for the North American colonist some nationality of his own; by elevating these small and unimportant communities into a society having some objects of national importance; and by thus giving their inhabitants a country which they would be unwilling to see absorbed even into one more powerful."

In the latter phrases Durham was referring to the threat being flung at each other by excited spokesmen of both races in the Canadian quarrel — the threat to secede from the British empire and ask for annexation by the United States rather than submit to any sort of domination by the other race in Canada itself. He went on to forsee that "it would be the tendency of a federation, sanctioned and consolidated by a monarchial government, gradually to become a complete legislative union; and thus, while conciliating the French of Lower Canada by leaving them the government of their own province and their own internal legislation, I might provide for the protection of British interests by the general government, and for the gradual transition of the provinces into a united and homogeneous community." This was clear prophecy in all but one word. The united community of Canada could never be homogeneous. Whatever happened, the French Canadians would retain their own community within the state, like the French of Switzerland, not a bit like the French absorbed in the determined melting pot of the United States.

The man who came out to Canada as governor-general in Durham's place was Charles Poulett Thomson, Baron Sydenham, another hero of the Reform movement in Britain. He arrived in October 1839. Since Durham's departure, the Hunters' lodges had created a greater uproar than the 1837 affair discussed in his report, and London took a stiffer view. Lord John Russell, Colonial Secretary in the British Cabinet, warned Sydenham not to countenance any Canadian movement "for what is absurdly called responsible government." The Montreal and the Toronto-Kingston cliques, the hyper-Tories with their fear and hatred of government by popular majorities, remained the loyal heart of the country in the eyes of the empire-conscious Colonial Office. Had not they proved it with arms in '37 and again in '38? Their voices were more powerful than ever now, and they were joined at this time by the powerful voices of the London bankers who had loaned so much money to Upper Canada for the construction of the canals. Their argument was for a union of Upper and Lower Canada—they pointed to Durham's report—and on special terms to keep the Reformers generally and the French-Canadian Reformers particularly in a position to do no further mischief in or out of Parliament.

With these old and new pressures emerging from the smoke of the rebellions, London tossed aside the principle of responsible government, which was the whole base of Durham's structure and which alone could make the rest of his recommendations palatable to the Reformers, French and English. On July 23, 1840, the British Parliament passed the Union Act, introduced by Russell. It was a triumph for the English-speaking bigots of the lower province and for the greedy Compact in the upper one. It created a single Province of Canada. It pooled the revenues of Lower Canada, whose debt was low, with those of Upper Canada, which had a huge debt and was bankrupt. It gave the united province an elective assembly of eighty-four members, of whom exactly half were to represent Upper Canada (with a population of 450,000) and half to represent Lower Canada (with a population of 650,000). It placed over the assembly a legislative council of the old style, with Crown-chosen members to be appointed for life. It gave the governor general the power of veto and the right to reserve any bill for London's sanction. It made English the only language to be used in recording the transactions of both houses. It required the assembly to provide £75,000 per year for the payment of the governor general, the judiciary, and the key men among the civil servants, all Crown appointees. Finally it authorized the governor general to appoint his own executive council.

When the first Parliament of the Province of Canada met at Kingston on June 14, 1841, the governor general's power of appointment was clearly shown in the composition of the upper House and the executive council. Of the two dozen legislative councilors, only eight were French Canadians. In the executive council there were none. Sydenham's excuse (which he mentioned privately in a dispatch to the Colonial Office) was that he could find few or no French Canadians of real ability who had not been identified in sympathy or action with the *Patriote* troubles. There was a good deal of truth in it.

And now, in the very moment of their apparent triumph, the Tories of Upper and Lower Canada were on the road to defeat. The rebellions, far from killing the Reform movement, had been a blessing in disguise. For one thing they had sloughed from the Reform body the irritating proud flesh of Mackenzie and Papineau and the other wild men who (whatever the honesty of their motives) had only been an embarrassment. For another thing the brutal persecution and repression by the Tories following the rebellions, which had driven thousands into exile, had awakened a strong feeling of revulsion in the general public. This had shown itself in a general chorus of Reform votes at the polls. But what was most important, the sober Reformers in all parts of the united province now recognized their common aims, in which the difference of race and religion had no part.

On the first day of the Kingston sessions Robert Baldwin, leader of the Reform majority in Upper Canada, and a member of the newly appointed executive council, demanded that the governor general remove the Tories from the council and replace them with Reformers, *including men from Lower Canada*. Sydenham refused and Baldwin at once resigned from the council. He was now free to oppose the rigged government of Sydenham's creation in and outside of the assembly. Outside of it he was promptly joined by Louis Hippolyte Lafontaine, leader of the Reformers in Lower

Canada, who already had challenged his own race to put aside
their ancient prejudice, to recognize that there were other Canadians besides themselves and that men of good will could work
together for the welfare of all.

By chance there was a golden opportunity to show that the Reformers, French and English, now stood together. By his political
enemies' use of the most flagrant violence and corruption at the
polls, Lafontaine had been outvoted at the Terrebonne polls in
the first elections for the united assembly. He could have found a
safe seat in Lower Canada, but in the autumn Robert Baldwin offered him one in the constituency of York, the very heart of Upper
Canada. When Lafontaine was confirmed a representative of York
the hyper-Tories rubbed their eyes. It was disturbing enough to see
Baldwin, a man of Protestant Irish blood and a former pupil of the
onetime schoolmaster Strachan, leading the radical party in Upper
Canada. To see a Catholic French Canadian, a former rebel under
Papineau, holding a seat in York was astounding. It was as if the
sky had fallen.

Two years later there was a chance to return the compliment, for
Baldwin lost his own seat in a personal defeat at the polls. Lafontaine provided him with one in the solidly French-Canadian
constituency of Rimouski, near the mouth of the St. Lawrence.
The times had changed indeed. Here was the solution of the old
political impasse between the two races in Canada, a bridge on
political party lines, something Durham had thought impossible.
So far there was nothing but an example. The practice would be
difficult. But Canada was a difficult country where nothing could
come easily.

CHAPTER 51

1837 — 1849

*The Reform movement in Nova Scotia — London concedes
responsible government — Montreal the capital of
Canada — The Rebellion Losses Bill — The burning
of Canada's House of Parliament — The
Annexation Manifesto*

I N THE salty atmosphere of the Maritime Provinces the cause
of Reform was being fought with heat by the Nova Scotians,
and with the usual bloody noses at the polls, but with no suggestion of rebellion. A Halifax Compact had ruled the province
since early colonial times with the same quasi-apostolic succession,
the same devout professions of loyalty to the Crown, and the same
easy and profitable manipulation of Crown patronage that had become so familiar in Lower and Upper Canada.

Here the champion of reform was Joseph Howe, son of a Loyalist,
printer of the *Nova Scotian*, a stocky energetic figure with a banker's
head for facts and figures, a ready pen, an eloquent tongue, and the
voice of a trumpet. His first clash with the Halifax Compact, a tight
cluster of wealthy merchants and officials, resulted in the time-hon-
ored gambit of such groups everywhere, a libel suit. Not a lawyer
in the city would defend him. The shock-haired printer undertook
his own defense and won his case in a crowded courtroom and with
a great crowd waiting in the street for the verdict. From that moment Howe never looked back and Privilege never looked comfortable. The road to Reform was a long and stony one, but Howe
was no wild-eyed revolutionist and he condemned the actions of
Mackenzie and Papineau. He entered the Nova Scotia assembly in
1837 and he saw from the first that Reform in all the Canadian
provinces was one cause. He made a telling contribution to that
cause in his famous open letters to Lord John Russell, which he
published in 1839.

Russell, like other successful Reformers in Britain, had put on the tinted spectacles of empire when he looked across the sea from his post as colonial secretary. The notion of colonial self-rule seemed a colonial illusion, impossible and unworkable within the imperial framework. Howe put before him with brilliant logic the case for colonial self-government, abjured the idea of separation from the empire because of it, and pointed out that the empire could not exist in the future without it. Russell was inclined to shuffle at the time (the powder smoke of the Canadian rebellions was drifting across the Atlantic long after the shooting ceased), but the effect of the letters was apparent in 1846 when he became head of the British ministry.

In that year the new colonial secretary, Lord Grey, received a dispatch from Sir John Harvey, lieutenant governor of Nova Scotia, setting forth the views of the Reform party led by Howe, and predicting that they would soon sweep into office. Here was the old colonial trouble coming to a head again, this time in a province where men were notably loyal and tough and shrewd—and whose capital was the chief British naval base in the western Atlantic, where good relations were vital. It was no time for quibbling and Grey's reply to Harvey stated in plain words a confession and a policy. *It is neither possible nor desirable to carry on the government of any of the British provinces in North America in opposition to the opinion of its inhabitants.* With this pronouncement Grey set out the changes by which the existing framework of government in the province could be made completely responsible to the electorate. It was almost exactly seventy years since the other thirteen colonies in the old coastal chain had seized the principle for themselves.

What was yielded to Nova Scotia naturally applied to all the other Canadian provinces. A new governor general of Canada, Lord Elgin, was about to sail from England to take up his post. Before leaving, he conferred with Grey and it was agreed that the policy would apply to any Canadian party that commanded a majority in its provincial assembly. At the moment the political affairs of the united Province of Canada were again out of balance. The elections of 1844 had been conducted in scenes of violent disorder. In Upper Canada the Orange cry had been raised against Baldwin's combination with the Papists of Lower Canada, and a resurgence of Toryism had carried the Draper government into power, leaving the Reformers with a minority largely composed of Lafontaine and his followers. It was the old bad situation of English-speaking Protestants versus French-speaking Catholics, with Governor General Metcalfe, a viceroy of the old school, leaning his weight heavily toward the English Protestants.

However the Draper government had now run into serious difficulties. The old and valuable British customs preference on Canadian wheat and timber vanished in 1846 when Lord John Russell's ministry put into practice the long-debated principle of free trade in Britain. Away went the famous Navigation laws and the Corn Law, under whose benefit the Canadians had built up their trade in those commodities, the mainstays of the country's business. A severe depression smote both just when Irish refugees from the potato famine, destitute and diseased with typhus, were pouring in Canada by tens of thousands to add to the confusion.

When Lord Elgin arrived in Canada in the bitter January of 1847 he found the Draper government floundering in these difficulties. Responsible government did not interest them so much as their other responsibilities, with which they could not cope. Elgin explained the British Government's decision as conveyed to the Nova Scotians, offered the Tory ministers his complete co-operation in the matter of appointments and patronage, and at the same time made it clear that he would do the same for the Reform party if and when they came to power. That event was very near. At the end of 1847 the Canadian Parliament was dissolved and in the following year Baldwin and Lafontaine rode into power on a tide of Liberal votes—for there were no Reform votes any more; Reform had come.

This, the second Baldwin-Lafontaine partnership in government, became known to Canadians in after years as the Great Administration. Its first test of strength came in 1849 when the long-sought principle of responsible government was put into full effect for the first time. The Nova Scotians had done this without disturbance in 1848. In the Province of Canada it came to birth in a hurricane. The occasion was the Rebellion Losses Bill.

Under a general amnesty many of the banished rebels of 1837–38 had come home and some (including Wolfred Nelson and Papineau) had re-entered politics. Papineau had spent years of his exile in Paris, cheek by jowl with the French *republicaines rouges*, and he had come back with all his old animosities tinged by the rub. This made him more than ever suspect to the Church and to many of the former *Patriotes*, including Lafontaine. For his part Papineau resented the new popularity and power of Lafontaine working in amity with *les sacrés anglais*. It stung the old lion in his most tender part, his vanity. He still had much popularity of his own and it was not long before he won a seat in the assembly. From this vantage point, and from his seigneury at Montebello in the old Two Mountains trouble spot, he was in a position to stir up trouble for the government, especially in those regions where homes, barns and churches had been burned by the soldiery during the rebellions.

Lafontaine and Baldwin recognized the menace to their *entente* at once, and saw the remedy in prompt and full repayment of the damages from government funds. It was just, but the matter was not merely one of justice or injustice. Nor was it merely a shrewd matter of party politics, although that was undoubtedly in the forefront of their minds. The thing really at stake was the newly found spirit of co-operation between men who spoke English and men who spoke French, a fragile seedling that would have to be nourished and shielded now and probably for generations before it could stand against all winds.

At the announcement of the Rebellion Losses Bill the Tory hurricane arose. It was obvious that most of the money would go to Lower Canada, where most of the damage had been done. Equally obvious was the difficulty, indeed the impossibility of making a nice distinction between innocent sufferers and men who had shouldered a pike or musket in the rebel ranks, evaded capture, and slipped back into the villages as simple *habitants* before the soldiers and torches appeared.

The amnesty to the banished rebels had been bad enough, said the Tories. There was Papineau, who should have been hanged, actually sitting in the assembly and raising his voice again. There was that crazy little printer Mackenzie, back in Upper Canada and planning to do the same thing. There was Lafontaine himself, one of the foremost *Patriotes*, who had fled to Paris after the rising of '37—Lafontaine with his strong facial resemblance to Napoleon, which everyone remarked (even Napoleon's old soldiers in the *Invalides*) and which he seemed to cultivate even to the drooping lock upon the forehead. And now the hard-earned tax money of loyal men was to be handed over to men like these who had plotted and fought against Her Majesty and the flag. A bounty for treason!

By an odd turn of fate the seat of government had been removed from Kingston to Montreal in 1844 because that city was more central and had better accommodation for the members. The Ste. Anne's Market Building had been taken over and remodeled for the Houses of Parliament, a limestone structure of three stories containing halls for the assembly and legislative council, a well-stocked library, and various offices. Gas jets hissed and flared throughout the building at night sessions. Portraits of Jacques Cartier, the third and fourth Georges, the young Victoria, and other worthies hung upon the walls. On the assembly table during sessions lay an eight-foot mace that had cost six hundred pounds.

All of this was in the heart of Montreal, the old nest of Governor Murray's "Licentious Fanaticks trading here," who had not changed much since 1763. The hard overriding spirit of the Nor'-westers, their successors, still hung over the place, and so did the current spirit of Adam Thom and the Doric Club. The new seat of government was the old site of friction between English (with a strong Scottish accent) and French in Canada; the one place in the country where interracial passion and prejudice were not merely things to be stirred up at election time but a daily order of life.

The debate on the Rebellion Losses Bill was long and furious and the halls and galleries buzzed with angry spectators. How could any English-speaking man hold his head up in the streets of Montreal if Lafontaine and his dupe Baldwin were allowed to scoop up tax money (which as everybody knew was collected mainly from the energetic and enterprising English) and fling it to a lot of greedy peasants, like slops to swine? At one stage in the debate the French-Canadian members heard themselves described as "aliens and rebels" by Sir Allan McNab, leader of the Tory party — the Family Compact in one flesh. Sir Allan had led a column against Montgomery's Tavern; he had ventured over to the American shore of the Niagara River in the winter of '37, captured the rebel steamer *Caroline*, and sent her drifting over the falls; if any man in the house was a Loyalist it was he, and his whole manner said so. He was answered with heat and eloquence by Hume Blake, M.P. of Toronto, who declared McNab a rebel himself. The two men passed from words to blows and the sergeant at arms had to separate them.

Through this and much more tumult the ministry held firmly on their course, and with their majority in the House the goal was certain. The bill passed its third reading. To make it law required the governor general's signature. To the excited Tory crowd in and outside of the building that was impossible. How could the Queen's own representative in Canada sign a bill rewarding treason? The mere suggestion was an insult. His first duty was to Her Majesty, and that being the case his next duty was to stay in his residence, "Monklands," outside the city, refusing to appear and put his name to the offensive document.

The born aristocrat at Monklands was only thirty-eight and his previous experience had been as governor of sunny Jamaica, dealing with the problems of freed slaves and planters. He was not a handsome man. He had a rectangular stubborn face framed in dark brushed locks and short side whiskers, with a pair of brooding wide-set eyes, a snowplow nose and a mouth whose lower lip was outthrust even in repose. He had married a daughter of "Radical Jack" Durham and the principle before him was one close to the hearts of his wife and himself. He wanted to see Durham vindicated, to put into effect the core of Durham's plan, which the British government had cut out of it in the Act of Union in 1840.

His private opinion of "paying rebels for rebellion" (as young William Ewart Gladstone put it) did not matter. If responsible government meant anything, it meant what Durham had said of it, that *"the Crown must submit to the necessary consequences of representative institutions; and if it has to carry on the government in unison with a representative body, it must consent to carry it on by means of those in whom that representative body has confidence."*

With this firmly in mind, Elgin got into his carriage and drove down to the city on the afternoon of April 25, 1849. It was a memorable date in Canadian history, for he signed the bill and in that one firm signature made clear that from now on Canada (and British governors general) were to be ruled by Canadians though the heavens fell.

And they fell. The gallery and the Tory members booed him in the House, and when he emerged a noisy throng shouted insults and spattered his carriage with rotten eggs and clods of mud. This was only the beginning. Handbills and an extra edition of the *Gazette* (which termed Elgin "the last governor of Canada") called a crowd of Tory sympathizers to an evening meeting in the Place d'Armes. About fifteen hundred men gathered there, a mixture of well-to-do merchants with their clerks and warehousemen, Orangemen wielding shillelaghs, large and small Tory placemen out of jobs since the last election, and the rabble, the toughs of the water-front and the streets, ready for anything that promised excitement. Various speakers played on the passions of this crowd. Finally the cry arose, "To Parliament!" and the whole mob pattered down to the big limestone building where, under the gaslights, the assembly was still in session.

They stormed inside, and as the members scrambled away for their lives an unidentified voice declared "this French Parliament" dissolved. To prove it, someone stole the mace. The mob then proceeded with the dissolution, smashing the furniture, the windows, the doors, tearing down hangings and portraits (young Sandford Fleming and three others managed to rescue Queen Victoria and carry her outside), and finally jerking the very gas jets from the walls. The last vandalism drove them from the building, for there was a hissing of gas, a series of small explosions, and then flames rushing through the whole interior. The fire brigade turned up with their engines, but the mob refused to let them work. All stood and watched the seat of Canadian Government burn to a blackened stone husk. The men who claimed a monopoly of loyalty had repeated at Montreal exactly what an invading army had done at Toronto in 1813.

Even this was not the end. The capital remained in a state of anarchy for days, with hooligans rushing about the streets attacking the homes of prominent liberals. Among others, Lafontaine's house was badly damaged and his household finally obliged to defend themselves with pistols. The small police force were helpless and the gentlemen of the city government were abetting the mobs. The assembly found temporary quarters, and the little old Château Ramezay became a temporary Government House. At the end of the third day of unchecked rioting the assembly prepared and approved an address to the governor general expressing their indignation at his treatment and the other outrages of the mob. The opposition voted against the address. In this, Allan McNab and Louis Papineau revealed themselves in the same camp, an association that seemed to prove what Hume Blake had said in debate before the riots—that McNab and his party were themselves rebels against the constitution and the country.

When Lord Elgin drove down to the Château Ramezay to receive this address in proper form his carriage was stoned and badly damaged, and troops had to clear the street before the building while a magistrate read the Riot Act. The governor general remained calm and determined. He refused to order the troops to put down the disorders in the city, for that would have been an assertion of imperial force in a civil matter, just what he was bound to avoid. Responsible government was a principle, and it applied to cities as much as provinces. Nor would he countenance the enlistment of special police among the French Canadians, the only law-abiding citizens to be found, pointing out in a letter to London; "all French Lower Canada is with us but the great object is to keep them quiet and to prevent collision between the races." Eventually a more sober Anglo-Montreal recruited a large force of special constables and brought order to the streets. It was a precarious order and there were sporadic riots in the city for another year.

Thus the government of Canada by the people of Canada was born in travail and christened with fire, an odd spectacle to the world at large. Some of the people now provided the world with an odder spectacle—a petition or demand for complete separation from the British empire and for complete annexation to the United States.

The gentlemen of Montreal who had so violently opposed the Rebellion Losses Bill called a gathering or convention at Kingston in July 1849, ostensibly to discuss the ills of the country. There were ills enough. The American financial crash of 1837 had affected Canada as much as the United States. The rebellions of '37 and '38 had been expensive affairs whose cost was still going on, as the obnoxious bill showed. Free trade in Britain had dealt a violent blow to the Canadian grain and timber trades. There was the flood of diseased and impoverished Irish, many of them dying like autumn flies in the hastily built lazarettos at Quebec, Montreal, and elsewhere. Thousands of Canadians had fled to the United States after the rebellions. Now there was another great exodus, this time fleeing hard times in Canada and drawn by the western boom in the United States.

The speeches at Kingston were long and dismal. The reporter of the Kingston *Whig* was reminded of an elderly Scotswoman at a radical meeting—"I couldna hae conceived I had been sae truly miserable hadna I been telled it." More to the point, perhaps, was a red-faced and lively old gentleman who "kicked up a little fun now and then by bawling that the chairman's address was a d——d pack of trash." The audience were certainly divided about the solution to all these ills. However one notable group drew up the famous Annexation Manifesto, with 325 signatures.

Most of those who signed it were from Montreal's mercantile and social *élite*, the very people who had so long proclaimed their devotion to King and flag and vied with each other in deference to the successive British governors general who were willing to play Canadian politics their way. (Now they would not admit Lord and Lady Elgin to their clubs and drawing rooms.) The rest of the signatures came from the old Tory groups in Toronto and Kingston and (not surprisingly) from radical French Canadians of Papineau's stamp. How few of them were serious in their expressed desire to live under the Stars and Stripes was soon apparent, for nearly all remained in their accustomed comfort where they were, under the old flag and the obnoxious new colonial government. The chief importance of the Manifesto was that it sounded the death rattle of the old Clique and Compact groups in Canada, who had so long made a fetish of Crown and flag and now stood condemned in their own words; and their tombstone was the blackened ruin in Montreal.

One of the young Tories who put his name to the Manifesto, John Abbott (who long afterward became a Prime Minister of Canada), dismissed the document in later years as "the outburst of a moment of petulance," which seems as good a description as any. Another young Tory present, a man of destiny, saw that the time had come to evolve a new Conservative party (he never afterward liked to be called a Tory) and with it a new policy. He had shouldered a musket as a loyal volunteer in 1837, and in his practice of law he had befriended the unfortunate Von Schultz at Kingston in '38. Behind the uproar of the mob in Montreal and behind this down-roar of old Tory die-hards at Kingston the voice of common sense was speaking in a tone that he heard plainly. The Baldwin-Lafontaine administration had created a bond, however precarious, between English and French and between Protestant and Catholic. From this time the opposition—any opposition—must do the same. Without that, it could never attain power or hold power when it got there. And if there was ever to be a great Canadian nation it must be laid upon the same broad base.

His name was John Alexander Macdonald. The 1849 Manifesto and what really came out of it he afterward put in this way:

"I was pressed to sign it but refused, and advocated the formation of the British America League as a more sensible procedure . . . A safety valve was found. Our first resolution was that we were resolved to maintain inviolate the connection with the mother country. The second proposition was that the true solution of the difficulty lay in the confederation of all the provinces. The third resolution was that we should attempt to form in such a confederation, or in Canada before confederation, a commercial national policy. The effects of the formation of the British America League were marvellous. Under its influence the annexation sentiment disappeared, the feeling of irritation died away, and the principles which were laid down by the British America League in 1850 are the lines on which the Conservative-Liberal party has moved ever since."

CHAPTER 52

1837 — 1849

The expansion of the United States — Border quarrels —
The Webster-Ashburton Treaty — American infiltration
into Oregon — "Fifty-Four-Forty or Fight"

WHILE the Canadians had been absorbed in the agitations and rebellions that led them finally to self-government, with their gaze always upon themselves and never a glance west of Fort William, the people of the United States were moving rapidly through the continental plains. This mass movement, forerun by resolute and well-armed pioneers, was soon pressing hard against the Mexicans, who had inherited the old Spanish possessions in Texas, New Mexico, Arizona, Nevada, and California. All of these were fated to be overrun before 1850 by the energetic new race pushing south and west from the Mississippi.

The earlier American pressure toward the north had been checked in 1812 but it was still there; the boundary of Maine was still only vaguely defined and open to argument, so was the northward limit of the Champlain pass, and west of Lake Superior ran a huge wild panorama of woods, prairies, and mountains with no boundary at all. The Canadian provinces concerned themselves only with the Maine line and with the north end of Lake Champlain. Since 1821 the former empire of the Nor'westers beyond Lake Superior had flown the British colors on the flagstaffs of the Hudson's Bay Company. In both cases any decision about a boundary would lie with officials in London.

The Treaty of Paris in 1783 had set the northwest limit of the United States at a line drawn from the headwaters of the Mississippi River to the nearest point on Lake Superior. Nobody knew exactly where the Mississippi rose. When the British handed over the Great Lakes forts to American troops in 1796 it was assumed that the Pigeon River, flowing into Lake Superior thirty miles below the present city of Fort William, lay in the latitude of the Mississippi source. It made a handy mark and the Americans promptly put a

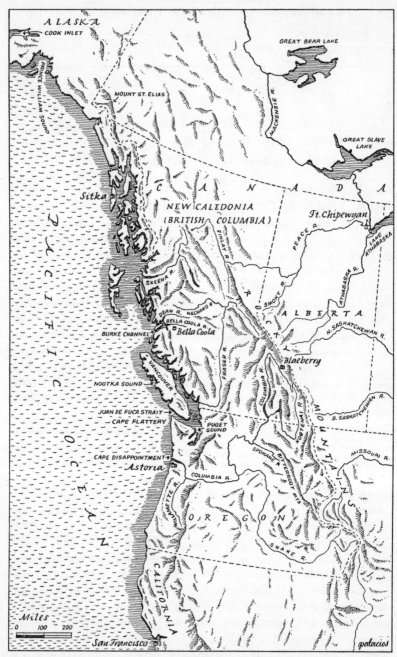

The Pacific coast of Canada including "Oregon"

customs guard on the Pigeon, forcing the Canadians off the Grand Portage in their traffic with the West. The true source of the Mississippi was discovered in 1832 sixty miles south of this latitude. A division on this, the true 1783 line, would have given the British a large slice of northern Minnesota, including most of the valuable Mesabi iron deposits, but by that time the Americans had become rooted on the Pigeon and had extended their hold along the south bank of the Rainy River, which ran westward in the same general line to Lake of the Woods.

Beyond this point lay the huge territories of the Hudson's Bay Company, including the Red River Valley reaching 350 miles straight south from Lake Winnipeg. In 1805 Thomas Jefferson (who already had sent Lewis and Clark across the plains to the Pacific) ordered Zebulon Pike to explore the upper Mississippi and find its source. Pike did not succeed but he visited the trading posts of the North West Company in that region and informed the Canadians that they were operating in United States territory. Nothing was done to molest them at this time. During the War of 1812 an American expedition came up the Mississippi as far as Prairie du Chien but it was driven back by Colonel McKay and his Canadian soldiers and Indians in 1814.

In 1815 under the terms of the peace treaty the last Canadian muskets were withdrawn from Wisconsin and Minnesota, and United States soldiers took possession of the country. They were followed closely by men of John Jacob Astor's aggressive American Fur Company. By the end of 1816 the Canadian traders had been forced out of all their old posts in Minnesota, which were taken over by Astor's men. In 1819 the United States Army established a post (Fort Snelling) on the site of the city of St. Paul. By 1823 steamboats were coming up the Mississippi to St. Paul, and in that year Major Long of the United States Army explored westward along the Minnesota Valley and crossed over the small divide to the Red River. Here he found British interests long established on the ground, for the Hudson's Bay Company maintained the old Nor'west trading posts in the Red River Valley and Lord Selkirk had planted his Highland settlers on its northern reach in 1812. There were no American settlers anywhere in this region. Even St. Paul itself as late as 1840 had no more than four hundred inhabitants, most of whom were French Canadians.

Now a tremendous question arose. By the gradual extension of their claims along the Rainy River to the south end of Lake of the Woods the Americans had pushed the limit of their territory up the map to Latitude 49°, more than one hundred miles farther north than the source of the Mississippi. The British had made no protest, and during the administration of President John Quincy Adams (1825–29) his government began suggestions to London that an international boundary should be drawn along Latitude 49 all the way to the Pacific. This would give the Americans the whole of "Oregon" (including the present state of Washington) in addition to much land along the way. London was not much concerned about the prairies, but "Oregon" was valuable and the British refused to recognize anything more than the joint-occupation compromise of 1818.

There matters stood until 1838, when the rebellions in Canada and other matters threatened to throw Britain and the United States into another war. At this time the American people were being galled by the published accounts of a number of supercilious British travelers portraying them as a nation of windy boors. The American financial panic of 1837 had brought a wide default of debts owned to British investors by state governments and a large number of companies, and the comments of British newspapers were caustic. Adding to these American irritations were three matters connected with Canada. One was more or less academic. At the north end of Lake Champlain the Canadian rebels and their American sympathizers had conveyed cannon and muskets across the border. But where exactly was the border? Certain marks had been set up, but the line had never been properly surveyed.

Very definite was the violation of American territory on the Niagara frontier in December 1837. After his flight across the river William Lyon Mackenzie had busied himself with other refugee rebels organizing a raid on the British army post at Chippewa. Using an American steamer, the *Caroline*, they seized Navy Island above Niagara Falls, and began to accumulate weapons and stores from their friends on the American side. Therefore on the night of December 29, 1837, a party of Canadian militia, led by Allan McNab, crossed in boats to the American side of the river, captured the *Caroline* after a brief fight, set her afire, and let her drift over the falls. Here was a direct attack on American property, in American territory, in which an American citizen had been killed. The frontier people of New York State were furious.

Even more serious, but quite unrelated to the Canadian revolt, was a border brawl between the state of Maine and the neighboring province of New Brunswick in the winter of 1838-39. Here the vague frontier mentioned in the Treaty of Paris in 1783 had never been settled on the ground. No one had worried much about it, although the Canadians realized that the general trend of Maine was a menace to their winter line of communication to the Maritime Provinces and the open sea. The British had tried to cure this by their march to the Penobscot during the War of 1812, but the Peace of Ghent dropped the problem back into their laps.

The area of danger happened to be good timber country, and in the year 1835 a fever of timber speculation spread on both sides of the undefined border. The major lumber operators, Canadian and American, were tough prehensile men, each commanding large crews of willing lumberjacks who drank much rum and enjoyed a fight as a relief from the dull round of slashing down the pine. The center of dispute was the tall forest along the banks of the Aroostook River. The British claimed it, so did the lumbermen of Maine. The matter had been referred to the King of the Netherlands for arbitration, but his compromise award, accepted by the British, was rejected by the U. S. Senate in 1832.

Meanwhile the lumbermen in the disputed area were busy swinging axes at the pine and fists at each other. It was a time when various Maine lumbermen were acquiring huge grants of timberland from the state government for little or nothing; and the state government was ready to grant them anything they wanted, whether the state itself had good title or not. Typical of the Maine lumbermen was "General" Sam Veazie, who had a railroad (built 1836) leading part way up the Penobscot River from Bangor. He owned or had bought control in fifty-two Maine sawmills, secured huge blocks of timberland for a few cents an acre, and persuaded a friendly legislature to set aside the whole of his own town of Veazie as a personal possession. Favored by a Family Compact government in Fredericton, the timber barons of New Brunswick were hardly less acquisitive, although their scale of operations was much smaller.

During the winter of 1838-39, while Upper and Lower Canada were still in an uproar from the Hunters' invasion, the "Aroostook War" suddenly became much more serious than a brawl of hilarious lumberjacks. Militia were called out in Maine and New Brunswick; British regular troops hurried from Halifax to the mouth of the

St. Croix; Nova Scotia made large defense appropriations; the U. S. Congress voted $10,000,000 for an emergency and authorized a force of 50,000 men.

The British War Office, looking beyond the petty squabbles of the lumbermen, saw that the full claims of the Maine legislature would cut away the precious Temiscouata road and corridor by which their troops made winter marches from the sea coast to the frozen St. Lawrence. Without it the whole of Canada along the St. Lawrence and the Great Lakes was isolated for five frosty months of the year. In a matter so vital there could be no hesitation and they prepared to fight.

At this point President Van Buren sent energetic General Winfield Scott to pour cold water on the fire. Scott traveled through the snows and persuaded the angry governors of Maine and New Brunswick to arrange a truce. The next step was another attempt to settle the border line. Both countries saw the folly of drifting into war over what was essentially a squabble of greedy woodcutters and eventually London and Washington agreed to refer the matter to a boundary commission.

In a spirit of armed truce the matter had dragged on until the spring of 1842, when London sent a special minister, Lord Ashburton, to confer at Washington with Secretary of State Daniel Webster. Ashburton was one of the great British banking family, the Barings, and his wife was the daughter of an American senator. Representatives from the states of Maine and Massachusetts (and eventually President Tyler himself) took part in the negotiations, which resulted in the so-called Webster-Ashburton Treaty of 1842.

Under this settlement the United States received about seven thousand of the twelve thousand square miles in the disputed region between Maine and New Brunswick, leaving the Canadians still in possession of the Temiscouata corridor but taking away almost the whole of the valuable Aroostook Valley. Also the border between Canada and the states of Vermont and New York was now set about half a mile north of Latitude 45°, in order to confirm to the United States a strip at the north end of Lake Champlain, on which their military engineers already had built fortifications. Most significant of all, the treaty confirmed the Pigeon and Rainy rivers as the U.S. boundary west of Lake Superior. As the Rainy flowed firmly on Latitude 49 . From this time they would insist with ever at a rising slant to Lake of the Woods, this placed the Americans greater vigor that Latitude 49° should form the international boundary all the way across the plains and mountains to the Pacific.

The treaty was unpopular in both Maine and New Brunswick, where the lumber interests remained dissatisfied. However from this time the loggers relieved their surplus energies in a purely private war in the frontier woods, a business of fists and ax handles which they enjoyed hugely and with no damage to anyone but themselves. In Britain the opponents of the government termed the treaty "Ashburton's Surrender."

All eyes now turned toward the Far West. Wagon trains of American settlers, following in the wake of their missionaries, were rolling in an almost continual procession over the now famous Oregon Trail. Old John McLoughlin of the Hudson's Bay Company, hitherto monarch of all he surveyed in those regions, began to see a hand writing on the Oregon wall—an American hand. Already the original Canadian settlers were far outnumbered. In another year they would be swamped. In June 1842 he sent James Douglas northward to seek an alternative base for the company's trade on Vancouver Island, which was not accessible to wagon wheels. Douglas selected a good harbor at the Indian village called Camosun, and in March 1843 he and fifteen Canadians, accompanied by the Jesuit missionary Father Bolduc, sailed there from the old headquarters (Fort Vancouver) on the Columbia River. When the Hudson's Bay Company's ship *Beaver* had landed them Father Bolduc celebrated mass, the first Christian service on Vancouver Island. By autumn fifty men were housed at Camosun and protected by a stout stockade. Eventually this post became headquarters of the Hudson's Bay Company on the Pacific coast, and its given name was that of the young queen, Victoria.

Meanwhile affairs were moving rapidly in "Oregon." In 1843 the American settlers formed a provisional government and appealed to their compatriots in the East for support. It came quickly. In 1844 the national convention of the Democratic party declared that the title of the United States "to the whole of the Territory of Oregon" was "clear and unquestionable." It was part of the fever of expansion now running in American veins. An infiltration of American settlers already had set up a republic in the old Mexican state of Texas as the first step to annexation by the United States. Other Americans were preparing to do the same in California. The old Spanish territories north of the Rio Grande and the Gulf of

California were doomed. So was the British possession of the Columbia basin. In his first annual address to the Congress in December 1845 President Polk denounced the old compromise of 1818 and claimed "Oregon" for the United States. For any future Canadian nation this was serious. What exactly was "Oregon"? The watershed of the Columbia River extended to California and Nevada on the south and in the other direction reached far north into the Canadian Rockies. The enthusiasts of national expansion in the United States were no longer content to halt their claims at the line of Latitude 49°. They had in mind the 1824 agreement with the Russians in which the United States had promised to make no claims north of Latitude 54° 40'. They now demanded American possession up to the fringe of the Russian settlements in Alaska.

This meant a Canada completely shut off from the Pacific. The British were alarmed, not merely at this, but at the whole American attitude. Where did the Americans intend to stop? John Sullivan, writing in the *United States Magazine and Democratic Review* in the summer of 1845, had expressed it boldly, referring to "the fulfillment of our manifest destiny to overspread the continent alloted by Providence for the free development of our yearly multiplying millions." He mentioned it in connection with Texas, but in December the New York *Morning News* used the phrase in its views on the Oregon dispute. A week later Robert Winthrop of Massachusetts, speaking in Congress on the Oregon affair expressed "the right of our manifest destiny to spread over this whole continent."

There were obvious and ominous preparations along the eastern frontiers of Canada. In 1844 the U.S.S. *Michigan*, an ironclad of six hundred tons, appeared on the Great Lakes. By that time United States army engineers had renovated and re-armed the forts at Niagara and Oswego, they were building new ones at Detroit and Buffalo, and they had commenced work on the formidable Fort Montgomery at the head of Lake Champlain. Were these works purely defensive or were they intended to guard preparations for a new war of conquest?

An economy-minded British Government was not anxious for a fort-building contest on the borders of Canada. Nor could the British regard the prospect of war with anything but horror. In an attempt to divert American ambitions, British diplomats began flirtations with Mexico and with the newly established republic of Texas. These maneuvers excited the more warlike American expansionists, who now claimed as an excuse that they were forestalling foreign attempts to evade the Monroe Doctrine. President Polk's strong stand on the Oregon matter had brought cheers and cries of "Fifty-four-forty or fight!" and the loudest cheers came from the old War Hawk states of the South and Middle West.

This was the dangerous state of affairs in December 1845 when the British Government suddenly abandoned all its rights in Oregon proper and offered to accept Latitude 49° as the boundary line. President Polk remained stiff, but in the early months of 1846 the demands and activities of the eager American venturers on the south and southwest turned the whole course of Manifest Destiny that way. The United States opened war on Mexico, the beginning of a campaign of conquest that was to last two years. A war on two fronts was out of the question even to the most ardent American expansionists, and in June the United States Senate accepted the British proposal. The Oregon Settlement was ratified in Washington on June 15, 1846. In this way, at the ultimate cost of the Mexicans, the Canadians retained what is now British Columbia.

The British hold on the Pacific coast was not yet safe however. The United States won their war in the south and in February 1848 the Mexicans signed away more than one million square miles of territory. Once more the American expansionists could turn their attention to the Northwest, for a die-hard group in the capital and in the Middle West still hankered for the whole Pacific territory to Alaska. The discovery of gold in the newly captured territory of California had started a new rush of Americans to the Pacific coast, prospectors wandered everywhere through the mountains panning the streams, and there were rumors of gold in British Columbia.

The Hudson's Bay Company were defenseless. There was not a single British soldier west of the Great Lakes except a small detachment in Manitoba, sent there to quiet another disturbance among the *métis*. The Canadian population in Oregon (including old John McLoughlin, the "father of Oregon") remained there and had become American citizens to all intents and purposes. There were no Canadian settlers in British Columbia except a handful of Bay men in the scattered trading posts. In American eyes it was not a British colony but simply the trading area of a private British company. Into such a vacuum a host of American settlers and gold seekers would soon be rushing as they had into California and Oregon, and with the same result.

In desperation the directors of the Hudson's Bay Company asked the British Government to proclaim at least Vancouver Island a British colony and to send out a governor at once. Meanwhile the Bay Company would arrange to send British settlers. Accordingly the government proclaimed the island a British colony in January 1849 and sent out a London lawyer, Richard Blanshard, as its first governor. It was a brave little whistle in the dark. Another ten years were to pass before any number of British settlers entered the country. But it served the purpose. The huge enlargement of the United States, the most remarkable event of the nineteenth century, had now run its course. The march beyond the Mississippi was inevitable, just as the American Revolution was inevitable in the first place, but not even the daring mind of Thomas Jefferson could have guessed how quickly it was to be accomplished. In only thirteen years, springing from the black depths of the financial crash in 1837, the Americans had carried their flag to the Pacific and into the heart of Mexico.

Much of this territory had been gained by an infiltration of traders and hunters, then a demand for American rights, then seizure by the threat of war or by war itself. These were precisely the methods by which the British had acquired much of their empire, and although they now feared American ambitions they had to admire the bold resolution of the American march across the west. Carlyle wrote to Emerson in 1849, "How beautiful to think of lean tough Yankee settlers, tough as gutta-percha, with most occult unsubduable fire in their belly, steering over the western mountains to annihilate the jungle and bring back corn and bacon out of it for the posterity of Adam! . . . Oh, if we were not a set of cant-ridden blockheads there is no myth of Athene or Hercules equal to this fact."

Lord Ashburton, who was one of Carlyle's few intimates, apparently felt the same.

CHAPTER 53

1850

The first railways — Joseph Howe — The Cunard Line —
The electric telegraph — A vision from sea to sea

AND so the calendar came to 1850. Tremendous things had happened in North America during the decade past. Another loomed suddenly, the growing internal quarrel over slavery in the United States which was to end in the tragedy of the Civil War. Meanwhile the finger of destiny had drawn a line across the continent, separating all that seemed warm and fertile and desirable from all that seemed rocky and barren and cold. North of that line the Canadians had won self-rule but they were still dependent on a British fleet and army to defend them. Among themselves there now existed a slender political bond between English and French; but they remained provinces with no sense of unity, without a heart in their own body (By Town was still a small village of no importance on the Ottawa) and without a view beyond the head of Lake Superior, as if the huge sprawl of the West and North had drifted away beyond the ken of mortal man. For the Nor'westers had vanished now—the lean tough Nor'westers with unsubduable fire who had ranged across the plains and mountains and tasted the salt of the Pacific when the Americans were still seeing nothing west of Ohio. Yet the Nor'westers' lesson survived—that nothing could be easy for the people who lived north of that line across the continent. So did the Nor'westers' motto engraved on those plates and glasses at Beaver Hall—Fortitude in Adversity.

Upper Canada (which received nearly all of the Canadian immigration from Europe) now had about a million people, surpassing the population of Lower Canada at last; but in the whole country from the Great Lakes to the Atlantic there were still less than two and one half millions. They had no magnificent Father of Waters

on which steamers could ride to the edge of the plains and there put
ashore pioneers and their covered wagons for the long roll to the
mountains. The rough barrier of the Shield stood between Fort
William and the sea of grass, just as it stood between Manitoba and
the shore of Hudson Bay. For years yet, the only practicable way to
the Canadian prairies must lie through American territory, up the
Mississippi and thence by Red River cart along the old buffalo trails;
and most people who went that way would find good land somewhere along the route and settle down as citizens of the United
States.

What was the solution? People in Britain had succumbed to the
railroad craze, as they had to the canal craze sixty years before.
People in the United States, in the seaboard states at least, were doing
the same thing — a host of small railway companies floating stocks,
selling bonds, building bits and pieces of lines between the main
inland cities and the ports; and then, as companies failed, floating
new companies and linking some of the bits and pieces together. A
really long line was undreamed until the late '40s. Durham's idea of
an "intercolonial" railroad all the way from the Great Lakes to
Nova Scotia had been regarded as the most fantastic item in his
famous report.

At the time he wrote, the only steam railway in Canada was the
Champlain & St. Lawrence, a portage line of sixteen miles linking the
St. Lawrence opposite Montreal with the navigable part of the
Richelieu River above St. Jean. Its lone wood-fired engine ran on
wooden rails, which jokers called "snake rails" because they warped
with heat and damp in spite of the strips of iron nailed along the
wearing surface. In the following year (1839) a colliery in Nova
Scotia built a line from the Albion mine a few miles to the ocean
shipping point. Its engine naturally burned coal — for years the only
coal-burning railway engine in the whole country. There was a tram-
way on the Niagara bank between Queenston and Chippewa, opened
in 1839 to pass goods around Niagara Falls (again supplementing a
canal), but its cars were drawn by horses because no steam engine of
the time could get up Queenston Heights.

The 1837–38 rebellions and the financial troubles that followed
made capital ventures in Canada more precarious than ever. In 1847
another modest steam railway appeared, an eight-mile track from
Montreal to Lachine, a rival to the little canal in passing goods
around the Lachine Rapids.

By 1844 the railway fever in Britain and the United States had
produced a corps of expert promoters and builders in search of
opportunity everywhere, and men were looking over greater distances, although in America they still looked in one direction —
from inland cities toward the Atlantic coast. Shrewd heads in Montreal now saw that a railway running south or southeast through the
New England states could carry their goods to or from an ice-free
port, at a distance of less than three hundred miles. Just as the Erie
Canal had sucked away much of their old carrying trade with the
Great Lakes, so the new American railways from New York to
Buffalo and from Baltimore to Ohio were threatening to take what
was left. In considering their problem they met with a shrewd and
able Yankee, John A. Poor, who steered their minds to the ice-free
harbor of Portland, Maine. The difficulty, as always in Canadian
affairs, was finance. The city of Montreal put up £125,000, the
Montreal Seminary £25,000, the British-American Land Company
another £25,000. The American contractors took most of their pay
in stock. Money was promised in Britain and elsewhere, but the
promises failed. In 1849 just forty miles of line had been built.

In Upper Canada there was a scheme for a railway to connect
Toronto with Collingwood on Lake Huron (the ultimate conception
of the old Indian portage and Simcoe's Yonge Street, by-passing the
long water route by way of Niagara and Detroit) with a prize to be
gained in the carrying trade of Chicago and the other growing cities
on the upper lakes. A rival group planned to tap the trade of Chicago
by building a line along the natural Canadian land bridge between
Detroit and Buffalo. In the Maritime Provinces men had their own
scheme for a railway connecting Canada with an ice-free seacoast.
This was to use the New Brunswick port of St. Andrew's, and in
the autumn of 1847 hopeful spades were breaking the first ground
for it.

Meanwhile Durham's old notion was revived in 1846, when the
three Canadian mainland provinces agreed to pay for a railway
survey from the St. Lawrence to Halifax. Here the British War
Office, watchful in the atmosphere of Fifty-four-forty-or-fight,
decided to take a hand. In military eyes the private Canadian schemes
for lines to Portland and St. Andrew's had a fatal fault; one lay
across American territory and the other ran so close to it that American troops could cut it in a day's march. For the effective defense of
Canada in a future war with the United States there must be a rail-

way from Halifax to Quebec at least, and it must describe a wide
loop through New Brunswick and across the Gaspé Peninsula to be
safe from American attack. Therefore the new survey was a military
one under Major Robinson of the Royal Engineers, who completed
it in 1848. By that time the Oregon matter had been settled and
the war scare had subsided. The intercolonial railway was a dream
that would be long in coming true; but when it came it would follow
"Major Robinson's line" from Quebec to Mont Joli on the St.
Lawrence, thence by the Matapedia valley to Chaleur Bay, and so on
down the coast and through the isthmus to Halifax.

The "intercolonial" railway had a champion at Halifax, the most
remarkable man in the Canadian provinces as the century drew
toward the halfway mark, Joseph Howe. His father was a pious
member of the strict Sandemanian sect and in politics a Tory of
Tories, a poor Loyalist printer who had fled from Boston while the
Revolution was still in progress. "Joe" Howe was born in 1804 in a
small cottage far outside the town of Halifax. He had no formal
education and in the early teens he became a "printer's devil" in a
shop on Bedford Row in the town. On an occasion well remembered
afterward the young apprentice was summoned as a witness in some
petty case being tried in the courtroom of Province House. The
judge regarded his ink-smudged face and fingers and smiled.

"So you're a devil," he said.

"Yes," said Joseph. "Not in the courthouse though."

It raised a laugh. The judge, a member of the Halifax Compact
like every other official of importance in the town, would have been
less amused if he could have seen the future. "Joe" Howe was to
prove himself a devil to the Compact and he was to make his first
demonstration in that very room.

In the printer's shop he worked from early morning into the
nights. Often on a sticky summer night he closed his labors by trot-
ting down a short lane to the harbor, tossing off his clothes behind
a wharf shed, and diving into the water for a swim by the light of the
stars. In just such a fashion later on he plunged into the murky tide
of provincial politics. At the age of twenty-four he went deeply
into debt also, raising enough money to buy the printing shop and its
moribund newspaper, the *Nova Scotian*. He wanted a weapon and
he had chosen his target. As in all the Canadian provinces the
assembly of Nova Scotia was a powerless body, overshadowed by

the legislative council, which was appointed by the Crown; and the province was ruled by a British governor and his Cabinet, termed the executive council. Howe saw that the successive governors, nearly all soldiers who knew little of government, were themselves governed partly by the Colonial Office in London and largely by the executive council. In Nova Scotia's case the council consisted of twelve wealthy Halifax merchants. Five of these were partners in a private banking enterprise, the Halifax Banking Company, the only bank in the province. The rest were closely related to the bankers by marriage or business interests. Among their other powers these men of the council appointed the bench of magistrates who ruled the town of Halifax itself. Thus twelve men had in their grip the province and its capital. All business, finance and law depended on their whim or their interest.

All of this made a wonderful target for the inky-fingered young man in Bedford Row. He let fly his first stone in 1835, a deliberately provocative attack on the Halifax magistrates in the pages of the *Nova Scotian*. Prodded from above, the magistrates sued Howe for libel, and the result was the famous trial in Province House, where the printer proved the magistrates guilty of gross corruption and neglect. The jury acquitted him of libel and the people cheered. His next and obvious step was to demand the incorporation of Halifax with a proper civic government — a measure long resisted by The Twelve. He won that also. The next step was the big one, the battle for responsible government of the province. Howe stood for election and took his seat in the assembly in 1837, the year of the rebellions in Upper and Lower Canada.

The Twelve and the people of Nova Scotia now began to discover what sort of creature Reform had thrown up in their midst. It was a complex one and no one ever fully understood it. Howe was not a handsome man, indeed he was plain to the point of ugliness, with a bulbous nose, a square stubborn face, shaggy brows, a shock of receding hair and the stocky muscular figure of a plowman. Self-educated, he had stocked that electric skull with history and the classics. He could make a speech in the lofty language of a Palmerston or he could set the whole assembly laughing, friends and enemies alike, with an apt anecdote in the salty idiom of the coast. He could dash off a well-scanned poem in praise of the Nova Scotian landscape or a lampoon that would curl a lieutenant governor's hair. When occasion called for platitudes he could reel them off in magnificent language for two hours at a stretch; yet he had a sharp mind for facts and he could meet the shrewd financiers of the executive council and mow them down with the grapeshot of their own statistics.

He was no respecter of persons or of groups, even among his own following. At various times he deliberately insulted not only lieutenant governors and the merchant aristocrats who ruled the governors but the powerful Baptist and Irish-Catholic bodies who had been his stoutest supporters, as well as the still more powerful Anglican group who had not. In an age when the Temperance Society was gathering multitudes into its fold and spoke almost with the voice of God, Joe Howe wrote verses in praise of wine, openly quaffed rum, and a temperance debate on the floor of the House declared, with a finger toward the sea, "Gentlemen, how beautiful is water — yet how dangerous!"

He could charm a great audience with an address on "The Moral Influence of Women" and yet make love to any pretty woman he met along the country roads. He was a good-natured and generous husband, the father of a large adoring family, and yet he sired at least one illegitimate child and jested broadly of such matters — thumbing his nose at the whole Victorian Age. He scorned the rebellions in the upper provinces, seeing them as a foolish blood-letting and what was worse, an admission of failure on the proper battlefield, the platform and the assembly floor. Yet personally he loved a fight, on the platform or anywhere else, and once he fought a duel with pistols in the woods of Point Pleasant, letting his opponent Haliburton take a deliberate aim and fire first. The shot missed, and Howe characteristically fired his own pistol into the air and walked off — a cliché, of course, but one that left Haliburton a political corpse in the shadow of the old Martello tower.

With all his complex nature Howe loved his province and his people. He spent weeks in the saddle on the rough country roads, chatting at farms and logging camps, at shipyards and fish wharves and smugglers' inns. He knew the Bluenoses, their faults, their virtues, and their capabilities, as no one has known them before or since. Many hated him, most loved him, and all could relish the keen point in whatever he had to say when the subject mattered to him. When he started the fight for responsible government the lieutenant governor snubbed him and The Twelve harped on "God Save the Queen" and the dangers of mob rule. Howe reminded them contemptuously of "the difference between curbing the insolence of the beadle and setting fire to the parish." When they warned him that Britain might cast off so fractious a colony, he replied in the tone of a Bluenose mate that "Nova Scotia would float if the Devil himself cut the tow-line." Yet he had a profound respect for the British connection. There was no provincial limit to his mind, and he was the first Canadian politician to point out clearly the conception of a commonwealth, each part of it self-governed.

And he could get things done. If Howe had not been a successful politician he could have been a successful business promoter. Until his time every government of Nova Scotia had stressed the importance of the soil, trying to create a population of farmers. Howe was the first man to point out that most of the province was rocky and that its natural crop was the forest. The future of Nova Scotia lay on the sea, not only in the fishery but in shipbuilding and world trade. The land was covered with good timber, easily floated down to the coast on the short rapid streams; the same streams turned the sawmills, and the immigration from Europe and a high native birth rate were filling the province with poor farmers who might as well be building and sailing ships. A few coastal communities had set the example from early times, but their success had been ignored in the constant cry of *Speed the Plow*. Howe hammered away at his theme and saw it come to life, especially after 1840, when the swift growth of world trade and the demand for ships and seamen made an opportunity for which Nova Scotia might have been created.

Even while this was going on he saw something else, the advantage of the steamship over the windjammer. Crossing the Atlantic in 1838, in the old packet brig of the time, he saw the new steamer *Sirius* come over the sky line and pass his own ship "with the speed of a hunter while we were moving with the rapidity of an ox-cart." As soon as he reached London he made for the Colonial Office to urge the need for rapid and reliable communication between Liverpool and Halifax. Within a few weeks the British Government called for tenders for a line of mail steamships on the North Atlantic run, but no single British shipping firm would undertake it. Eventually it was another Nova Scotian, Samuel Cunard, already rich on lumber and sailing ships, who stepped into the transatlantic scene, persuaded some British shipping men to join him, and formed the famous Cunard Line. In 1840 their first ship, the *Unicorn*, steamed into Halifax harbor fourteen days from Liverpool.

So it was, too, with the telegraph. Elderly Nova Scotians could remember the first telegraph system in North America, the Duke of Kent's chain of visual-signal stations from Halifax to Fredericton. Nothing else had appeared until the American inventor Morse perfected his electric telegraph and built a line from Washington to Baltimore in 1844. Within a few years his metallic web had spread through the eastern states and into New Brunswick; and Howe, in the face of violent criticism, used Nova Scotia government funds to extend the line to Halifax in the autumn of 1849. Within a year the line was paying 5 per cent on the investment, for Halifax as the first port of call for the Cunard steamers was the first recipient of news from Europe, vital to the stock exchange and the great newspapers of the United States, and Nova Scotia was on the map as it had never been before.

Howe's vision went inland also. In 1841 he made a careful tour of the upper Canadian provinces — "lingering at the falls of Niagara for a couple of days till the mighty cataract had roared down the discordant voices of the Canadian politicians" — and he came back deeply impressed. "You feel at every step that Canada must become a great nation." His own battle for responsible government was still to be won, he could sympathize with the Reformers wherever he found them, and of Canada he remarked shrewdly, "Whether she will take her stand by the side of Britain, respected, free, confiding, or whether she shall be held by the strong hand of power until she breaks away ... is the problem which will probably be worked out within the next five years."

The problem was worked out in seven, and it was Howe's success in Nova Scotia that paved the way for it. The prospect of Canada as a great nation never diminished in his mind, although in later years he changed his mind twice on the prospect of Nova Scotia as part of it. He had some sage advice for the British-American League when they met at Kingston in '49 to discuss a confederation of all the provinces and (on the part of many) to sign the Annexation Manifesto.

"A confederation of the colonies may be the desire of your convention ... We are not indisposed to union or a confederation, but we must know with whom we are dealing and have securities for the blessings we enjoy. We desire free trade among all the provinces under our national flag, with one coin, one measure, one tariff, one post office. We feel that the courts, the press, the educational institutions of [British] North America would be elevated by union;

and that, if such a combination of interests were achieved wisely and with proper guards, the foundations of a great nation, in friendly connection with the mother country, would be laid on an indestructible basis."

He had something else to say. After all, Nova Scotia was a miniature Canada with a French minority, the original settlers of the province, once savagely persecuted. In the long time since the English-speaking Nova Scotian Protestant had learned to live in complete amity with his French-Catholic neighbor, respecting his religion and language and quick to defend his rights; and in return the *acadien* had learned to trust the other and to work with him unselfishly for the good of all. This happy state of affairs impressed Howe when he looked up the St. Lawrence, and in his letter to Kingston he added:

"We hear a great deal about anglifying the French-Canadians; and a union of the provinces is sometimes advocated with a view to swamping and controlling that portion of the population . . . On this point we had better understand each other. We have no desire to form part of a nation with a helot and inferior race within its bosom. The Anglo-Saxons of Canada may, if they are strong enough and have the disposition, try this unpromising experiment for themselves. The Nova Scotians will never aid them nor consent."

Here was wisdom. It must have added to the anger of the rabid wing of the league who had burned down the House of Parliament in Montreal. To the cooler heads it offered considerable thought, not least to John Alexander Macdonald.

But whatever the prospect of a political union between the Canadian provinces, it seemed to Howe that first there must be a tangible bond in the form of a railway for the interpassage of goods and mails, summer and winter. He had advocated a railway between Nova Scotia and New Brunswick as early as 1835, and he was one of the few who saw Durham's "intercolonial" line as an actual possibility and never let anyone forget it. More, he was the first to do anything about it, driven by the restless energy that rose behind all his visions. He sailed for England in 1850 to request an imperial guarantee to back the necessary loans for railway construction, so that the provinces could borrow the money at a low rate of interest. On that basis Howe proposed "to bind the Colonial Governments and Legislatures to make a great highway from Western Canada to the ocean through British territory."

In Britain his plan had a mixed reception. The single-minded professional soldiers at the War Office saw an urgent need of the railway for Canadian defense. The Colonial Office was stiffly aware that the provinces had long agitated and lately won the principle of self-government, but that they were assuming no responsibility for their own defense. The "Little Englanders" were now in power in Britain with their notion that an empire was not worth the trouble of its upkeep, and Grey had expressed their sentiments to Lord Elgin in 1848: "To us except the loss of prestige (no small one I admit) the loss of Canada would be the loss of little but a source of heavy expense and great anxiety."

Therefore the imperial government blew hot and then cold on the Canadian railway scheme. The Nova Scotian came back undaunted. He set himself the task of persuading the provincial governments to borrow the money on their own risk and build the line themselves. In Halifax he declared confidently; "Within five years we shall make the journey hence to Quebec and Montreal." In this he was disappointed. The path of the intercolonial railway was a long and stony one in all ways and the tale was to run for almost a generation. But he was not content with a single prophecy. To most Canadians "Western Canada" meant the peninsula of Ontario, and their railway promoters looked only toward the Atlantic. The enthusiast in Nova Scotia faced the other way and saw far past the Great Lakes. At a public meeting in Halifax on his return from England, Howe urged the Nova Scotians to build their own link in the railway to the upper provinces, and added one of his clairvoyant flashes: "I believe that many in this room will live to hear the whistle of the steam engine in the passes of the Rocky Mountains and to make the journey from Halifax to the Pacific in five or six days."

In 1850 this was fantastic and Howe did not live to see it true; but many in that room did.

CHAPTER 54

1763 — 1850

The march of communications — "Wooden ships and iron men" — Canadian literature of the period

EIGHTY-SEVEN years, the span of a hale man's lifetime, had passed since France resigned her "acres of snow" to the British conquerors. In the beginning there were few roads in the wilderness. By means of the *corvée* the old French regime had made and maintained a highway from Quebec to Montreal, with staging houses and stables at regular intervals along the way. Even this was so bad that in winter travelers drove their carioles along the smoother ice of the St. Lawrence. Elsewhere the roads were mere tracks, often on the site of Indian paths or cut through the woods to a width measured easily and conveniently by the span of a man's outstretched arms. The snows of winter made them passable for small sleds of the "jumper" sort, and in the neighborhood of the settlements a liberal use of small tree trunks or branches thrown down in the water holes made them passable for wagons.

The period had been a time of wars, one after another, and the passage of armies during the Conquest, the American Revolution, and the War of 1812 had opened many new roads or improved and lengthened old ones. Even the interludes of peace had been shadowed by threat of war — Simcoe's ambitious "streets" through the woods of Upper Canada had been surveyed and cut in such a time.

Water was always the best means of getting anywhere and roads were a last consideration until the waterfront had been taken up and men had to hew their way inland. Even then the least effort necessary to make a wagon track was enough. The same careless measure applied to main highways. Basil Hall, traveling the coach road between Kingston and York in the summer of 1827 observed that "the horrible corduroy roads again made their appearance in a more formidable shape by the addition of deep inky holes, which almost swallowed up the forewheels of the wagon and bathed its hinder axle-tree."

A traveler moving west from Hamilton in 1837, the year of Queen Victoria's coronation and of the Canadian rebellion, found that "the roads were throughout so execrably bad that no words can give you any idea of them. We often sank in mudholes above the axle-tree; then over trunks of trees laid across swamps, called corduroy roads, where my poor bones dislocated. A wheel here and there, or a broken shaft lying by the roadside, told of former wrecks and disasters. When I arrived at Blandford my hands were swelled and blistered by continually grasping with all my strength an iron bar in the front of my vehicle to prevent myself from being flung out."

In Lower Canada things had been no better in 1833 when Adam Fergusson found on a coach journey along the St. Lawrence: "The planks of the bridges were frequently so loose and so crazy that I am yet at a loss to conjecture how our bulky machine and the four high-mettled steeds escaped without falling through. A sufficient supply of stone for repairs lay along the roadside . . . as gathered from the land, while timber for the bridges was certainly not far to seek. The period of annual repair had not, however, yet come round, and even then no metal would be applied; the road would merely receive a sort of levelling, often, as I was assured, with the plough."

After 1825 the practice of charging tolls for the upkeep of main highways, common in Britain, was adopted in Upper Canada. These so-called turnpike roads became numerous in the peninsula of Ontario during the next twenty-five years. On some the maintenance was merely a plowing and scraping of dirt from the sides to the crown of the road, with corduroy bridges flung across the streams and swamp holes. After 1840 many were graveled. By 1850, when sawmills whined everywhere and three-inch plank was cheap, a good many wooden turnpikes stretched between the towns. All of these toll roads were maintained by private individuals or companies, with a tollgate every four or five miles in the settled districts to make sure that no one used the way without paying the fee. The system continued on some roads well into the twentieth century.

Water transport had improved much more rapidly. At the Conquest a few schooners and sloops plied on the St. Lawrence between Quebec and Montreal. For the rest of the country the *bateau* and bark canoe had to suffice. During the American Revolution the sailing vessels of the Provincial Marine appeared on Lake Ontario. By 1810 there were small fleets of privately owned schooners on Lake Ontario and Lake Erie, and from Detroit the fur traders were operating schooners to the foot of Lake Michigan and the head of Lake Huron. In 1809 Molson launched the first steamer on the lower St. Lawrence and in 1816–17 the steamers *Frontenac* and *Charlotte* made their appearance on Lake Ontario. By 1822 J. J. Rigby observed on Lake Huron "a very large and splendid steamer — the first vessel of the kind ever seen there. Red men and white flocked to see her from great distances... The steamship arrived at the appointed day crowded with fashionables from the Atlantic shores of the United States, eager to penetrate so safely and agreeably into the far Indian solitudes." In 1836 the first grain cargo from Chicago came down the lakes to Buffalo in a steamer loaded with three thousand bushels of wheat. By that time the blue wood smoke of steamers could be seen everywhere on the lakes, on the Ottawa, and on the St. Lawrence rapids as far down as the Long Sault. Most of them now had high-pressure engines, to the distress of impressionable Mrs. Jameson, who found that they made "a horrible and perpetual snorting like the engine on a railroad."

By 1846 Sir Richard Bonnycastle found steam travel in Canadian waters a luxurious affair. "You can have every convenience on board a Lake Ontario mail-packet, which is about as large as a small frigate and has the usual sea equipment of masts, sails and iron rigging. The fare is five dollars in the cabin and two dollars in the steerage. In the former you have tea and breakfast, in the latter nothing but what is bought at the bar. By paying a dollar extra you may have a stateroom... where you find a good bed, a large looking-glass, washing stand and towels, and a night-lamp if required. The captains are generally part owners and are kind, obliging and communicative, sitting at the head of their table where places for females and families are always reserved. The stewards and waiters are coloured people, clean, neat and active. The ladies' cabin has generally a large cheval glass and a piano, with a white lady to wait, who is always decked out in flounces and furbelows and usually good-looking."

With improved roads, with stagecoaches rattling along every main highway, with steamers snorting up and down the lakes and rivers, with the electric telegraph clicking busily, the life and business of the provinces had struck a lively pace by 1850 when the all-conquering railways loomed upon the scene. The grain and timber trades were recovering from the shock of Britain's free-trade policy and realizing that they must compete in the market with the rest of the world. The Niagara and St. Lawrence canals left much to be desired, but a busy traffic moved through them for all that, and in 1847 the sailing ship *New Brunswick* of St. Catharines, Ontario, passed down the waterway and carried her cargo of grain to England, the first lake vessel to cross the Atlantic. In this venture, which cut out the old vexatious costs of trans-shipment, there was a tremendous promise for the future.

On the broad ocean the sailing ship could still compete for freights against the coal-devouring steamer of the period, for the winds were free and canvas was cheaper far than boilers and pistons; indeed the sailing ship with its clipper design was now reaching the peak of its size, speed, and utility. The gold rush around the Horn to California and the continued swarming of European emigrants to the eastern ports of North America created a demand for ships unprecedented in world history; and a sailing ship could be built cheaply wherever there was a handy supply of timber on the stump, a stream to turn a sawmill, and a river or a tide deep enough to carry the ship away. For such an industry the eastern coasts of Canada were ideal.

By 1850 the banks of the lower St. Lawrence and the tidal creeks of New Brunswick and Nova Scotia were ringing with the sounds of ship carpentry; sparmakers, sailmakers, blacksmiths, blockmakers, riggers and caulkers all found work behind the slips; in the seaports a growing host of shipping merchants and chandlers looked after the supplies, the marine insurance, and the charters; and in the amphibious population of the coast it was easy to find crews. The "wooden ships and iron men" of the Maritime Provinces were to be seen in ports all over the globe. Nova Scotia alone, with her 2500 vessels (including fishing craft) could claim place among the great shipping nations of the world; and already the profits had made the Bluenoses per capita the wealthiest people in British North America.

Meanwhile emigrants from Britain and Ireland were still coming up the St. Lawrence at the rate of 30,000 a year. In the season of 1850 the Montrealers counted 222 ships from overseas loading or discharging cargo at their wharves. Since 1841 the population of Upper Canada had more than doubled. The times were still hard in the interior. Trade was struggling; a hostile tariff shut Canadian goods out of the United States, and across the width of the Atlantic it was difficult to compete with French and Russian grain in the British market; but there was a new hopeful feeling in the air.

There was no boom in the finer things of life. A pioneer people just emerging from bare subsistence and filled now with the go-ahead spirit of their North American neighbors had little time or thought for such matters. Free schools were still only a dream. There was a large proportion of illiterates among the English-speaking population and still more among the *habitants*, although the intellectual group in French Canada was far larger and more active than any to be found in the English-speaking provinces. A literary and philosophical society in Toronto in the 1840s lasted no more than a year.

Yet by 1850 there was a native literature of sorts, chiefly notable for its promise of better things to come. Remarkable among the writers in English were a small group of young Nova Scotians who in 1828 formed what they called The Club, in which they wrote and read and sometimes published papers in the manner of Blackwood's *Noctes Ambrosianae*. Of these men Joseph Howe and Thomas Haliburton became famous. Howe poured out a stream of essays and verse to inspire in his Bluenoses a love of their province. These efforts on the whole were marred by the pompous and turgid style which any politician of the day found necessary on the platform, but the essays and many of Howe's letters show a mastery of English prose unmatched in the Canada of his time.

Haliburton had the greater success as a man of letters. He was of the Tory caste and his youthful history of Nova Scotia (published by Howe in 1829) was spoiled by a Tory bias and careless research. Like Howe, he had a deep love of his native province and a longing to see the Bluenoses become something more than mere "colonials," but his own method of rousing their self-respect was to lash their faults. For the purpose he invented "Sam Slick," a shrewd Yankee pedlar selling gimcrack wooden clocks to the gullible Bluenoses and at the same time uttering aside a stream of acrid comment on their habits, dress, and manners. As *The Clockmaker* appeared by installments in Howe's newspaper, Haliburton carried his satire further, darting his pen abroad with equal malice at bumptious Yankeedom and pompous British officialdom. When the first volume appeared in 1837 the Nova Scotians themselves received it with indifference, but the effect in the world outside was remarkable. "Sam Slick" blew into

the stuffy early Victorian literary world like a boisterous and salty
gale from the Nova Scotia coast. Briton and Yankee alike discovered
a capacity for laughing at themselves; and the medium was utterly
new, for *The Clockmaker* spoke in the racy and pungent language
of North America, which could paint a scene in one picturesque
sentence and flay a prig or a fool in a phrase.

Haliburton, somewhat astonished, found himself famous almost
overnight in Britain and the United States. For the next twenty years
his wit was to be quoted in every British drawing room. In the
United States his books could be found everywhere from Philadelphia drawing rooms to hundreds of remote Mississippi cabins. "Sam
Slick's" style and idiom founded a school of American colloquial
humor in which, among many, Artemus Ward and Mark Twain
were to stand out by themselves. No Canadian author since has had
a success or an influence so widespread or so long lived, for "Sam
Slick" is still read today.

In French Canada since the conquest there had been a smattering
of poems and essays mostly in hopeful imitation of the authors of
old France, and printed in *La Gazette de Quebec* (1764), *La Gazette
Littéraire* (1778), *Le Canadien* (1806), and other periodicals. As in
Nova Scotia there was an awakening in the late 1820s, with the same
local consciousness, the same desire to arouse a native pride. Satire
aimed primarily at themselves was not a French-Canadian weapon
and no Haliburton arose. Even solemn self-criticism, such as Michel
Bibaud's *l'Histoire du Canada*, did not meet with a good reception.
There was criticism enough of that kind from the English-speaking
merchants and officials, large and small, who never lost a chance to
tell the *canadien* that he was ignorant, primitive, superstitious and
lazy, and that he had no past and no future. Lord Durham had
described this *anglais* attitude well when he said, "It is not anywhere
a virtue of the English race to look with complacency on any
manners, customs or laws which appear strange to them; accustomed
to form a high estimate of their own superiority, they take no pains
to conceal from others their contempt and intolerance of their
usages." And yet he reflected a view of these very critics when he
said of the French Canadians; "They are a people with no history
and literature."

It was inevitable, then, that when competent French-Canadian
writers arose they should strive to create a literature and a history
extolling the deeds and virtues of their own race. The first was

François Xavier Garneau, a law clerk in Quebec who enlarged his outlook with tours of Canada, the United States, Britain and France, and then settled down to a careful study of Canadian historical documents. It was a dedicated labor that took many years, but when the first volume of his *History of Canada from the Discovery to Our Times* appeared in 1845 it was clearly the best Canadian work of its kind in French or English.

In the field of fiction Philippe Aubert de Gaspé published the first French-Canadian romance, *L'Influence d'un Livre* in 1837. Joseph Doutre produced another, *Les Fiancées de 1812* seven years later. A far more serious and better written novel, *Charles Guérin*, written by Pierre Chauveau, appeared in 1846 in the *Revue Canadienne*. Their public was small. The readers of these works naturally were people of the language in Canada and to some extent in France. The day was far in the future when organized bookselling could make English translations profitable and enable the French-Canadian author to reach the great markets of the United States and Britain.

Nevertheless the basis of a French-Canadian literature had been set by these books and by some excellent essays, short stories, and poems contributed to the periodicals. By 1850 Octave Crémazie, with his ugly face and handsome well-stocked mind, had gathered about him in the back room of the family bookshop in Quebec the group of poets, historians, and essayists whose work was to flower in the '60s. Nowhere else in the Canadian provinces did such a group exist (in Halifax "The Club" had dissolved long ago) and nowhere was there such a volume of good literary work in the making.

The only English work in Lower Canada worth notice was an early and exotic flower, that of Frances Brooke, wife of the Church of England chaplain to the Quebec garrison in the years between the Conquest and the end of the American Revolution. Her novels *The History of Lady Julia Mandeville* (1763) and *The History of Emily Montague* (1769) gave some detail of the Quebec scene and of the light and mildly scandalous side of garrison life; but the style was imitative (her chief model was Samuel Richardson) and even as imitations the books were poor. The lady in person was much more remarkable. Her erudition in the garrison staff circle earned her the title "Queen of the Blue Stockings," although an unfortunate squint and a figure both short and fat made her anything but queenly in appearance. She made up for this with a lively manner, and one of the winter sights of Quebec was that of the chaplain's gossipy wife, wrapped in sables and a scarlet capote, flying about the narrow streets in a cariole on her visits from parlor to parlor. The garrison wits called her Little Miss Riding Hood.

Upper Canada in the period had produced two native writers. Julia Beckwith was remarkable only because at the age of seventeen she wrote the first novel by a born Canadian. A native of New Brunswick, she had moved as a child to Kingston with her family. Her *St. Ursula's Convent or The Nun of Canada* was published in two volumes there in 1824, eleven years after she wrote it. The novel had little merit. After marriage she spent much of her life in the United States, where she did some further writing, none of it distinguished. Eventually she returned to New Brunswick and died at Fredericton in 1867.

John Richardson was the first Canadian writer of worth except the incomparable Haliburton. He was a native of the Niagara frontier, where his father was a surgeon in the Queen's Rangers. In 1812 at the age of sixteen he enlisted in the 41st Regiment, saw much action against the Americans, was captured, escaped after a year, rejoined his regiment, and subsequently moved with it to Spain, France, and England. After his army service he returned to his native province and in 1832 published *Wacousta*, a tale of Pontiac's rebellion, traditions of which were still told on the Niagara when he was a boy. Afterward he wrote several other historical novels and a poem in four cantos, *Tecumseh or The Warrior of the West*, a eulogy of the great chief with whom his regiment had been so closely associated. Indeed his best resource lay in his memories of the late war. To these he added much research and compiled his *War of 1812*, a history first published at Brockville in 1842. It was his most enduring work. He had no luck in his business affairs or with his pen. Eventually he drifted away to New York and perished there, starving and ill, in 1852.

The Strickland sisters, Mrs. Moodie and Mrs. Traill, were Englishwomen of education who came to Upper Canada with their husbands in the early 1830s, lived on rude farms in the backwoods, and wrote about their adventures in the earliest Canadian magazine, the *Literary Garland*, between 1838 and 1847. Their books belong to a later period. Another literary Englishwoman, Mrs. Anna Jameson, came to the province with her husband in 1836, stayed two years, and later published the observing and lively *Winter Studies and Summer Rambles in Canada.*

Quite apart from provincial efforts various books were published during the period by explorers of the North West Company and the Hudson's Bay Company. Chief among these were Samuel Hearne, who published in 1795 his *Journey from ... Hudson's Bay to the Northern Ocean*: Alexander Mackenzie, who published in 1801 his *Voyages from Montreal through ... the Continent of North America to the Frozen and Pacific Oceans*: and Alexander Henry, who published in 1809 his *Travels and Adventures in Canada and the Indian Territories.*

Numerous other travel accounts by English visitors formed part of the frothy spate of such books poured out by globe-trotting Britons during the nineteenth century. Much more valuable, but unpublished before 1850, were the carefully written journals of traders and explorers in the Canadian North in the period after 1818, when the real search for the Northwest Passage drew many able men into the bleak coasts and barrens first seen by Hearne and Mackenzie.

On the whole, Canadian writing between 1763 and 1850 was fugitive and spotty, with no expression of a native spirit except by the Nova Scotians and French Canadians, in both cases a spirit purely provincial.

CHAPTER 55

1763 — 1850

The arts in Canada

ART in the period flourished best among the French Canadians. Their skill and taste showed itself in architecture and in wood carving, at which they were particularly adept, as they were in the household arts of rugmaking, basketry, leatherwork, embroidery, weaving, and the designing and making of home furniture. Handicrafts had been taught by the Ursuline nuns for generations before the conquest. Bishop Laval had established about the year 1675 his École des Arts et Métieres, bringing over from France a staff of architects, masons, woodcarvers, coppersmiths and silversmiths. The school had vanished since, but its work, like that of the Ursulines, took root in the population and by 1763 had produced a widespread native craftsmanship which had no counterpart in the English-speaking provinces and colonies in North America. These skills reached their finest work between 1763 and 1850, when the machine age intruded on handicrafts everywhere.

The French-Canadian skill in architecture had shown itself at an early time in the design of the typical Quebec farmhouse, sturdy, rectangular, long and low, with its steep pitched roof and wide outcurved eaves (the so-called bellcast roof) to shed the heavy winter snows. It showed itself also in the design and construction of buildings for the Church, many of which were destroyed during the conquest and were patiently replaced in the long years of British occupation. Notable examples surviving are the well-proportioned Church of Ste. Jean-de-Chantal on Ile Perrot, the Ursuline monastery and the chapel of the Hôpital General at Quebec, the Church of the Visitation at Sault au Récollet, and the Church of St. Jean at Port-Joli. All of these are rich with fine carvings from ceilings to doors, enclosed within their simple beauty of structure.

French-Canadian art has expressed itself best in the strength and rhythm of its wood carving, especially much statuary for the Church.

Often the craft was handed down generation after generation from father to son, as in the case of the celebrated Baillairgé family, which produced fine carving from 1741 almost without a pause until 1849. Notable among the metalworkers were the silversmiths Ranvoyzé and Amiot, the first of whom died in 1819, the second twenty years later. Their best work was for the Church, and such things as their chalices and incense pots remain unsurpassed to the present time.

In painting the French Canadians were not so fortunate. In this field, mostly religious, there was a large production which, however devout, had little of the divine touch of art itself. Nevertheless this period saw the work of the first Canadian-born painter, Abbé Aide-Créquy, a native of Quebec, and of the portrait artists De Beaucourt and Plamondon, both of whom had a merit that survived their day.

In the Maritime Provinces art found its most fertile field in Halifax, where merchants made prosperous by the wars and well-to-do officers of the Army and Navy gave it a patronage not to be found elsewhere. Even so it had a narrow range, confined almost entirely to the crayon and brush. There were no handicrafts worth mention; even the few silversmiths and goldsmiths who fled from New York and other American cities with the Loyalists found small market for their work in "Nova Scarcity."

Before the Loyalist influx two visitors may be mentioned. Richard Short, an officer of the fleet, made some excellent drawings of Halifax in 1759. These were engraved and published in London in 1764. His drawings of Quebec, made during and after the siege, were engraved in London in 1761. The other was J. F. W. Desbarres, a British officer engaged in surveying the Nova Scotia coast from 1763 to 1773. His splendid collection of charts, *The Atlantic Neptune*, illustrated by aquatint engravings from his own drawings of Halifax, Annapolis, Louisburg, and other provincial towns and scenes, were published in London in 1780–81, and Nelson possessed a set. Desbarres died in Halifax in 1824.

Among the impoverished Loyalists who came to Nova Scotia were Gilbert Stuart and his family, who arrived in 1775. His son Gilbert, then twenty, had to earn his living for a time as a common seaman in Nova Scotia ships, and although none of it survives, undoubtedly his earliest drawing and painting were done in these ships and in the Nova Scotia farmhouse where his parents had made their home. He soon made his way to London and studied under Benjamin West, who put him on the road to fame. After five busy years in Europe he removed to the United States, where he spent the rest of his life. His paintings of great Americans remain his best memorial, and his "Athenaeum" head of George Washington is still the accepted likeness.

His nephew Gilbert Stuart Newton, born in Halifax in 1795, also made his way to England as a young man, studied at the Royal Academy, and was elected an academician in 1832. He remained in England and died there in 1835. In this man Nova Scotia exported its one native genius in the field of art. The painters of note in Nova Scotia during the period were nearly all Englishmen and only one of them spent the greater part of his life in the province.

Best among them was Robert Field, who lived in Halifax from 1808 to 1818. He had been painting and engraving successfully in the United States for some years when Governor Wentworth induced him to come to Nova Scotia. Here he painted all the notables of the day, army, naval and civil. Many of them were members of the exclusive Rockingham Club, whose quarters were on the Duke of Kent's old estate at Bedford Basin, some miles out of Halifax. As Kneller had done for the famous Kit-cat Club in London, so Field made portraits of wealthy Rockingham members to be hung on the walls of the clubhouse. He returned to England, exhibited some of his work in the Royal Academy, and died in Jamaica in 1819.

One of the more itinerant English artists, John Poad Drake, had seen Napoleon on board the *Bellerophon* in Plymouth Sound in 1815. He brought a painting of that memorable deck scene with him to America, where it gave him an immediate public interest. In 1819 the bench and magistrates of Halifax commissioned him to paint a full-length portrait of Chief Justice Blowers in his robes. There was some disagreement over the payment and apparently Drake took a high tone. The magistrates finally paid the fee in ha'pennies and the disgruntled artist had to send a man with a wheelbarrow to carry it away.

The best topographical artist of the period was William Eager, an Irishman who came to Halifax in 1834 and made many drawings of the provincial scene. These were published as lithographs in 1839–40, many of the plates drawn directly on stone by Eager himself.

An American teacher of art, W. H. Jones, was on the staff of Dalhousie College for some years and in 1830 he arranged an exhibition there, the first in Canada. The artist who worked longest in

Nova Scotia during the period was William Valentine, a young Englishman who came to Halifax about the time of Field's departure in 1818 and spent the rest of his life in the city. He arrived at a time when the rich financial flush of the wars had paled (which was probably the reason for Field's departure) and poor Valentine, during the many hard years that followed, had to eke out a living with sign painting and house decorating. Nevertheless he was a skilled artist in oils and he left many good portraits of the Haligonians of his time. Toward the end of his life Daguerre's invention of photography rang the knell of the portrait painters except those with a wealthy clientele. Daguerreotypes were taken in Quebec as early as 1840, and about four years later Valentine himself turned to portrait photography. He died at Halifax in 1849.

Upper Canada, the youngest of the Canadian provinces in 1850, had produced little art, and that only with brush and pencil. What it had was chiefly owed to John Howard, who came from England to teach drawing at Upper Canada College in 1832. He organized the Society of Artists and Amateurs in Toronto in 1834. Most of them were amateurs and none were good, and in the pragmatic society of the provincial capital his society languished for lack of support. Howard tried again with the Upper Canada Society in 1841. That failed also, and so did another he formed in 1847.

The only kind of art worthy of note in Upper Canada was common to all the provinces — the topographical drawings and sketches made by British soldiers and explorers in the course of mapping the country, and by one notable civilian, W. H. Bartlett. The soldiers who did the best work in Upper Canada were Lieutenant Colonel J. P. Cockburn, Major W. J. Bennett, Major Davis, and Captain Hancock. The English civilian Bartlett outshone them all. He came to Nova Scotia in 1836 when he was twenty-nine and made carefully observed sketches of the provincial landscape there, in Lower and Upper Canada, and in the eastern United States. In 1842 he published the collection of lithographs entitled *Canadian Scenery* which, with the corresponding *American Scenery* (1840), made him famous.

Nothing remarkable was done in the West until the period was drawing to a close. In 1845, when the Oregon dispute was getting hot, Captain Herbert Warre of the British Army traveled with a survey party from Manitoba to Vancouver Island and also examined the Oregon Trail. On these journeys Warre made many excellent pencil-and-wash drawings, some of which later were lithographed. He was followed independently by Paul Kane, who was a Canadian artist in all but his birthplace.

Kane as a boy of eight had come from Ireland to Upper Canada in 1818. He grew up in Toronto with an itching foot as well as an artist's eye and hand. He made tours of the United States and of Europe, and he returned fired with a desire to do for the Indians of the Canadian prairies and mountains what George Catlin had done for them in the American West, traveling their country thoroughly, studying their life, and recording it in a collection of pictures taken before the onrush of "civilization" could change them.

He set out from Toronto in 1845, but the Hudson's Bay Company staff at Sault Ste. Marie managed to persuade him that a lone journey beyond that point was foolhardy. In the following spring he joined the Bay Company's canoe "brigade" on their annual trip with supplies for the posts across the West. With them he traveled up Lake Superior, through the wild forests of the Shield to Lake Winnipeg, and by the Saskatchewan River across the prairies. He crossed the Rockies on horseback and passed down the Columbia River to old Fort Vancouver, reaching Oregon just when the whole country south of the 49th parallel was passing into Americans hands for ever.

Kane got back to Toronto in 1848, battered and gaunt, but he had with him more than five hundred sketches made along the way. From these he made many oil paintings and years later (1859) published his book *Wanderings of an Artist*. He was by no means the best artist of his period, even in Canada; but in historical value his work placed him ahead of the rest by the width of a continent.

CHAPTER 56

1850

The air of destiny

WHEN the period began, George III was on the throne at twenty-five, with his mother's whispered "George, be a king!" in his ears, and determined to be a king at all costs. At its close, the throne held a pious and matronly woman who had such a memory of dislike for "the wicked uncles" and the House of Hanover generally that she refused to name any of her sons George. Victoria was determined to be a queen and a queen she was, but a queen always served by able ministers who deferred to her suavely in small matters and managed to do what they pleased in the big ones. Democracy was not a favorite British word, least of all with Queen Victoria, but whatever polite disguise it wore, the principle was in the British saddle now and finding its feet in the stirrups.

Across the sea it rode a Canadian saddle. The Canadians did not know yet what they would do with it or with the half continent that the long strange march of events had left at their disposal. Newfoundland, oldest of the colonies, stood aloof in the sea with a gaze fixed toward Britain, having no trade or any other common interest with the mainland provinces. Nova Scotia, New Brunswick, and Prince Edward Island remained a geographical extension of New England, with close ties of blood and trade with the Yankees and none whatever with the people on the St. Lawrence and the Great Lakes. (Long after Upper Canada became officially Ontario the Bluenoses with their seafaring logic went on calling it by the old name, for the adjective was true in all ways; the journey there was usually upwind, always upstream and — when the railway was built — upgrade.)

The Lower Canadians remained a sensitive enclave of Catholic French in an English-speaking and largely Protestant continent, with an instinct to tie their faith and race together in one tight inviolate knot. Upper Canada was a typical midwestern American state paradoxically flying the Union Jack. Energetic, ambitious, go-getting and money-making, the Upper Canadians spoke with an Ulster-American accent and (with their bitter memories of 1812) held a constant suspicion of everything "Yankee," whether good, bad, or innocuous, and by the same token regarded with a mystical devotion everything British.

Manitoba ("where-the Great-Spirit-speaks") was a small clan of half-wild Scots almost lost in the growing swarm of *métis*, the New Nation, who considered themselves the true owners of the plains, no matter what the distant and still mysterious *anglais* of the East might say. In 1846 they were so unruly that the Hudson's Bay Company felt obliged to call in troops by way of the bay. The British soldiers stayed two years and then withdrew as they had in 1817. In the solitudes of the plains the Great Spirit continued to speak with a strong *métis* accent.

Far to the north the indomitable Franklin had vanished in the Arctic and now many men were there in search of him and his crews. Eventually the world would know that Franklin died in 1847, that his crews had abandoned their ice-locked ships in 1848 and tried to reach the Canadian settlements overland, and that all had perished on the way. In the meantime explorers of the Hudson's Bay Company searched the hitherto unknown stretches of the Arctic coast line and mapped it as they went, while half a dozen ship expeditions crept among the maze of bleak islands that stretched from Canada toward the Pole. The quest for Franklin was leading now to the discovery of the Northwest Passage, to the mapping of the whole Canadian North, and to a keen awareness of Canada's third ocean that Franklin alive could never have aroused.

Far southward stretched the barrens, the sub-Arctic forest, and then the wide sweep of the prairies, dotted with H.B.C. posts and with the camps of wandering Indians and *métis*, but without a settler's chimney beyond Red River. In the Rockies and beyond the mountains the same was true. A handful of Canadian settlers and H.B.C. employees on Vancouver Island marked the tenuous British hold on the Pacific coast. North of them sat the tough and uncommunicative Russians, southward the exuberant emigrants of the Oregon Trail, the roaring gold-panning forty-niners of California.

What was to come out of all this? In 1850 the notion of a political league was stirring in the Canadian provinces, but its westward view was lost in the mists of Lake Superior. A Canadian nation whose writ ran all the way to the Pacific and the Arctic lay beyond the bounds of imagination, just as Howe's fantastic train whistles in the Rockies were beyond all hope of possibility. A Canadian nation even in the settled East was improbable. Although some men dreamed of it, the facts were all against them. Wise heads in London were convinced now that the destiny of the Canadian provinces was to be part of the United States, either by conquest or by a voluntary absorption. Also they foresaw that the slavery problem, already sharp, eventually must split the United States in two parts, North and South. The twin prospects made a curious sum. The British had just escaped by the narrowest of margins a ruinous war with the Americans. It was apparent now that the swiftly rising transatlantic power would soon be the greatest in the world, and with a deep-rooted hostility to everything British. To suppose that this colossus would rest content in a world that still contained a British empire was folly. Sooner or later the clash would come. The only hope was that the Americans might divide themselves into two nations, mutually hostile, absorbed in their own affairs.

It was in this spirit of cold calculation that Lord Grey wrote to Elgin in Canada in 1849: "If we refuse to afford all the facilities we can for commercial intercourse between Canada and her powerful neighbor we must certainly create discontent inconsistent with our retention of the Colony — if on the other hand we encourage that intercourse there is every probability that Canada ere long will be Americanized by the influx of Yankees. Between the two I have no hesitation in preferring the latter, and if ultimately it should lead to the separation of these Provinces from the British Empire let us hope that this may take place by amicable arrangement instead of by war, and may lead to a division of the Union — British America with some of the Northern States forming one Nation and the Southern States another. This would be no such bad result and in the meantime our trade would prosper and emigration would flourish."

The Colonial Office had now come full cycle. It was less than seventy years since Lord Shelburne's agent had accepted in secret from Benjamin Franklin the principle that no permanent peace could exist between the British and the Americans unless Canada were part of the United States. It was a sentiment now held by most of the "Little Englanders" at Westminster. The repeated American threats of war between 1838 and 1846 had frightened them badly. The Canadian insistence on self-government, just conceded, seemed to offer London a heaven-sent line of retreat from this dangerous political and military liability in North America; and while Lord John Russell in a speech on February 8, 1850, made it plain that the retreat would be graceful and gradual, there was no doubt about its direction.

Although the patient Elgin had warned them that it was the last wild gesture of a group discredited by the riots in Montreal, the British Government were much impressed by the Annexation Manifesto. Peering into the North American future they saw the growing rift between North and South in the United States. They failed to see that so long as the Union held together, the southern states would veto any addition of non-slave states — for such the Canadian provinces were bound to be. For that reason annexation was now impossible and the old wild doctrine of Manifest Destiny was dead.

Moreover to Canadians the hard-won principle of self-government, which London had granted them at last, was not to be thrown away for a government in Washington or anywhere else. Most Canadians and some Americans knew this, and so did Lord Elgin. They saw something else. The Canadians were coming of age. It was time for them to bury the old interprovincial jealousies and band together for the huge tasks that lay ahead of them. And it was time for Canadians and Americans to sweep away the old hostility and with it the trade barriers that shut them off from each other; for it was evident now that no single people were to rule the continent. The hand of destiny had marked out two at least, and for their own good they must learn to live with each other under the continental roof.

Index

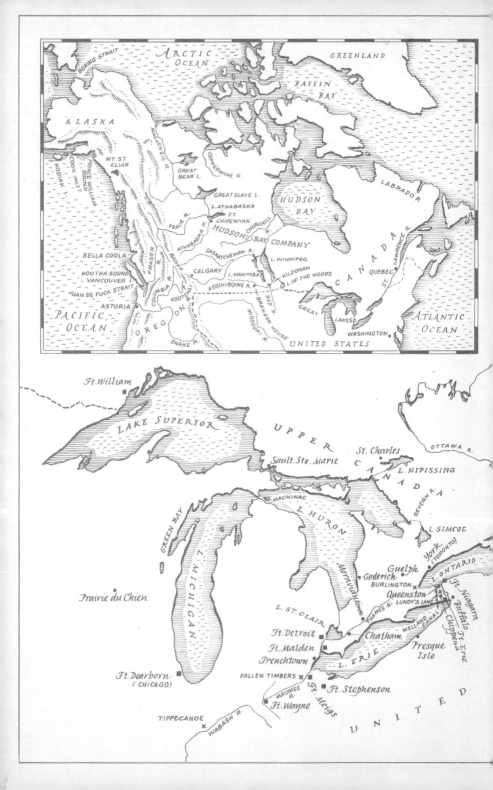